DATE DUE

electric girl

by Michael Brennan

3

AIT★PLANET LAR

San Francisco

Electric Girl volume 3
by Michael Brennan

Published by
AiT/Planet Lar
2034 47th Avenue
San Francisco, CA 94116
www.ait-planetlar.com

First Edition August 2005
10 9 8 7 6 5 4 3 2 1

Written and Drawn by Michael Brennan
Cover Design by Christine Gleason
Cover Art by Michael Brennan

ISBN 1-932051-38-4

Printed and bound in Canada by Quebecor Printing, Inc.

Thanks to everyone who helped make these books possible.

electric girl #9

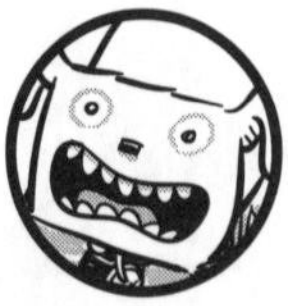 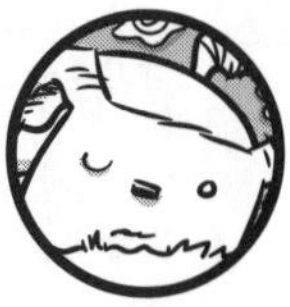 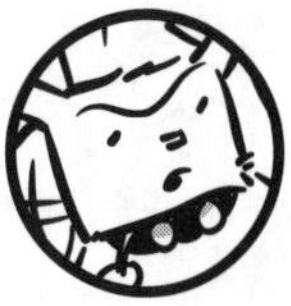

Originally published in Spring 2002

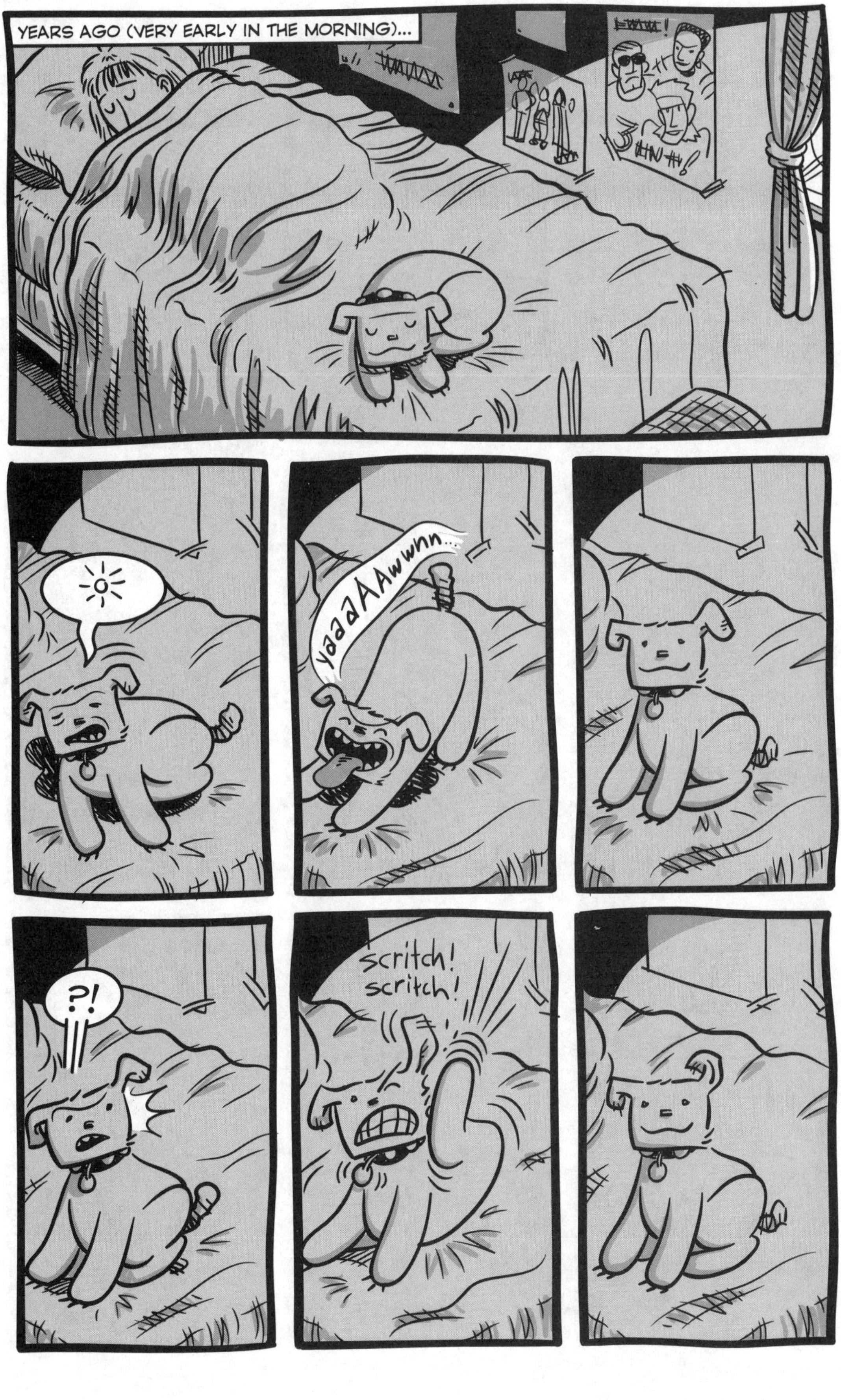
YEARS AGO (VERY EARLY IN THE MORNING)...
yaaaAAwwhn...
?!
scritch! scritch!

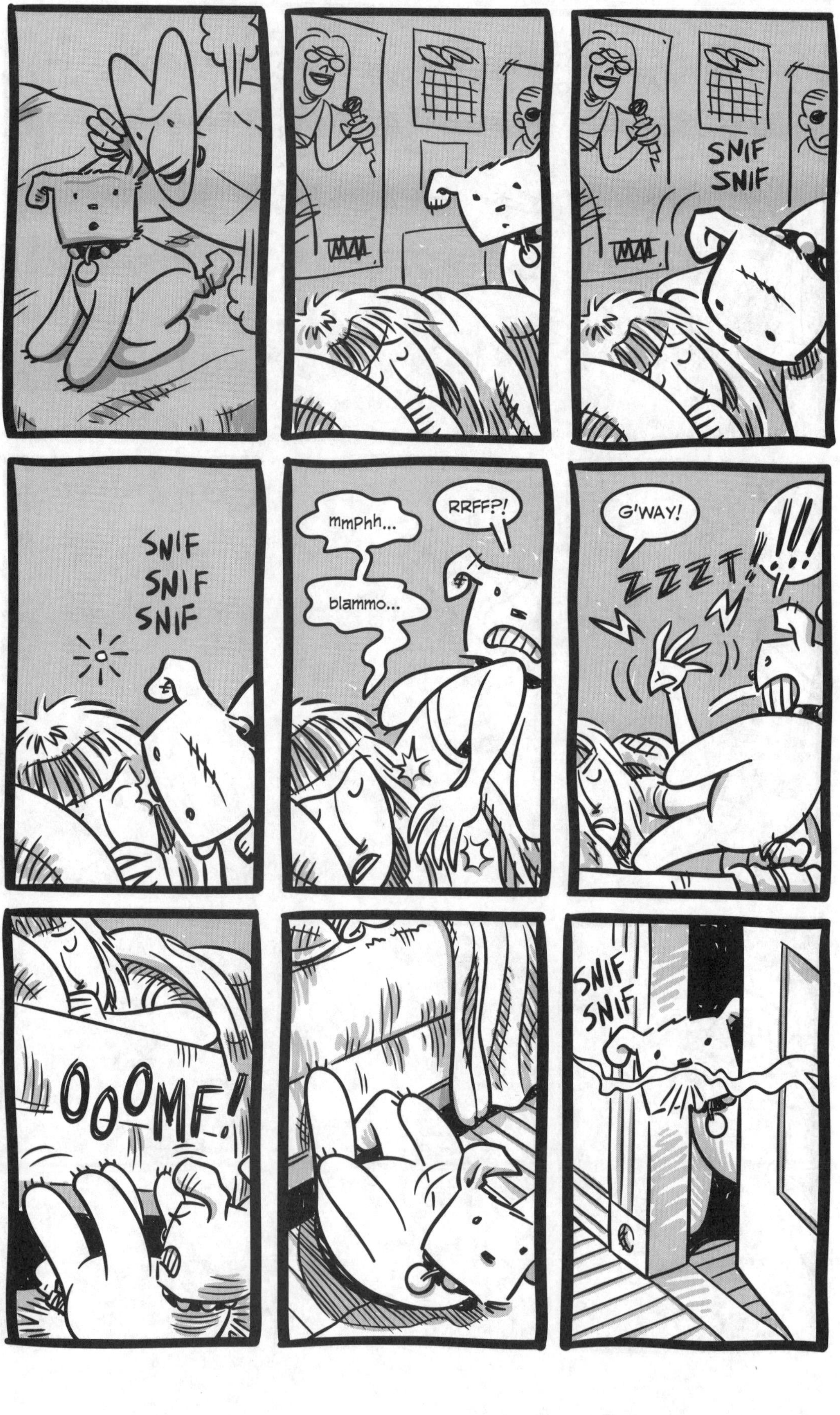
SNIF
SNIF
SNIF
SNIF
SNIF
mmphh...
blammo...
RRFF?!
G'WAY!
ZZZT!
!!!
OOOMF!
SNIF
SNIF

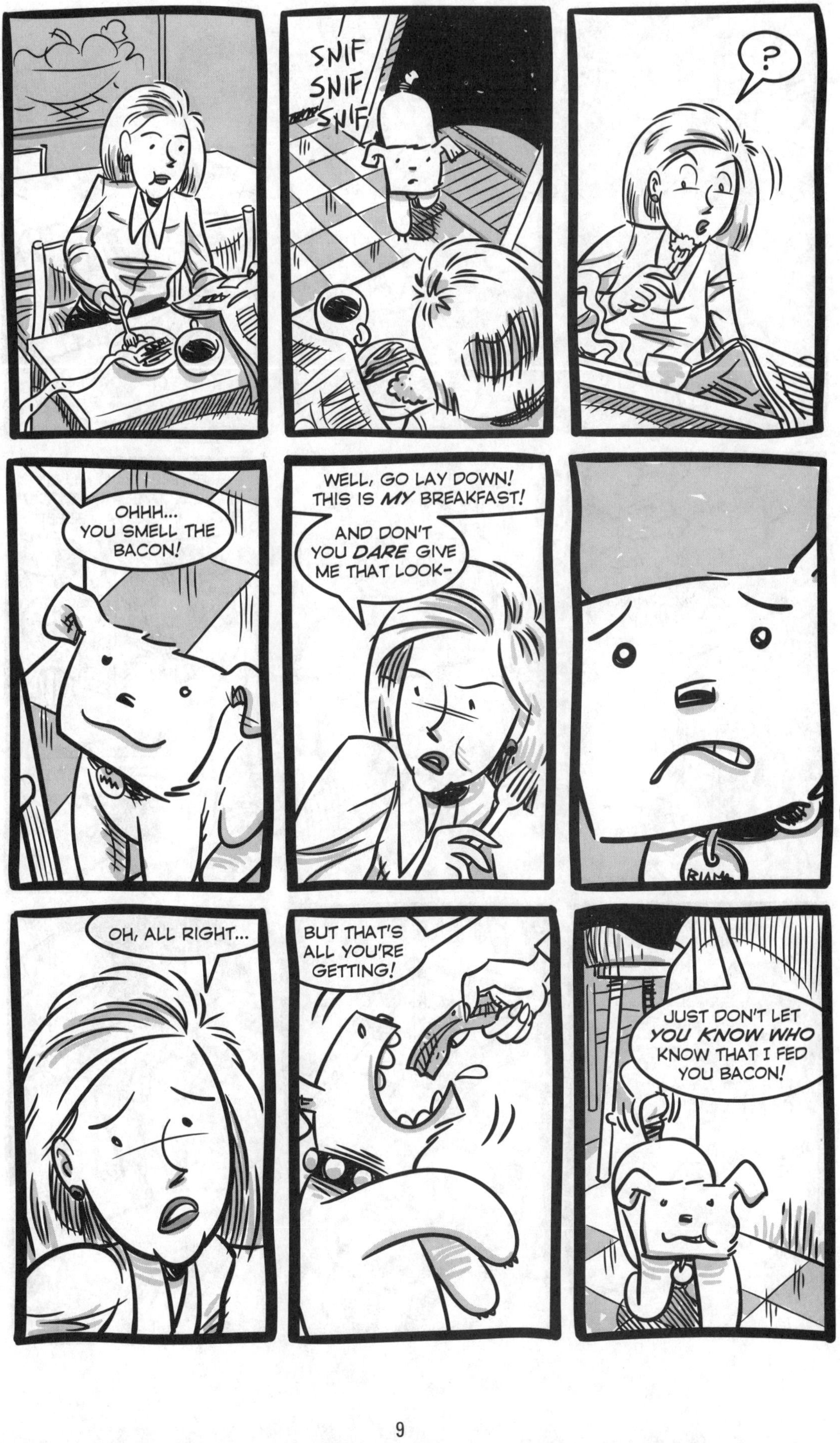
SNIF
SNIF
SNIF
?
OHHH... YOU SMELL THE BACON!
WELL, GO LAY DOWN! THIS IS *MY* BREAKFAST!
AND DON'T YOU *DARE* GIVE ME THAT LOOK-
OH, ALL RIGHT...
BUT THAT'S ALL YOU'RE GETTING!
JUST DON'T LET *YOU KNOW WHO* KNOW THAT I FED YOU BACON!

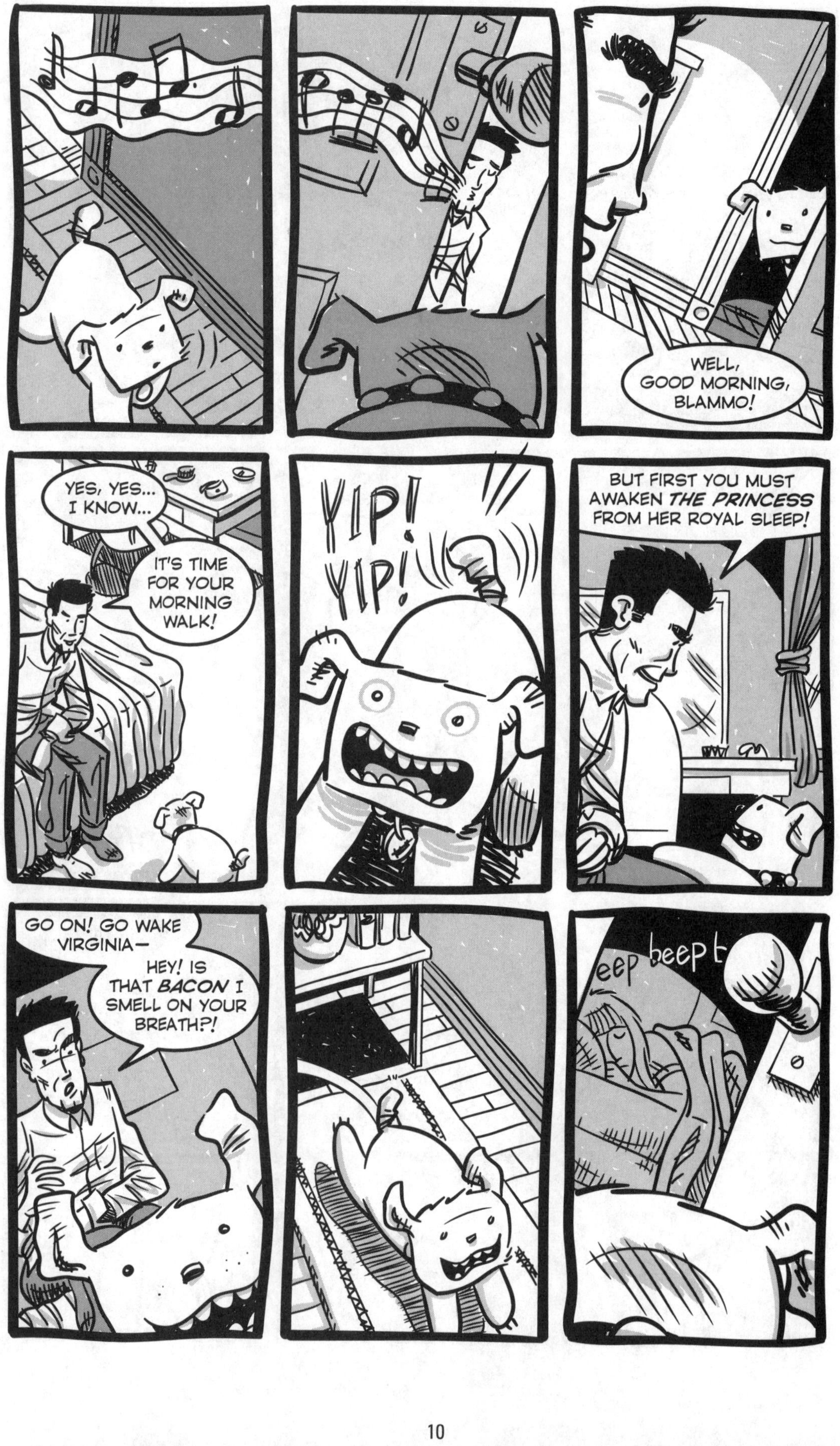
WELL, GOOD MORNING, BLAMMO!
YES, YES... I KNOW...
IT'S TIME FOR YOUR MORNING WALK!
YIP! YIP!
BUT FIRST YOU MUST AWAKEN THE PRINCESS FROM HER ROYAL SLEEP!
GO ON! GO WAKE VIRGINIA—
HEY! IS THAT BACON I SMELL ON YOUR BREATH?!
eep beept

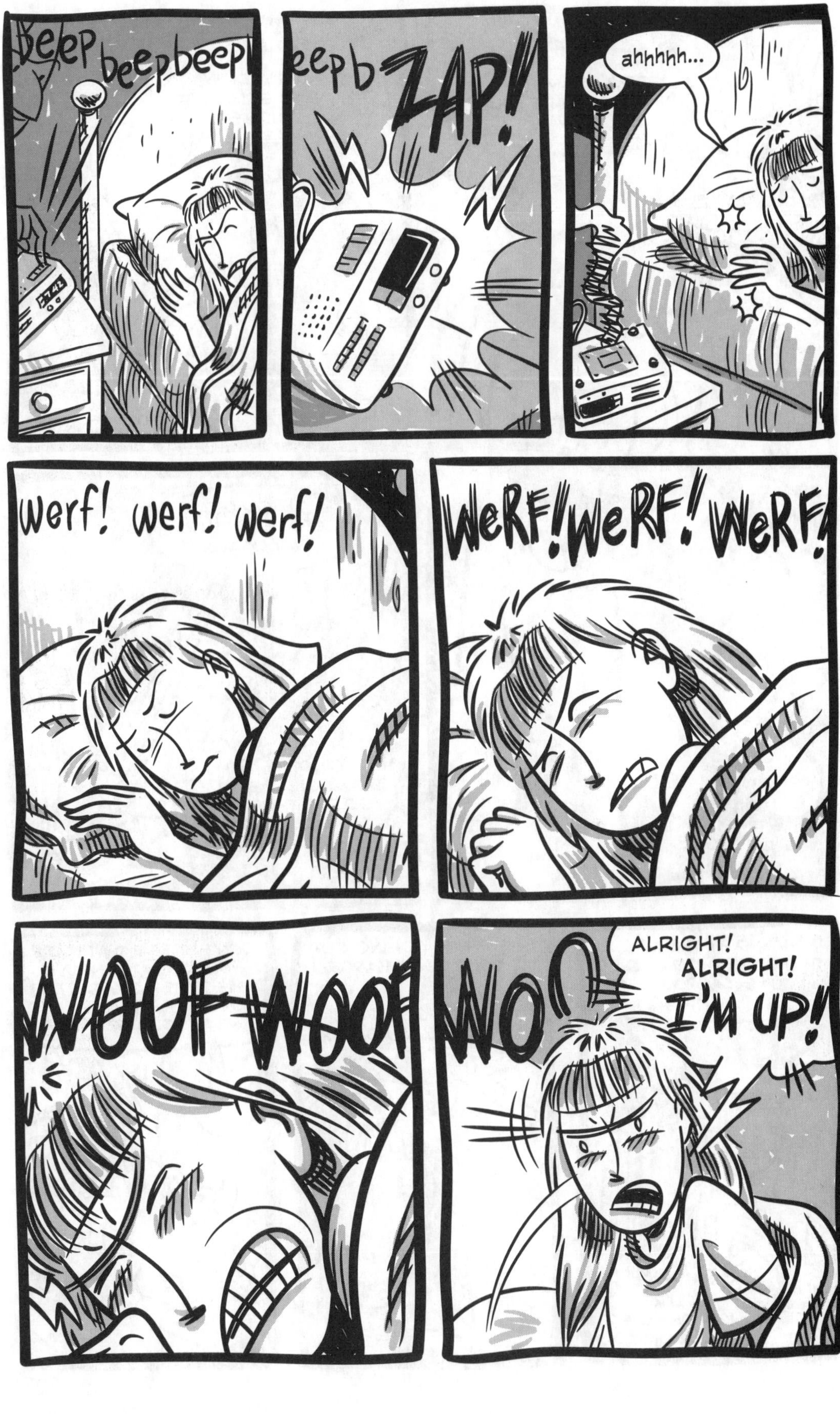
beep beepbeepbeepb
eepb ZAP!
ahhhhh...
werf! werf! werf!
WERF! WERF! WERF!
WOOF WOOF
WO
ALRIGHT!
ALRIGHT!
I'M UP!!

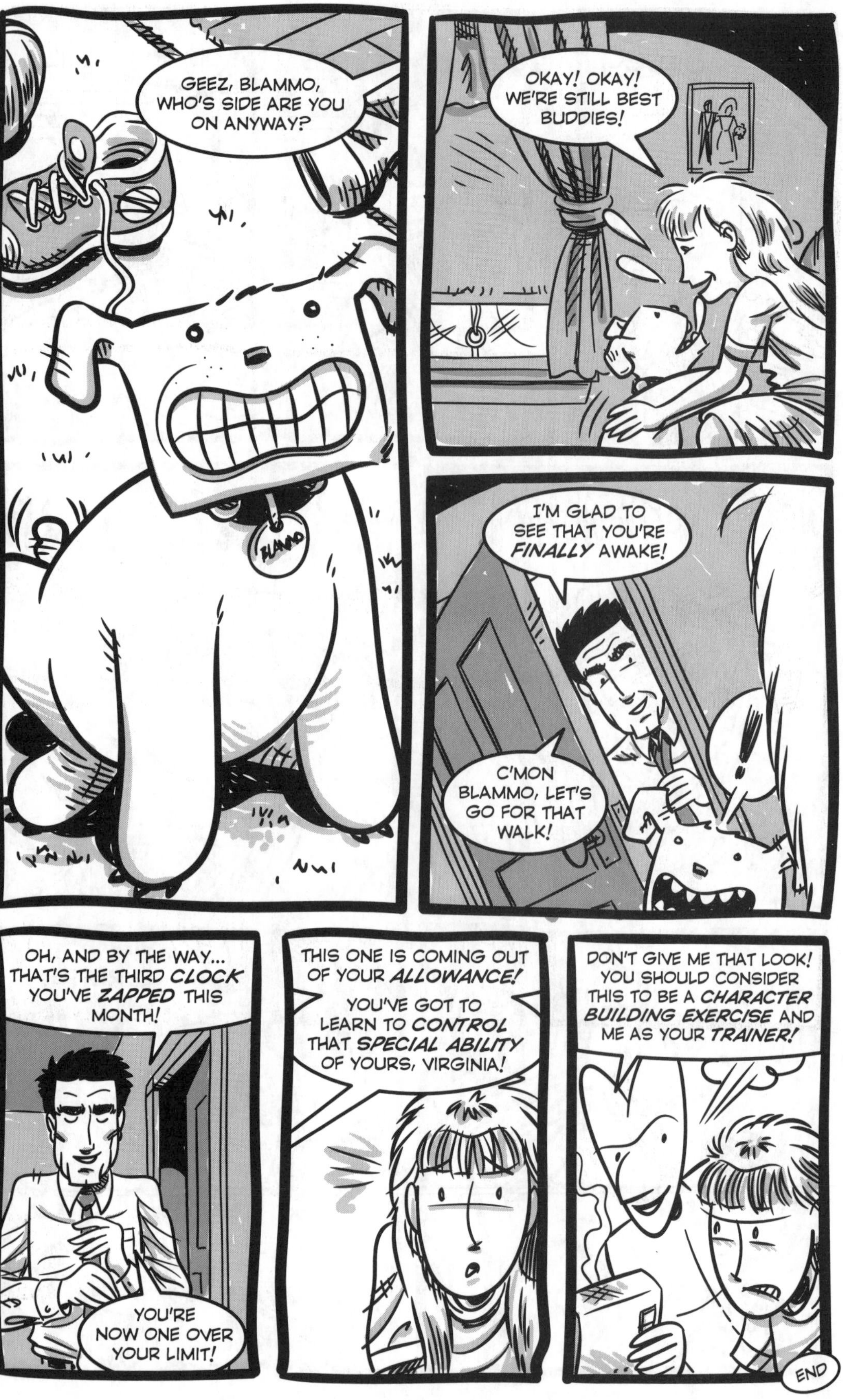
GEEZ, BLAMMO, WHO'S SIDE ARE YOU ON ANYWAY?
BLAMMO
OKAY! OKAY! WE'RE STILL BEST BUDDIES!
I'M GLAD TO SEE THAT YOU'RE *FINALLY* AWAKE!
C'MON BLAMMO, LET'S GO FOR THAT WALK!
OH, AND BY THE WAY... THAT'S THE THIRD *CLOCK* YOU'VE *ZAPPED* THIS MONTH!
YOU'RE NOW ONE OVER YOUR LIMIT!
THIS ONE IS COMING OUT OF YOUR *ALLOWANCE!*
YOU'VE GOT TO LEARN TO *CONTROL* THAT *SPECIAL ABILITY* OF YOURS, VIRGINIA!
DON'T GIVE ME THAT LOOK! YOU SHOULD CONSIDER THIS TO BE A *CHARACTER BUILDING EXERCISE* AND ME AS YOUR *TRAINER!*
END

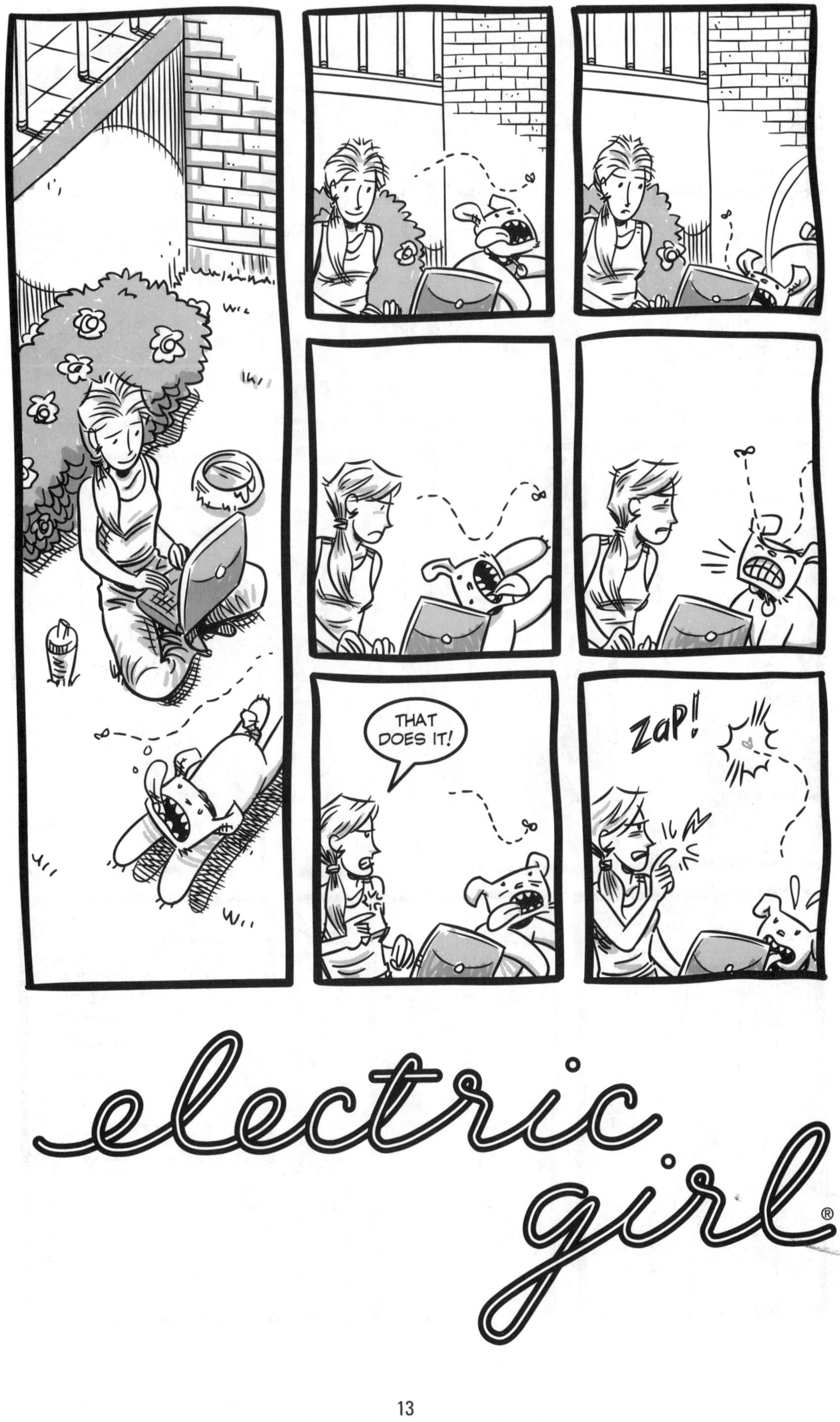
THAT DOES IT!
ZAP!

electric girl®

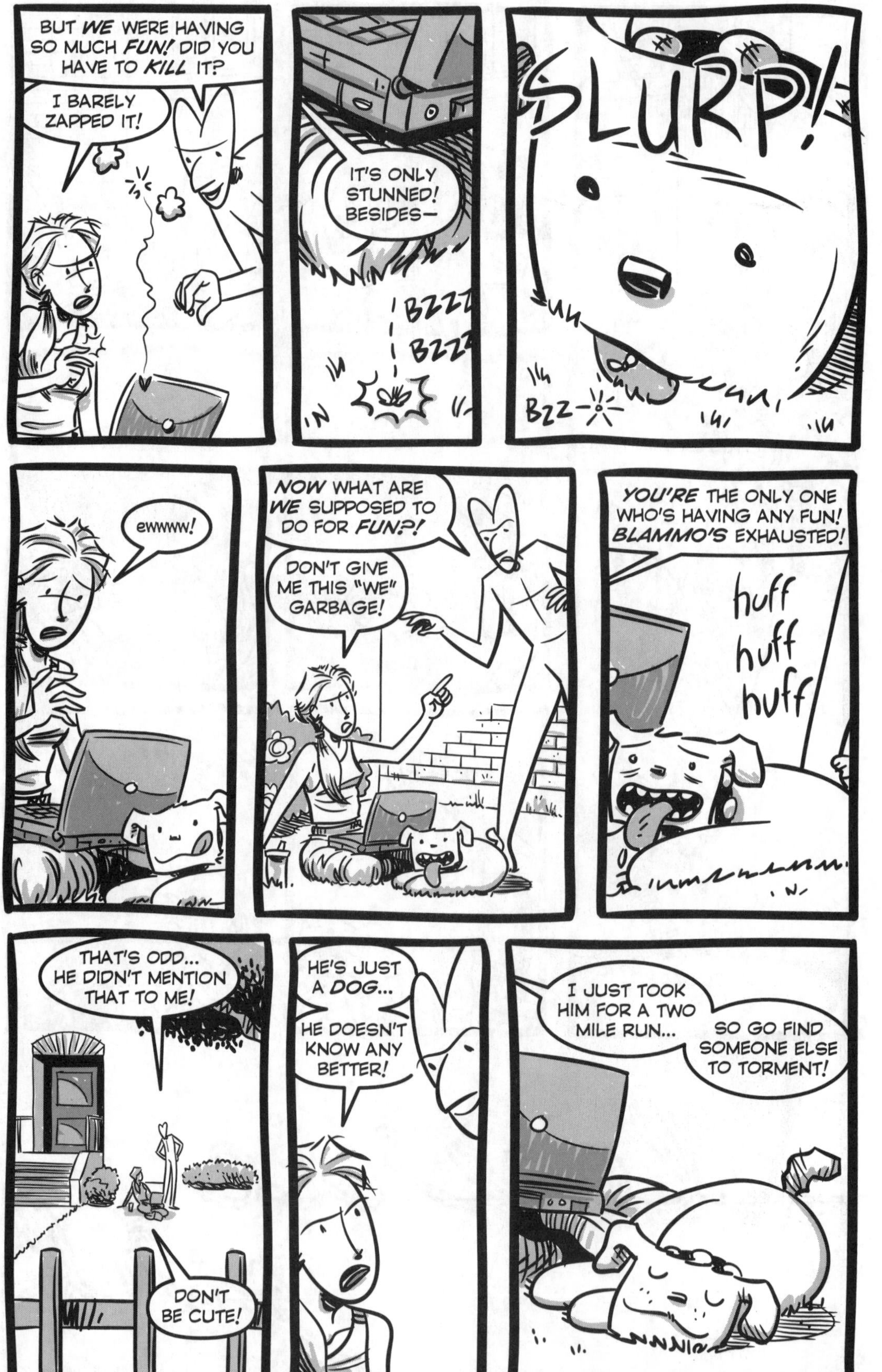
BUT WE WERE HAVING SO MUCH FUN! DID YOU HAVE TO KILL IT?
I BARELY ZAPPED IT!
IT'S ONLY STUNNED! BESIDES—
BZZZ
BZZZ
SLURP!
BZZ
ewwww!
NOW WHAT ARE WE SUPPOSED TO DO FOR FUN?!
DON'T GIVE ME THIS "WE" GARBAGE!
YOU'RE THE ONLY ONE WHO'S HAVING ANY FUN! BLAMMO'S EXHAUSTED!
huff huff huff
THAT'S ODD... HE DIDN'T MENTION THAT TO ME!
DON'T BE CUTE!
HE'S JUST A DOG...
HE DOESN'T KNOW ANY BETTER!
I JUST TOOK HIM FOR A TWO MILE RUN...
SO GO FIND SOMEONE ELSE TO TORMENT!

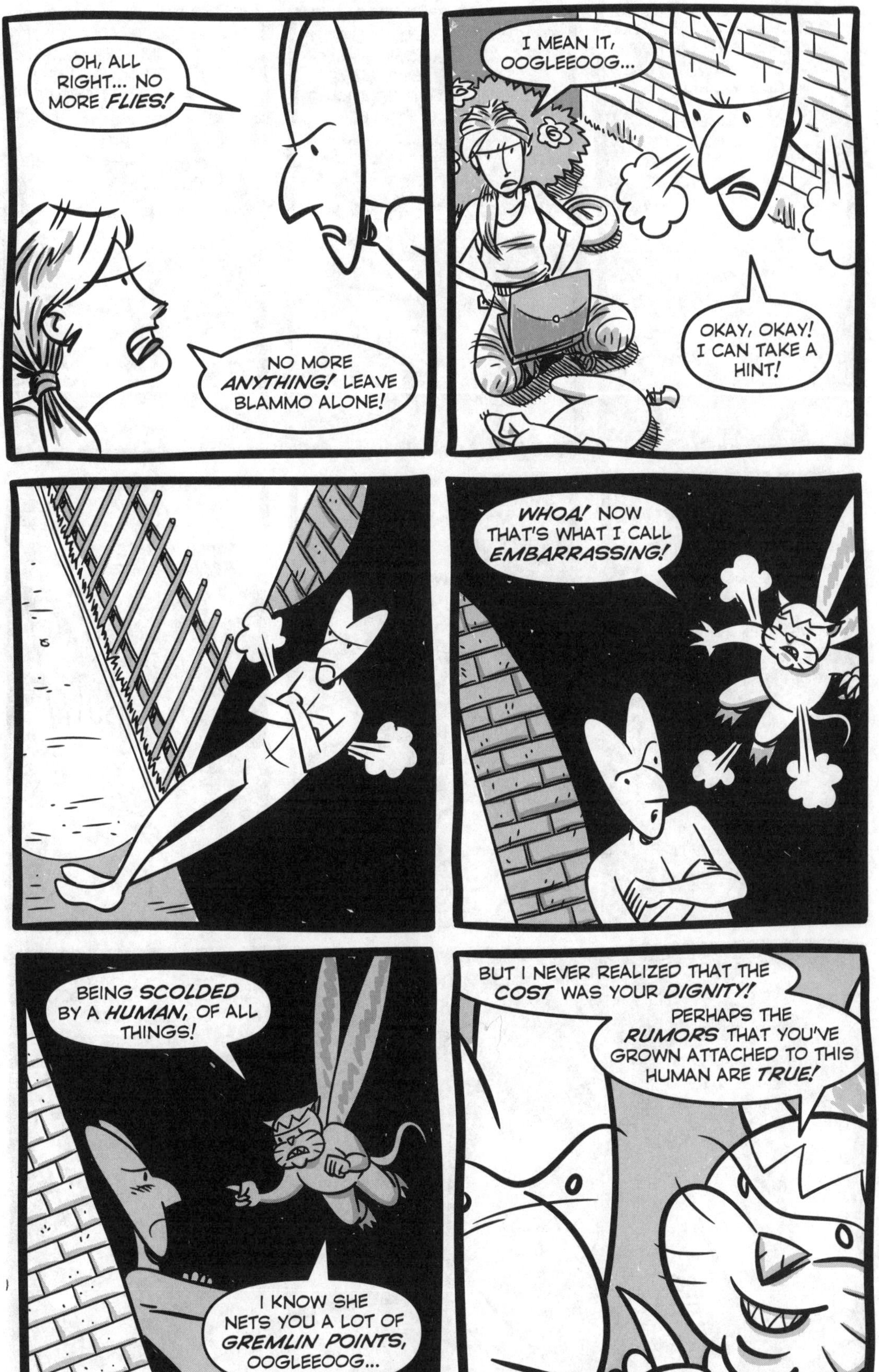
OH, ALL RIGHT... NO MORE FLIES!
NO MORE ANYTHING! LEAVE BLAMMO ALONE!
I MEAN IT, OOGLEEOOG...
OKAY, OKAY! I CAN TAKE A HINT!
WHOA! NOW THAT'S WHAT I CALL EMBARRASSING!
BEING SCOLDED BY A HUMAN, OF ALL THINGS!
I KNOW SHE NETS YOU A LOT OF GREMLIN POINTS, OOGLEEOOG...
BUT I NEVER REALIZED THAT THE COST WAS YOUR DIGNITY!
PERHAPS THE RUMORS THAT YOU'VE GROWN ATTACHED TO THIS HUMAN ARE TRUE!

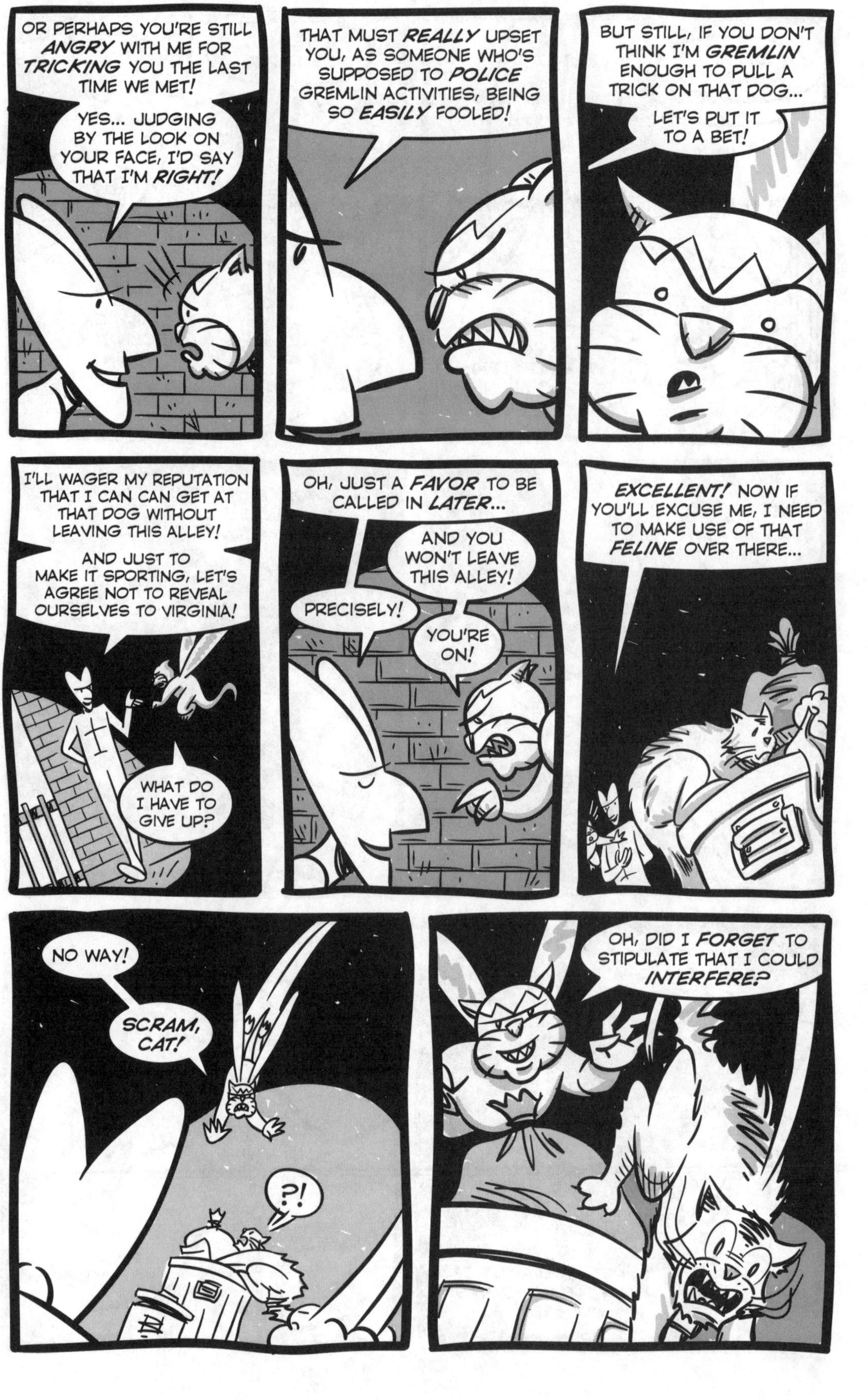
OR PERHAPS YOU'RE STILL ANGRY WITH ME FOR TRICKING YOU THE LAST TIME WE MET!
YES... JUDGING BY THE LOOK ON YOUR FACE, I'D SAY THAT I'M RIGHT!
THAT MUST REALLY UPSET YOU, AS SOMEONE WHO'S SUPPOSED TO POLICE GREMLIN ACTIVITIES, BEING SO EASILY FOOLED!
BUT STILL, IF YOU DON'T THINK I'M GREMLIN ENOUGH TO PULL A TRICK ON THAT DOG...
LET'S PUT IT TO A BET!
I'LL WAGER MY REPUTATION THAT I CAN CAN GET AT THAT DOG WITHOUT LEAVING THIS ALLEY!
AND JUST TO MAKE IT SPORTING, LET'S AGREE NOT TO REVEAL OURSELVES TO VIRGINIA!
WHAT DO I HAVE TO GIVE UP?
OH, JUST A FAVOR TO BE CALLED IN LATER...
AND YOU WON'T LEAVE THIS ALLEY!
PRECISELY!
YOU'RE ON!
EXCELLENT! NOW IF YOU'LL EXCUSE ME, I NEED TO MAKE USE OF THAT FELINE OVER THERE...
NO WAY!
SCRAM, CAT!
?!
OH, DID I FORGET TO STIPULATE THAT I COULD INTERFERE?

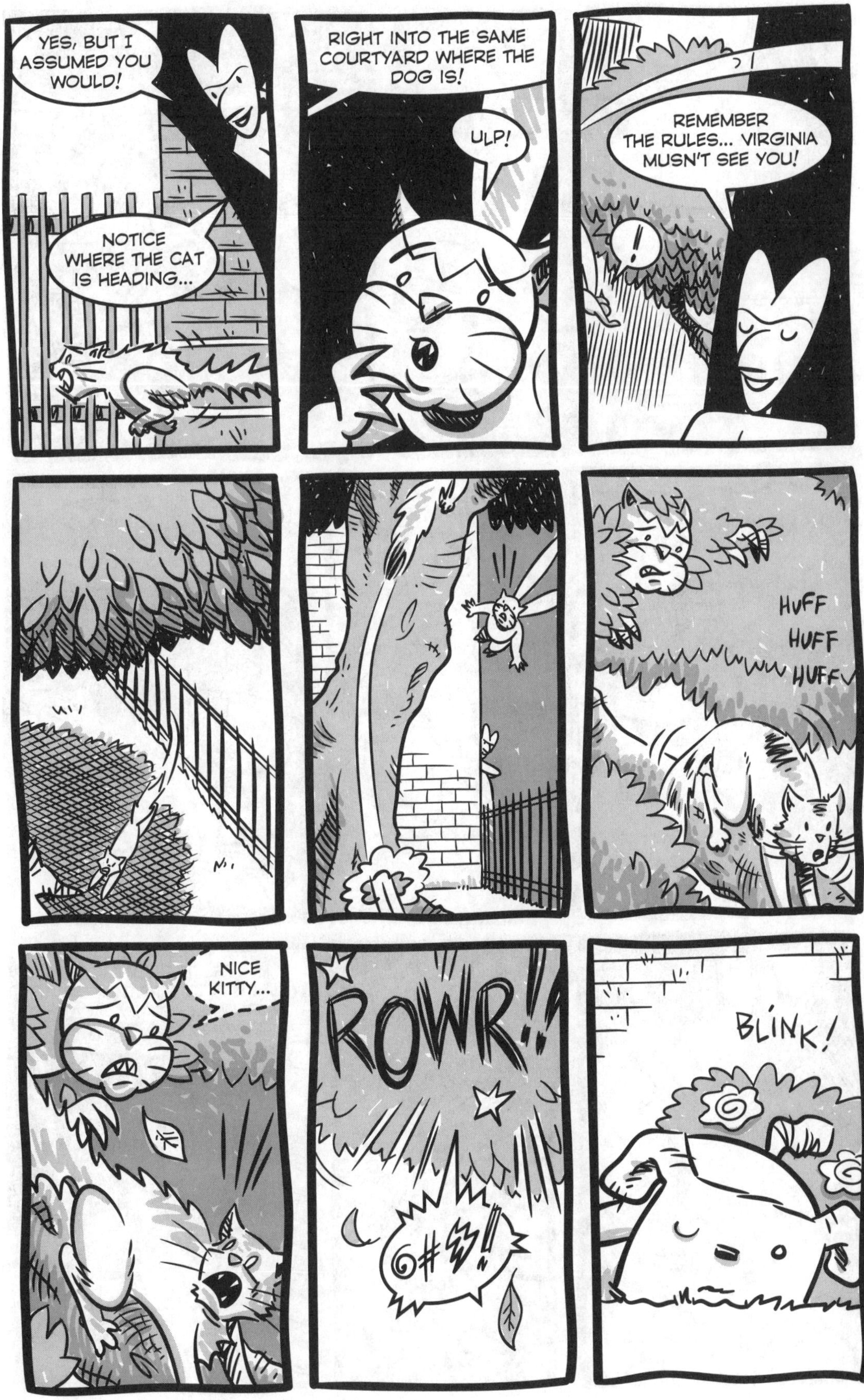
YES, BUT I ASSUMED YOU WOULD!
NOTICE WHERE THE CAT IS HEADING...
RIGHT INTO THE SAME COURTYARD WHERE THE DOG IS!
ULP!
REMEMBER THE RULES... VIRGINIA MUSN'T SEE YOU!
HUFF
HUFF
HUFF
NICE KITTY...
ROWR!!
@#$!
BLINK!

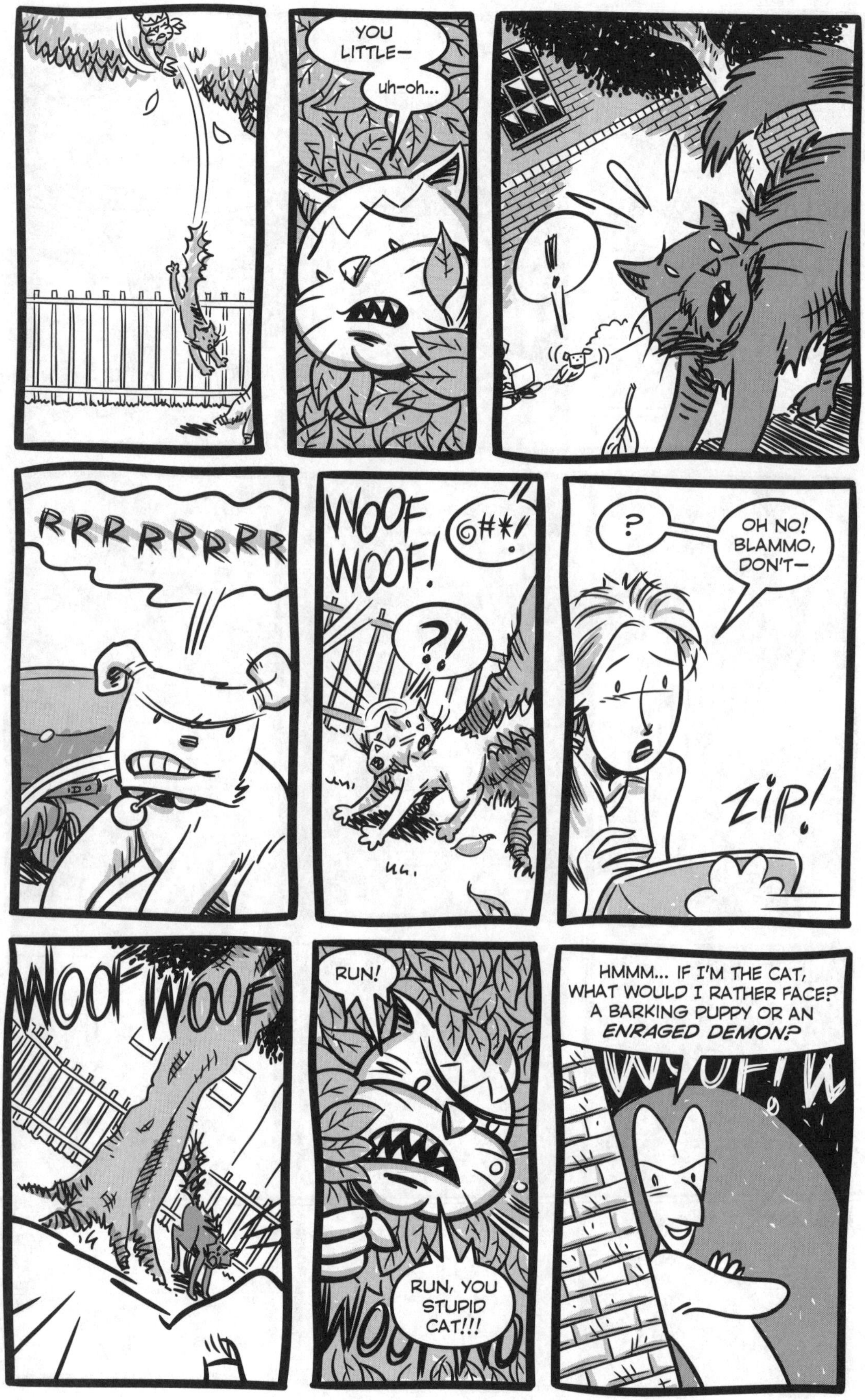
YOU LITTLE—
uh-oh...
RRRRRRRRR
WOOF WOOF!
@#*!
?!
?
OH NO! BLAMMO, DON'T—
ZIP!
WOOF WOOF
RUN!
RUN, YOU STUPID CAT!!!
HMMM... IF I'M THE CAT, WHAT WOULD I RATHER FACE? A BARKING PUPPY OR AN *ENRAGED DEMON?*

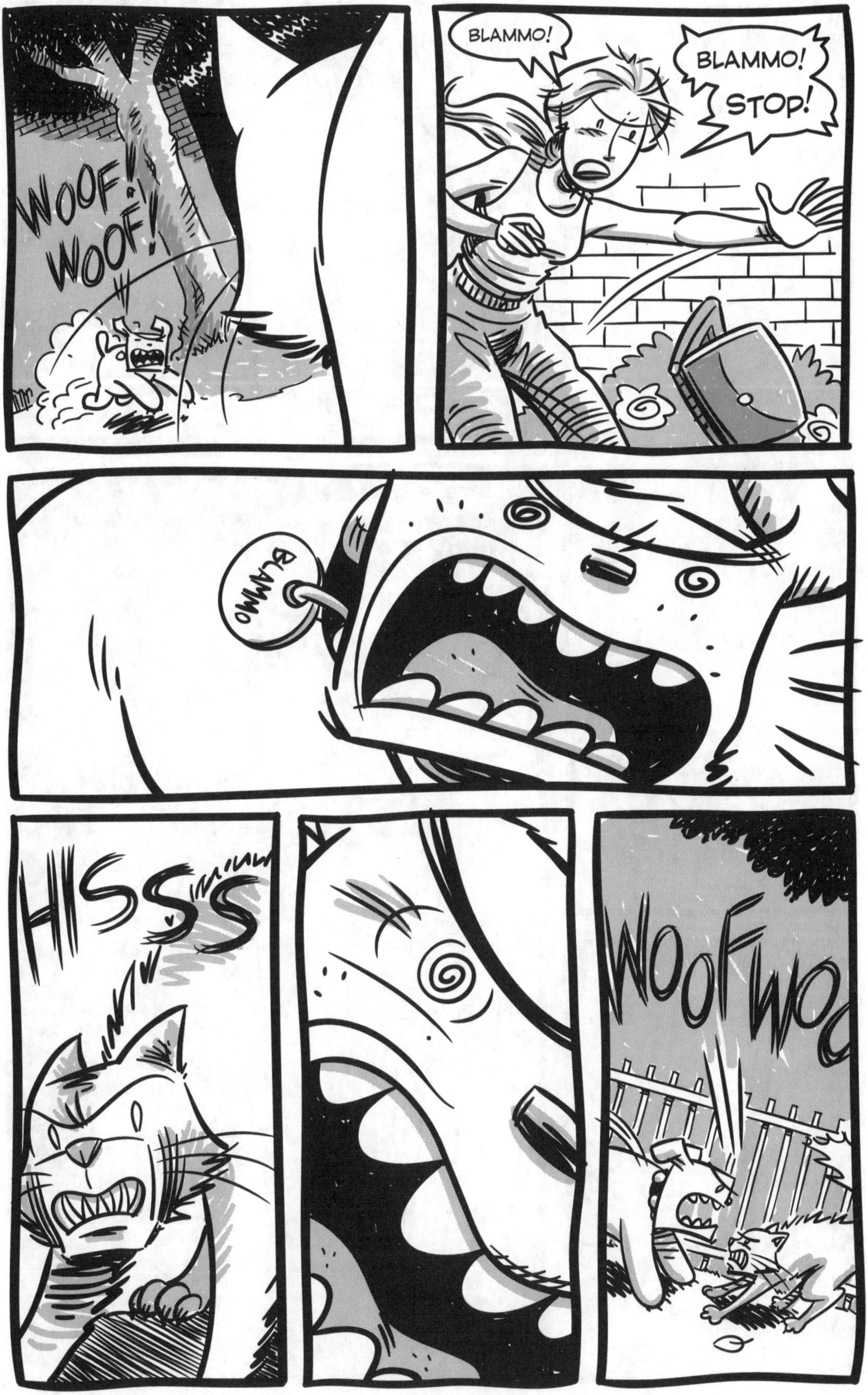
WOOF! WOOF!
BLAMMO!
BLAMMO! STOP!
BLAMMO
HISSS
WOOF WOO

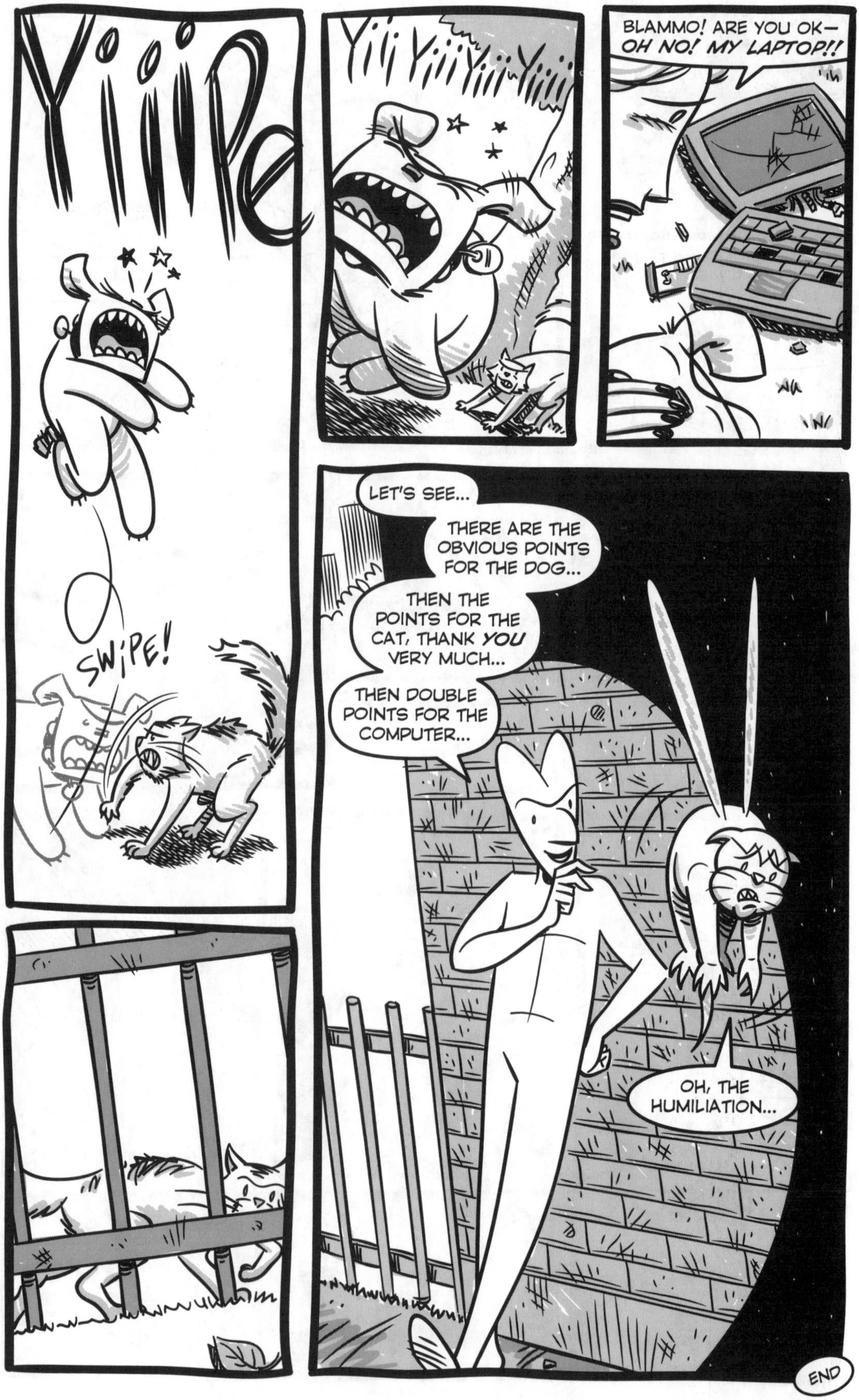
YIIIPE
SWIPE!
YIII YIIIYIIIIYIII
BLAMMO! ARE YOU OK—
OH NO! MY LAPTOP!!
LET'S SEE...
THERE ARE THE OBVIOUS POINTS FOR THE DOG...
THEN THE POINTS FOR THE CAT, THANK YOU VERY MUCH...
THEN DOUBLE POINTS FOR THE COMPUTER...
OH, THE HUMILIATION...
END

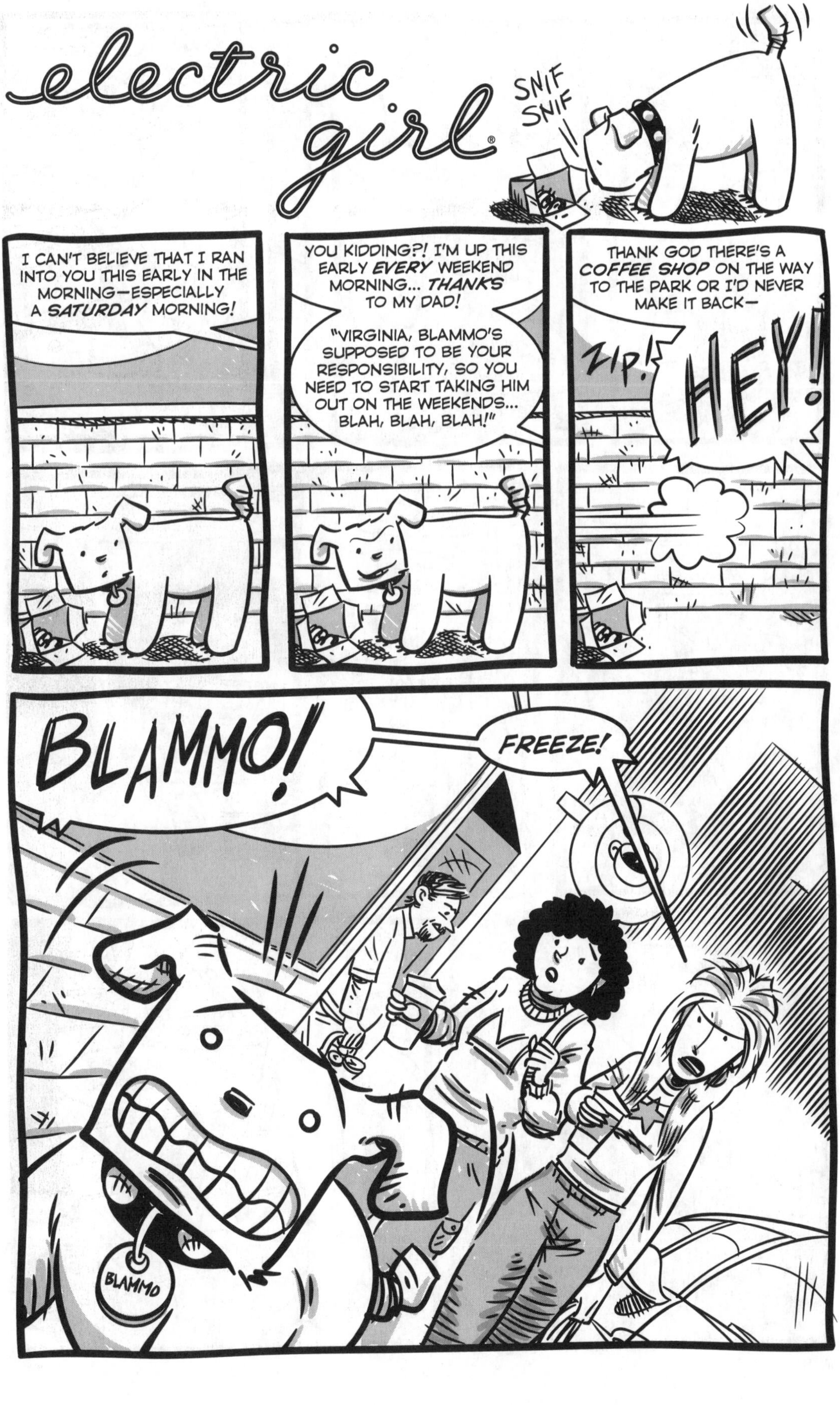
electric girl®
SNIF SNIF
I CAN'T BELIEVE THAT I RAN INTO YOU THIS EARLY IN THE MORNING—ESPECIALLY A *SATURDAY* MORNING!
YOU KIDDING?! I'M UP THIS EARLY *EVERY* WEEKEND MORNING... *THANKS* TO MY DAD!
"VIRGINIA, BLAMMO'S SUPPOSED TO BE YOUR RESPONSIBILITY, SO YOU NEED TO START TAKING HIM OUT ON THE WEEKENDS... BLAH, BLAH, BLAH!"
THANK GOD THERE'S A *COFFEE SHOP* ON THE WAY TO THE PARK OR I'D NEVER MAKE IT BACK—
ZIP!
HEY!
BLAMMO!
FREEZE!
BLAMMO

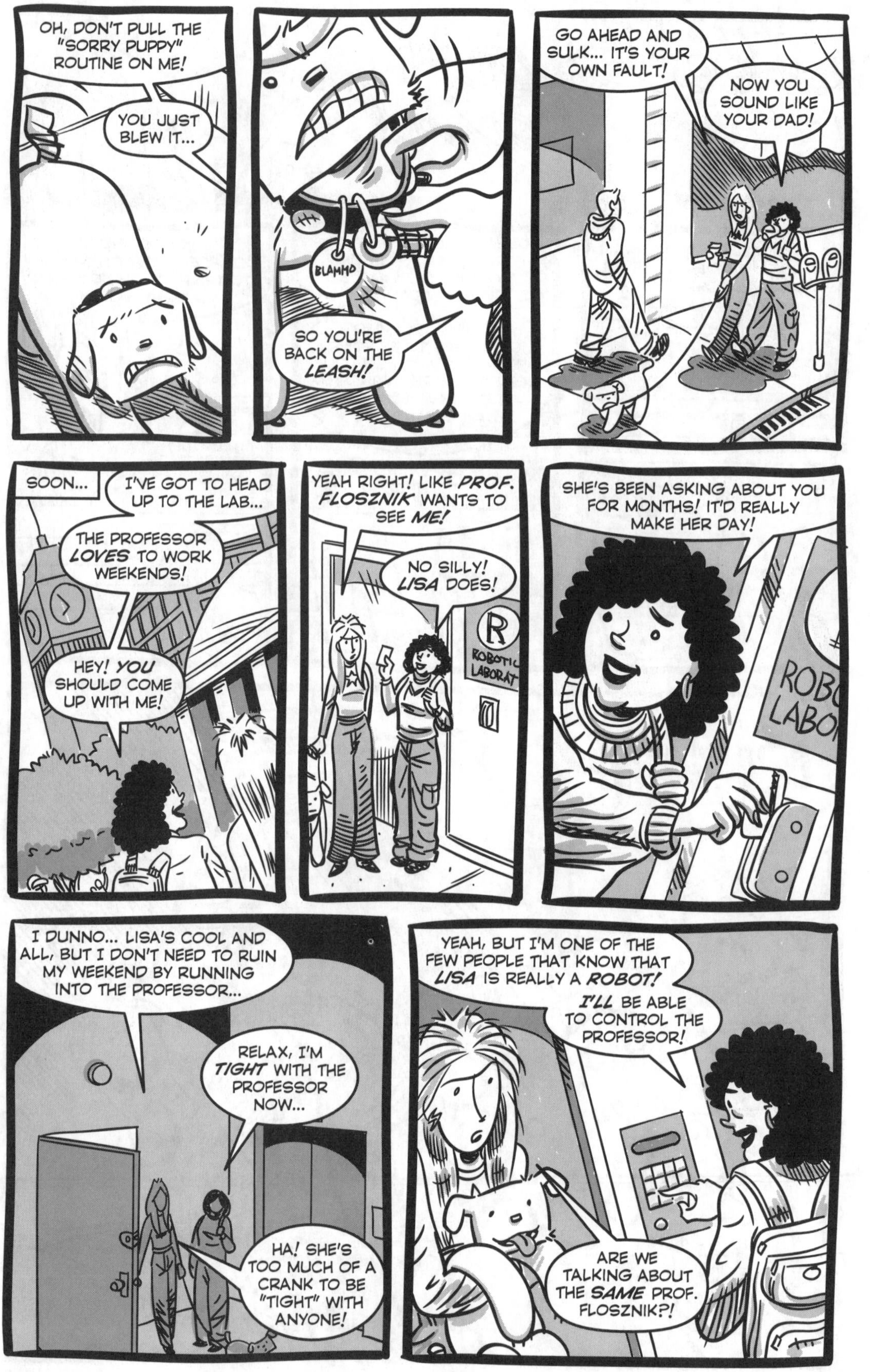
OH, DON'T PULL THE "SORRY PUPPY" ROUTINE ON ME!
YOU JUST BLEW IT...
BLAMMO
SO YOU'RE BACK ON THE *LEASH!*
GO AHEAD AND SULK... IT'S YOUR OWN FAULT!
NOW YOU SOUND LIKE YOUR DAD!
SOON...
I'VE GOT TO HEAD UP TO THE LAB...
THE PROFESSOR *LOVES* TO WORK WEEKENDS!
HEY! *YOU* SHOULD COME UP WITH ME!
YEAH RIGHT! LIKE *PROF. FLOSZNIK* WANTS TO SEE *ME!*
NO SILLY! *LISA* DOES!
SHE'S BEEN ASKING ABOUT YOU FOR MONTHS! IT'D REALLY MAKE HER DAY!
I DUNNO... LISA'S COOL AND ALL, BUT I DON'T NEED TO RUIN MY WEEKEND BY RUNNING INTO THE PROFESSOR...
RELAX, I'M *TIGHT* WITH THE PROFESSOR NOW...
HA! SHE'S TOO MUCH OF A CRANK TO BE "TIGHT" WITH ANYONE!
YEAH, BUT I'M ONE OF THE FEW PEOPLE THAT KNOW THAT *LISA* IS REALLY A *ROBOT!*
I'LL BE ABLE TO CONTROL THE PROFESSOR!
ARE WE TALKING ABOUT THE *SAME* PROF. FLOSZNIK?!

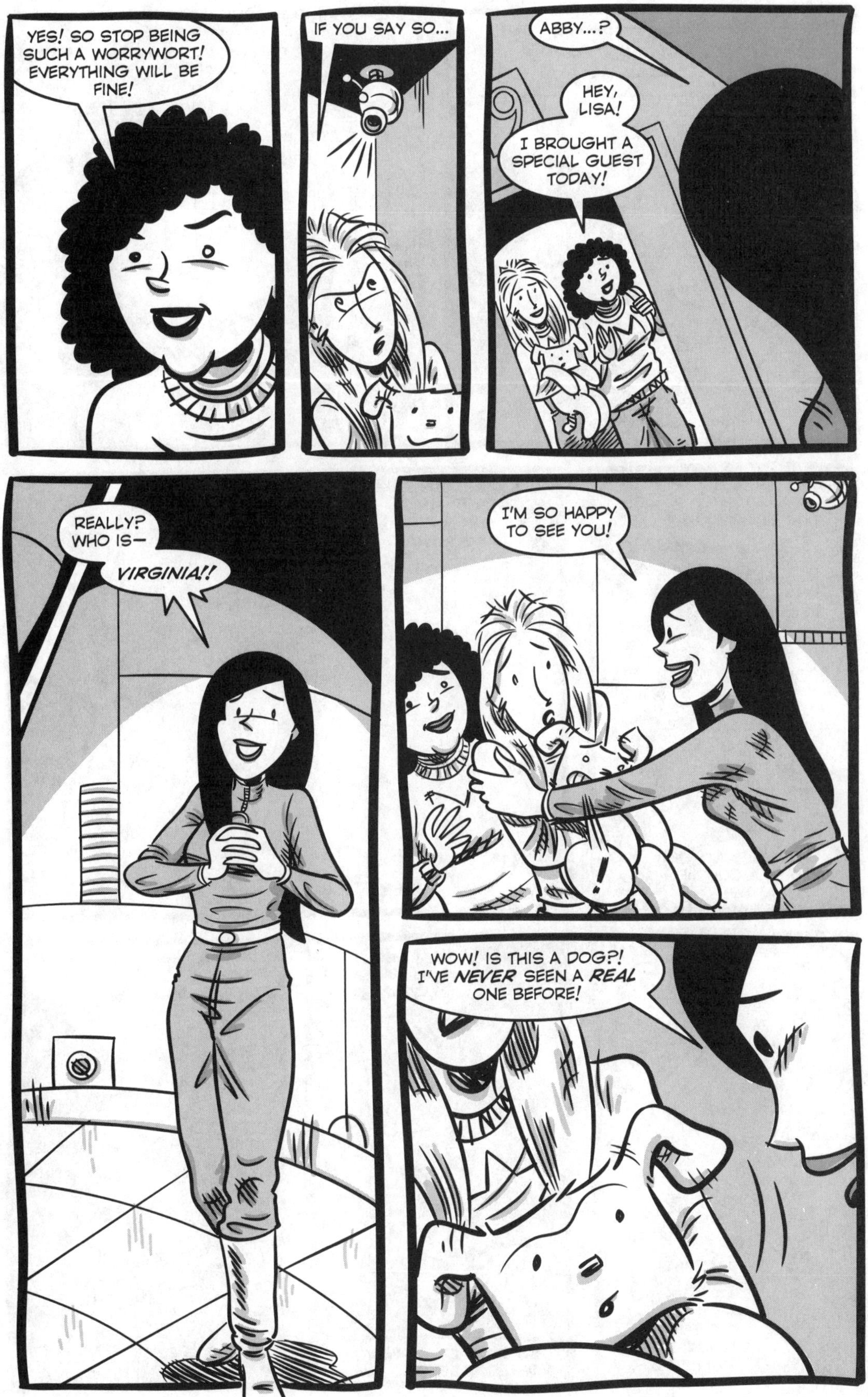
YES! SO STOP BEING SUCH A WORRYWORT! EVERYTHING WILL BE FINE!
IF YOU SAY SO...
ABBY...?
HEY, LISA!
I BROUGHT A SPECIAL GUEST TODAY!
REALLY? WHO IS—
VIRGINIA!!
I'M SO HAPPY TO SEE YOU!
!
WOW! IS THIS A DOG?! I'VE NEVER SEEN A REAL ONE BEFORE!

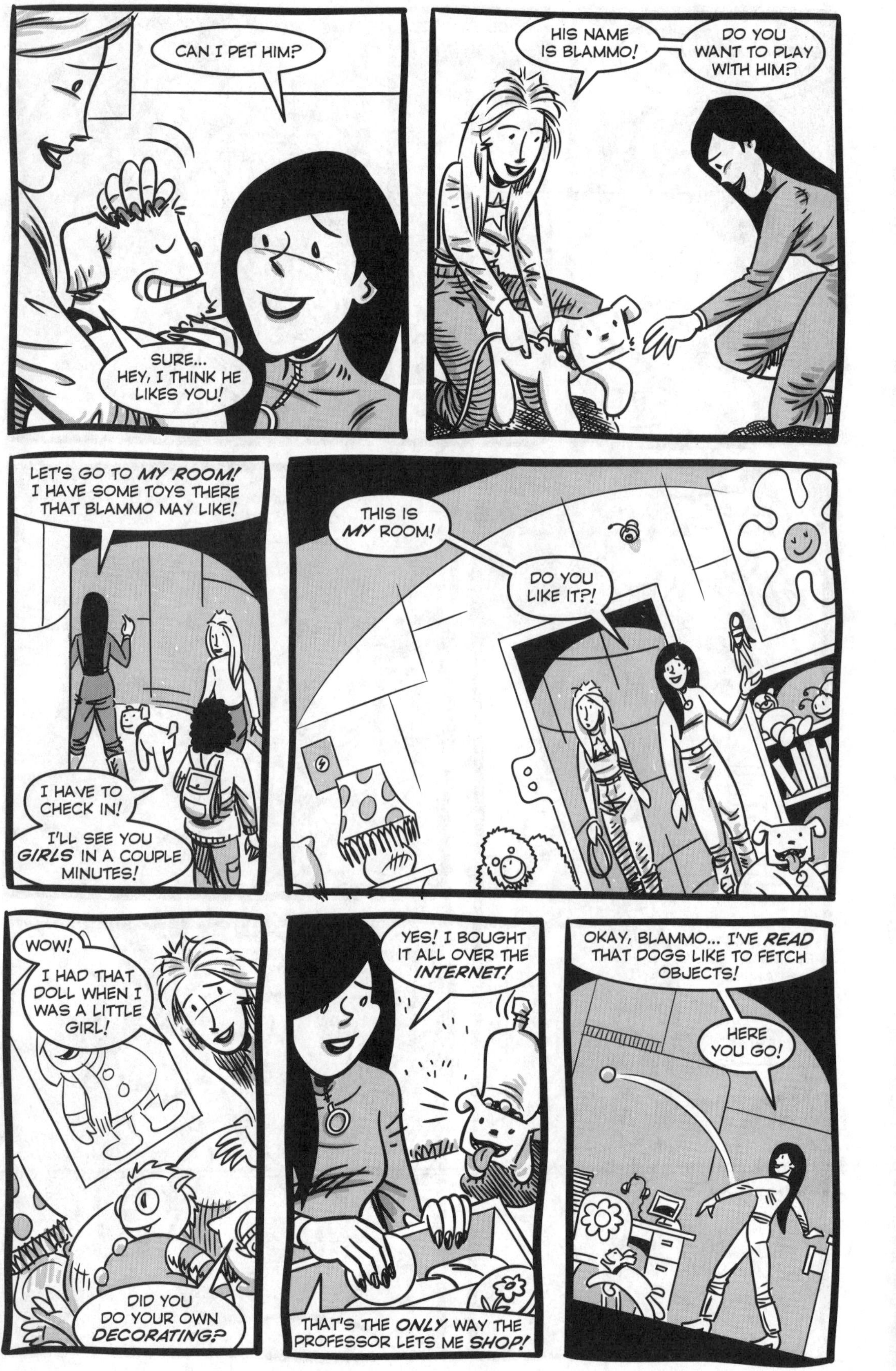
CAN I PET HIM?
SURE... HEY, I THINK HE LIKES YOU!
HIS NAME IS BLAMMO!
DO YOU WANT TO PLAY WITH HIM?
LET'S GO TO MY ROOM! I HAVE SOME TOYS THERE THAT BLAMMO MAY LIKE!
I HAVE TO CHECK IN!
I'LL SEE YOU GIRLS IN A COUPLE MINUTES!
THIS IS MY ROOM!
DO YOU LIKE IT?!
WOW!
I HAD THAT DOLL WHEN I WAS A LITTLE GIRL!
DID YOU DO YOUR OWN DECORATING?
YES! I BOUGHT IT ALL OVER THE INTERNET!
THAT'S THE ONLY WAY THE PROFESSOR LETS ME SHOP!
OKAY, BLAMMO... I'VE READ THAT DOGS LIKE TO FETCH OBJECTS!
HERE YOU GO!

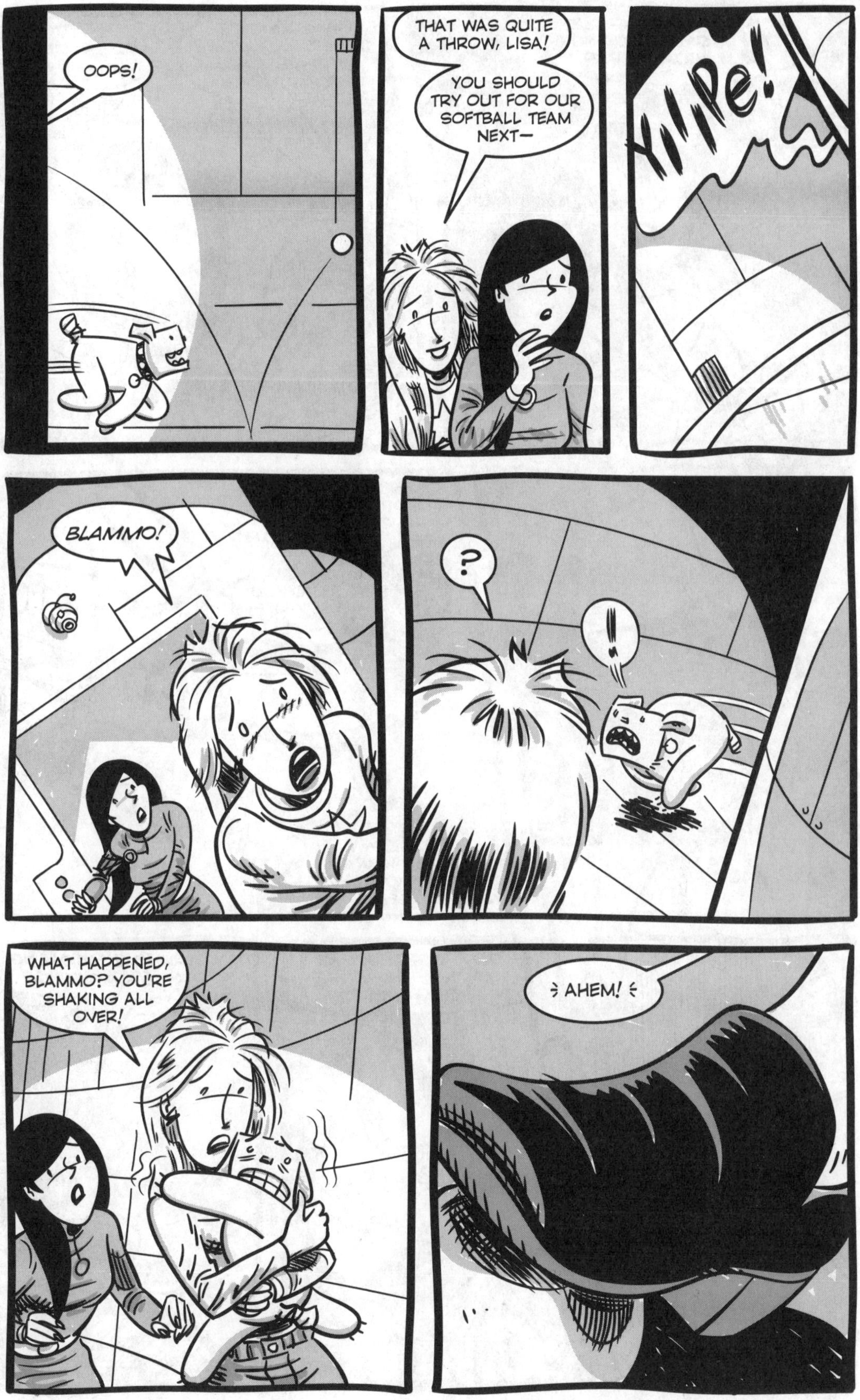
OOPS!
THAT WAS QUITE A THROW, LISA!
YOU SHOULD TRY OUT FOR OUR SOFTBALL TEAM NEXT—
YIIPE!
BLAMMO!
?
!
WHAT HAPPENED, BLAMMO? YOU'RE SHAKING ALL OVER!
AHEM!

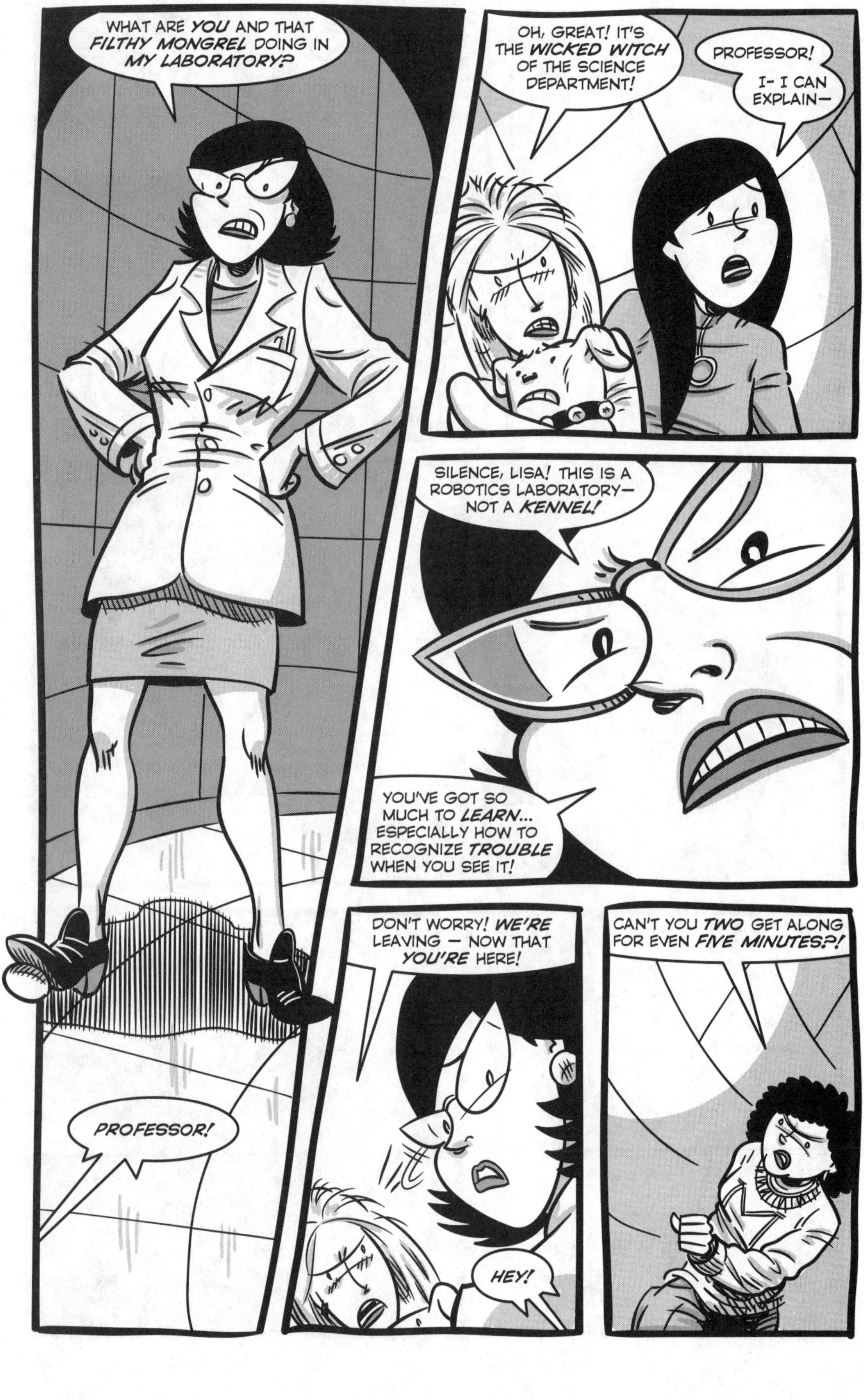
WHAT ARE YOU AND THAT FILTHY MONGREL DOING IN MY LABORATORY?
OH, GREAT! IT'S THE WICKED WITCH OF THE SCIENCE DEPARTMENT!
PROFESSOR!
I- I CAN EXPLAIN—
SILENCE, LISA! THIS IS A ROBOTICS LABORATORY— NOT A KENNEL!
YOU'VE GOT SO MUCH TO LEARN... ESPECIALLY HOW TO RECOGNIZE TROUBLE WHEN YOU SEE IT!
PROFESSOR!
DON'T WORRY! WE'RE LEAVING — NOW THAT YOU'RE HERE!
HEY!
CAN'T YOU TWO GET ALONG FOR EVEN FIVE MINUTES?!

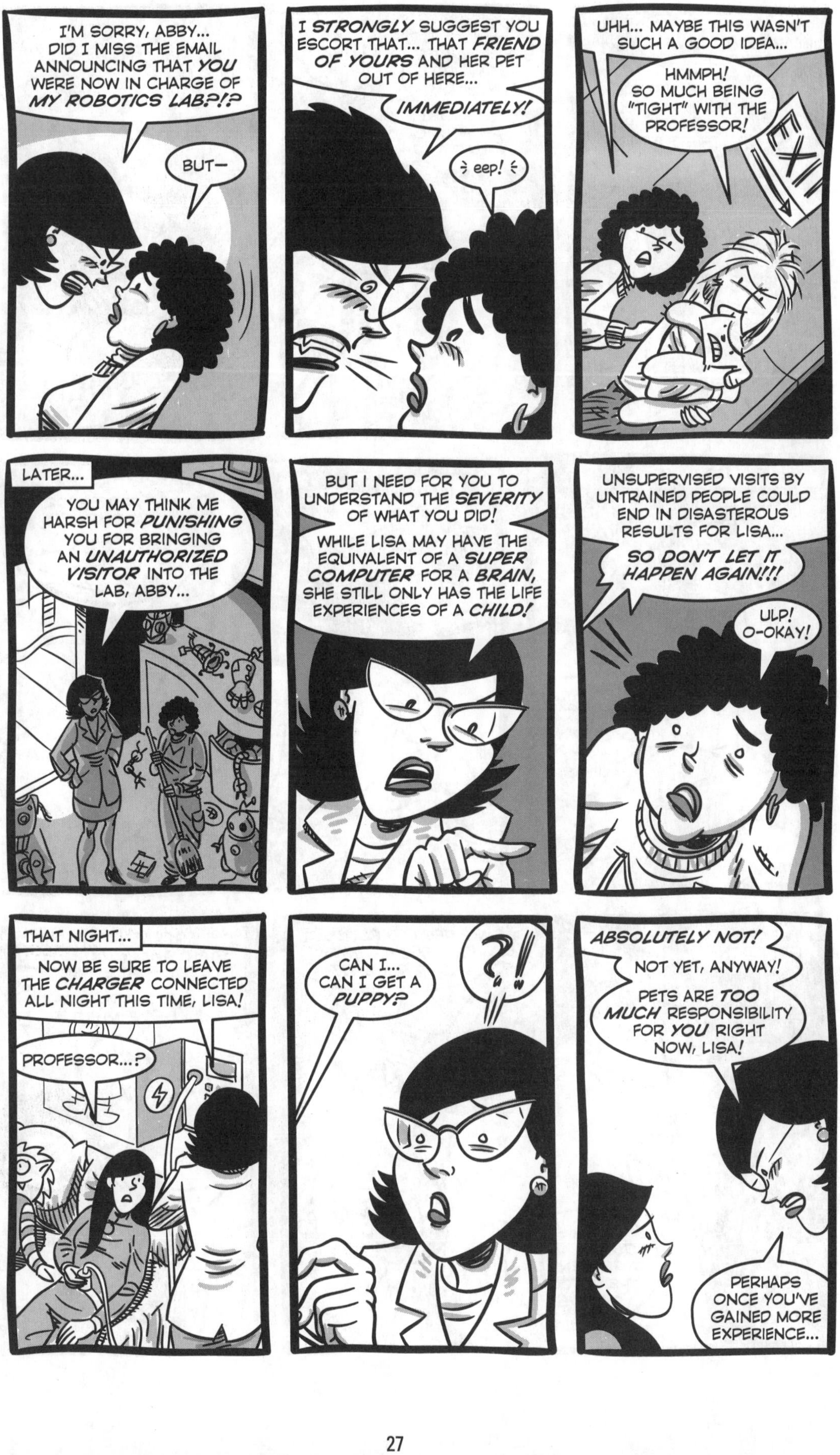
I'M SORRY, ABBY... DID I MISS THE EMAIL ANNOUNCING THAT YOU WERE NOW IN CHARGE OF MY ROBOTICS LAB?!?
BUT—
I STRONGLY SUGGEST YOU ESCORT THAT... THAT FRIEND OF YOURS AND HER PET OUT OF HERE...
IMMEDIATELY!
eep!
UHH... MAYBE THIS WASN'T SUCH A GOOD IDEA...
HMMPH! SO MUCH BEING "TIGHT" WITH THE PROFESSOR!
EXIT
LATER...
YOU MAY THINK ME HARSH FOR PUNISHING YOU FOR BRINGING AN UNAUTHORIZED VISITOR INTO THE LAB, ABBY...
BUT I NEED FOR YOU TO UNDERSTAND THE SEVERITY OF WHAT YOU DID!
WHILE LISA MAY HAVE THE EQUIVALENT OF A SUPER COMPUTER FOR A BRAIN, SHE STILL ONLY HAS THE LIFE EXPERIENCES OF A CHILD!
UNSUPERVISED VISITS BY UNTRAINED PEOPLE COULD END IN DISASTEROUS RESULTS FOR LISA...
SO DON'T LET IT HAPPEN AGAIN!!!
ULP! O-OKAY!
THAT NIGHT...
NOW BE SURE TO LEAVE THE CHARGER CONNECTED ALL NIGHT THIS TIME, LISA!
PROFESSOR...?
CAN I... CAN I GET A PUPPY?
?!!
ABSOLUTELY NOT!
NOT YET, ANYWAY!
PETS ARE TOO MUCH RESPONSIBILITY FOR YOU RIGHT NOW, LISA!
PERHAPS ONCE YOU'VE GAINED MORE EXPERIENCE...

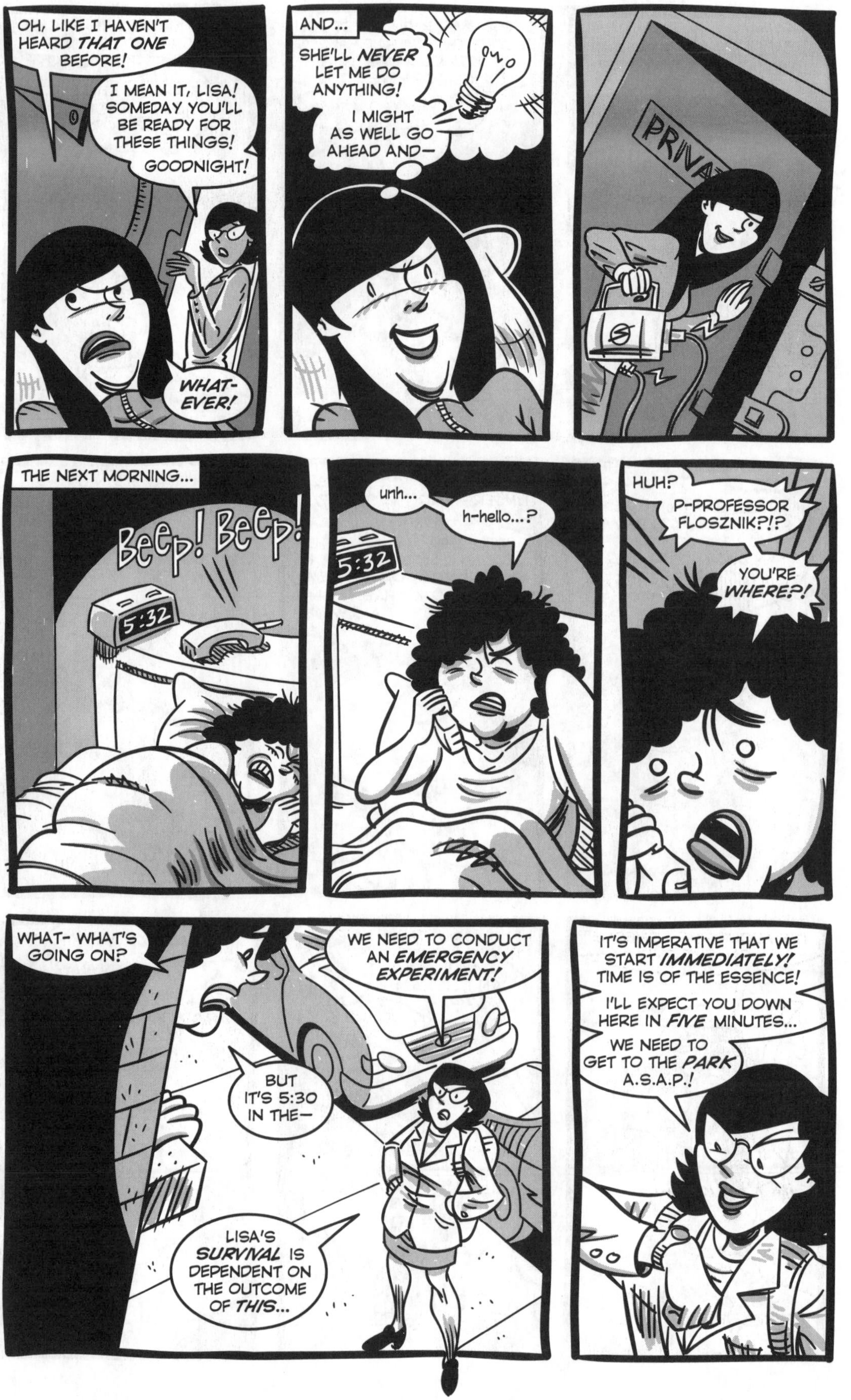
OH, LIKE I HAVEN'T HEARD *THAT ONE* BEFORE!
I MEAN IT, LISA! SOMEDAY YOU'LL BE READY FOR THESE THINGS!
GOODNIGHT!
WHAT-EVER!
AND...
SHE'LL *NEVER* LET ME DO ANYTHING!
I MIGHT AS WELL GO AHEAD AND–
THE NEXT MORNING...
Beep! Beep!
5:32
unh...
h-hello...?
HUH?
P-PROFESSOR FLOSZNIK?!?
YOU'RE *WHERE?!*
WHAT- WHAT'S GOING ON?
WE NEED TO CONDUCT AN *EMERGENCY EXPERIMENT!*
BUT IT'S 5:30 IN THE–
LISA'S *SURVIVAL* IS DEPENDENT ON THE OUTCOME OF *THIS...*
IT'S IMPERATIVE THAT WE START *IMMEDIATELY!* TIME IS OF THE ESSENCE!
I'LL EXPECT YOU DOWN HERE IN *FIVE* MINUTES...
WE NEED TO GET TO THE *PARK* A.S.A.P.!

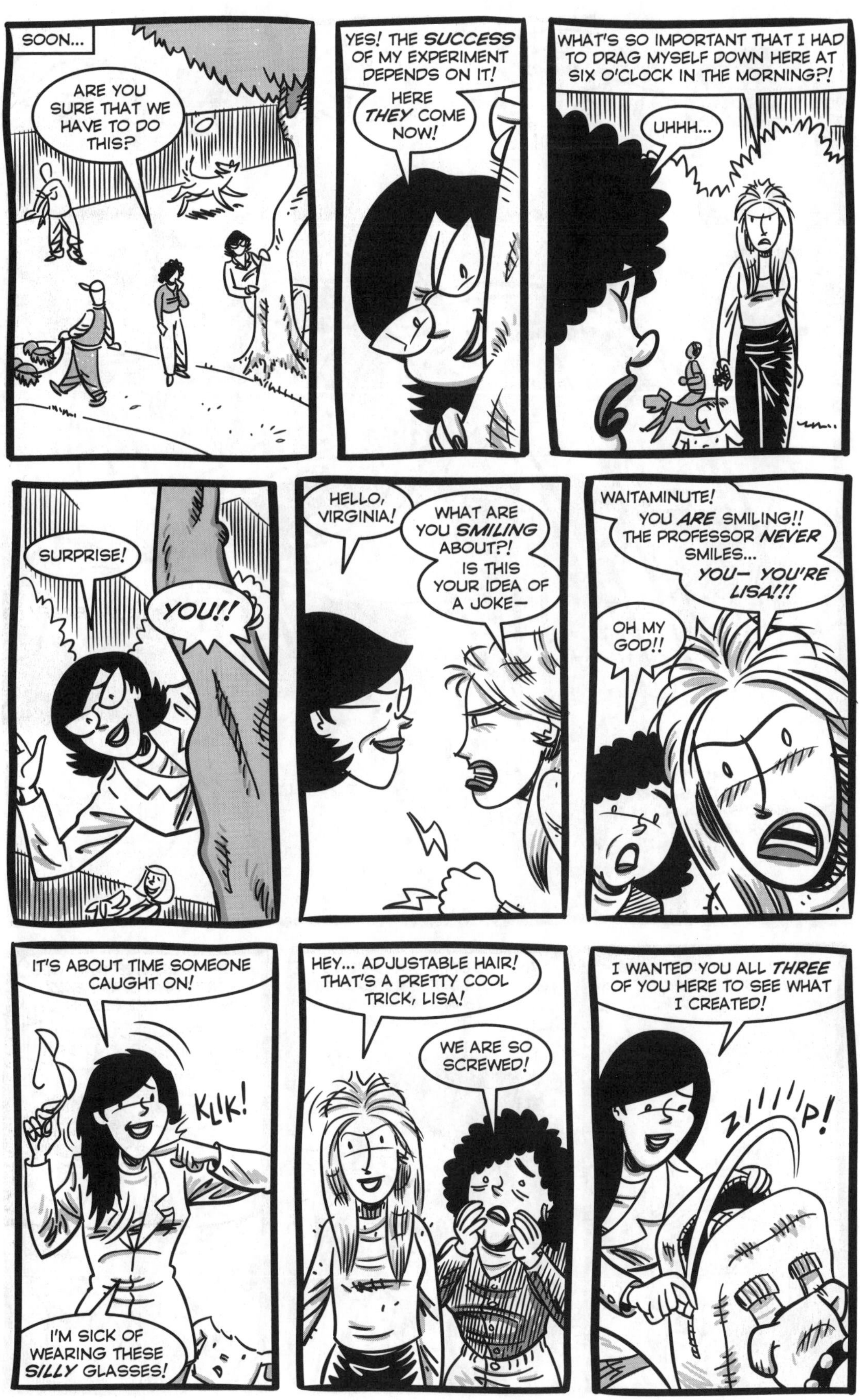
SOON...
ARE YOU SURE THAT WE HAVE TO DO THIS?
YES! THE SUCCESS OF MY EXPERIMENT DEPENDS ON IT!
HERE THEY COME NOW!
WHAT'S SO IMPORTANT THAT I HAD TO DRAG MYSELF DOWN HERE AT SIX O'CLOCK IN THE MORNING?!
UHHH...
SURPRISE!
YOU!!
HELLO, VIRGINIA!
WHAT ARE YOU SMILING ABOUT?!
IS THIS YOUR IDEA OF A JOKE–
WAITAMINUTE!
YOU ARE SMILING!! THE PROFESSOR NEVER SMILES...
YOU– YOU'RE LISA!!!
OH MY GOD!!
IT'S ABOUT TIME SOMEONE CAUGHT ON!
KLIK!
I'M SICK OF WEARING THESE SILLY GLASSES!
HEY... ADJUSTABLE HAIR! THAT'S A PRETTY COOL TRICK, LISA!
WE ARE SO SCREWED!
I WANTED YOU ALL THREE OF YOU HERE TO SEE WHAT I CREATED!
ZIIIIP!

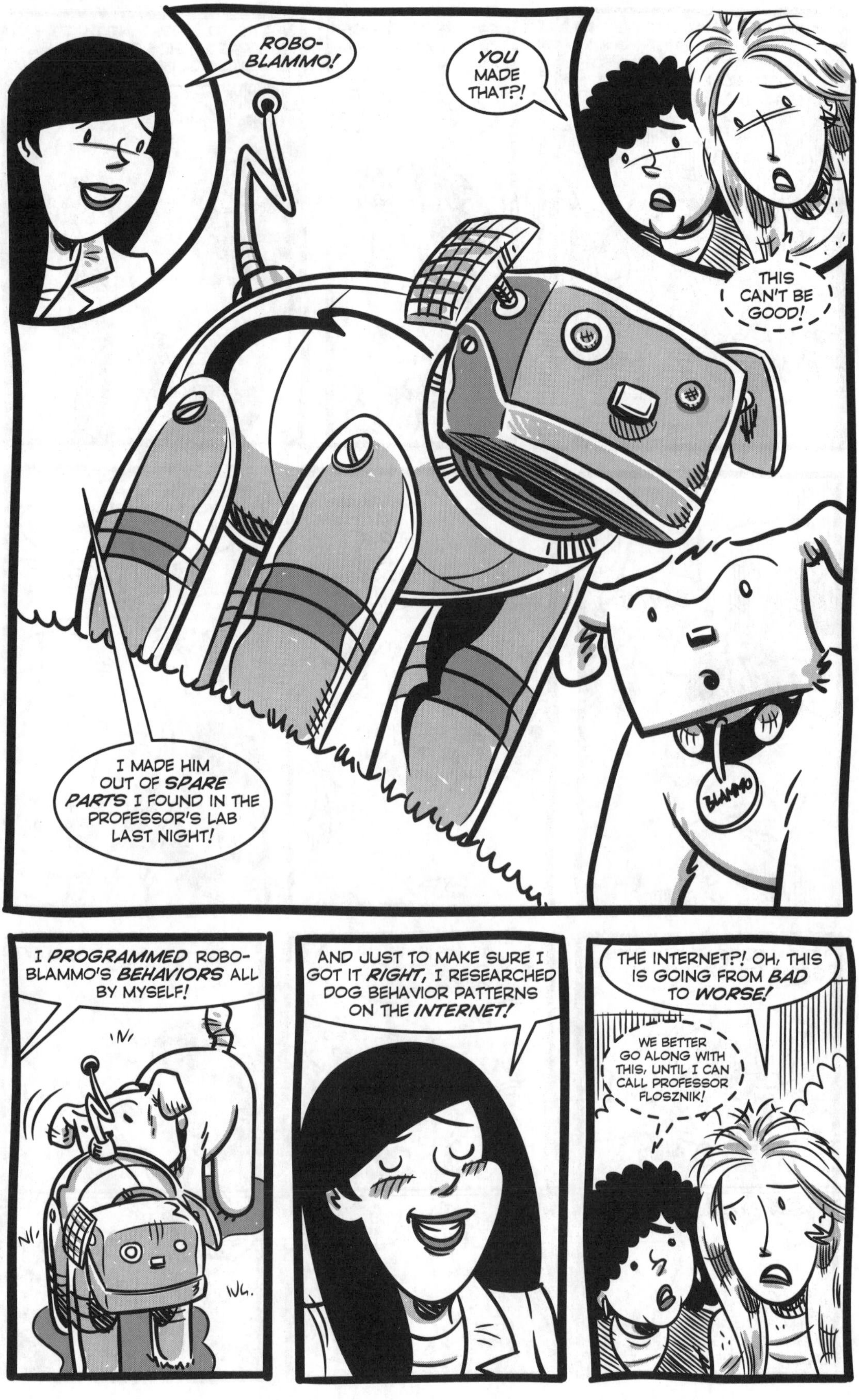
ROBO-BLAMMO!
YOU MADE THAT?!
THIS CAN'T BE GOOD!
I MADE HIM OUT OF SPARE PARTS I FOUND IN THE PROFESSOR'S LAB LAST NIGHT!
BLAMMO
I PROGRAMMED ROBO-BLAMMO'S BEHAVIORS ALL BY MYSELF!
AND JUST TO MAKE SURE I GOT IT RIGHT, I RESEARCHED DOG BEHAVIOR PATTERNS ON THE INTERNET!
THE INTERNET?! OH, THIS IS GOING FROM BAD TO WORSE!
WE BETTER GO ALONG WITH THIS, UNTIL I CAN CALL PROFESSOR FLOSZNIK!

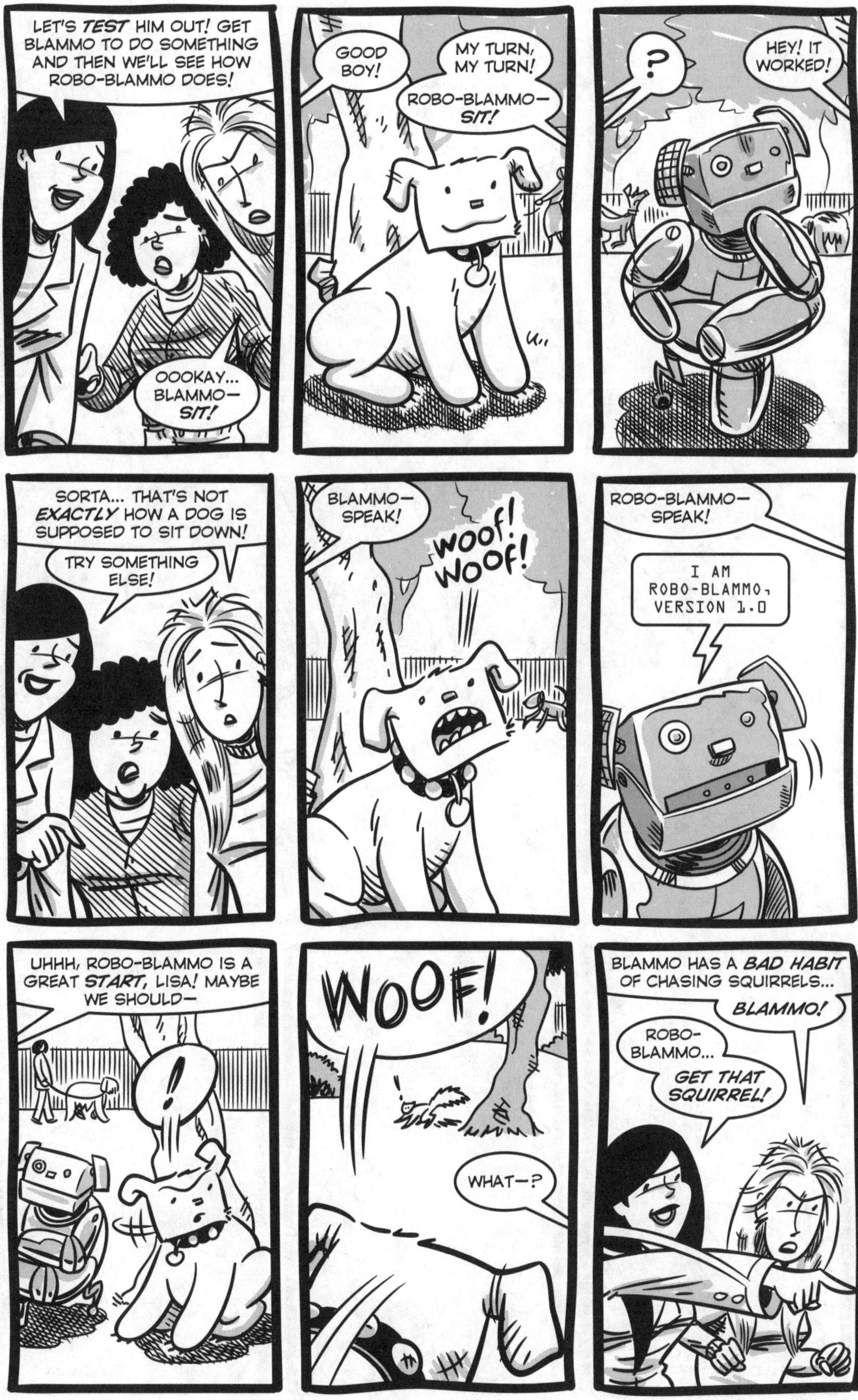
LET'S TEST HIM OUT! GET BLAMMO TO DO SOMETHING AND THEN WE'LL SEE HOW ROBO-BLAMMO DOES!
OOOKAY... BLAMMO— SIT!
GOOD BOY!
MY TURN, MY TURN!
ROBO-BLAMMO— SIT!
?
HEY! IT WORKED!
SORTA... THAT'S NOT EXACTLY HOW A DOG IS SUPPOSED TO SIT DOWN!
TRY SOMETHING ELSE!
BLAMMO— SPEAK!
WOOF! WOOF!
ROBO-BLAMMO— SPEAK!
I AM ROBO-BLAMMO, VERSION 1.0
UHHH, ROBO-BLAMMO IS A GREAT START, LISA! MAYBE WE SHOULD—
!
WOOF!
WHAT—?
BLAMMO HAS A BAD HABIT OF CHASING SQUIRRELS...
BLAMMO!
ROBO-BLAMMO... GET THAT SQUIRREL!

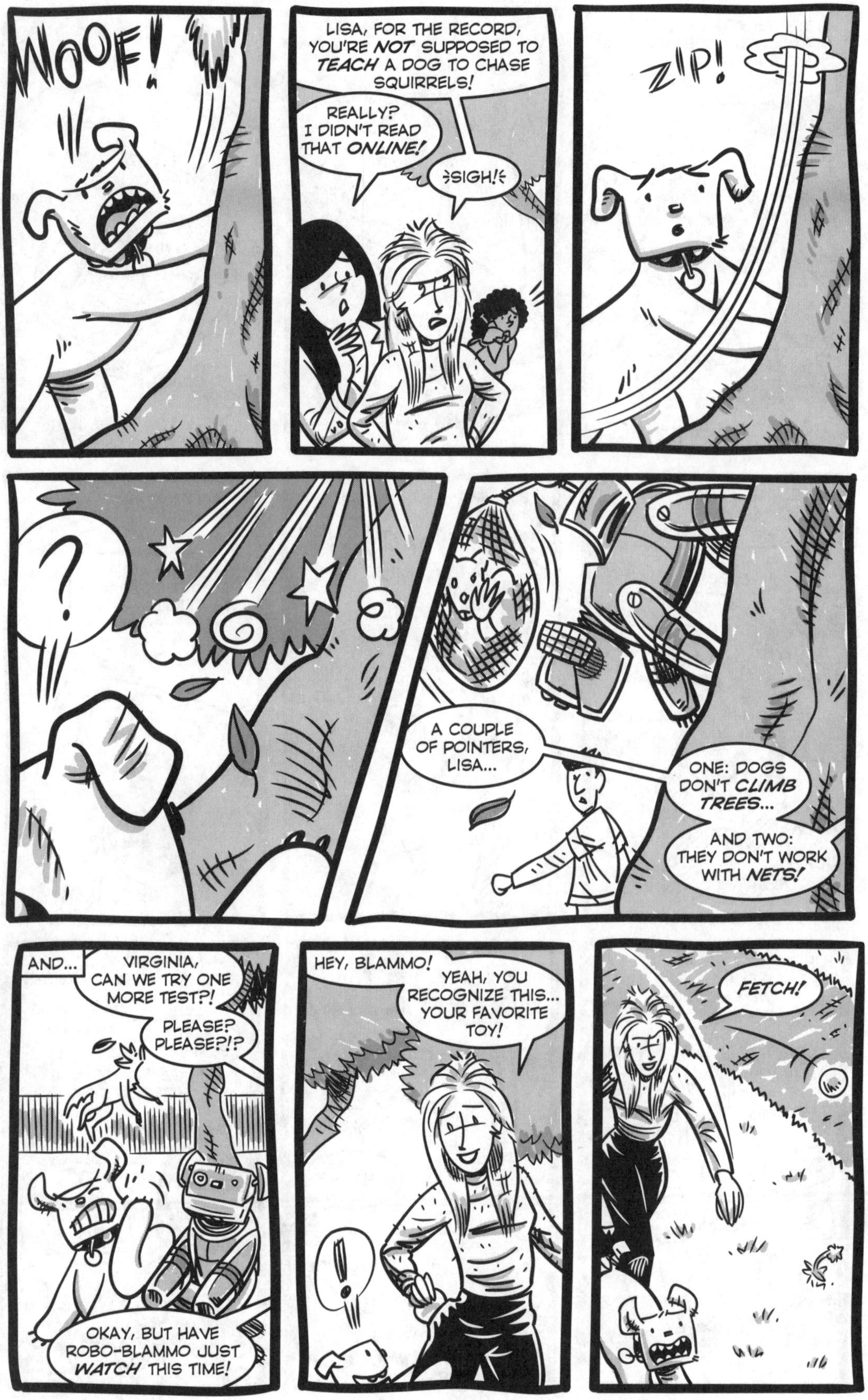
WOOF!
LISA, FOR THE RECORD, YOU'RE NOT SUPPOSED TO TEACH A DOG TO CHASE SQUIRRELS!
REALLY? I DIDN'T READ THAT ONLINE!
SIGH!
ZIP!
?
A COUPLE OF POINTERS, LISA...
ONE: DOGS DON'T CLIMB TREES...
AND TWO: THEY DON'T WORK WITH NETS!
AND...
VIRGINIA, CAN WE TRY ONE MORE TEST?!
PLEASE? PLEASE?!?
OKAY, BUT HAVE ROBO-BLAMMO JUST WATCH THIS TIME!
HEY, BLAMMO!
YEAH, YOU RECOGNIZE THIS... YOUR FAVORITE TOY!
!
FETCH!

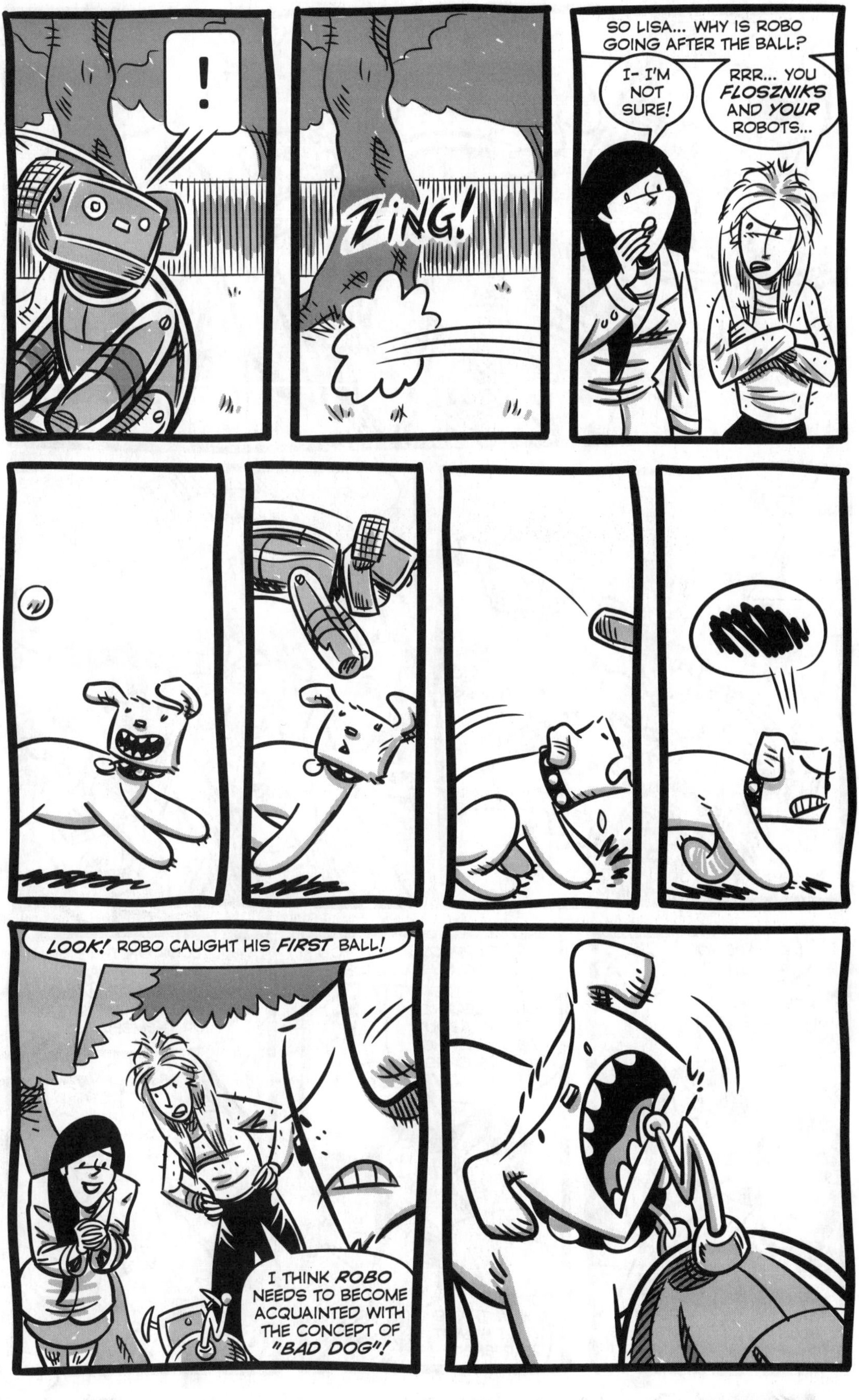
!
ZING!
SO LISA... WHY IS ROBO GOING AFTER THE BALL?
I- I'M NOT SURE!
RRR... YOU FLOSZNIKS AND YOUR ROBOTS...
LOOK! ROBO CAUGHT HIS FIRST BALL!
I THINK ROBO NEEDS TO BECOME ACQUAINTED WITH THE CONCEPT OF "BAD DOG"!

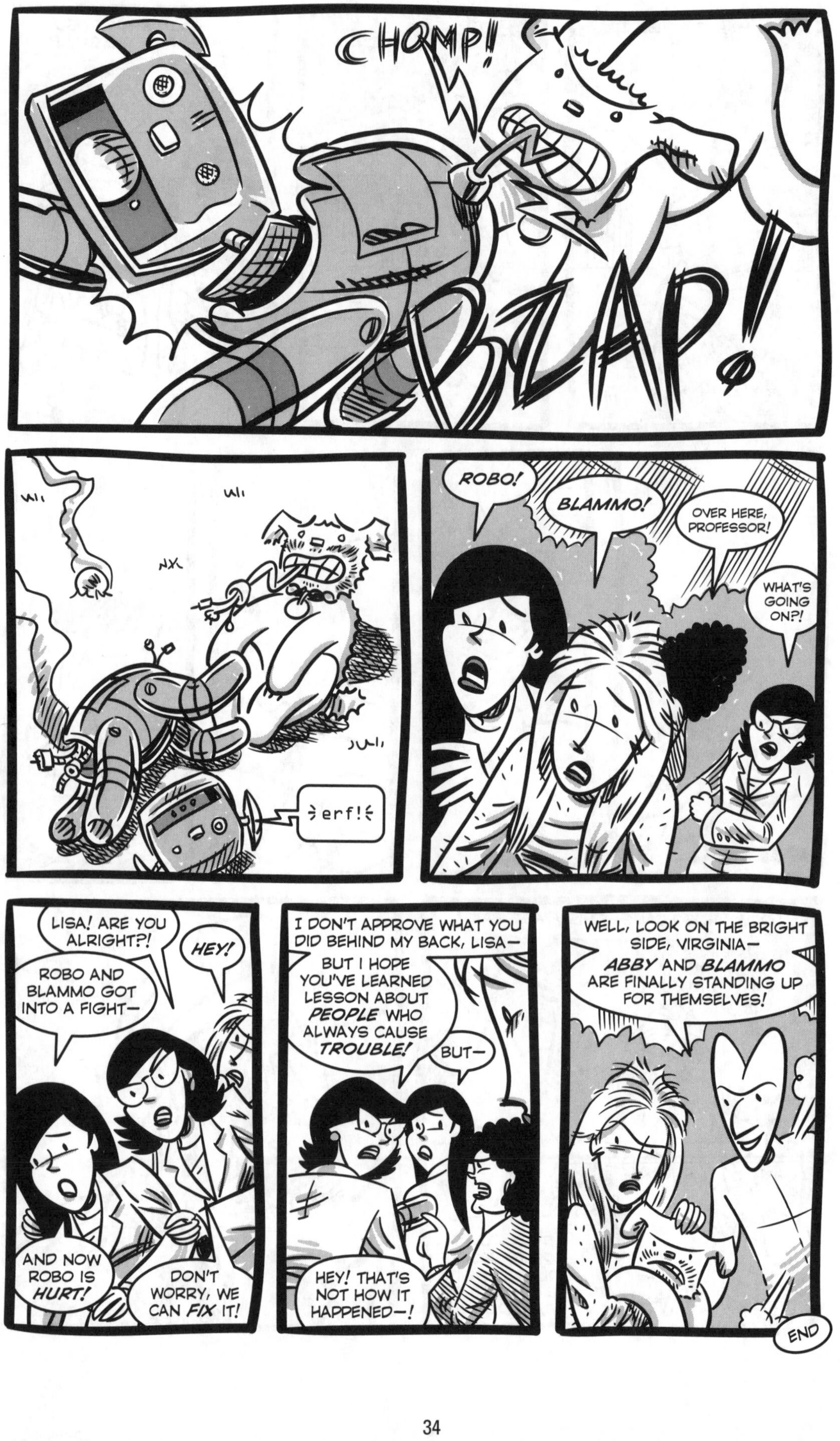
CHOMP!
BZAP!
erf!
ROBO!
BLAMMO!
OVER HERE, PROFESSOR!
WHAT'S GOING ON?!
LISA! ARE YOU ALRIGHT?!
HEY!
ROBO AND BLAMMO GOT INTO A FIGHT—
AND NOW ROBO IS HURT!
DON'T WORRY, WE CAN FIX IT!
I DON'T APPROVE WHAT YOU DID BEHIND MY BACK, LISA—
BUT I HOPE YOU'VE LEARNED LESSON ABOUT PEOPLE WHO ALWAYS CAUSE TROUBLE!
BUT—
HEY! THAT'S NOT HOW IT HAPPENED—!
WELL, LOOK ON THE BRIGHT SIDE, VIRGINIA— ABBY AND BLAMMO ARE FINALLY STANDING UP FOR THEMSELVES!
END

electric girl #10

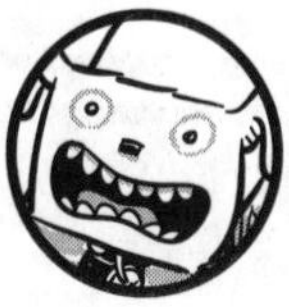 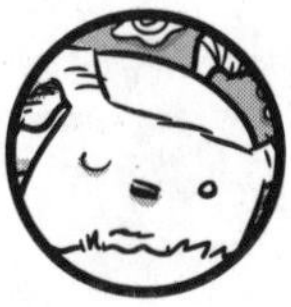 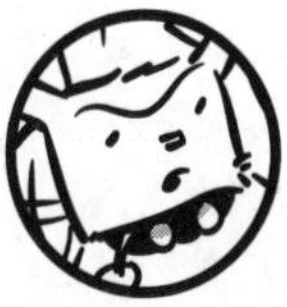

Originally published in Fall 2002

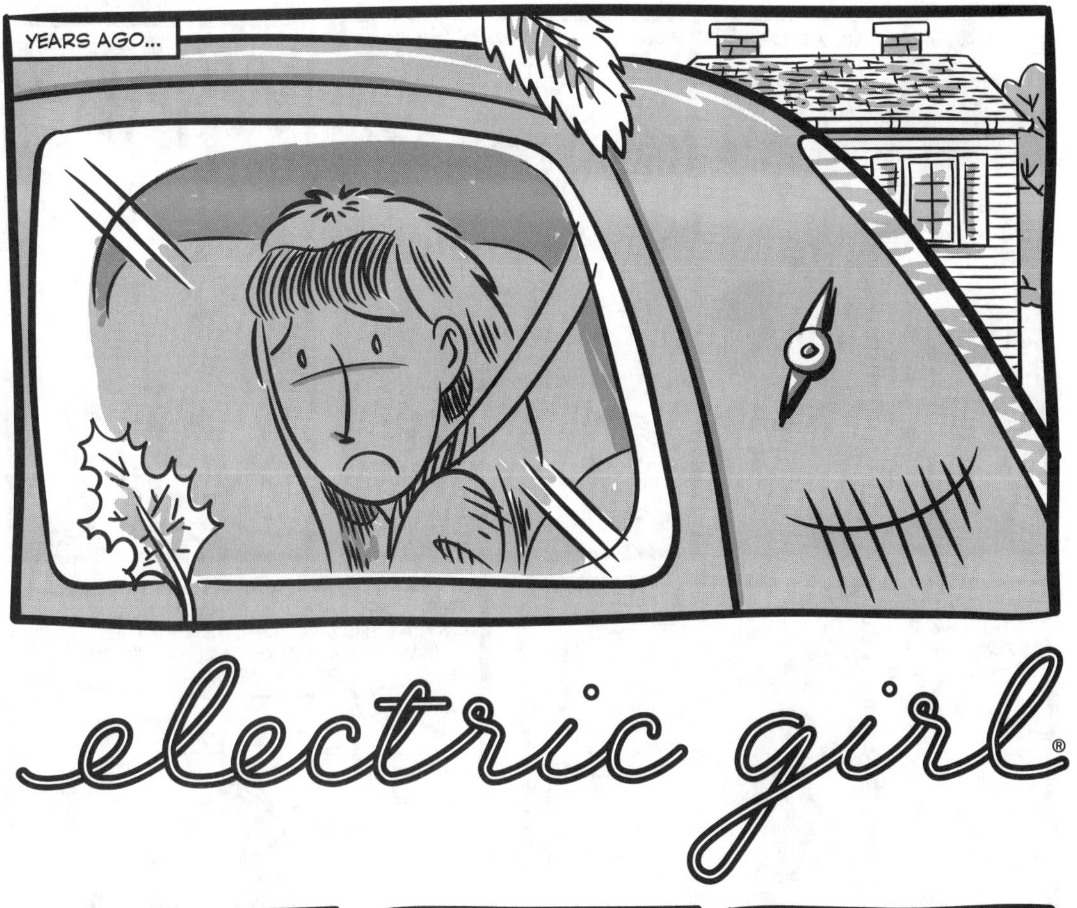
YEARS AGO...

electric girl®

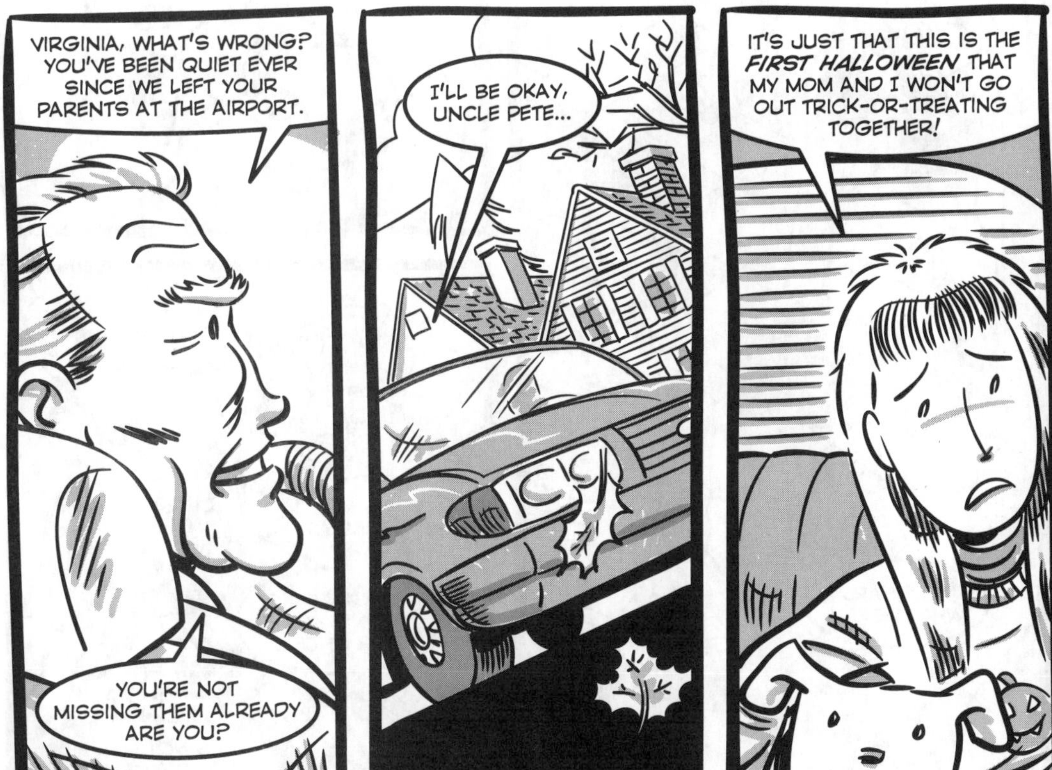
VIRGINIA, WHAT'S WRONG? YOU'VE BEEN QUIET EVER SINCE WE LEFT YOUR PARENTS AT THE AIRPORT.
YOU'RE NOT MISSING THEM ALREADY ARE YOU?
I'LL BE OKAY, UNCLE PETE...
IT'S JUST THAT THIS IS THE *FIRST HALLOWEEN* THAT MY MOM AND I WON'T GO OUT TRICK-OR-TREATING TOGETHER!

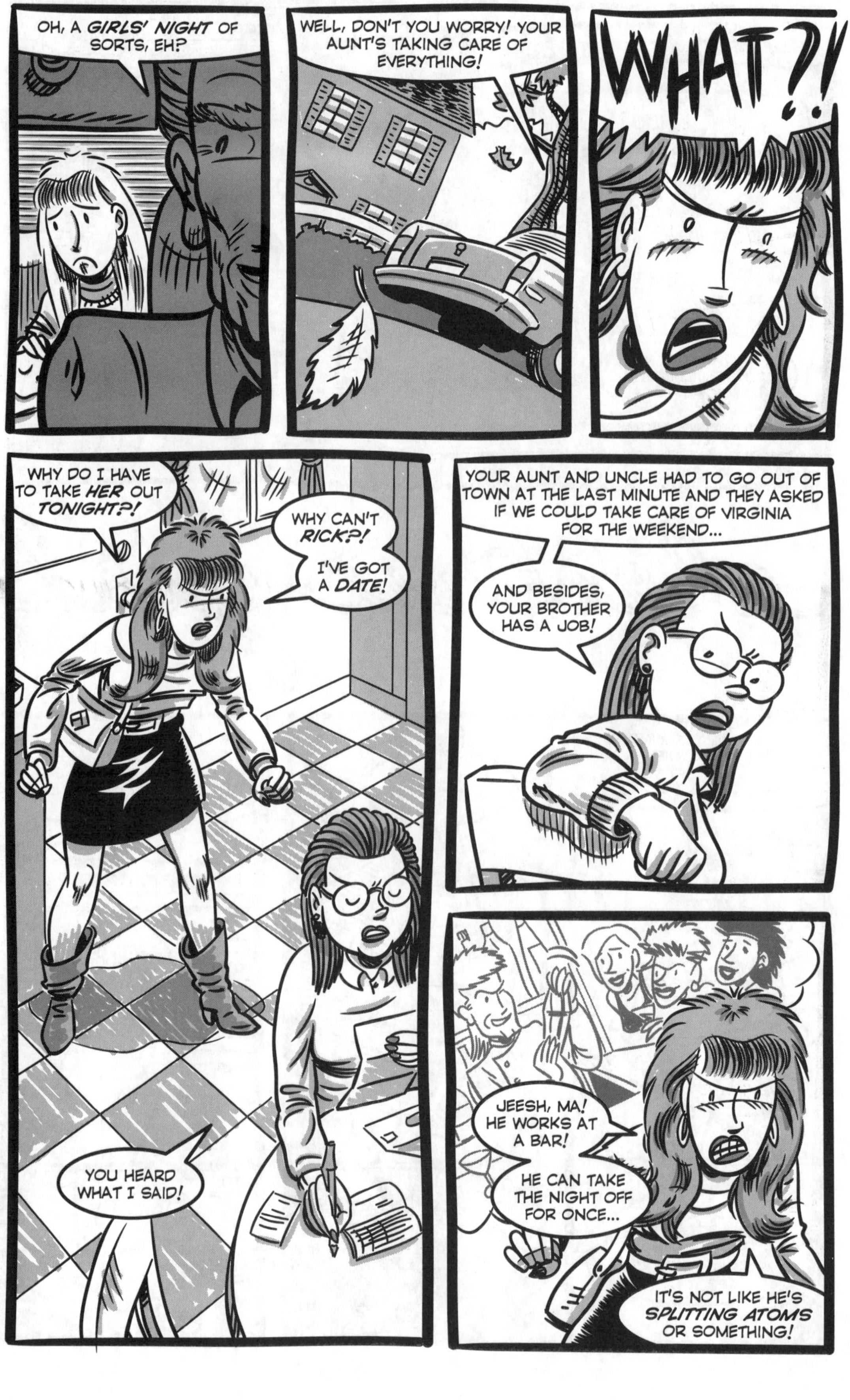
OH, A *GIRLS' NIGHT* OF SORTS, EH?
WELL, DON'T YOU WORRY! YOUR AUNT'S TAKING CARE OF EVERYTHING!
WHAT?!
WHY DO I HAVE TO TAKE *HER* OUT *TONIGHT?!*
WHY CAN'T *RICK?!*
I'VE GOT A *DATE!*
YOU HEARD WHAT I SAID!
YOUR AUNT AND UNCLE HAD TO GO OUT OF TOWN AT THE LAST MINUTE AND THEY ASKED IF WE COULD TAKE CARE OF VIRGINIA FOR THE WEEKEND...
AND BESIDES, YOUR BROTHER HAS A JOB!
JEESH, MA! HE WORKS AT A BAR!
HE CAN TAKE THE NIGHT OFF FOR ONCE...
IT'S NOT LIKE HE'S *SPLITTING ATOMS* OR SOMETHING!

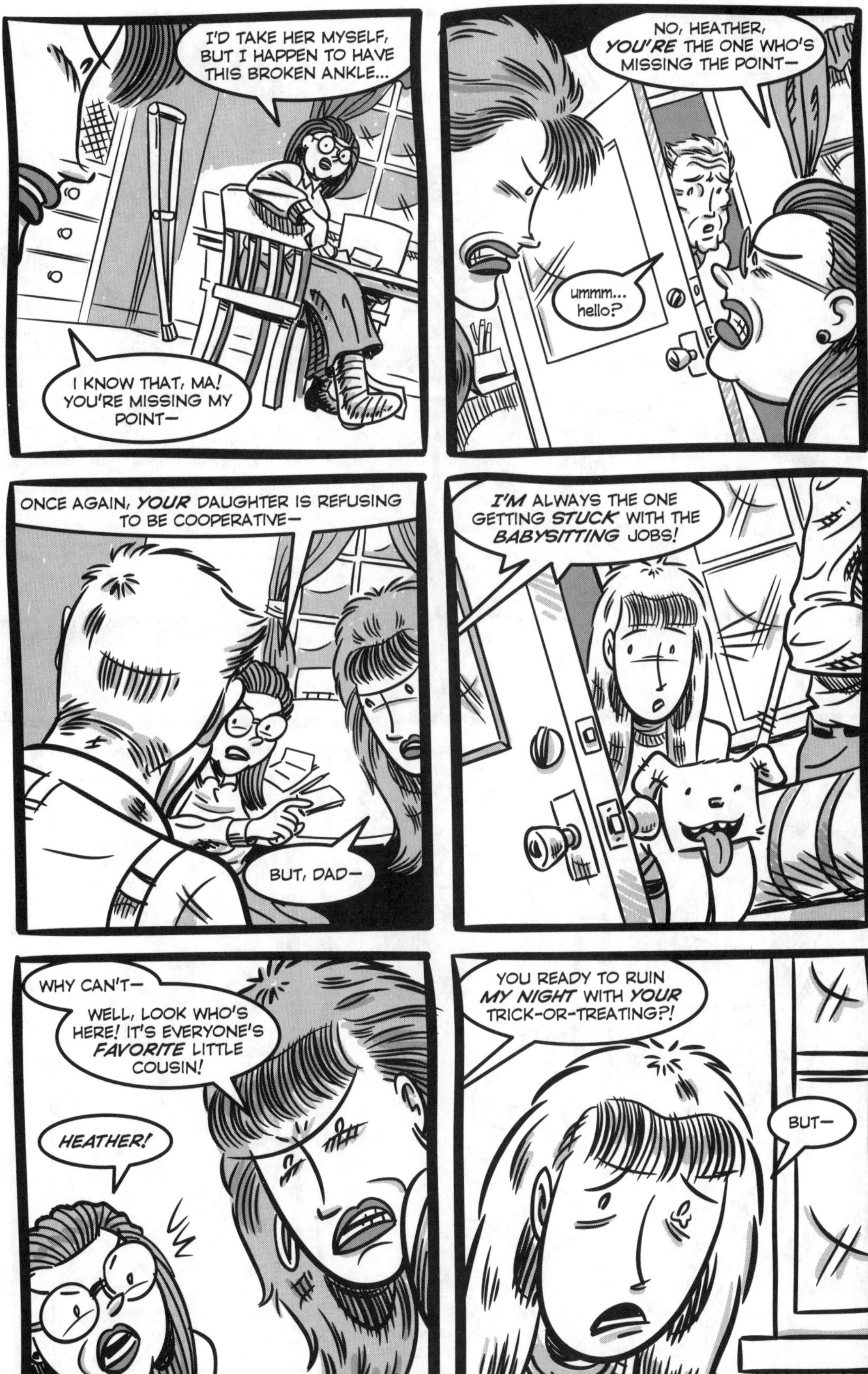
I'D TAKE HER MYSELF, BUT I HAPPEN TO HAVE THIS BROKEN ANKLE...
I KNOW THAT, MA! YOU'RE MISSING MY POINT—
NO, HEATHER, YOU'RE THE ONE WHO'S MISSING THE POINT—
ummm... hello?
ONCE AGAIN, YOUR DAUGHTER IS REFUSING TO BE COOPERATIVE—
BUT, DAD—
I'M ALWAYS THE ONE GETTING STUCK WITH THE BABYSITTING JOBS!
WHY CAN'T—
WELL, LOOK WHO'S HERE! IT'S EVERYONE'S FAVORITE LITTLE COUSIN!
HEATHER!
YOU READY TO RUIN MY NIGHT WITH YOUR TRICK-OR-TREATING?!
BUT—

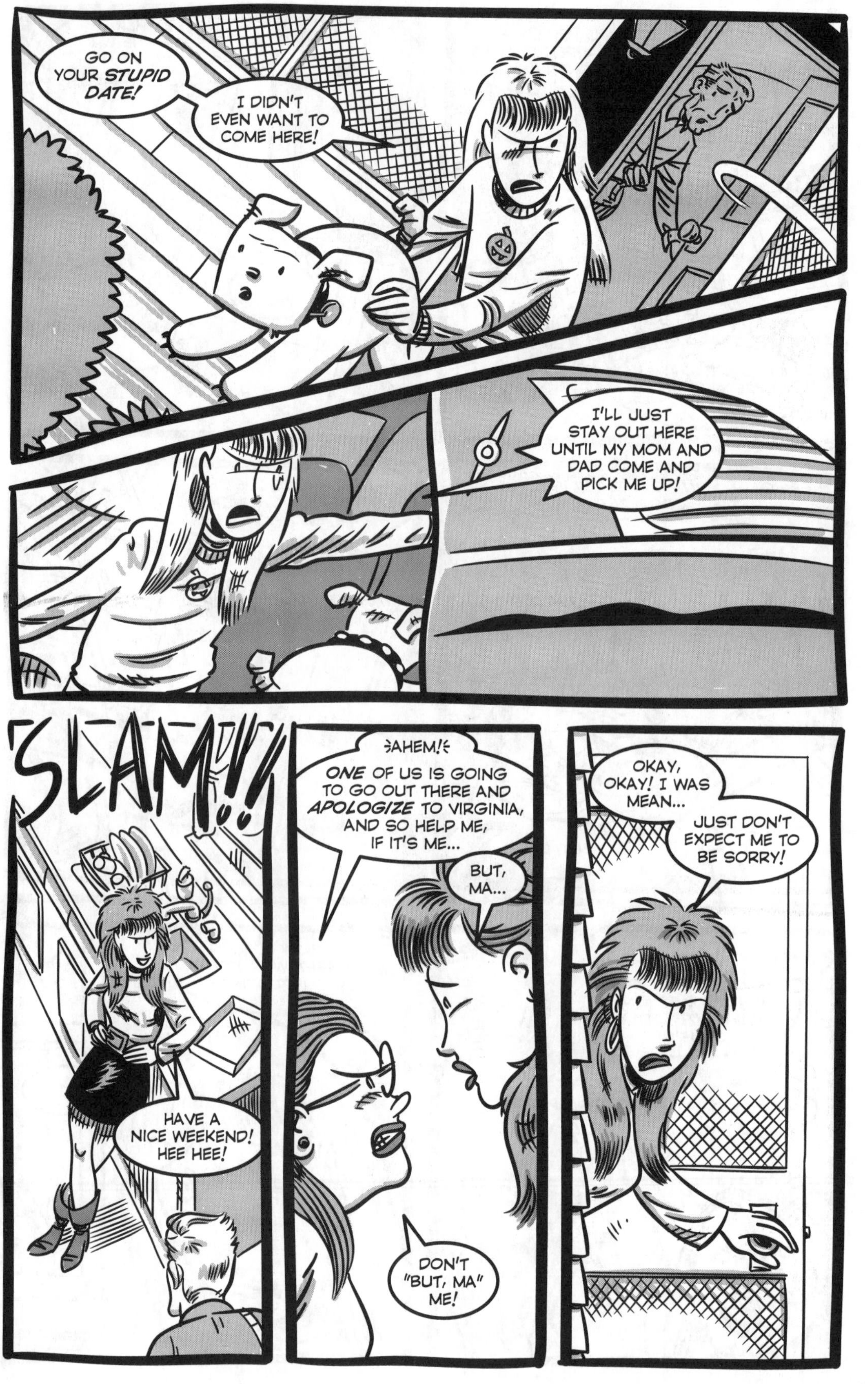
GO ON YOUR STUPID DATE!
I DIDN'T EVEN WANT TO COME HERE!
I'LL JUST STAY OUT HERE UNTIL MY MOM AND DAD COME AND PICK ME UP!
SLAM!!
HAVE A NICE WEEKEND! HEE HEE!
AHEM!
ONE OF US IS GOING TO GO OUT THERE AND APOLOGIZE TO VIRGINIA, AND SO HELP ME, IF IT'S ME...
BUT, MA...
DON'T "BUT, MA" ME!
OKAY, OKAY! I WAS MEAN...
JUST DON'T EXPECT ME TO BE SORRY!

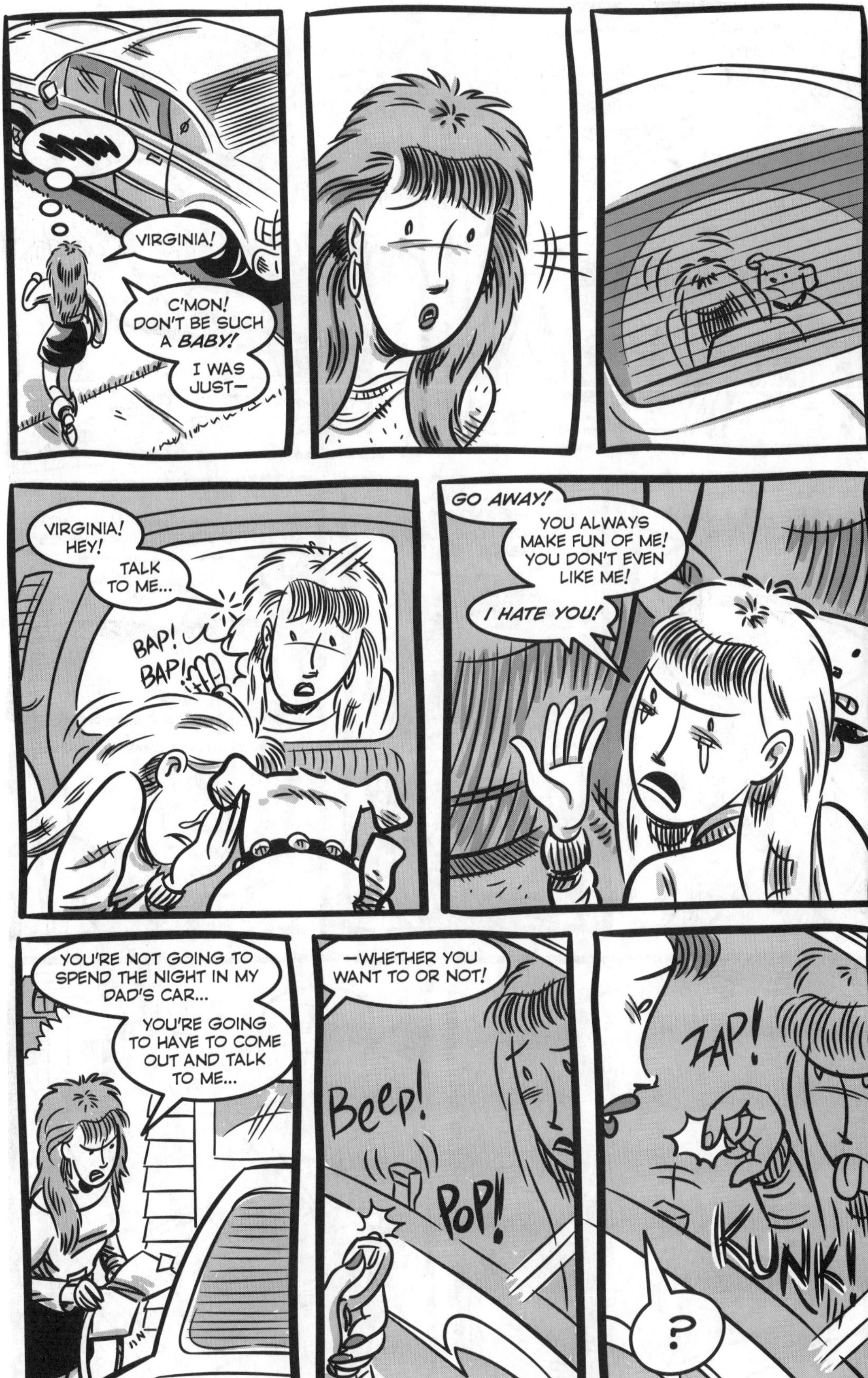
VIRGINIA!
C'MON! DON'T BE SUCH A *BABY!*
I WAS JUST—
VIRGINIA! HEY!
TALK TO ME...
BAP! BAP!
GO AWAY!
YOU ALWAYS MAKE FUN OF ME! YOU DON'T EVEN LIKE ME!
I HATE YOU!
YOU'RE NOT GOING TO SPEND THE NIGHT IN MY DAD'S CAR...
YOU'RE GOING TO HAVE TO COME OUT AND TALK TO ME...
—WHETHER YOU WANT TO OR NOT!
Beep!
POP!
ZAP!
KUNK!
?

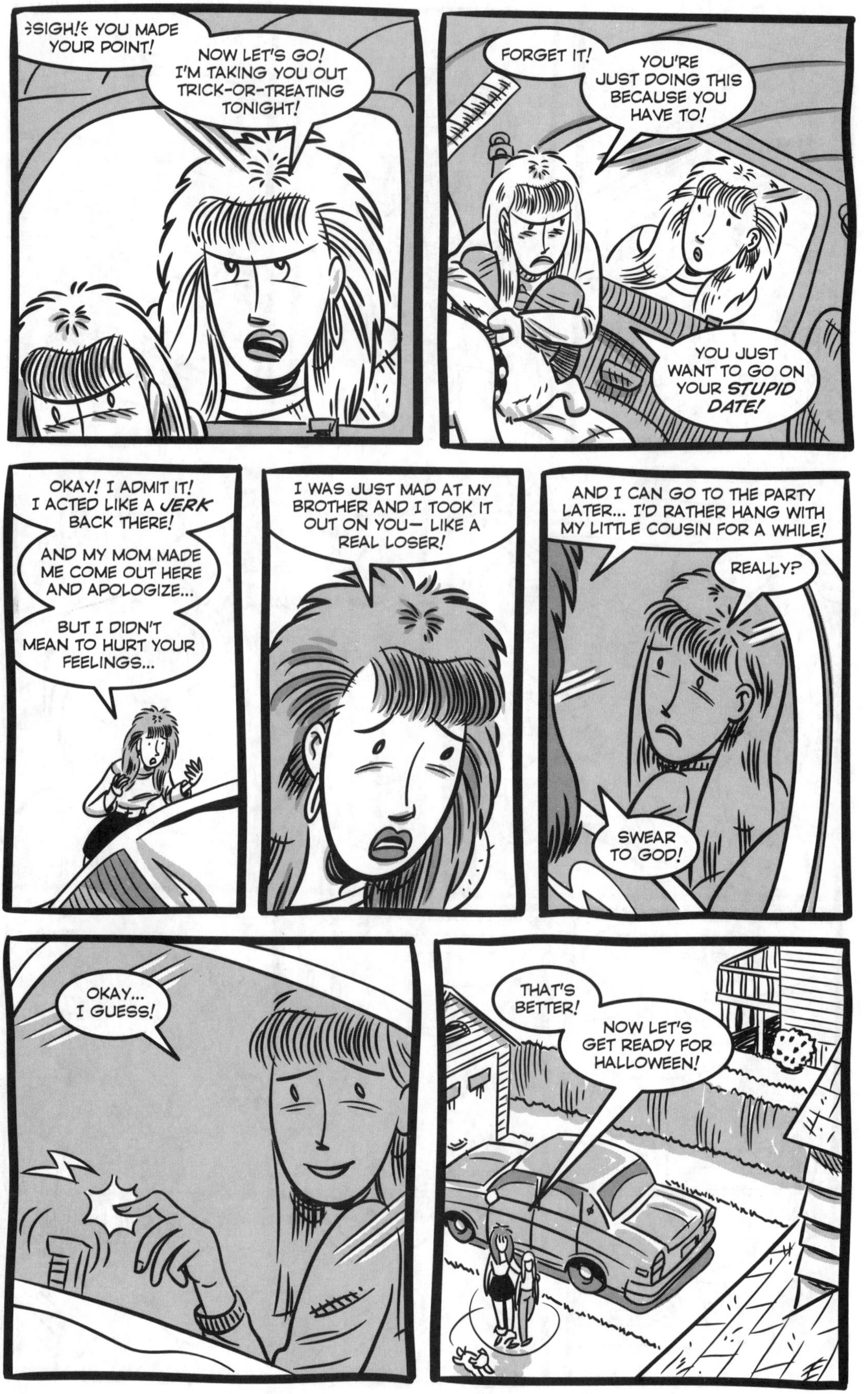

SIGH! YOU MADE YOUR POINT!
NOW LET'S GO! I'M TAKING YOU OUT TRICK-OR-TREATING TONIGHT!
FORGET IT!
YOU'RE JUST DOING THIS BECAUSE YOU HAVE TO!
YOU JUST WANT TO GO ON YOUR STUPID DATE!
OKAY! I ADMIT IT! I ACTED LIKE A JERK BACK THERE!
AND MY MOM MADE ME COME OUT HERE AND APOLOGIZE...
BUT I DIDN'T MEAN TO HURT YOUR FEELINGS...
I WAS JUST MAD AT MY BROTHER AND I TOOK IT OUT ON YOU— LIKE A REAL LOSER!
AND I CAN GO TO THE PARTY LATER... I'D RATHER HANG WITH MY LITTLE COUSIN FOR A WHILE!
REALLY?
SWEAR TO GOD!
OKAY... I GUESS!
THAT'S BETTER!
NOW LET'S GET READY FOR HALLOWEEN!

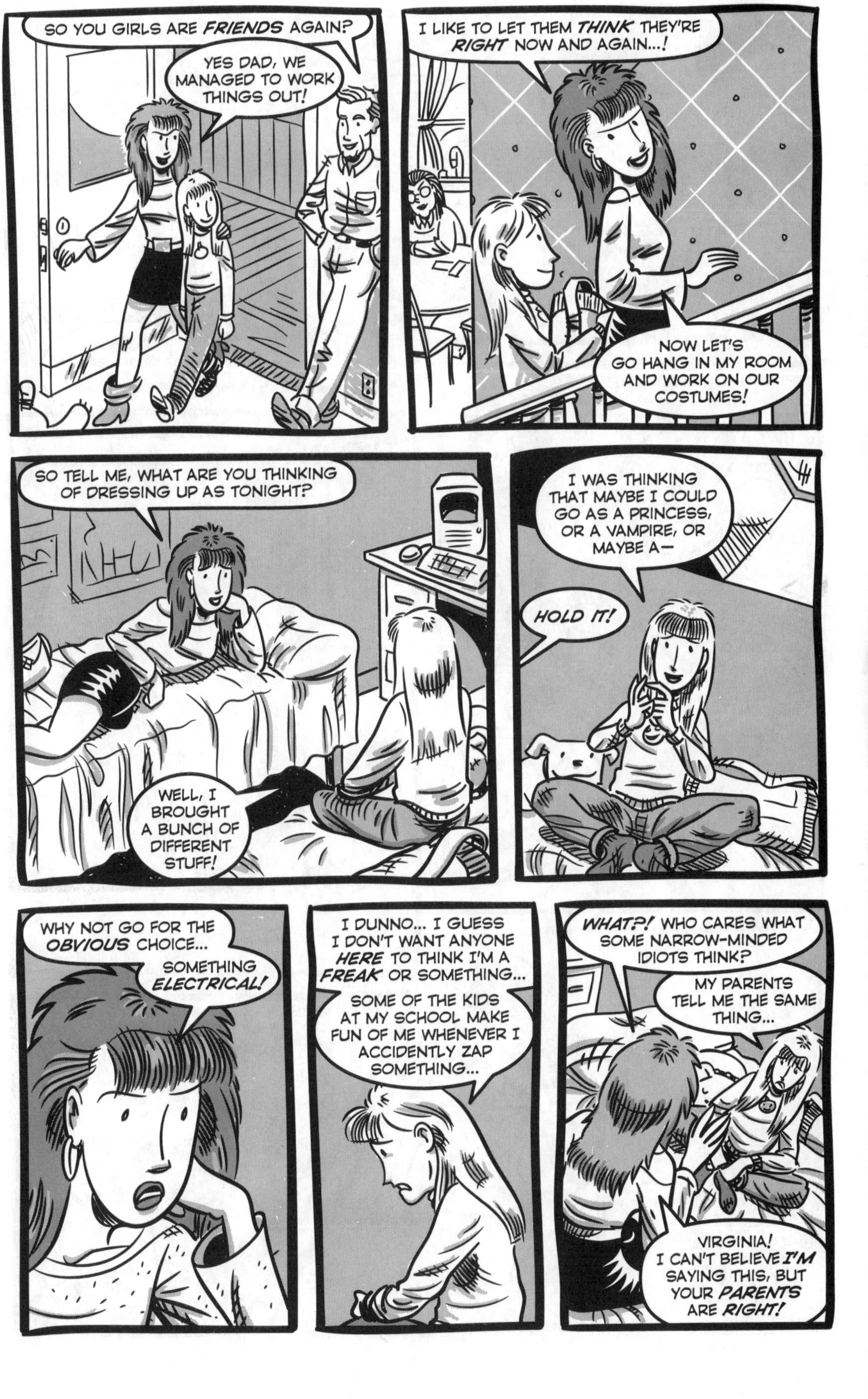
SO YOU GIRLS ARE *FRIENDS* AGAIN?
YES DAD, WE MANAGED TO WORK THINGS OUT!
I LIKE TO LET THEM *THINK* THEY'RE *RIGHT* NOW AND AGAIN...!
NOW LET'S GO HANG IN MY ROOM AND WORK ON OUR COSTUMES!
SO TELL ME, WHAT ARE YOU THINKING OF DRESSING UP AS TONIGHT?
WELL, I BROUGHT A BUNCH OF DIFFERENT STUFF!
I WAS THINKING THAT MAYBE I COULD GO AS A PRINCESS, OR A VAMPIRE, OR MAYBE A—
HOLD IT!
WHY NOT GO FOR THE *OBVIOUS* CHOICE...
SOMETHING *ELECTRICAL!*
I DUNNO... I GUESS I DON'T WANT ANYONE *HERE* TO THINK I'M A *FREAK* OR SOMETHING...
SOME OF THE KIDS AT MY SCHOOL MAKE FUN OF ME WHENEVER I ACCIDENTLY ZAP SOMETHING...
WHAT?! WHO CARES WHAT SOME NARROW-MINDED IDIOTS THINK?
MY PARENTS TELL ME THE SAME THING...
VIRGINIA! I CAN'T BELIEVE *I'M* SAYING THIS, BUT YOUR *PARENTS* ARE *RIGHT!*

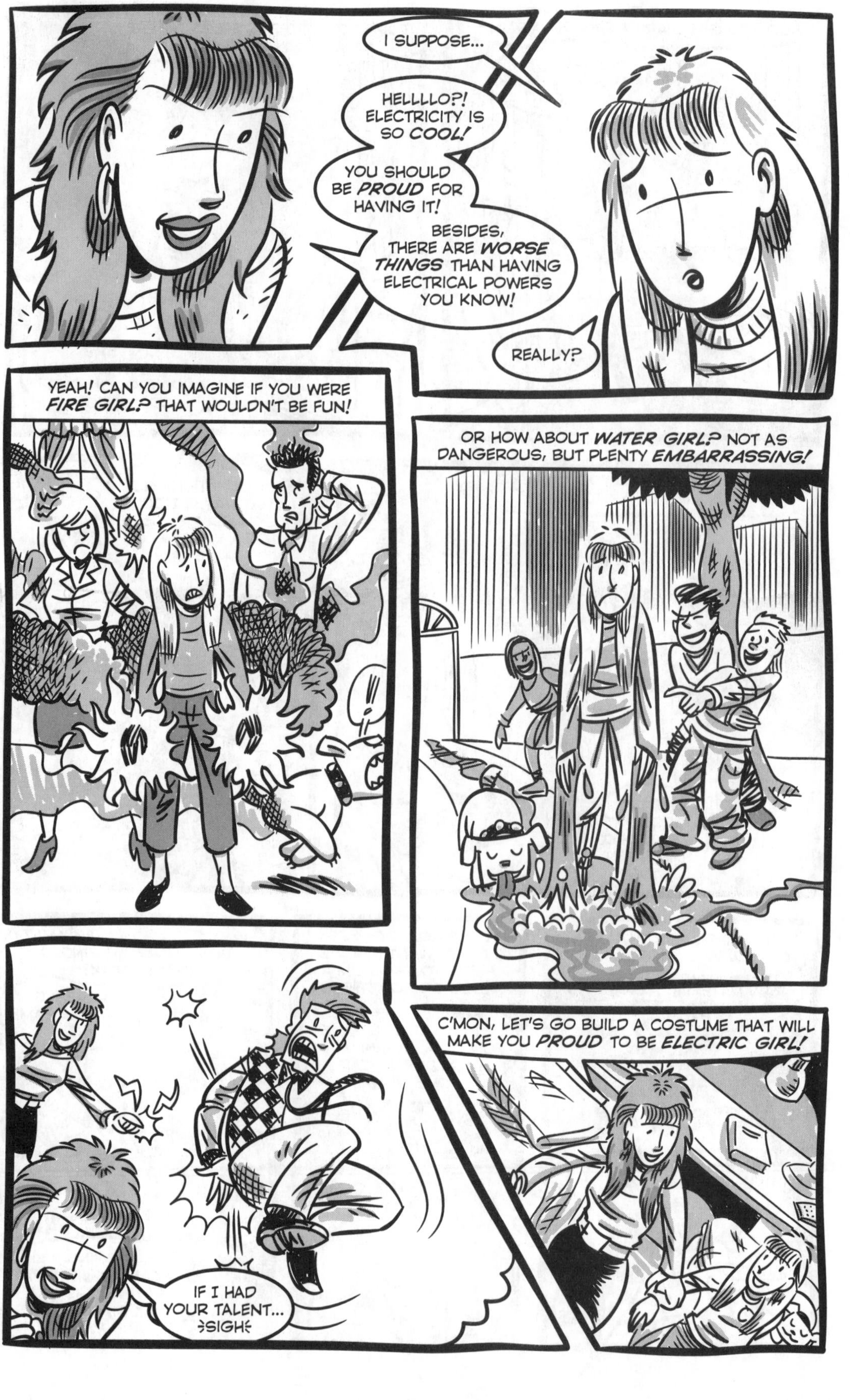
I SUPPOSE...
HELLLLO?! ELECTRICITY IS SO COOL!
YOU SHOULD BE PROUD FOR HAVING IT!
BESIDES, THERE ARE WORSE THINGS THAN HAVING ELECTRICAL POWERS YOU KNOW!
REALLY?
YEAH! CAN YOU IMAGINE IF YOU WERE FIRE GIRL? THAT WOULDN'T BE FUN!
OR HOW ABOUT WATER GIRL? NOT AS DANGEROUS, BUT PLENTY EMBARRASSING!
IF I HAD YOUR TALENT... SIGH
C'MON, LET'S GO BUILD A COSTUME THAT WILL MAKE YOU PROUD TO BE ELECTRIC GIRL!

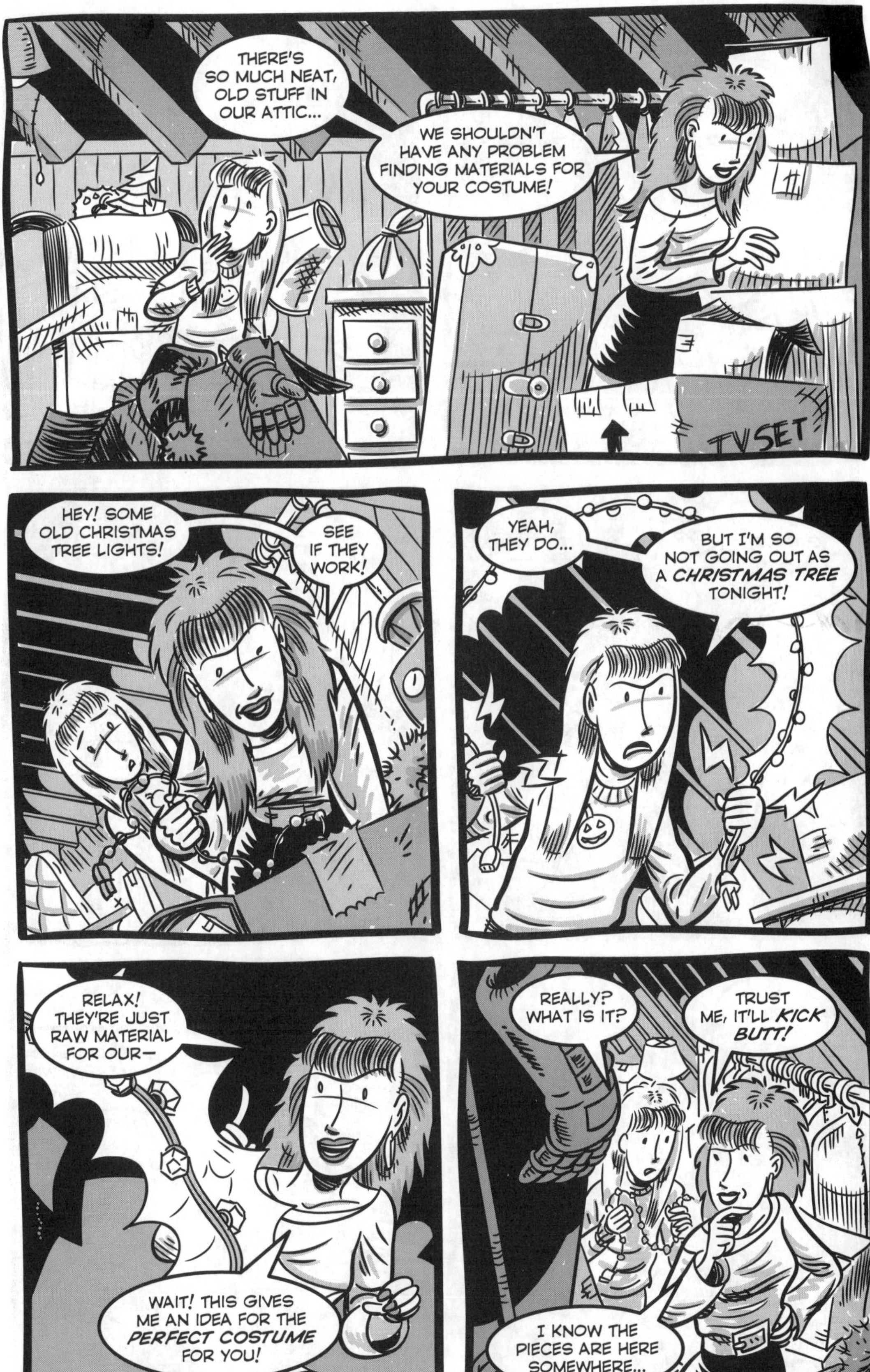
THERE'S SO MUCH NEAT, OLD STUFF IN OUR ATTIC...
WE SHOULDN'T HAVE ANY PROBLEM FINDING MATERIALS FOR YOUR COSTUME!
TV SET
HEY! SOME OLD CHRISTMAS TREE LIGHTS!
SEE IF THEY WORK!
YEAH, THEY DO...
BUT I'M SO NOT GOING OUT AS A *CHRISTMAS TREE* TONIGHT!
RELAX! THEY'RE JUST RAW MATERIAL FOR OUR—
WAIT! THIS GIVES ME AN IDEA FOR THE *PERFECT COSTUME* FOR YOU!
REALLY? WHAT IS IT?
TRUST ME, IT'LL *KICK BUTT!*
I KNOW THE PIECES ARE HERE SOMEWHERE...

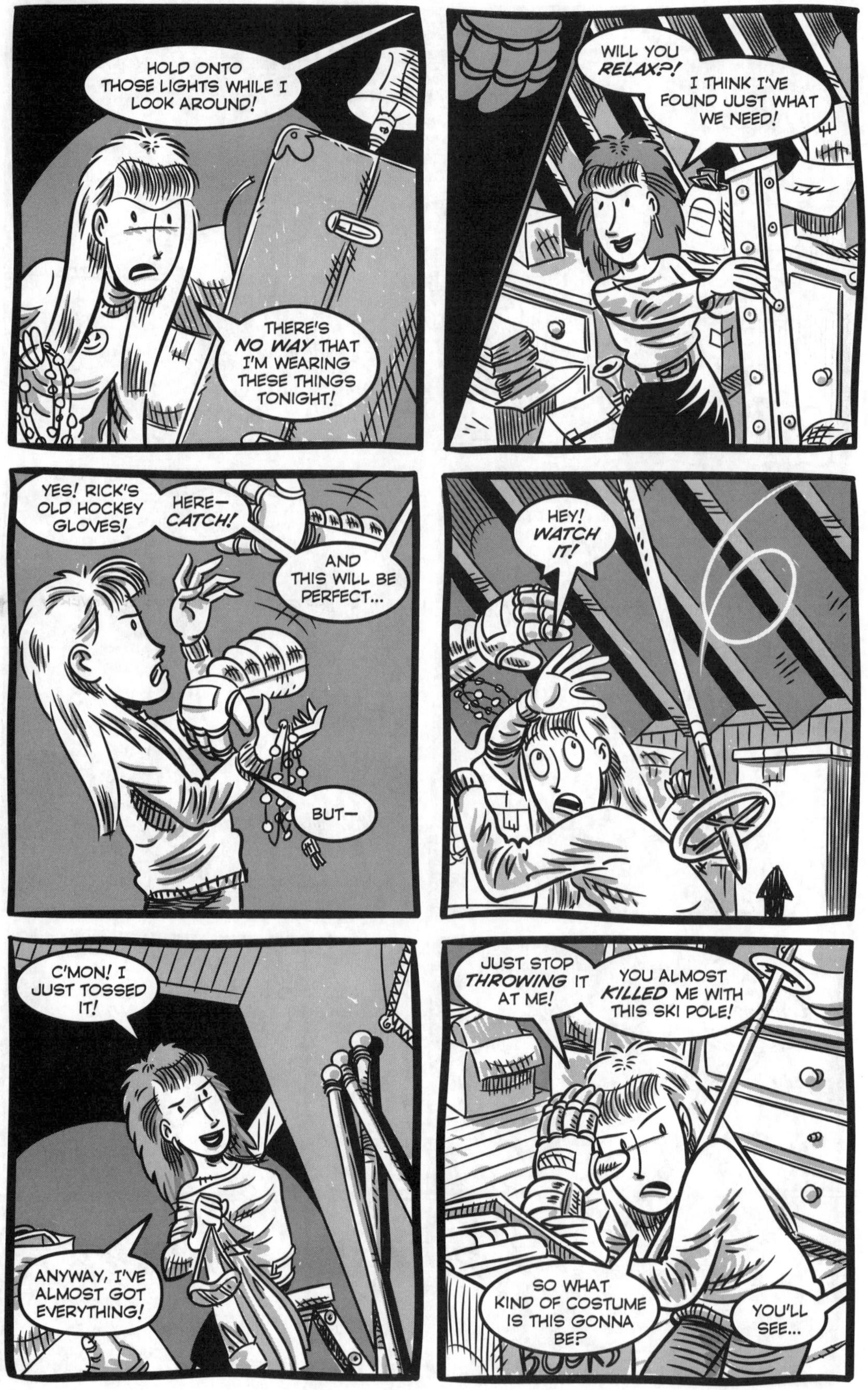
HOLD ONTO THOSE LIGHTS WHILE I LOOK AROUND!
THERE'S NO WAY THAT I'M WEARING THESE THINGS TONIGHT!
WILL YOU RELAX?!
I THINK I'VE FOUND JUST WHAT WE NEED!
YES! RICK'S OLD HOCKEY GLOVES!
HERE— CATCH!
AND THIS WILL BE PERFECT...
BUT—
HEY! WATCH IT!
C'MON! I JUST TOSSED IT!
ANYWAY, I'VE ALMOST GOT EVERYTHING!
JUST STOP THROWING IT AT ME!
YOU ALMOST KILLED ME WITH THIS SKI POLE!
SO WHAT KIND OF COSTUME IS THIS GONNA BE?
YOU'LL SEE...

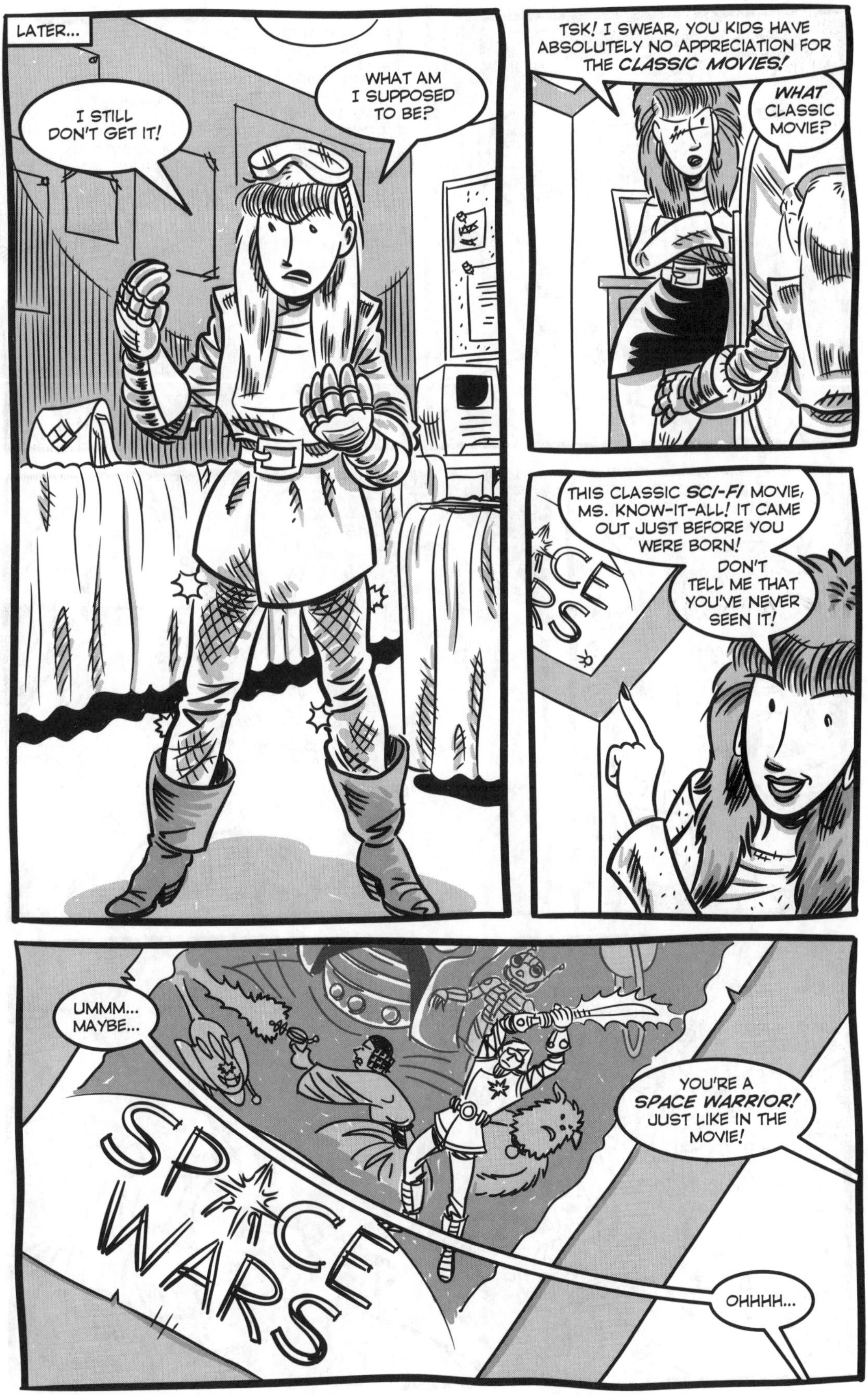
LATER...
I STILL DON'T GET IT!
WHAT AM I SUPPOSED TO BE?
TSK! I SWEAR, YOU KIDS HAVE ABSOLUTELY NO APPRECIATION FOR THE CLASSIC MOVIES!
WHAT CLASSIC MOVIE?
THIS CLASSIC SCI-FI MOVIE, MS. KNOW-IT-ALL! IT CAME OUT JUST BEFORE YOU WERE BORN!
DON'T TELL ME THAT YOU'VE NEVER SEEN IT!
UMMM... MAYBE...
YOU'RE A SPACE WARRIOR! JUST LIKE IN THE MOVIE!
SPACE WARS
OHHHH...

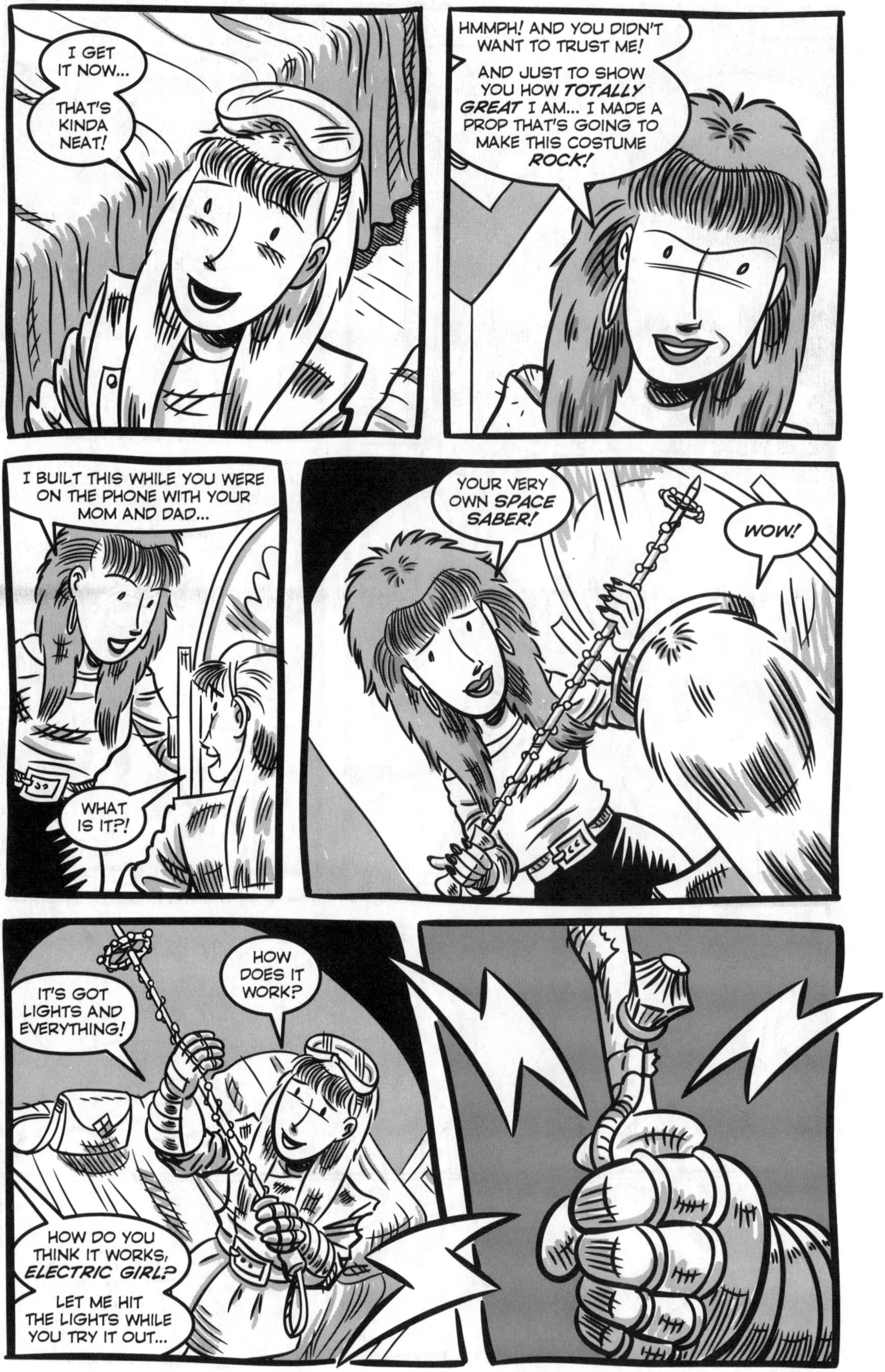
I GET IT NOW...
THAT'S KINDA NEAT!
HMMPH! AND YOU DIDN'T WANT TO TRUST ME!
AND JUST TO SHOW YOU HOW TOTALLY GREAT I AM... I MADE A PROP THAT'S GOING TO MAKE THIS COSTUME ROCK!
I BUILT THIS WHILE YOU WERE ON THE PHONE WITH YOUR MOM AND DAD...
WHAT IS IT?!
YOUR VERY OWN SPACE SABER!
WOW!
IT'S GOT LIGHTS AND EVERYTHING!
HOW DOES IT WORK?
HOW DO YOU THINK IT WORKS, ELECTRIC GIRL?
LET ME HIT THE LIGHTS WHILE YOU TRY IT OUT...

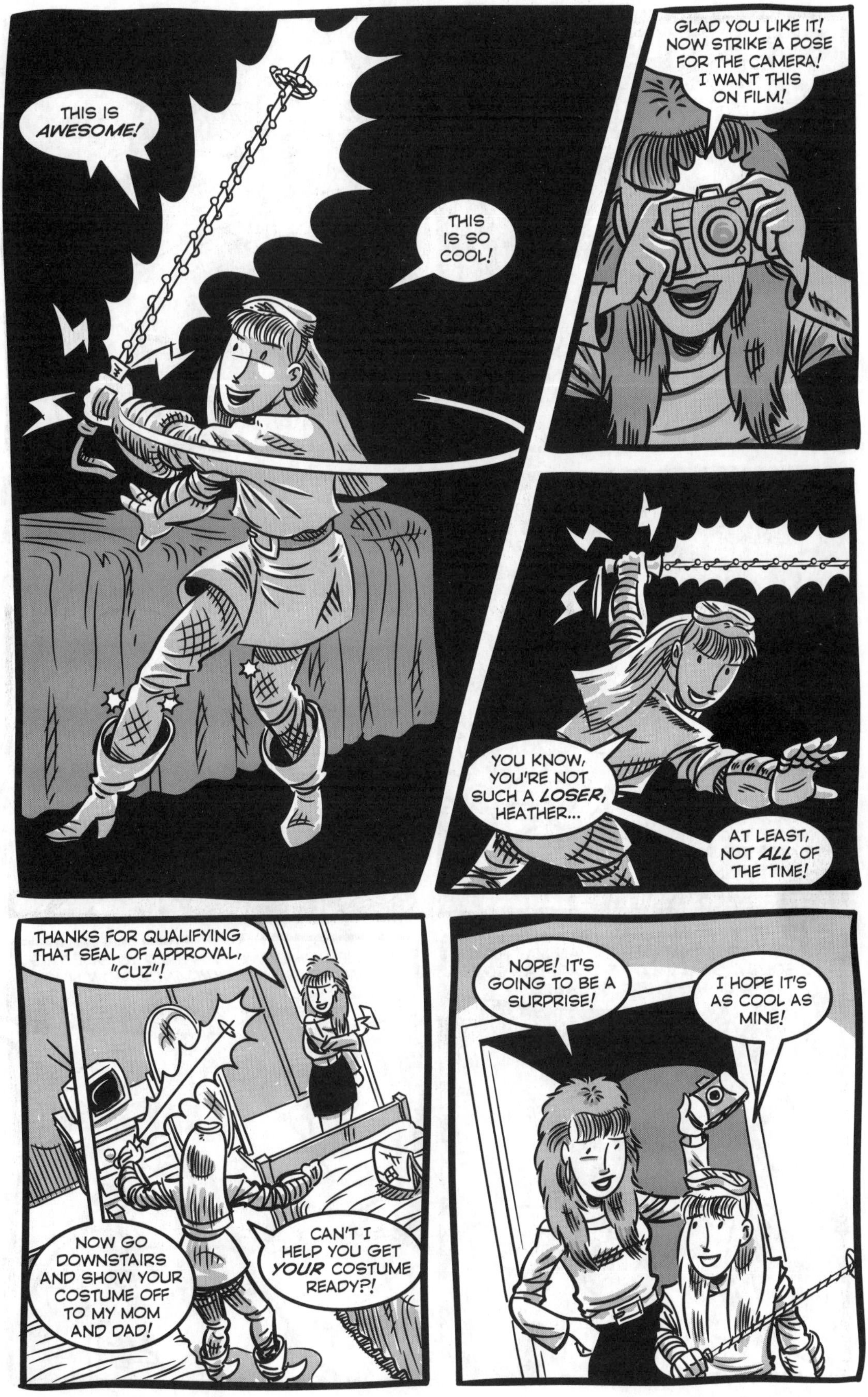
THIS IS AWESOME!
THIS IS SO COOL!
GLAD YOU LIKE IT! NOW STRIKE A POSE FOR THE CAMERA! I WANT THIS ON FILM!
YOU KNOW, YOU'RE NOT SUCH A LOSER, HEATHER...
AT LEAST, NOT ALL OF THE TIME!
THANKS FOR QUALIFYING THAT SEAL OF APPROVAL, "CUZ"!
NOW GO DOWNSTAIRS AND SHOW YOUR COSTUME OFF TO MY MOM AND DAD!
CAN'T I HELP YOU GET YOUR COSTUME READY?!
NOPE! IT'S GOING TO BE A SURPRISE!
I HOPE IT'S AS COOL AS MINE!

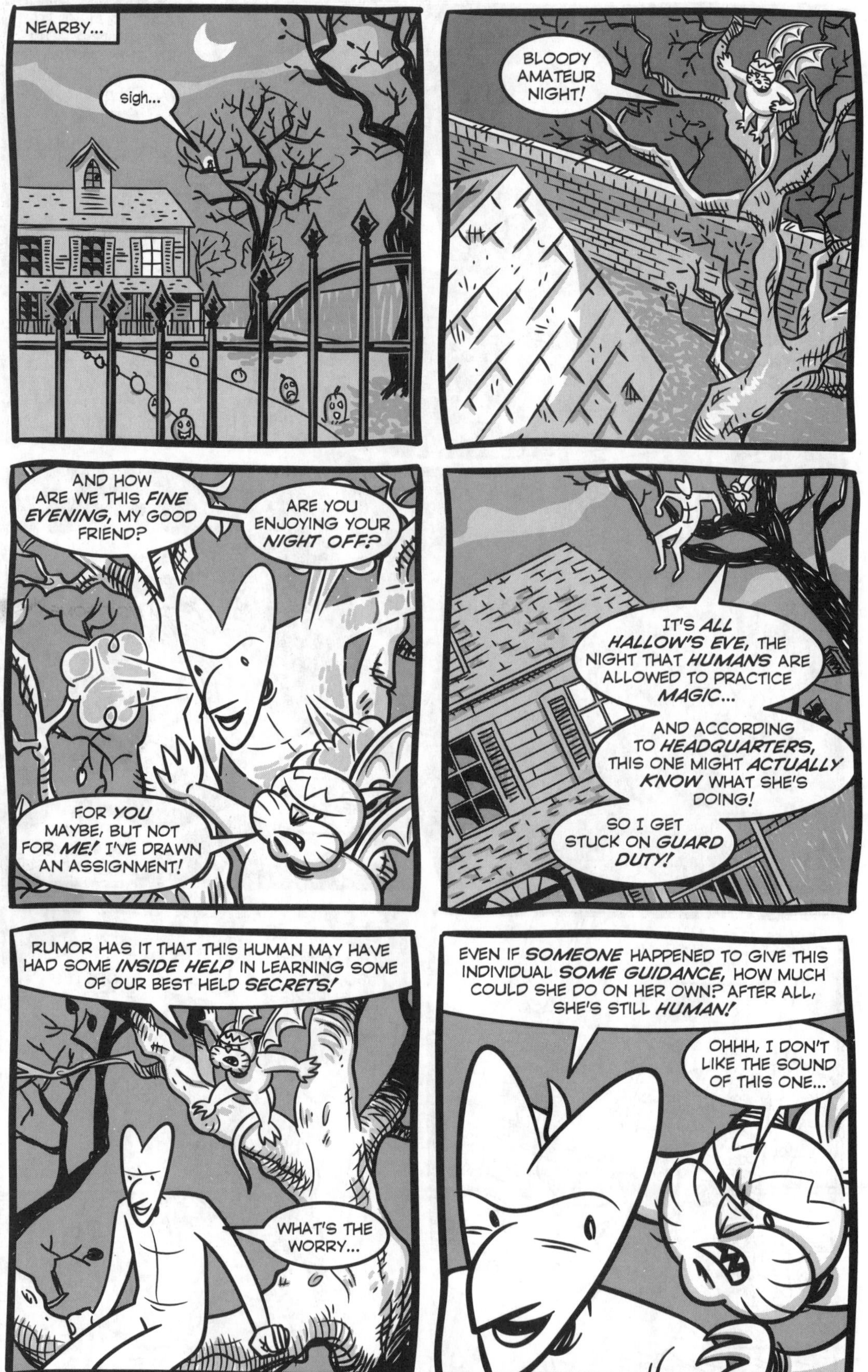
NEARBY...
sigh...
BLOODY AMATEUR NIGHT!
AND HOW ARE WE THIS FINE EVENING, MY GOOD FRIEND?
ARE YOU ENJOYING YOUR NIGHT OFF?
FOR YOU MAYBE, BUT NOT FOR ME! I'VE DRAWN AN ASSIGNMENT!
IT'S ALL HALLOW'S EVE, THE NIGHT THAT HUMANS ARE ALLOWED TO PRACTICE MAGIC...
AND ACCORDING TO HEADQUARTERS, THIS ONE MIGHT ACTUALLY KNOW WHAT SHE'S DOING!
SO I GET STUCK ON GUARD DUTY!
RUMOR HAS IT THAT THIS HUMAN MAY HAVE HAD SOME INSIDE HELP IN LEARNING SOME OF OUR BEST HELD SECRETS!
WHAT'S THE WORRY...
EVEN IF SOMEONE HAPPENED TO GIVE THIS INDIVIDUAL SOME GUIDANCE, HOW MUCH COULD SHE DO ON HER OWN? AFTER ALL, SHE'S STILL HUMAN!
OHHH, I DON'T LIKE THE SOUND OF THIS ONE...

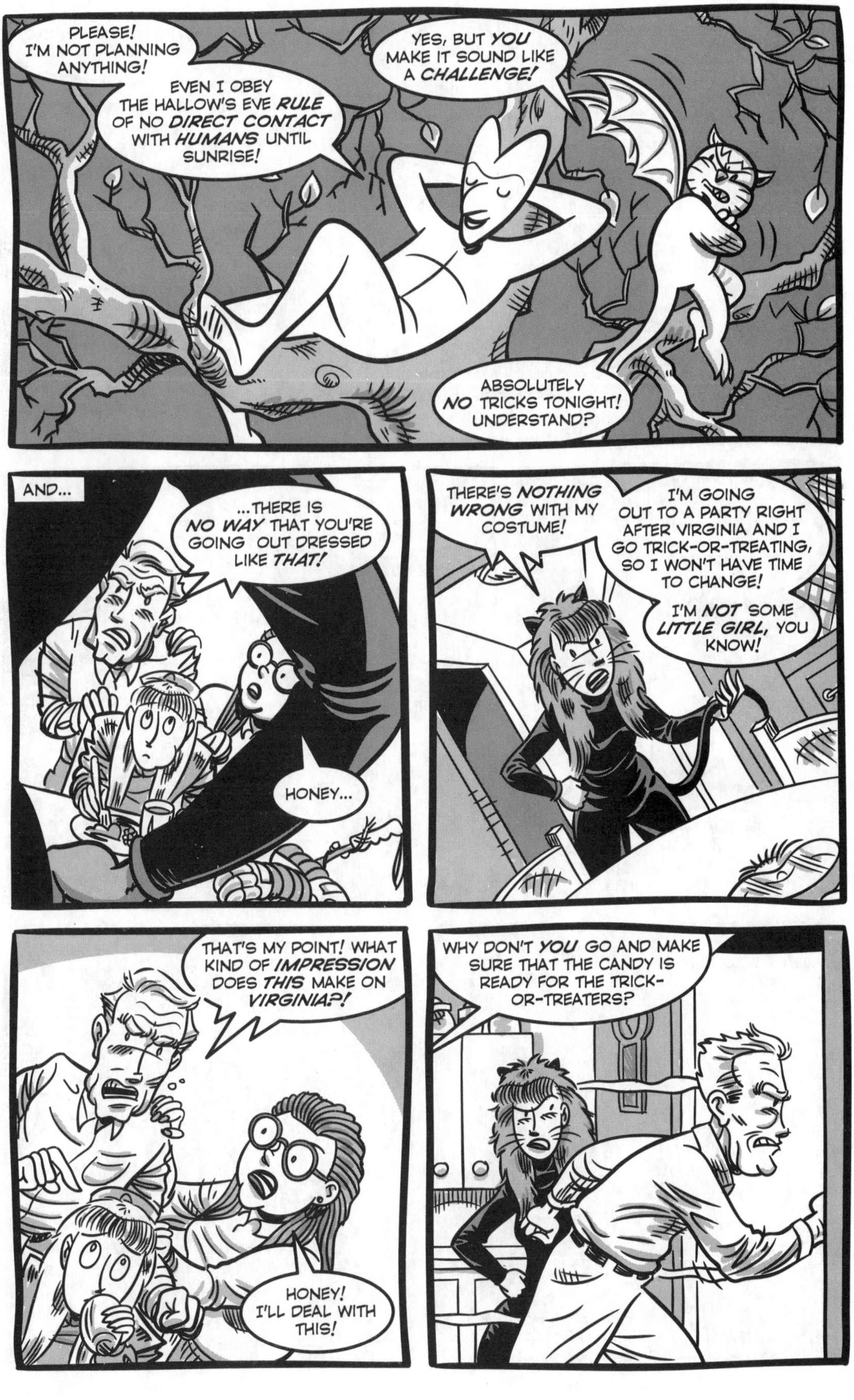
PLEASE! I'M NOT PLANNING ANYTHING!
EVEN I OBEY THE HALLOW'S EVE RULE OF NO DIRECT CONTACT WITH HUMANS UNTIL SUNRISE!
YES, BUT YOU MAKE IT SOUND LIKE A CHALLENGE!
ABSOLUTELY NO TRICKS TONIGHT! UNDERSTAND?
AND...
...THERE IS NO WAY THAT YOU'RE GOING OUT DRESSED LIKE THAT!
HONEY...
THERE'S NOTHING WRONG WITH MY COSTUME!
I'M GOING OUT TO A PARTY RIGHT AFTER VIRGINIA AND I GO TRICK-OR-TREATING, SO I WON'T HAVE TIME TO CHANGE!
I'M NOT SOME LITTLE GIRL, YOU KNOW!
THAT'S MY POINT! WHAT KIND OF IMPRESSION DOES THIS MAKE ON VIRGINIA?!
HONEY! I'LL DEAL WITH THIS!
WHY DON'T YOU GO AND MAKE SURE THAT THE CANDY IS READY FOR THE TRICK-OR-TREATERS?

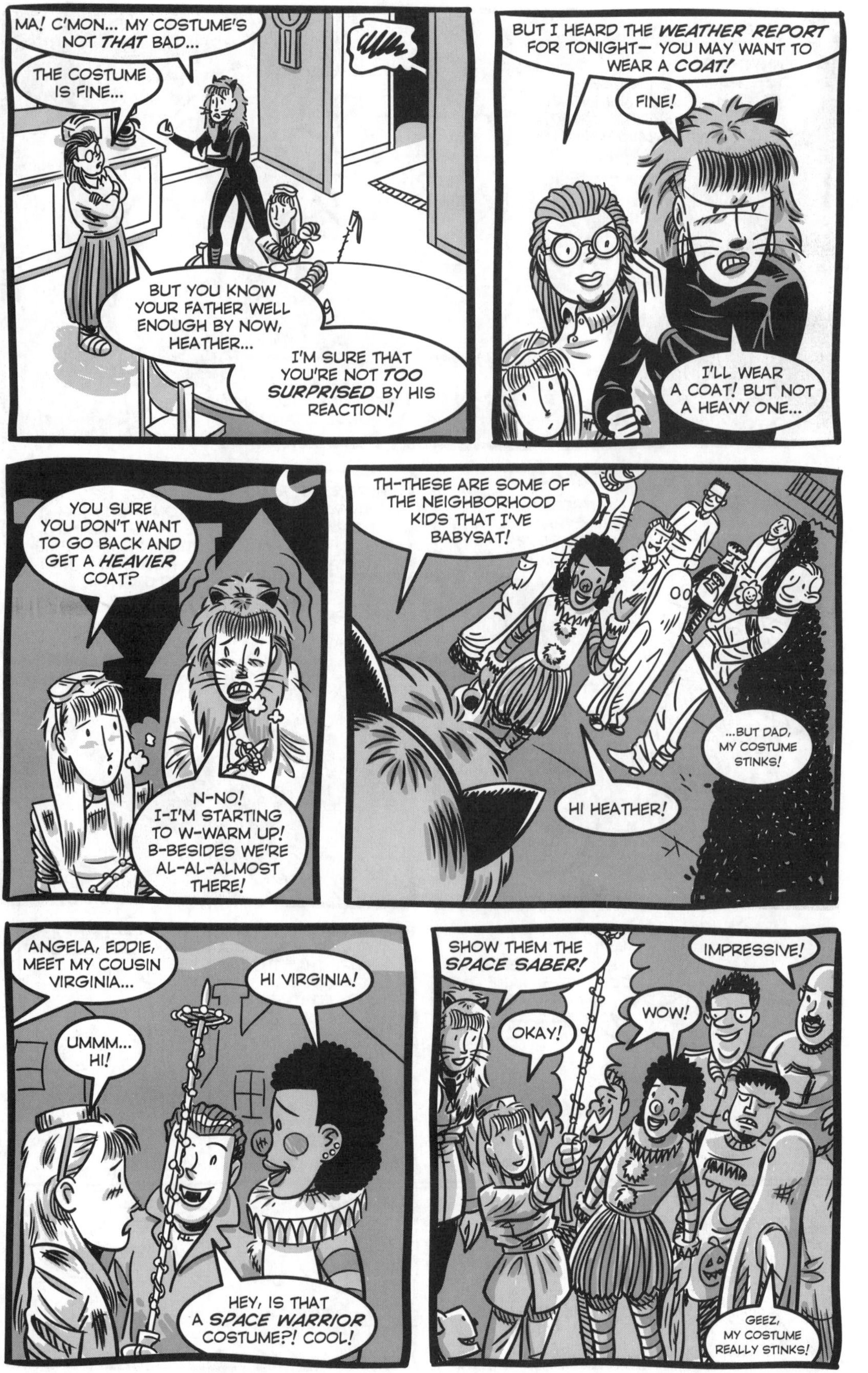
MA! C'MON... MY COSTUME'S NOT THAT BAD...
THE COSTUME IS FINE...
BUT YOU KNOW YOUR FATHER WELL ENOUGH BY NOW, HEATHER...
I'M SURE THAT YOU'RE NOT TOO SURPRISED BY HIS REACTION!
BUT I HEARD THE WEATHER REPORT FOR TONIGHT— YOU MAY WANT TO WEAR A COAT!
FINE!
I'LL WEAR A COAT! BUT NOT A HEAVY ONE...
YOU SURE YOU DON'T WANT TO GO BACK AND GET A HEAVIER COAT?
N-NO! I-I'M STARTING TO W-WARM UP! B-BESIDES WE'RE AL-AL-ALMOST THERE!
TH-THESE ARE SOME OF THE NEIGHBORHOOD KIDS THAT I'VE BABYSAT!
...BUT DAD, MY COSTUME STINKS!
HI HEATHER!
ANGELA, EDDIE, MEET MY COUSIN VIRGINIA...
HI VIRGINIA!
UMMM... HI!
HEY, IS THAT A SPACE WARRIOR COSTUME?! COOL!
SHOW THEM THE SPACE SABER!
IMPRESSIVE!
WOW!
OKAY!
GEEZ, MY COSTUME REALLY STINKS!

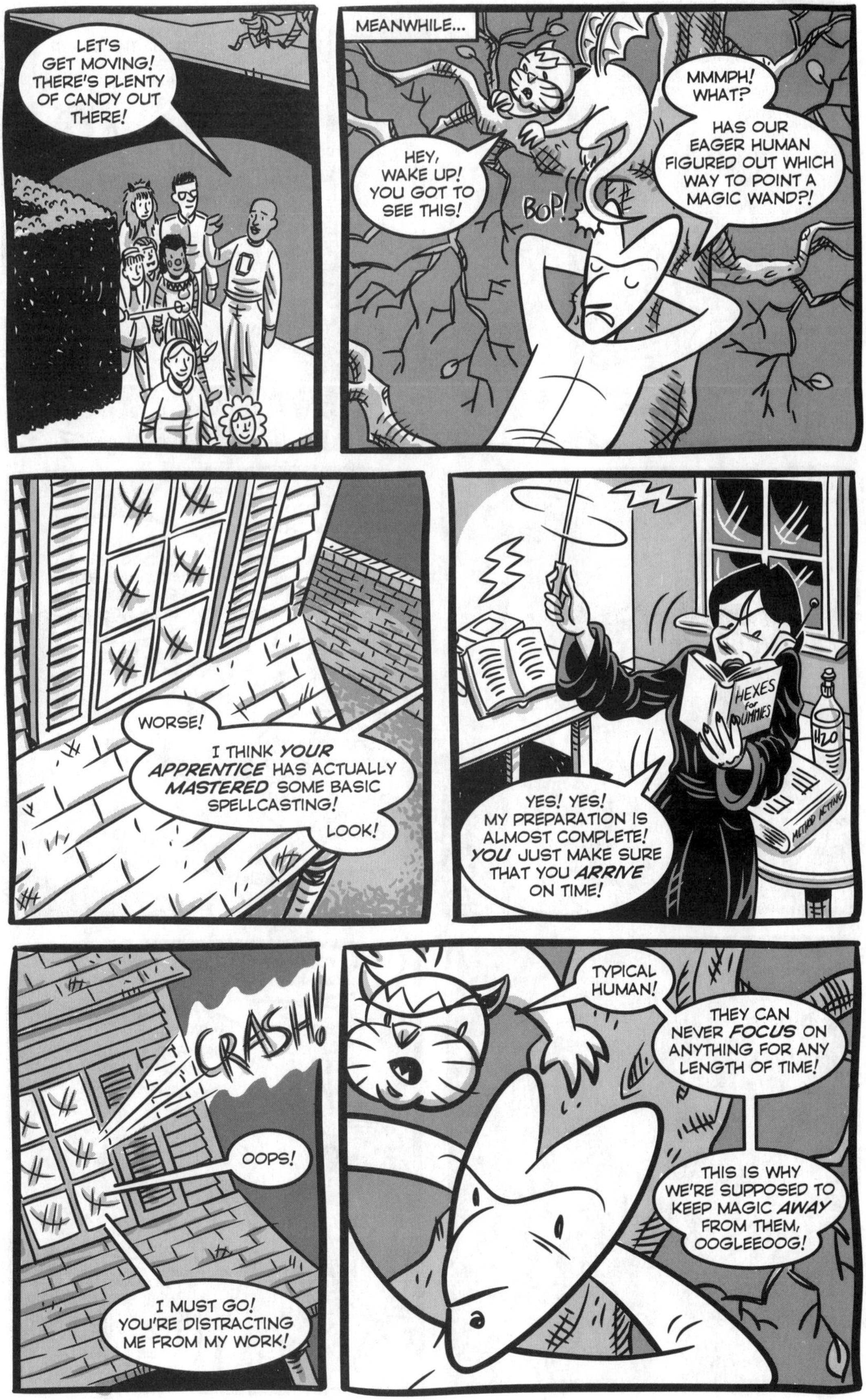
LET'S GET MOVING! THERE'S PLENTY OF CANDY OUT THERE!
MEANWHILE...
HEY, WAKE UP! YOU GOT TO SEE THIS!
BOP!
MMMPH! WHAT?
HAS OUR EAGER HUMAN FIGURED OUT WHICH WAY TO POINT A MAGIC WAND?!
WORSE!
I THINK YOUR APPRENTICE HAS ACTUALLY MASTERED SOME BASIC SPELLCASTING!
LOOK!
HEXES for DUMMIES
H2O
METHOD ACTING
YES! YES! MY PREPARATION IS ALMOST COMPLETE! YOU JUST MAKE SURE THAT YOU ARRIVE ON TIME!
CRASH!
OOPS!
I MUST GO! YOU'RE DISTRACTING ME FROM MY WORK!
TYPICAL HUMAN!
THEY CAN NEVER FOCUS ON ANYTHING FOR ANY LENGTH OF TIME!
THIS IS WHY WE'RE SUPPOSED TO KEEP MAGIC AWAY FROM THEM, OOGLEEOOG!

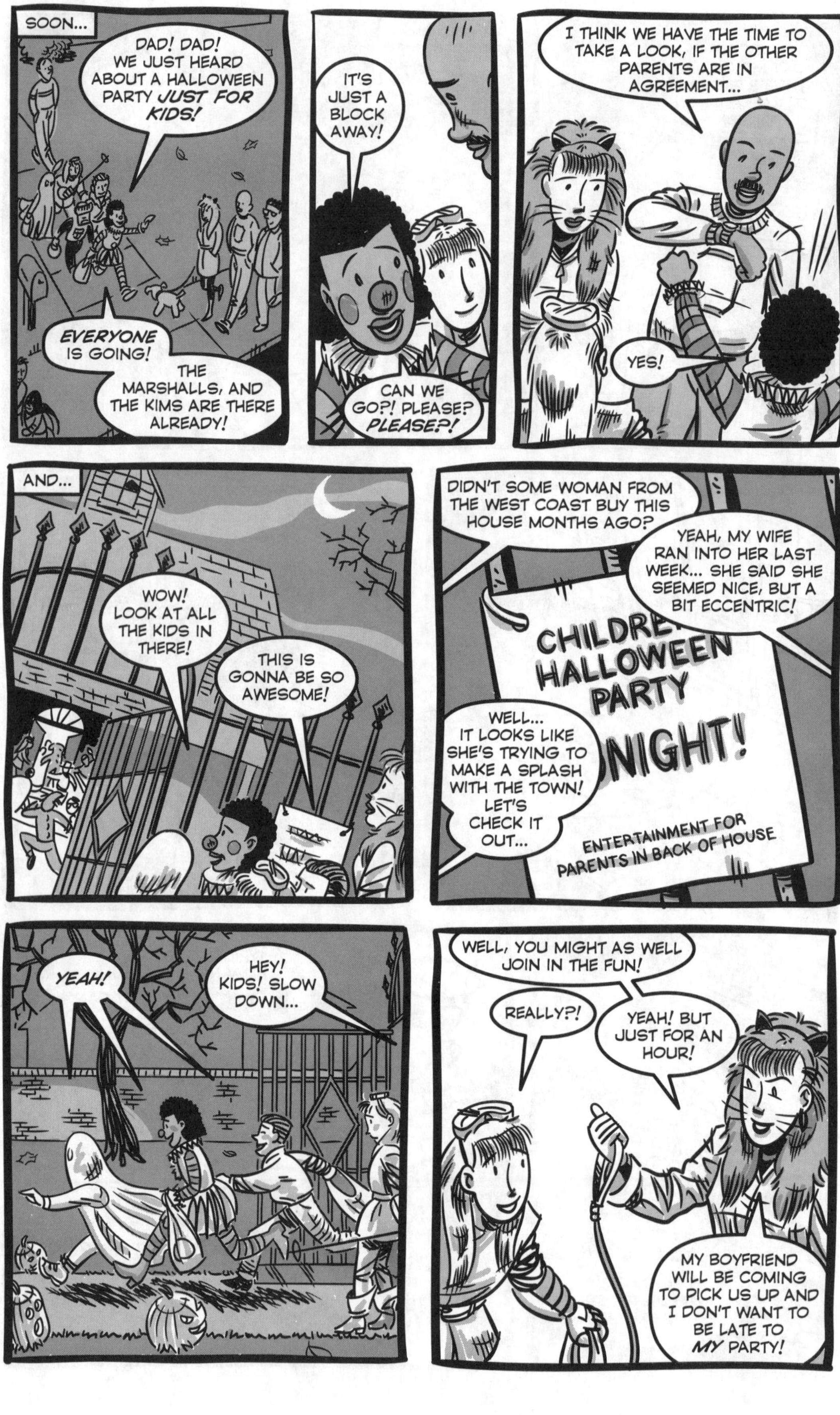
SOON...
DAD! DAD! WE JUST HEARD ABOUT A HALLOWEEN PARTY *JUST FOR KIDS!*
EVERYONE IS GOING!
THE MARSHALLS, AND THE KIMS ARE THERE ALREADY!
IT'S JUST A BLOCK AWAY!
CAN WE GO?! PLEASE? *PLEASE?!*
I THINK WE HAVE THE TIME TO TAKE A LOOK, IF THE OTHER PARENTS ARE IN AGREEMENT...
YES!
AND...
WOW! LOOK AT ALL THE KIDS IN THERE!
THIS IS GONNA BE SO AWESOME!
DIDN'T SOME WOMAN FROM THE WEST COAST BUY THIS HOUSE MONTHS AGO?
YEAH, MY WIFE RAN INTO HER LAST WEEK... SHE SAID SHE SEEMED NICE, BUT A BIT ECCENTRIC!
CHILDRE
HALLOWEEN
PARTY
NIGHT!
ENTERTAINMENT FOR PARENTS IN BACK OF HOUSE
WELL... IT LOOKS LIKE SHE'S TRYING TO MAKE A SPLASH WITH THE TOWN! LET'S CHECK IT OUT...
YEAH!
HEY! KIDS! SLOW DOWN...
WELL, YOU MIGHT AS WELL JOIN IN THE FUN!
REALLY?!
YEAH! BUT JUST FOR AN HOUR!
MY BOYFRIEND WILL BE COMING TO PICK US UP AND I DON'T WANT TO BE LATE TO *MY* PARTY!

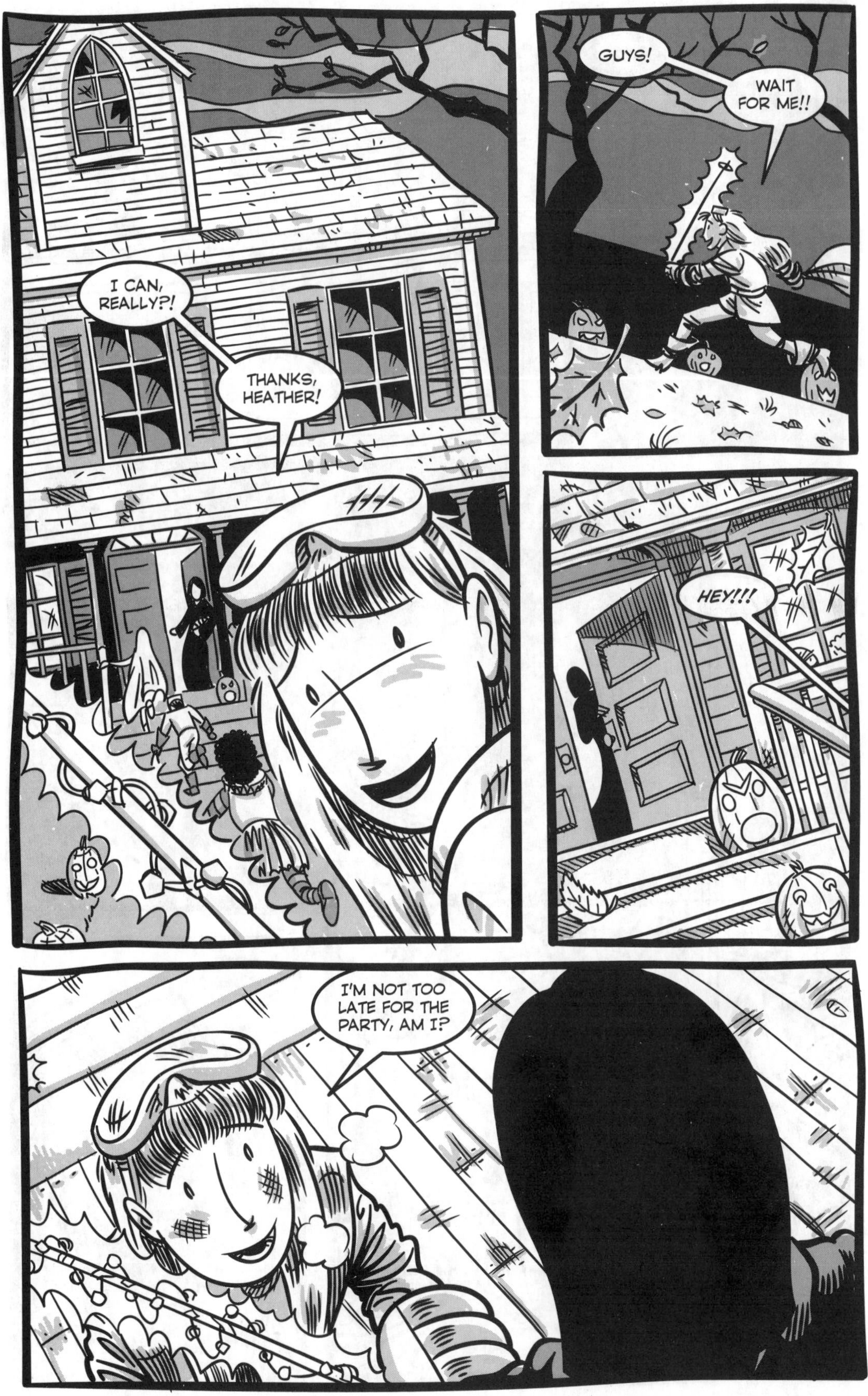
I CAN, REALLY?!
THANKS, HEATHER!
GUYS!
WAIT FOR ME!!
HEY!!!
I'M NOT TOO LATE FOR THE PARTY, AM I?

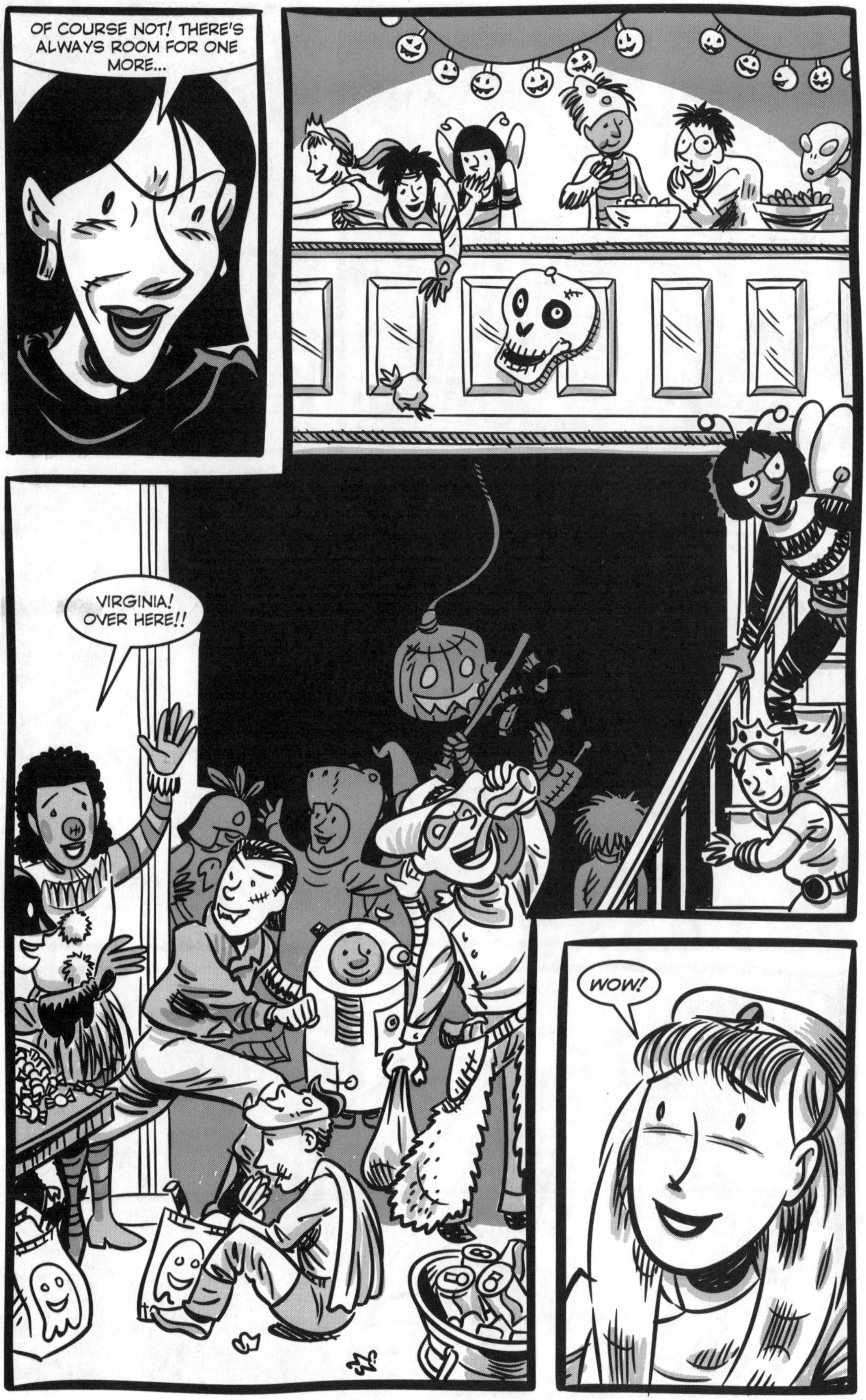
OF COURSE NOT! THERE'S ALWAYS ROOM FOR ONE MORE...
VIRGINIA! OVER HERE!!
WOW!

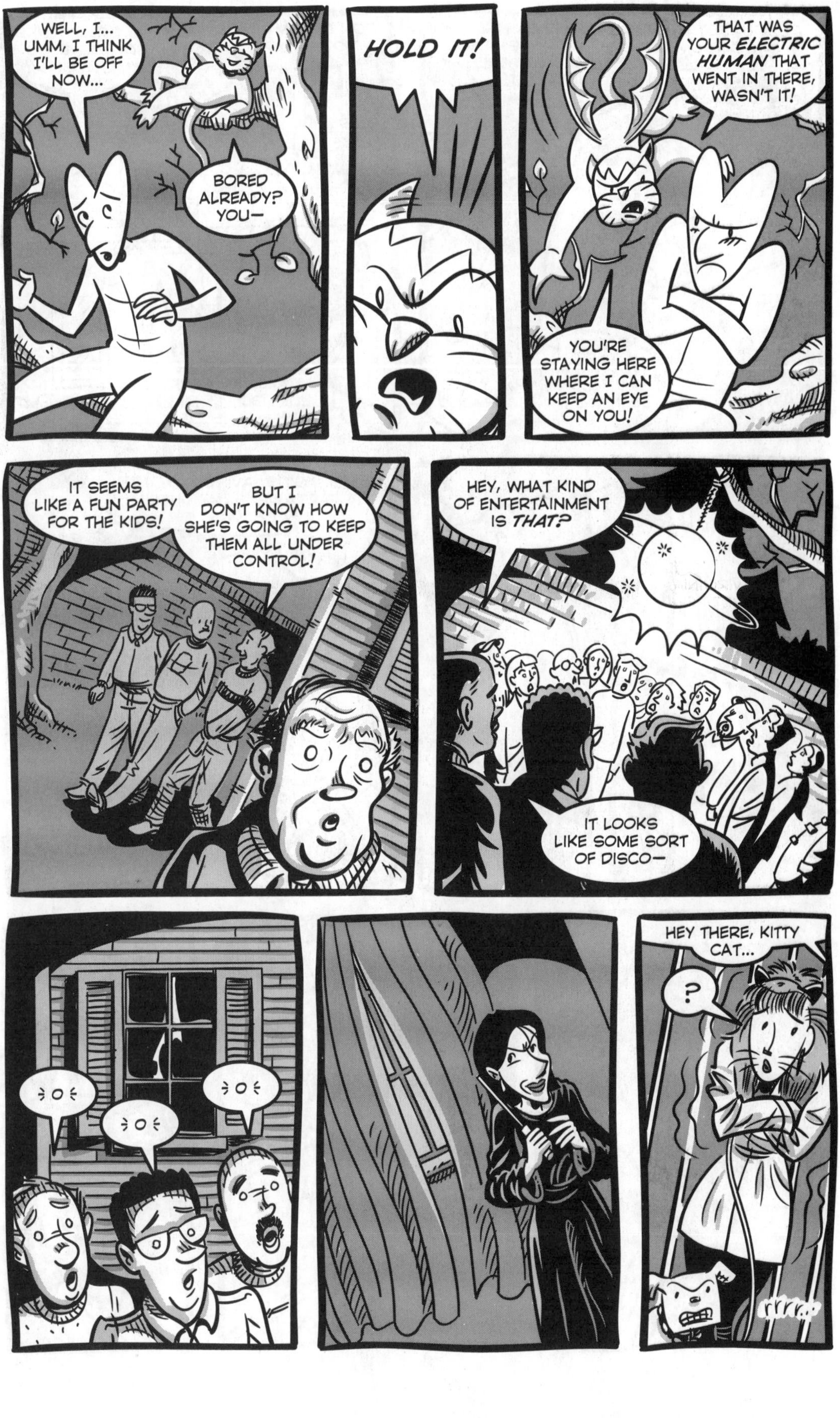
WELL, I... UMM, I THINK I'LL BE OFF NOW...
BORED ALREADY? YOU—
HOLD IT!
THAT WAS YOUR *ELECTRIC HUMAN* THAT WENT IN THERE, WASN'T IT!
YOU'RE STAYING HERE WHERE I CAN KEEP AN EYE ON YOU!
IT SEEMS LIKE A FUN PARTY FOR THE KIDS!
BUT I DON'T KNOW HOW SHE'S GOING TO KEEP THEM ALL UNDER CONTROL!
HEY, WHAT KIND OF ENTERTAINMENT IS *THAT?*
IT LOOKS LIKE SOME SORT OF DISCO—
HEY THERE, KITTY CAT...
?
rrrr..

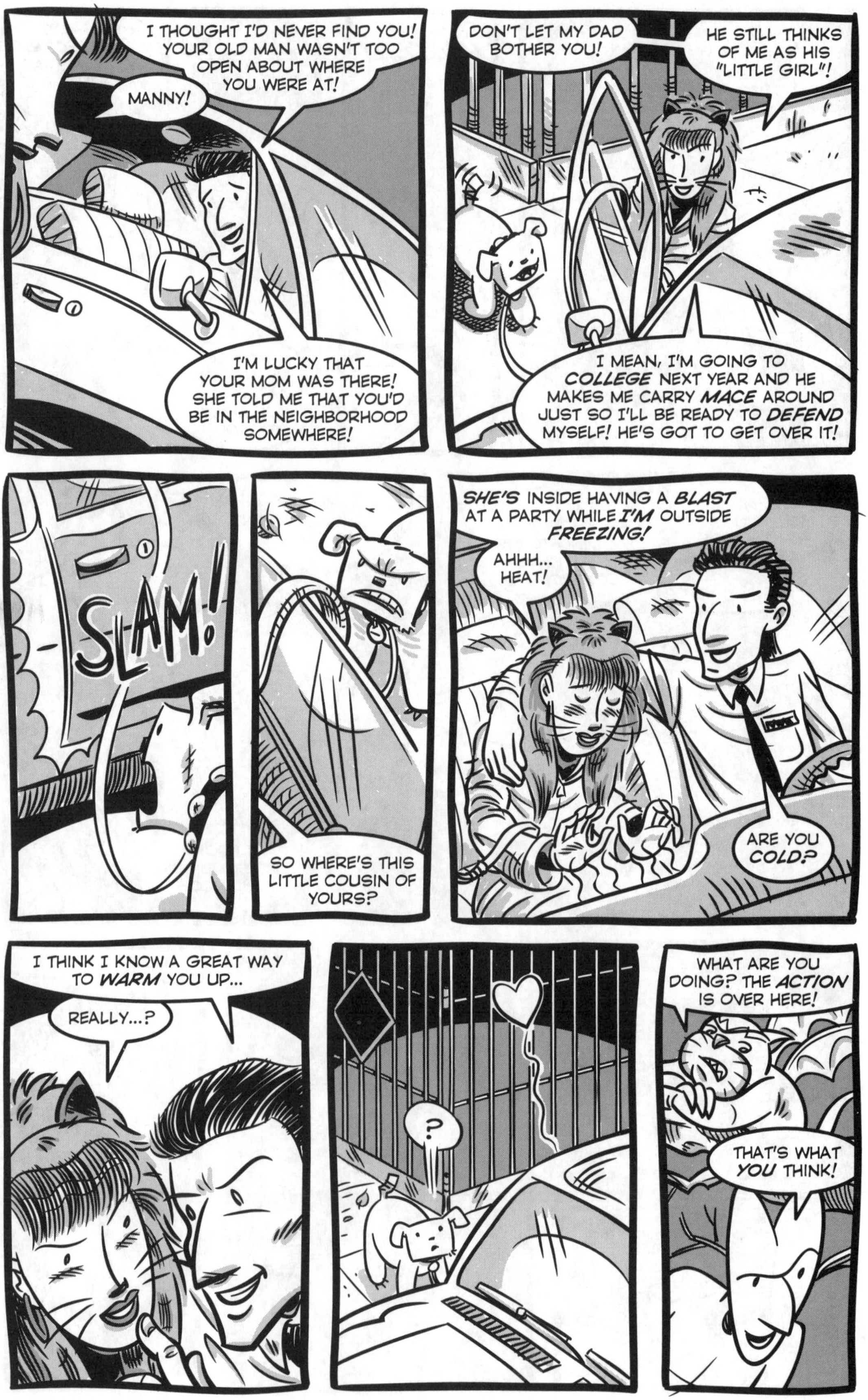
MANNY!
I THOUGHT I'D NEVER FIND YOU! YOUR OLD MAN WASN'T TOO OPEN ABOUT WHERE YOU WERE AT!
I'M LUCKY THAT YOUR MOM WAS THERE! SHE TOLD ME THAT YOU'D BE IN THE NEIGHBORHOOD SOMEWHERE!
DON'T LET MY DAD BOTHER YOU!
HE STILL THINKS OF ME AS HIS "LITTLE GIRL"!
I MEAN, I'M GOING TO COLLEGE NEXT YEAR AND HE MAKES ME CARRY MACE AROUND JUST SO I'LL BE READY TO DEFEND MYSELF! HE'S GOT TO GET OVER IT!
SLAM!
SO WHERE'S THIS LITTLE COUSIN OF YOURS?
SHE'S INSIDE HAVING A BLAST AT A PARTY WHILE I'M OUTSIDE FREEZING!
AHHH... HEAT!
ARE YOU COLD?
I THINK I KNOW A GREAT WAY TO WARM YOU UP...
REALLY...?
?
WHAT ARE YOU DOING? THE ACTION IS OVER HERE!
THAT'S WHAT YOU THINK!

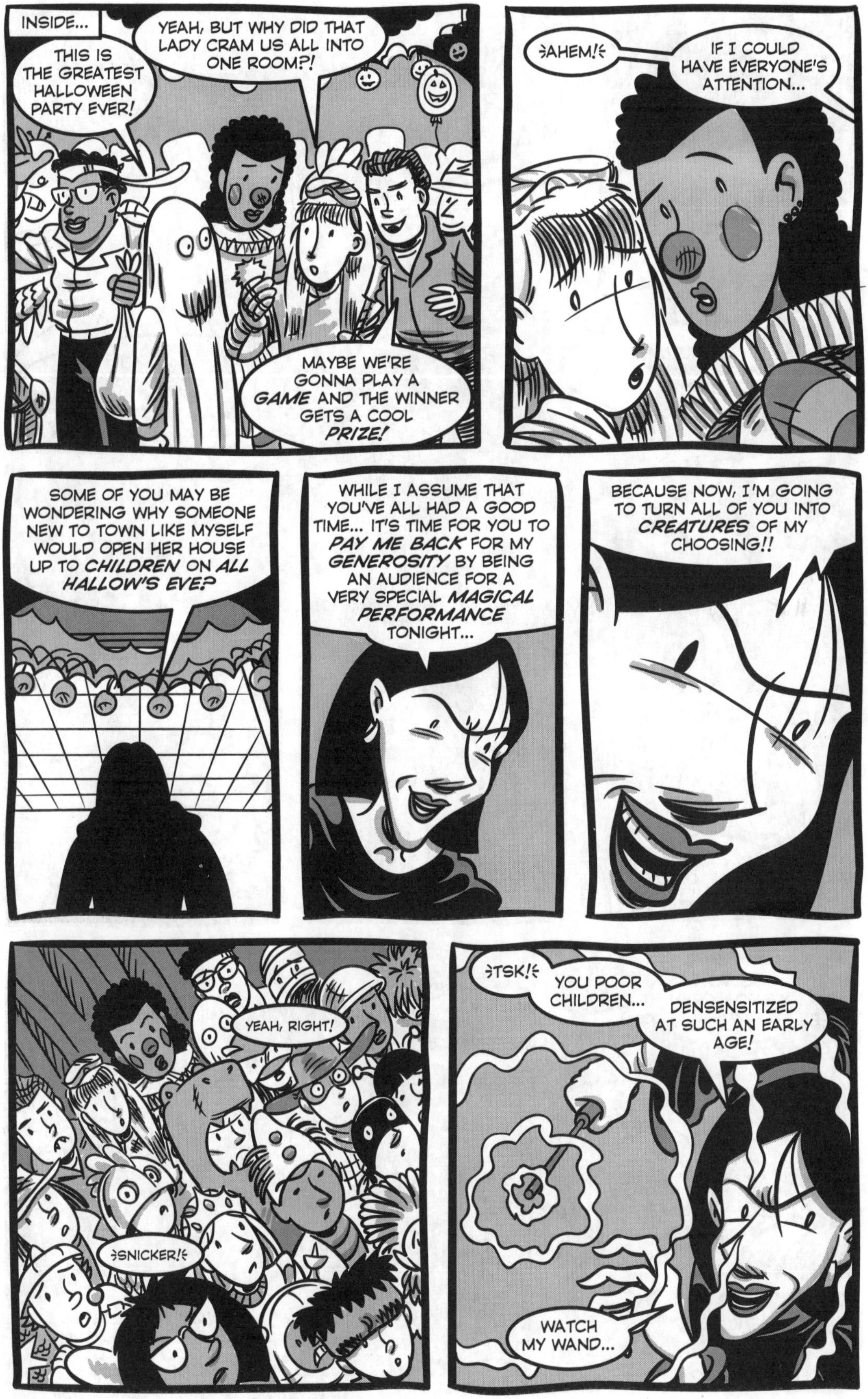
INSIDE...
THIS IS THE GREATEST HALLOWEEN PARTY EVER!
YEAH, BUT WHY DID THAT LADY CRAM US ALL INTO ONE ROOM?!
MAYBE WE'RE GONNA PLAY A *GAME* AND THE WINNER GETS A COOL *PRIZE!*
AHEM!
IF I COULD HAVE EVERYONE'S ATTENTION...
SOME OF YOU MAY BE WONDERING WHY SOMEONE NEW TO TOWN LIKE MYSELF WOULD OPEN HER HOUSE UP TO *CHILDREN* ON *ALL HALLOW'S EVE?*
WHILE I ASSUME THAT YOU'VE ALL HAD A GOOD TIME... IT'S TIME FOR YOU TO *PAY ME BACK* FOR MY *GENEROSITY* BY BEING AN AUDIENCE FOR A VERY SPECIAL *MAGICAL PERFORMANCE* TONIGHT...
BECAUSE NOW, I'M GOING TO TURN ALL OF YOU INTO *CREATURES* OF MY CHOOSING!!
YEAH, RIGHT!
SNICKER!
TSK!
YOU POOR CHILDREN...
DENSENSITIZED AT SUCH AN EARLY AGE!
WATCH MY WAND...

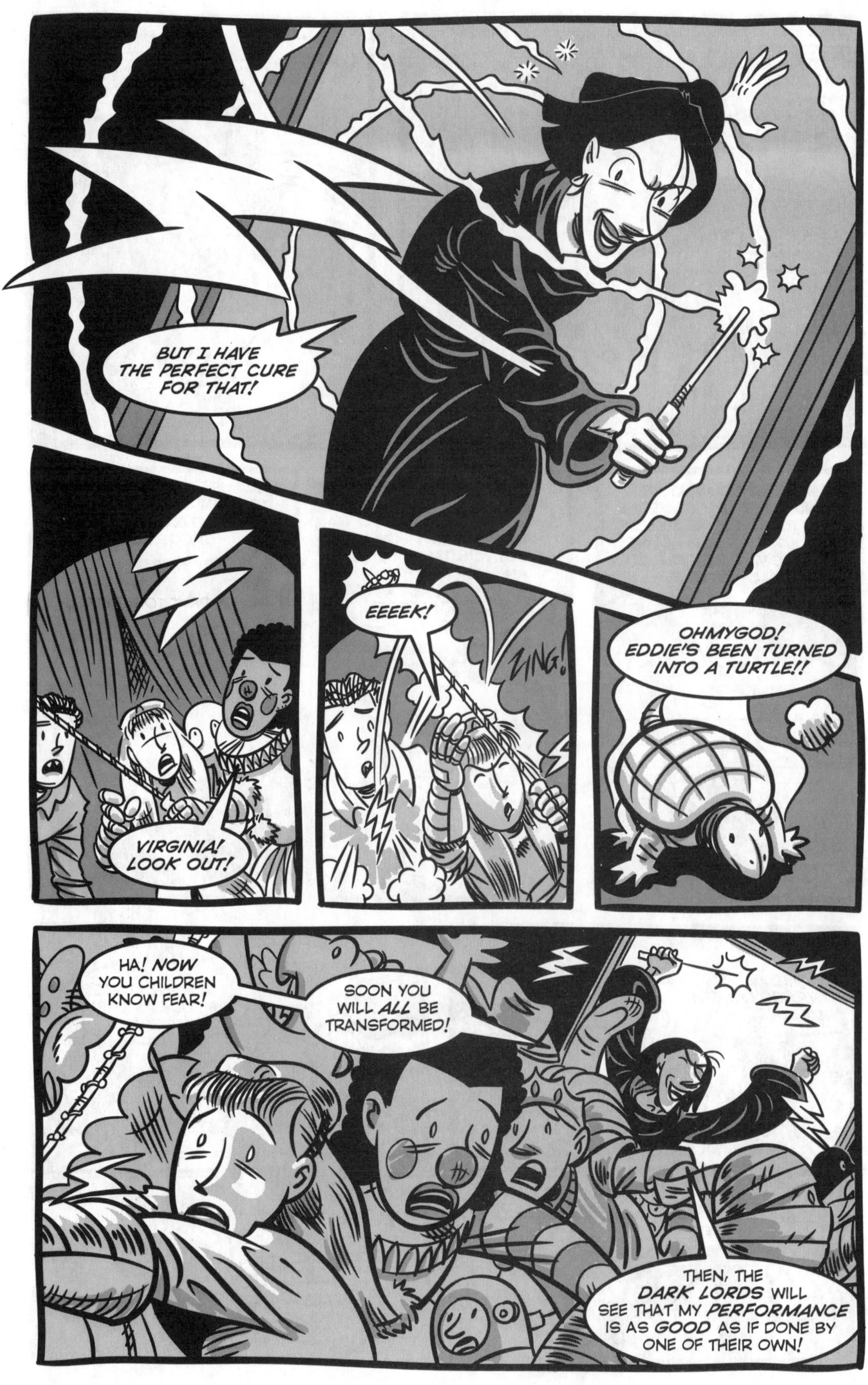

BUT I HAVE THE PERFECT CURE FOR THAT!
VIRGINIA! LOOK OUT!
EEEEK!
ZING!
OHMYGOD! EDDIE'S BEEN TURNED INTO A TURTLE!!
HA! NOW YOU CHILDREN KNOW FEAR!
SOON YOU WILL ALL BE TRANSFORMED!
THEN, THE DARK LORDS WILL SEE THAT MY PERFORMANCE IS AS GOOD AS IF DONE BY ONE OF THEIR OWN!

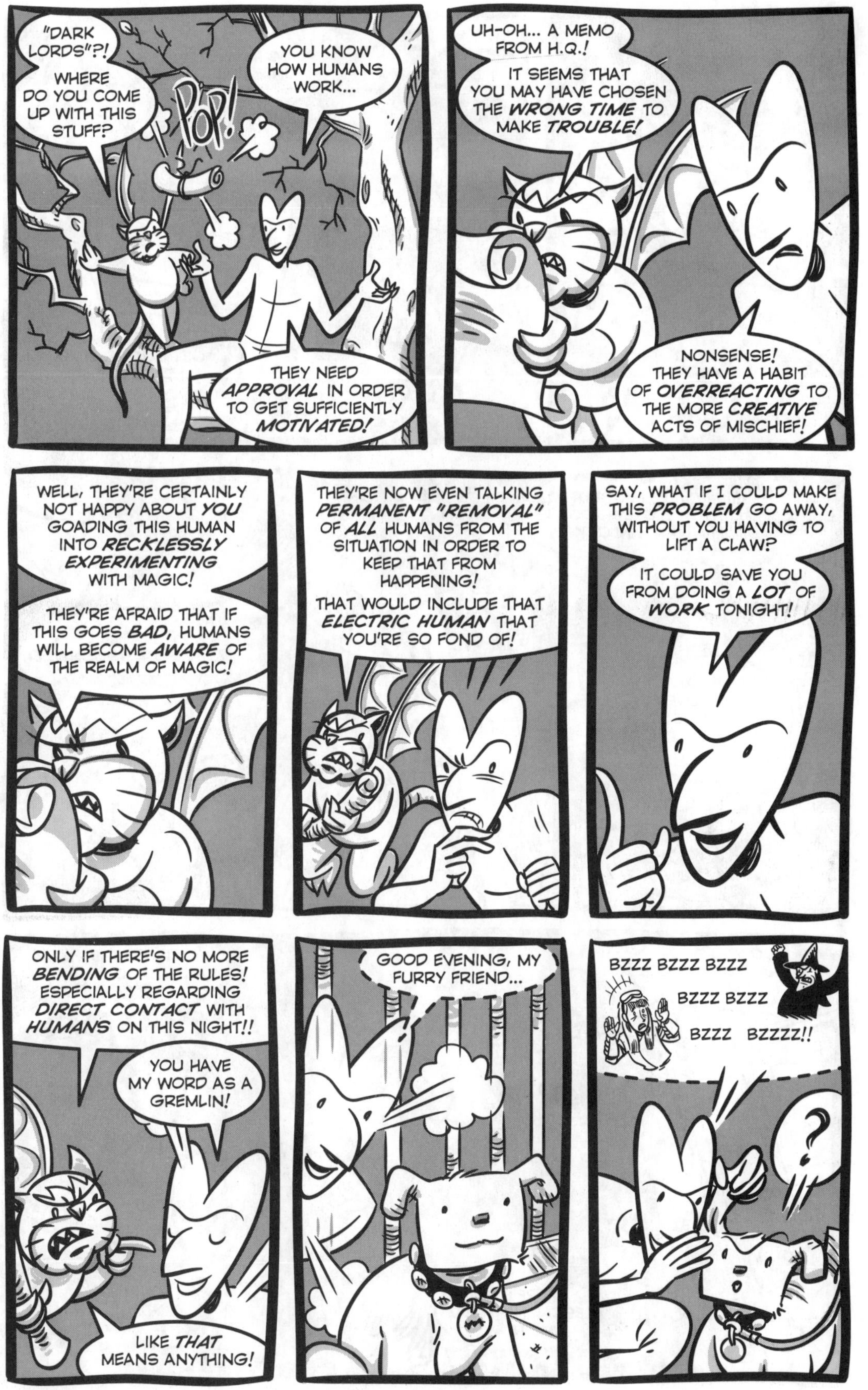
"DARK LORDS"?!
WHERE DO YOU COME UP WITH THIS STUFF?
POP!
YOU KNOW HOW HUMANS WORK...
THEY NEED APPROVAL IN ORDER TO GET SUFFICIENTLY MOTIVATED!
UH-OH... A MEMO FROM H.Q.!
IT SEEMS THAT YOU MAY HAVE CHOSEN THE WRONG TIME TO MAKE TROUBLE!
NONSENSE! THEY HAVE A HABIT OF OVERREACTING TO THE MORE CREATIVE ACTS OF MISCHIEF!
WELL, THEY'RE CERTAINLY NOT HAPPY ABOUT YOU GOADING THIS HUMAN INTO RECKLESSLY EXPERIMENTING WITH MAGIC!
THEY'RE AFRAID THAT IF THIS GOES BAD, HUMANS WILL BECOME AWARE OF THE REALM OF MAGIC!
THEY'RE NOW EVEN TALKING PERMANENT "REMOVAL" OF ALL HUMANS FROM THE SITUATION IN ORDER TO KEEP THAT FROM HAPPENING!
THAT WOULD INCLUDE THAT ELECTRIC HUMAN THAT YOU'RE SO FOND OF!
SAY, WHAT IF I COULD MAKE THIS PROBLEM GO AWAY, WITHOUT YOU HAVING TO LIFT A CLAW?
IT COULD SAVE YOU FROM DOING A LOT OF WORK TONIGHT!
ONLY IF THERE'S NO MORE BENDING OF THE RULES! ESPECIALLY REGARDING DIRECT CONTACT WITH HUMANS ON THIS NIGHT!!
YOU HAVE MY WORD AS A GREMLIN!
LIKE THAT MEANS ANYTHING!
GOOD EVENING, MY FURRY FRIEND...
BZZZ BZZZ BZZZ
BZZZ BZZZ
BZZZ BZZZZ!!
?

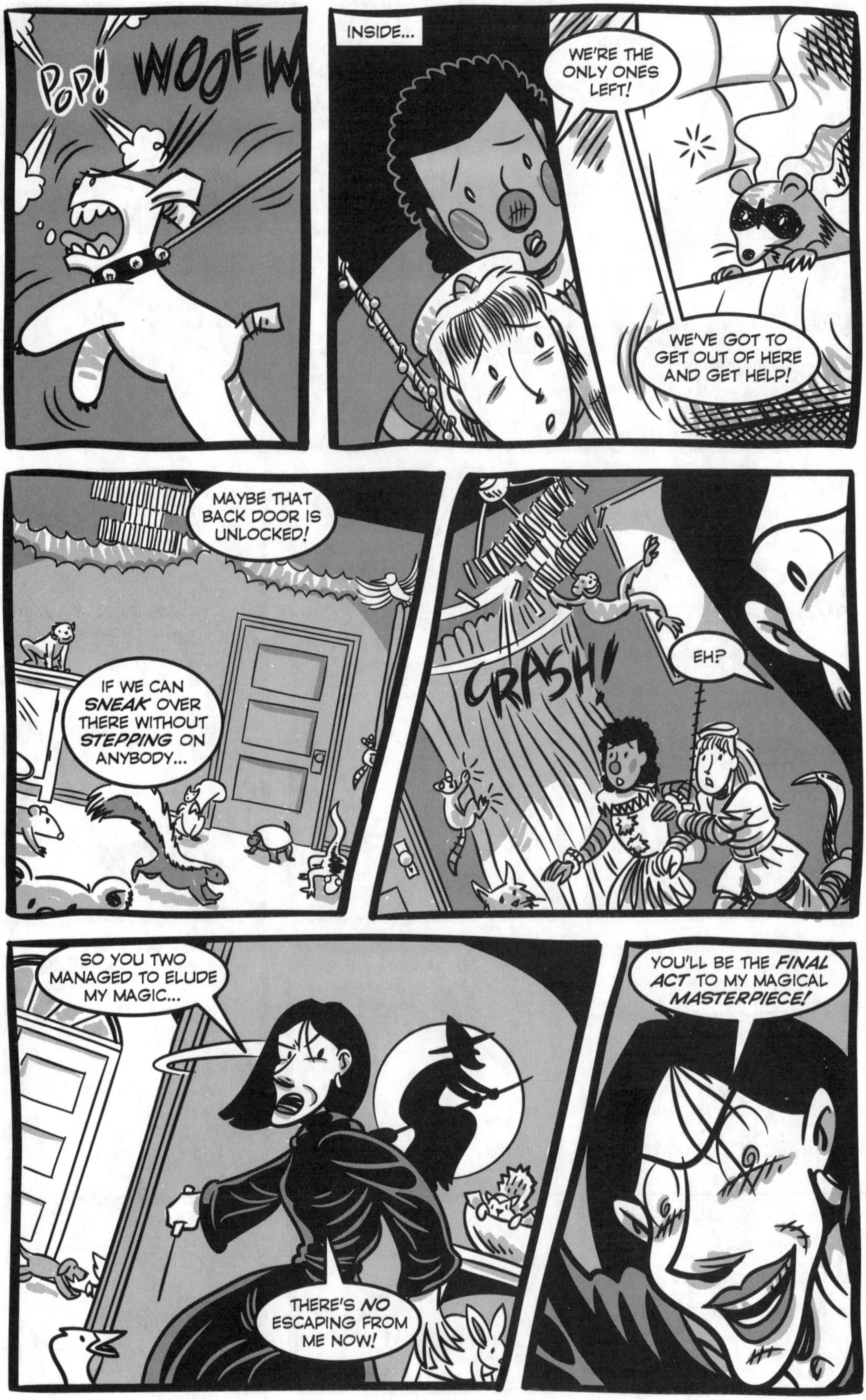
POP!
WOOF W
INSIDE...
WE'RE THE ONLY ONES LEFT!
WE'VE GOT TO GET OUT OF HERE AND GET HELP!
MAYBE THAT BACK DOOR IS UNLOCKED!
IF WE CAN SNEAK OVER THERE WITHOUT STEPPING ON ANYBODY...
CRASH!
EH?
SO YOU TWO MANAGED TO ELUDE MY MAGIC...
THERE'S NO ESCAPING FROM ME NOW!
YOU'LL BE THE FINAL ACT TO MY MAGICAL MASTERPIECE!

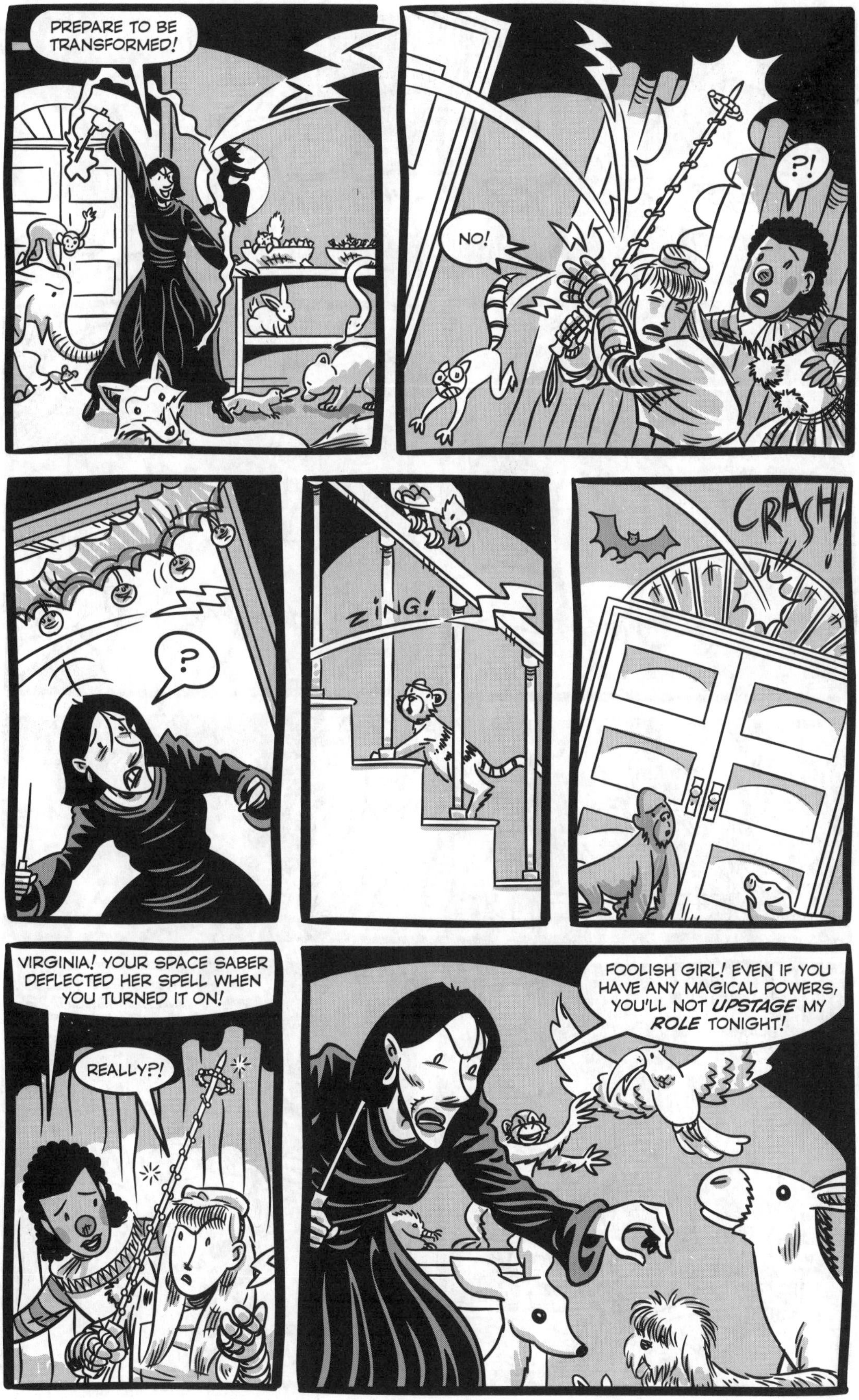
PREPARE TO BE TRANSFORMED!
NO!
?!
?
ZING!
CRASH!
VIRGINIA! YOUR SPACE SABER DEFLECTED HER SPELL WHEN YOU TURNED IT ON!
REALLY?!
FOOLISH GIRL! EVEN IF YOU HAVE ANY MAGICAL POWERS, YOU'LL NOT *UPSTAGE* MY *ROLE* TONIGHT!

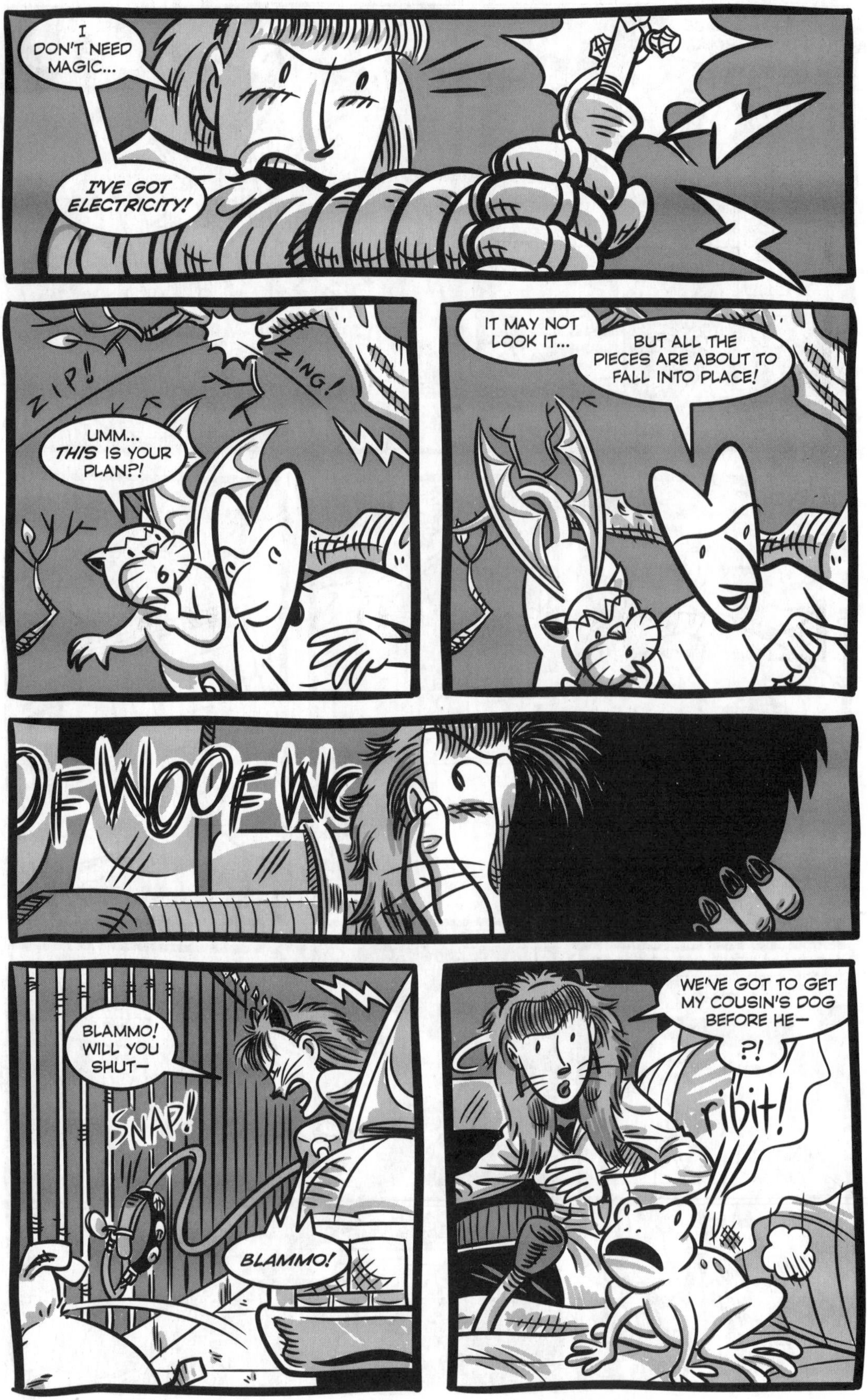
I DON'T NEED MAGIC...
I'VE GOT ELECTRICITY!
ZIP!
ZING!
UMM... THIS IS YOUR PLAN?!
IT MAY NOT LOOK IT...
BUT ALL THE PIECES ARE ABOUT TO FALL INTO PLACE!
OF WOOF WO
BLAMMO! WILL YOU SHUT—
SNAP!
BLAMMO!
WE'VE GOT TO GET MY COUSIN'S DOG BEFORE HE—
?!
ribit!

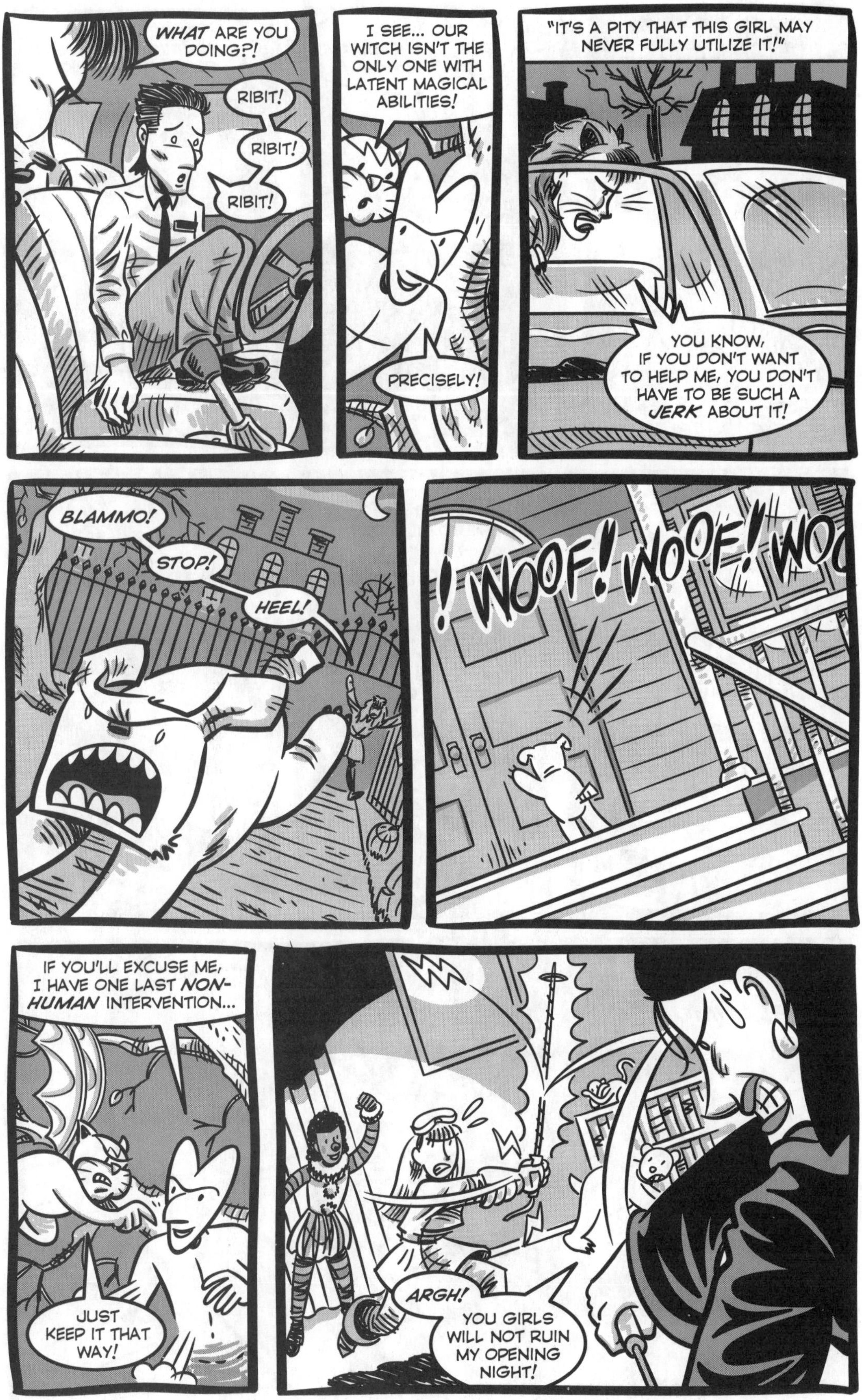
WHAT ARE YOU DOING?!
RIBIT!
RIBIT!
RIBIT!
I SEE... OUR WITCH ISN'T THE ONLY ONE WITH LATENT MAGICAL ABILITIES!
PRECISELY!
"IT'S A PITY THAT THIS GIRL MAY NEVER FULLY UTILIZE IT!"
YOU KNOW, IF YOU DON'T WANT TO HELP ME, YOU DON'T HAVE TO BE SUCH A JERK ABOUT IT!
BLAMMO!
STOP!
HEEL!
! WOOF! WOOF! WOO
IF YOU'LL EXCUSE ME, I HAVE ONE LAST NON-HUMAN INTERVENTION...
JUST KEEP IT THAT WAY!
ARGH!
YOU GIRLS WILL NOT RUIN MY OPENING NIGHT!

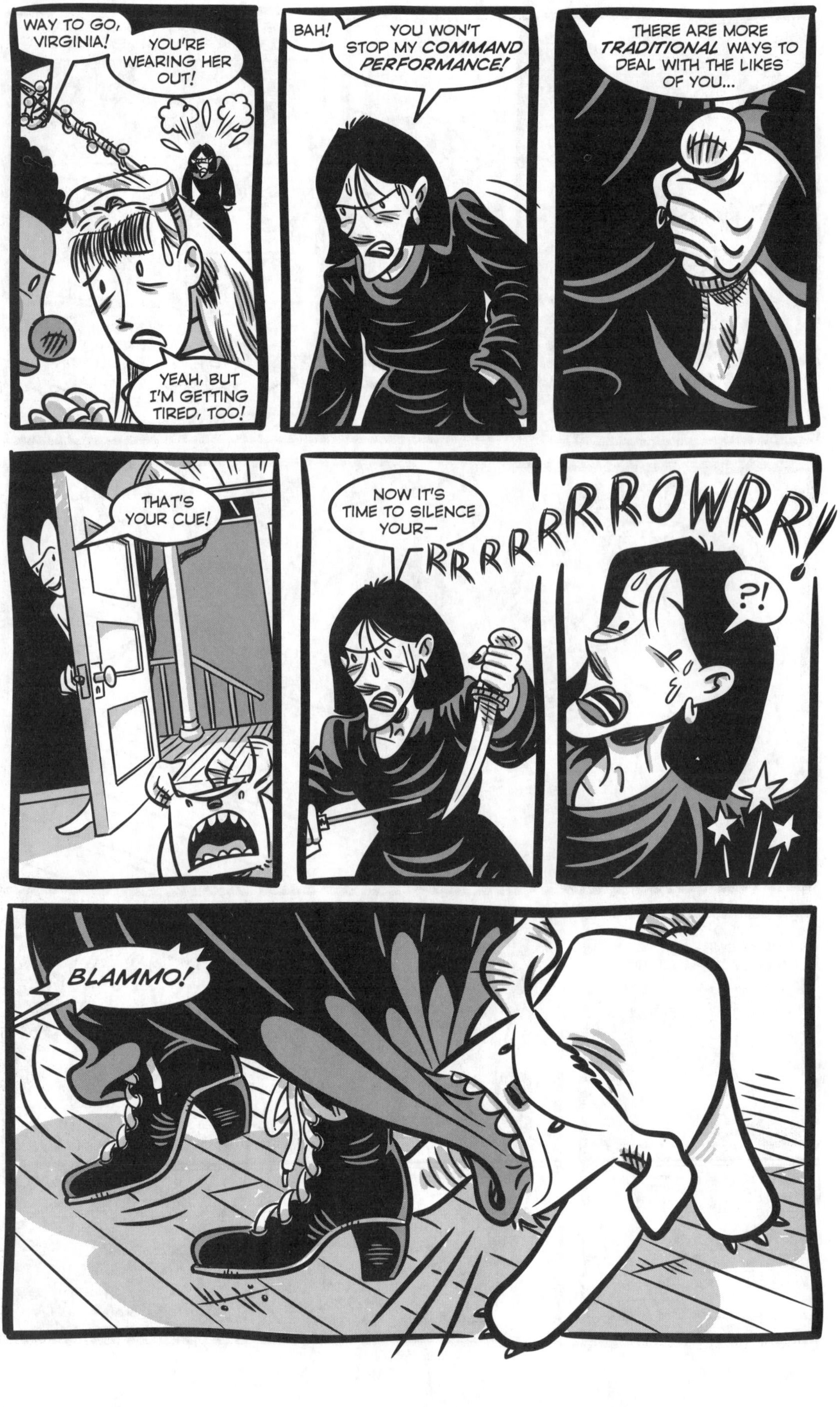
WAY TO GO, VIRGINIA!
YOU'RE WEARING HER OUT!
YEAH, BUT I'M GETTING TIRED, TOO!
BAH!
YOU WON'T STOP MY COMMAND PERFORMANCE!
THERE ARE MORE TRADITIONAL WAYS TO DEAL WITH THE LIKES OF YOU...
THAT'S YOUR CUE!
NOW IT'S TIME TO SILENCE YOUR—
RRRRRRROWRR!
?!
BLAMMO!

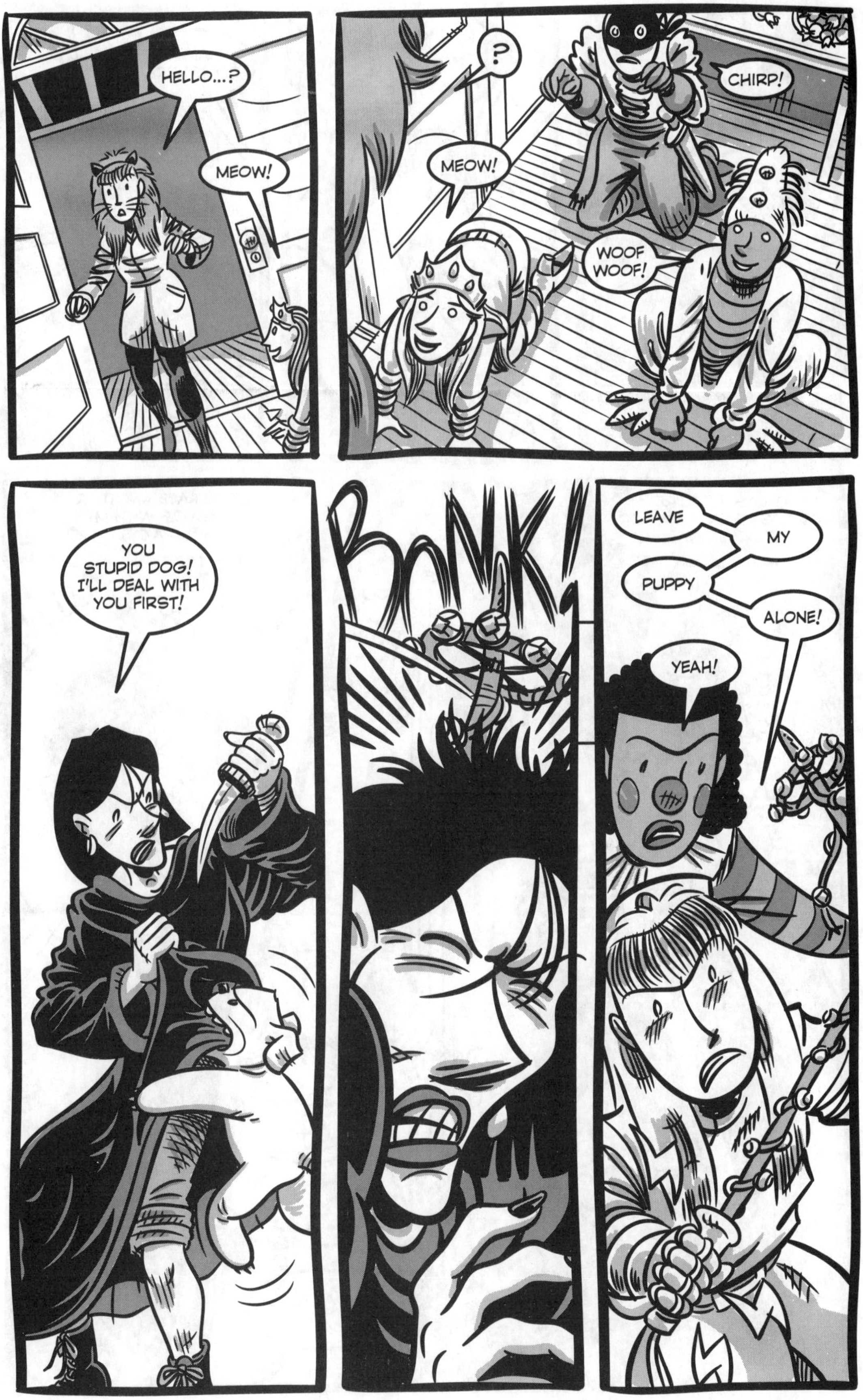
HELLO...?
MEOW!
?
CHIRP!
MEOW!
WOOF WOOF!
YOU STUPID DOG! I'LL DEAL WITH YOU FIRST!
BONK!
LEAVE
MY
PUPPY
ALONE!
YEAH!

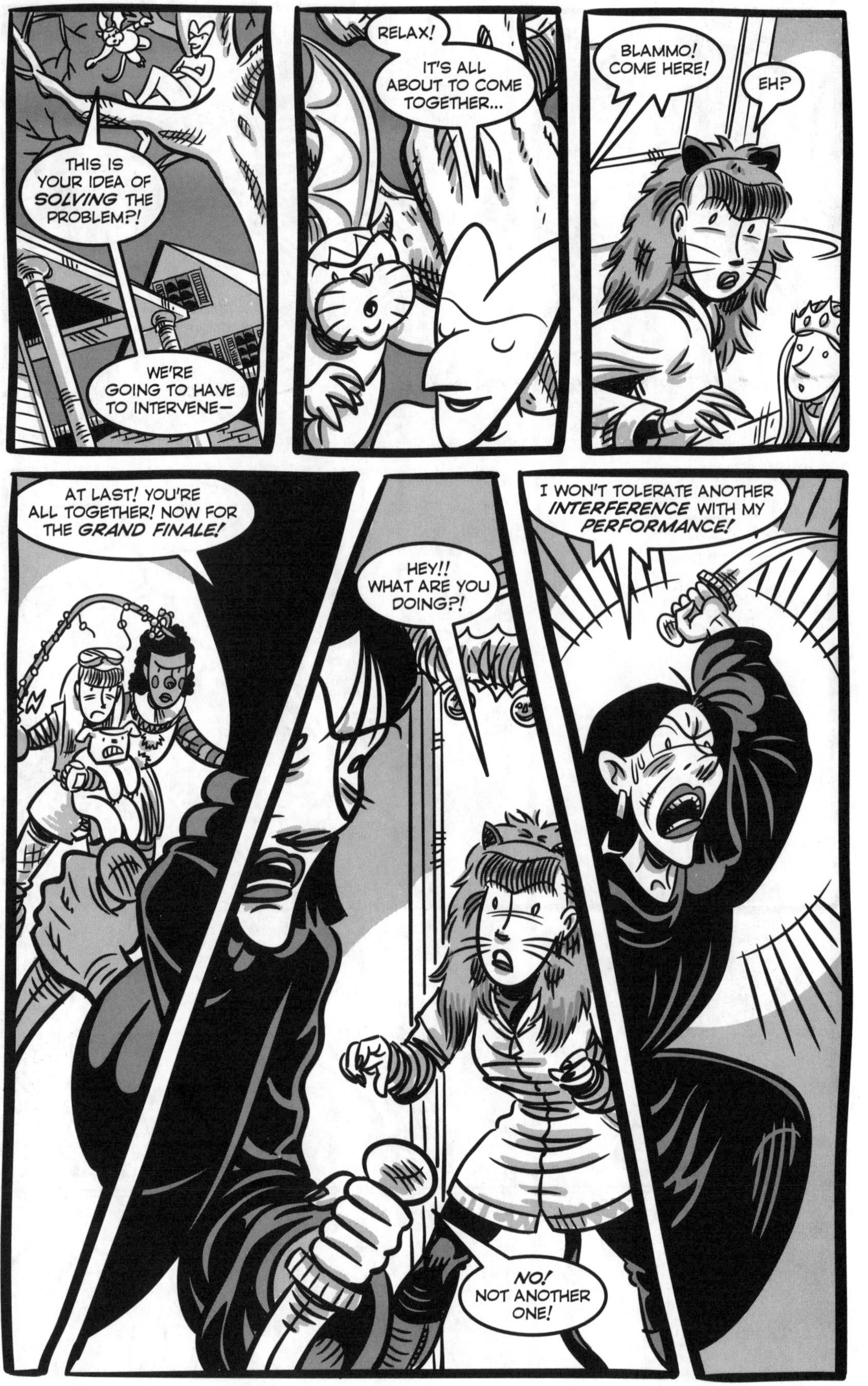
THIS IS YOUR IDEA OF *SOLVING* THE PROBLEM?!
WE'RE GOING TO HAVE TO INTERVENE—
RELAX!
IT'S ALL ABOUT TO COME TOGETHER...
BLAMMO! COME HERE!
EH?
AT LAST! YOU'RE ALL TOGETHER! NOW FOR THE *GRAND FINALE!*
HEY!! WHAT ARE YOU DOING?!
I WON'T TOLERATE ANOTHER *INTERFERENCE* WITH MY *PERFORMANCE!*
NO! NOT ANOTHER ONE!

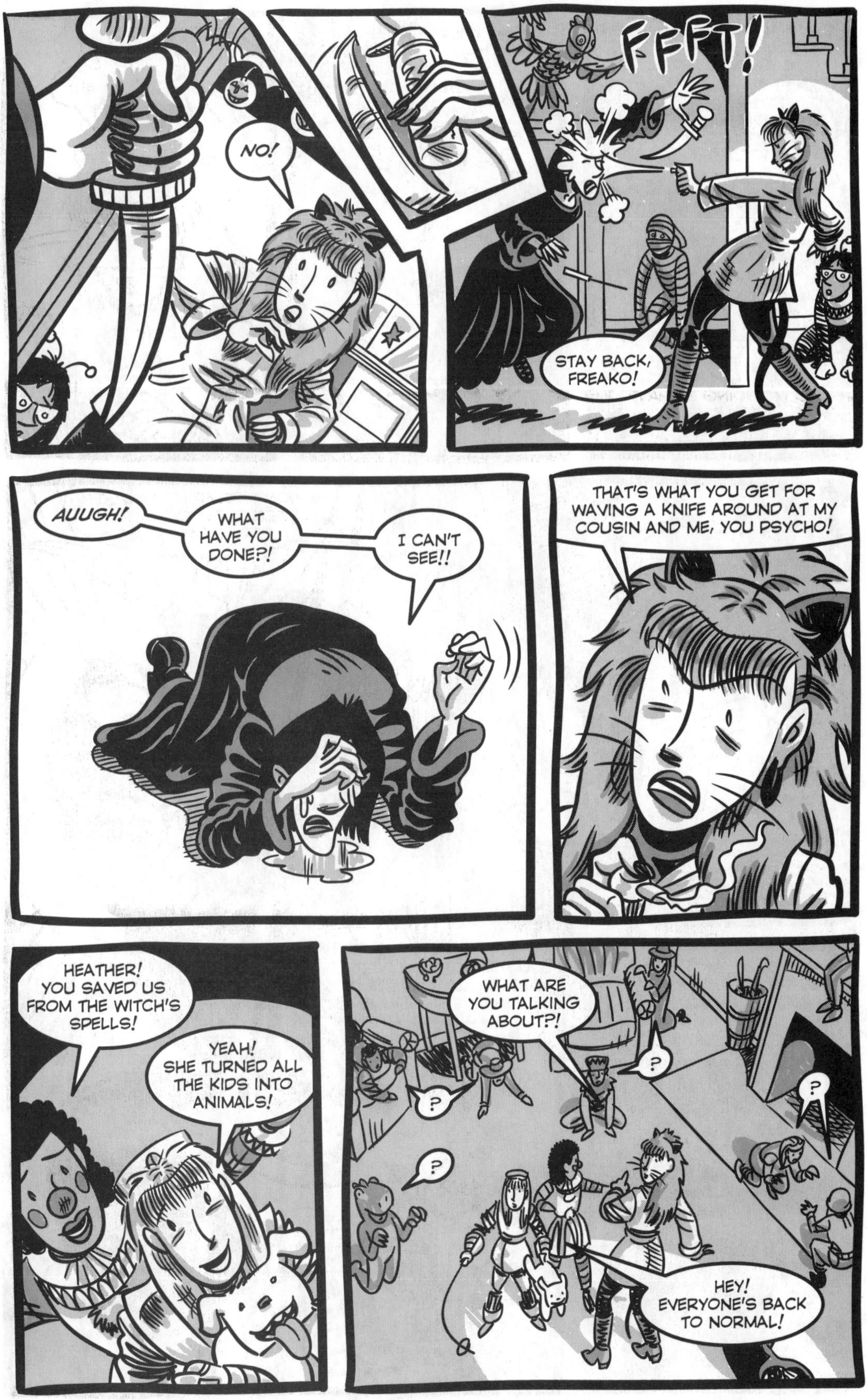
NO!
FFFT!
STAY BACK, FREAKO!
AUUGH!
WHAT HAVE YOU DONE?!
I CAN'T SEE!!
THAT'S WHAT YOU GET FOR WAVING A KNIFE AROUND AT MY COUSIN AND ME, YOU PSYCHO!
HEATHER! YOU SAVED US FROM THE WITCH'S SPELLS!
YEAH! SHE TURNED ALL THE KIDS INTO ANIMALS!
WHAT ARE YOU TALKING ABOUT?!
?
?
?
?
HEY! EVERYONE'S BACK TO NORMAL!

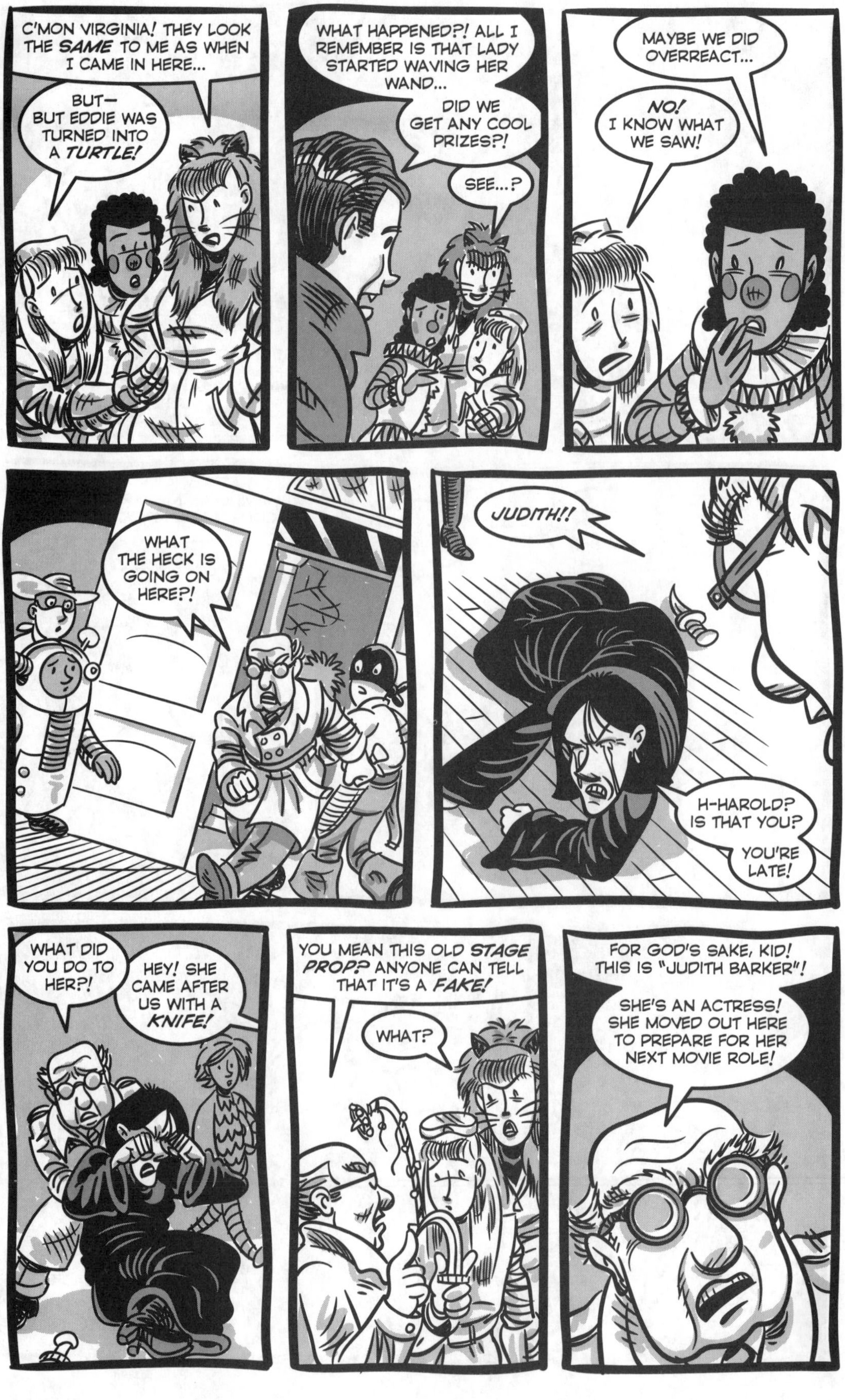
C'MON VIRGINIA! THEY LOOK THE *SAME* TO ME AS WHEN I CAME IN HERE...
BUT— BUT EDDIE WAS TURNED INTO A *TURTLE!*
WHAT HAPPENED?! ALL I REMEMBER IS THAT LADY STARTED WAVING HER WAND...
DID WE GET ANY COOL PRIZES?!
SEE...?
MAYBE WE DID OVERREACT...
NO! I KNOW WHAT WE SAW!
WHAT THE HECK IS GOING ON HERE?!
JUDITH!!
H-HAROLD? IS THAT YOU?
YOU'RE LATE!
WHAT DID YOU DO TO HER?!
HEY! SHE CAME AFTER US WITH A *KNIFE!*
YOU MEAN THIS OLD *STAGE PROP?* ANYONE CAN TELL THAT IT'S A *FAKE!*
WHAT?
FOR GOD'S SAKE, KID! THIS IS "JUDITH BARKER"!
SHE'S AN ACTRESS! SHE MOVED OUT HERE TO PREPARE FOR HER NEXT MOVIE ROLE!

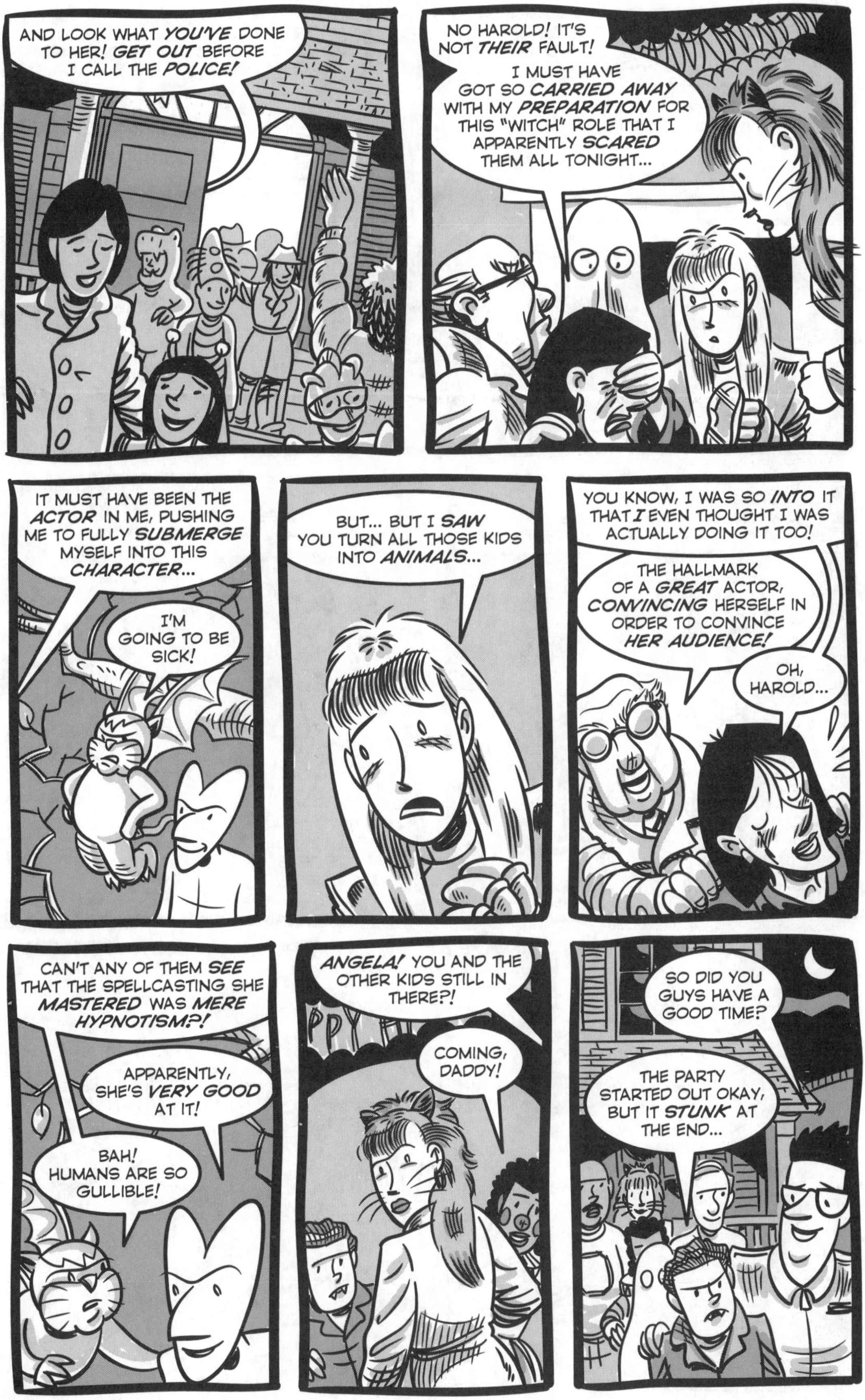
AND LOOK WHAT YOU'VE DONE TO HER! GET OUT BEFORE I CALL THE POLICE!
NO HAROLD! IT'S NOT THEIR FAULT!
I MUST HAVE GOT SO CARRIED AWAY WITH MY PREPARATION FOR THIS "WITCH" ROLE THAT I APPARENTLY SCARED THEM ALL TONIGHT...
IT MUST HAVE BEEN THE ACTOR IN ME, PUSHING ME TO FULLY SUBMERGE MYSELF INTO THIS CHARACTER...
I'M GOING TO BE SICK!
BUT... BUT I SAW YOU TURN ALL THOSE KIDS INTO ANIMALS...
YOU KNOW, I WAS SO INTO IT THAT I EVEN THOUGHT I WAS ACTUALLY DOING IT TOO!
THE HALLMARK OF A GREAT ACTOR, CONVINCING HERSELF IN ORDER TO CONVINCE HER AUDIENCE!
OH, HAROLD...
CAN'T ANY OF THEM SEE THAT THE SPELLCASTING SHE MASTERED WAS MERE HYPNOTISM?!
APPARENTLY, SHE'S VERY GOOD AT IT!
BAH! HUMANS ARE SO GULLIBLE!
ANGELA! YOU AND THE OTHER KIDS STILL IN THERE?!
COMING, DADDY!
SO DID YOU GUYS HAVE A GOOD TIME?
THE PARTY STARTED OUT OKAY, BUT IT STUNK AT THE END...

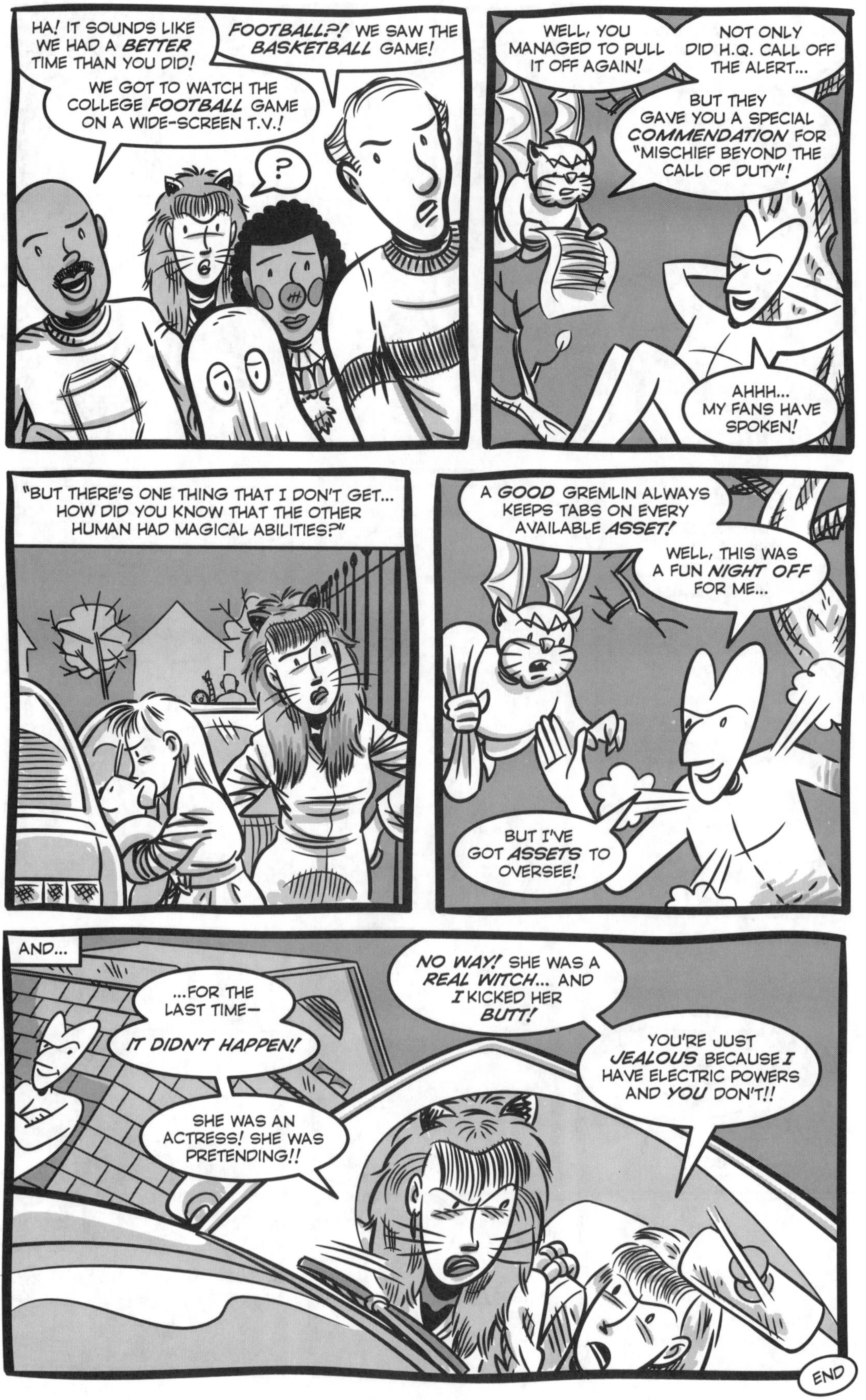

HA! IT SOUNDS LIKE WE HAD A BETTER TIME THAN YOU DID!
WE GOT TO WATCH THE COLLEGE FOOTBALL GAME ON A WIDE-SCREEN T.V.!
FOOTBALL?! WE SAW THE BASKETBALL GAME!
?
WELL, YOU MANAGED TO PULL IT OFF AGAIN!
NOT ONLY DID H.Q. CALL OFF THE ALERT...
BUT THEY GAVE YOU A SPECIAL COMMENDATION FOR "MISCHIEF BEYOND THE CALL OF DUTY"!
AHHH... MY FANS HAVE SPOKEN!
"BUT THERE'S ONE THING THAT I DON'T GET... HOW DID YOU KNOW THAT THE OTHER HUMAN HAD MAGICAL ABILITIES?"
A GOOD GREMLIN ALWAYS KEEPS TABS ON EVERY AVAILABLE ASSET!
WELL, THIS WAS A FUN NIGHT OFF FOR ME...
BUT I'VE GOT ASSETS TO OVERSEE!
AND...
...FOR THE LAST TIME—
IT DIDN'T HAPPEN!
SHE WAS AN ACTRESS! SHE WAS PRETENDING!!
NO WAY! SHE WAS A REAL WITCH... AND I KICKED HER BUTT!
YOU'RE JUST JEALOUS BECAUSE I HAVE ELECTRIC POWERS AND YOU DON'T!!
END

new stories

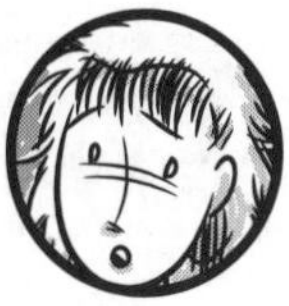

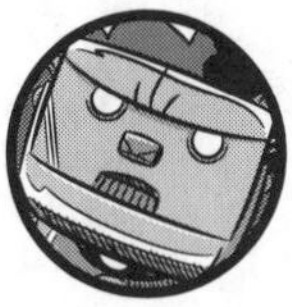

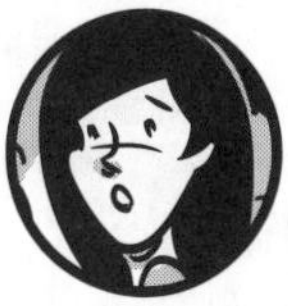

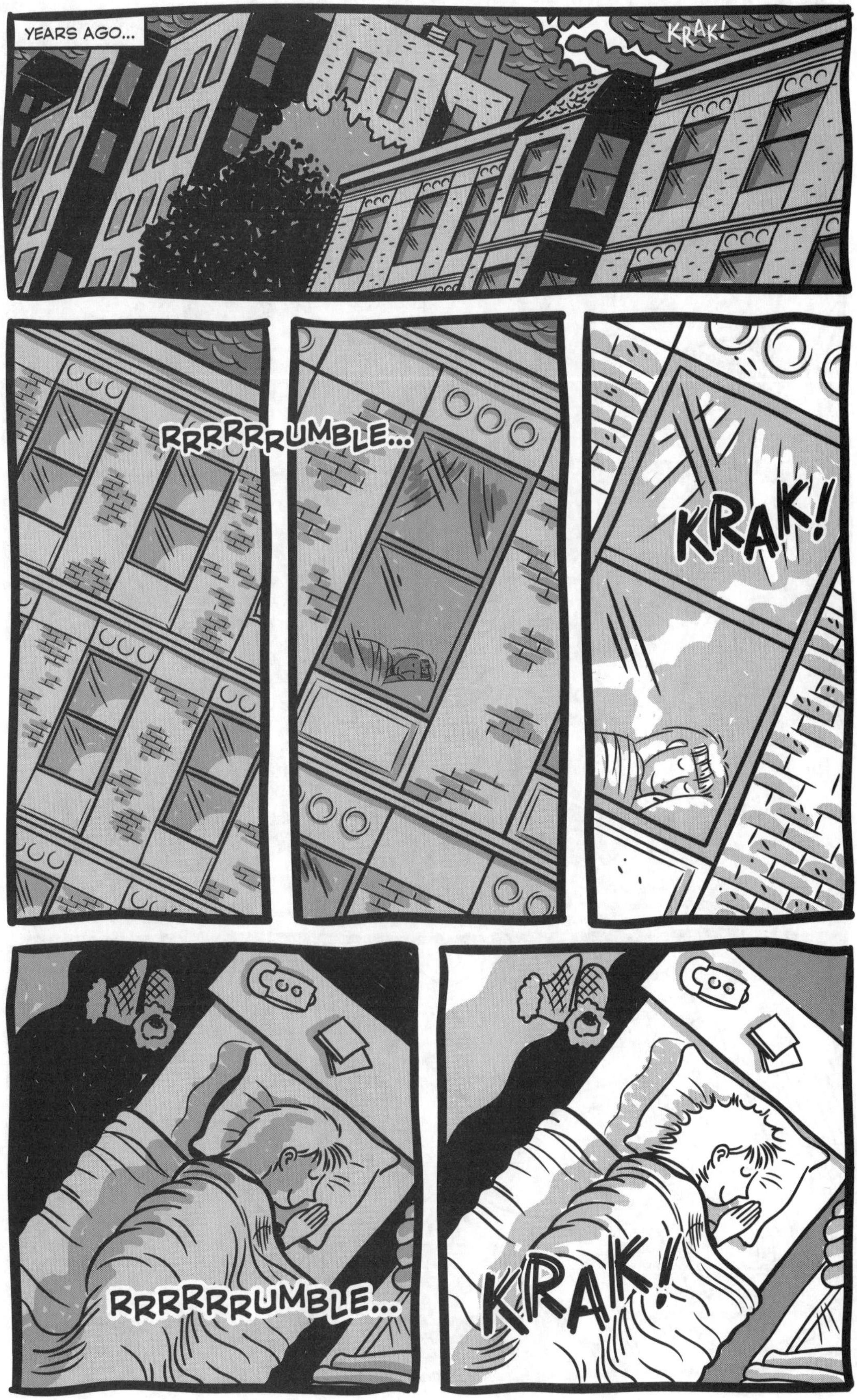
YEARS AGO...
KRAK!
RRRRRRUMBLE...
KRAK!
RRRRRRUMBLE...
KRAK!

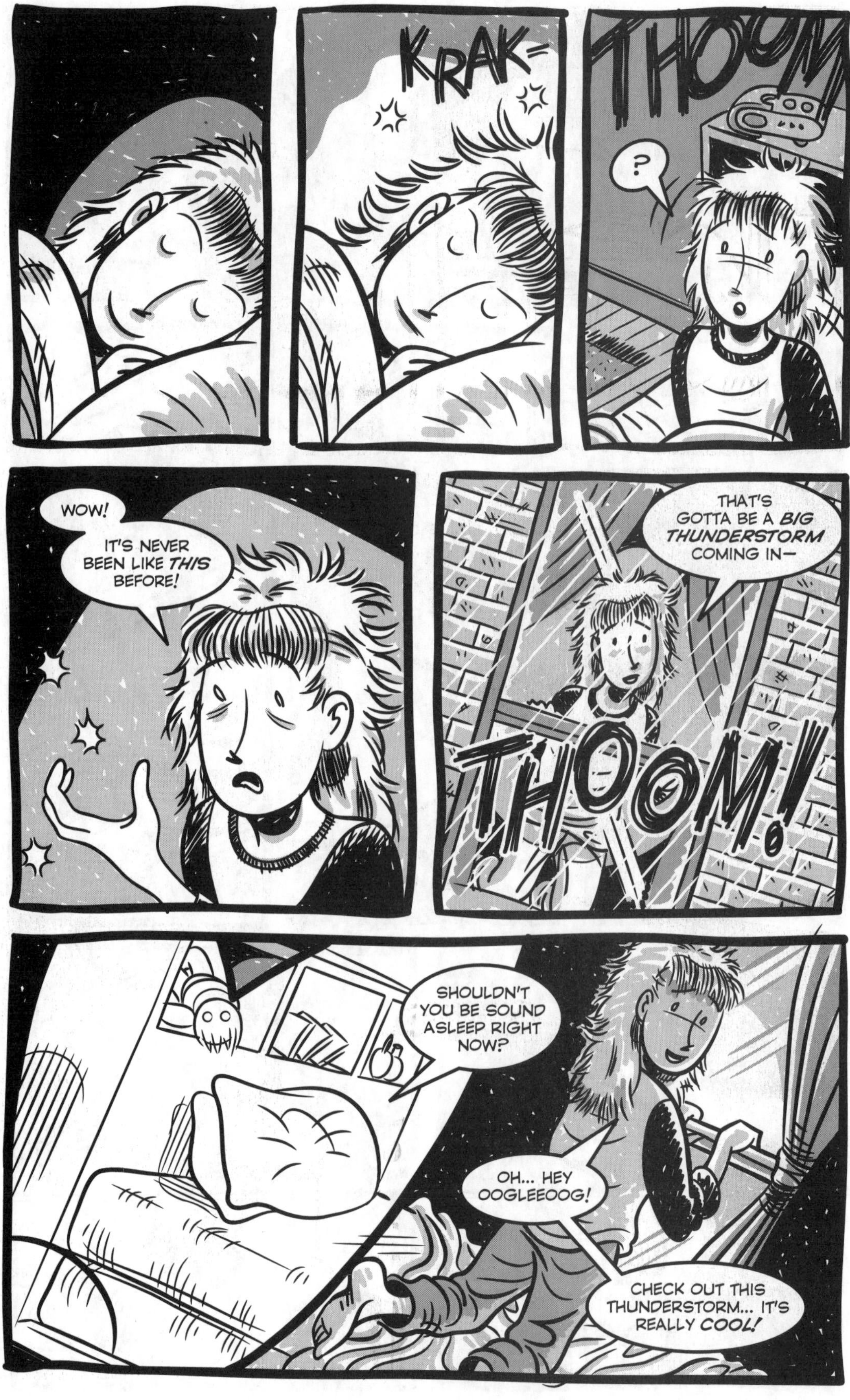
KRAK-
THOOM
?
WOW!
IT'S NEVER BEEN LIKE *THIS* BEFORE!
THAT'S GOTTA BE A *BIG THUNDERSTORM* COMING IN—
THOOM!
SHOULDN'T YOU BE SOUND ASLEEP RIGHT NOW?
OH... HEY OOGLEEOOG!
CHECK OUT THIS THUNDERSTORM... IT'S REALLY *COOL!*

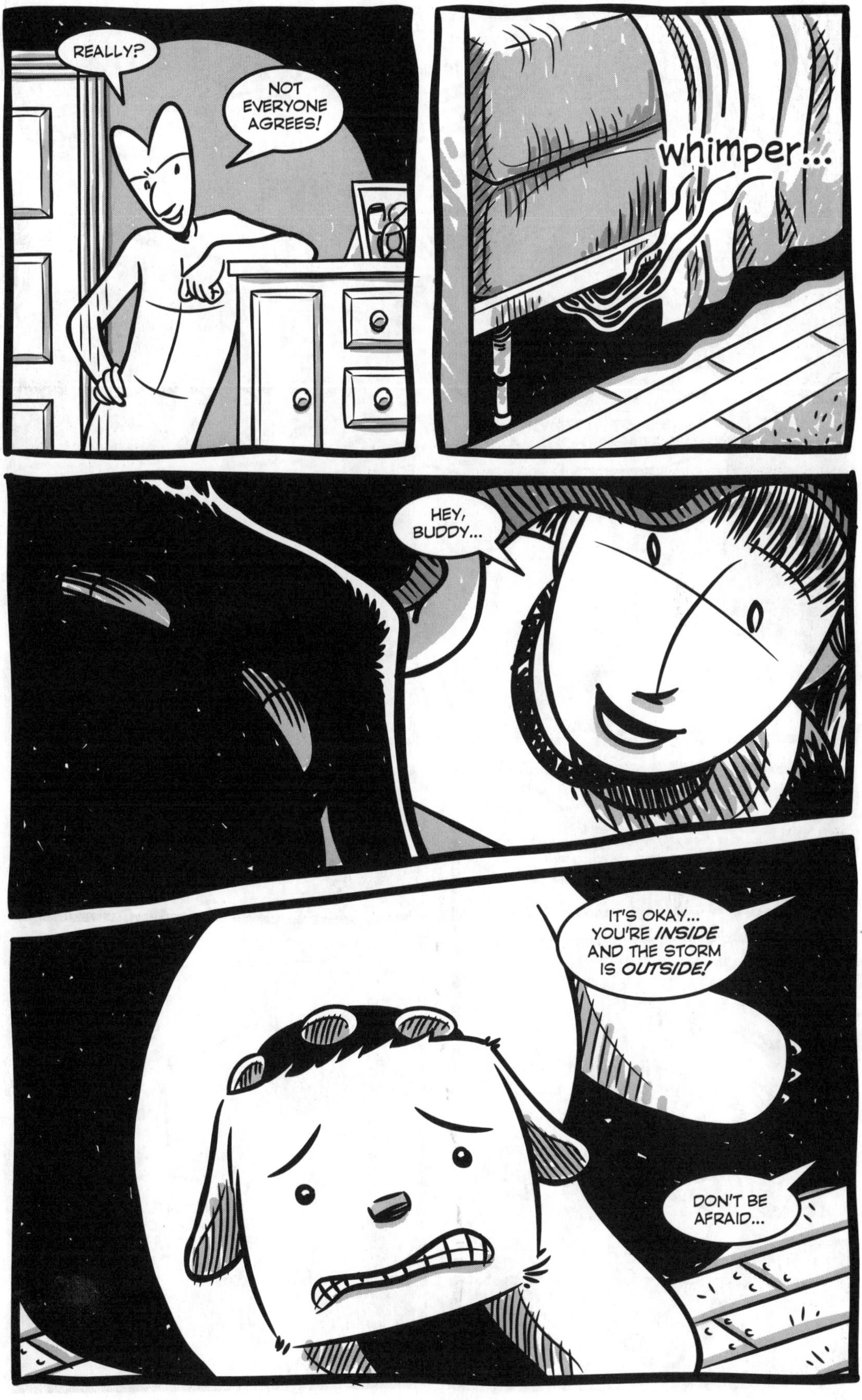
REALLY?
NOT EVERYONE AGREES!
whimper...
HEY, BUDDY...
IT'S OKAY... YOU'RE *INSIDE* AND THE STORM IS *OUTSIDE!*
DON'T BE AFRAID...

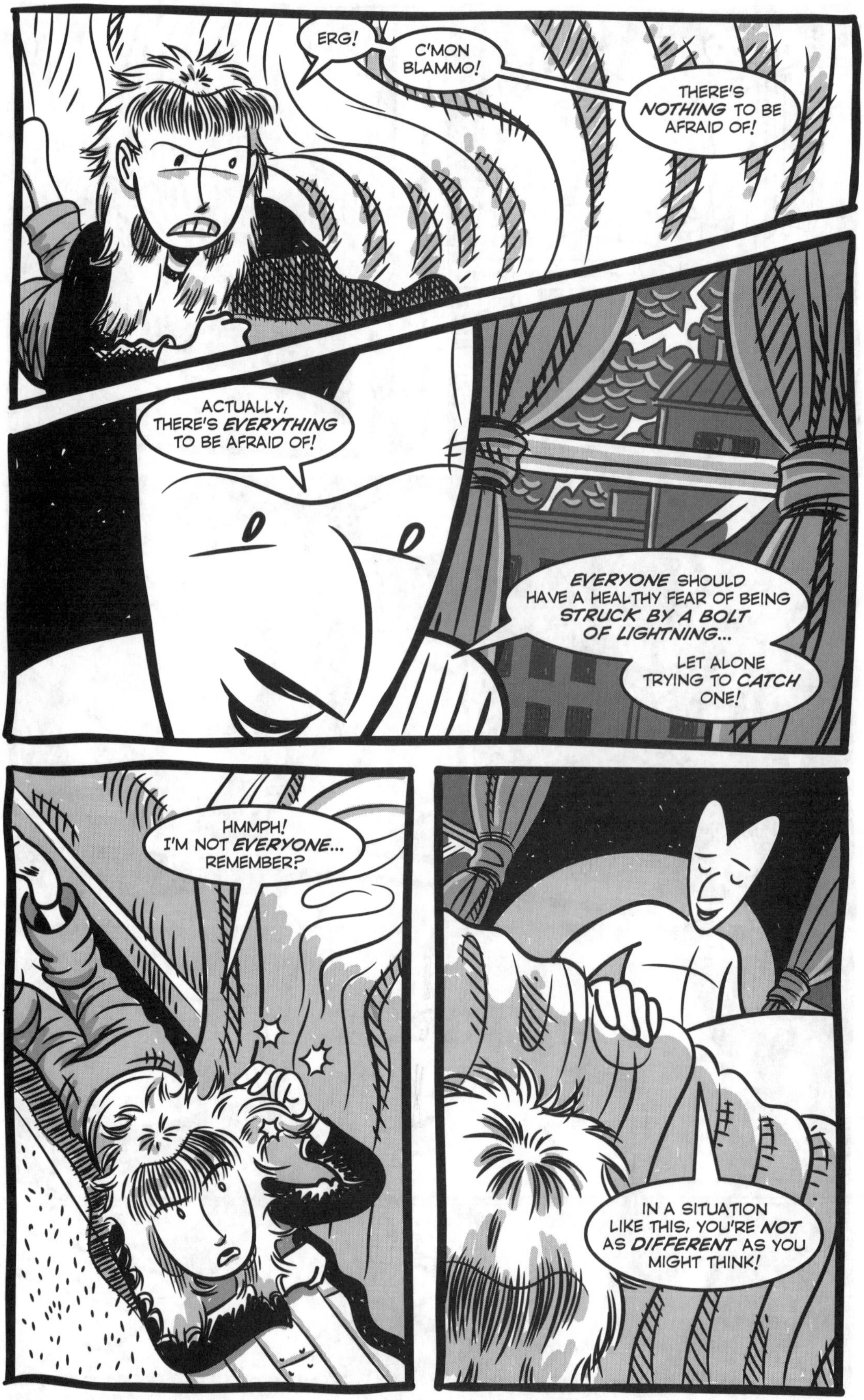
ERG!
C'MON BLAMMO!
THERE'S NOTHING TO BE AFRAID OF!
ACTUALLY, THERE'S EVERYTHING TO BE AFRAID OF!
EVERYONE SHOULD HAVE A HEALTHY FEAR OF BEING STRUCK BY A BOLT OF LIGHTNING...
LET ALONE TRYING TO CATCH ONE!
HMMPH! I'M NOT EVERYONE... REMEMBER?
IN A SITUATION LIKE THIS, YOU'RE NOT AS DIFFERENT AS YOU MIGHT THINK!

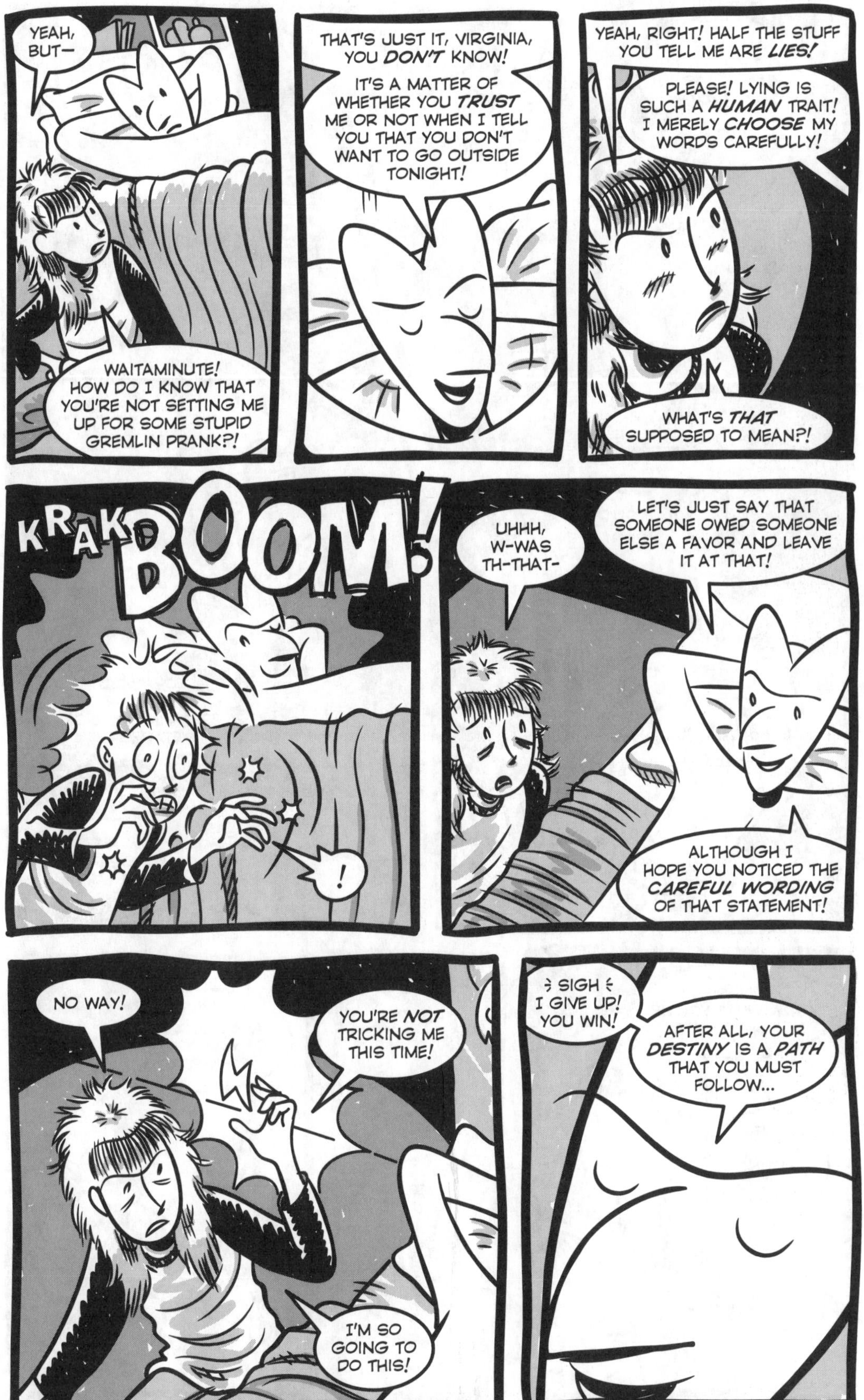
YEAH, BUT—
WAITAMINUTE! HOW DO I KNOW THAT YOU'RE NOT SETTING ME UP FOR SOME STUPID GREMLIN PRANK?!
THAT'S JUST IT, VIRGINIA, YOU DON'T KNOW!
IT'S A MATTER OF WHETHER YOU TRUST ME OR NOT WHEN I TELL YOU THAT YOU DON'T WANT TO GO OUTSIDE TONIGHT!
YEAH, RIGHT! HALF THE STUFF YOU TELL ME ARE LIES!
PLEASE! LYING IS SUCH A HUMAN TRAIT! I MERELY CHOOSE MY WORDS CAREFULLY!
WHAT'S THAT SUPPOSED TO MEAN?!
KRAKBOOM!
!
UHHH, W-WAS TH-THAT-
LET'S JUST SAY THAT SOMEONE OWED SOMEONE ELSE A FAVOR AND LEAVE IT AT THAT!
ALTHOUGH I HOPE YOU NOTICED THE CAREFUL WORDING OF THAT STATEMENT!
NO WAY!
YOU'RE NOT TRICKING ME THIS TIME!
I'M SO GOING TO DO THIS!
SIGH
I GIVE UP! YOU WIN!
AFTER ALL, YOUR DESTINY IS A PATH THAT YOU MUST FOLLOW...

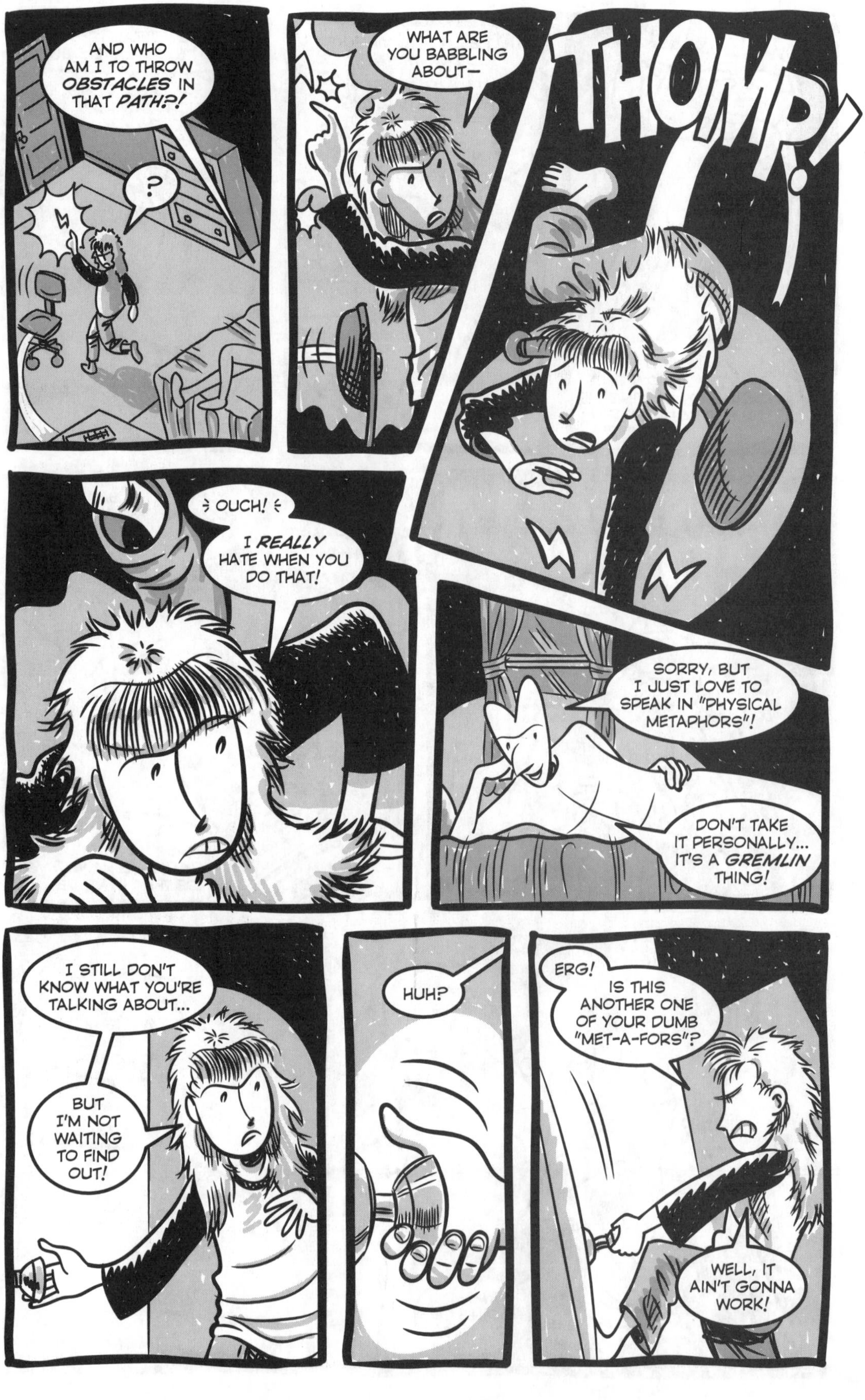
AND WHO AM I TO THROW OBSTACLES IN THAT PATH?!
?
WHAT ARE YOU BABBLING ABOUT—
THOMP!
OUCH!
I REALLY HATE WHEN YOU DO THAT!
SORRY, BUT I JUST LOVE TO SPEAK IN "PHYSICAL METAPHORS"!
DON'T TAKE IT PERSONALLY... IT'S A GREMLIN THING!
I STILL DON'T KNOW WHAT YOU'RE TALKING ABOUT...
BUT I'M NOT WAITING TO FIND OUT!
HUH?
ERG!
IS THIS ANOTHER ONE OF YOUR DUMB "MET-A-FORS"?
WELL, IT AIN'T GONNA WORK!

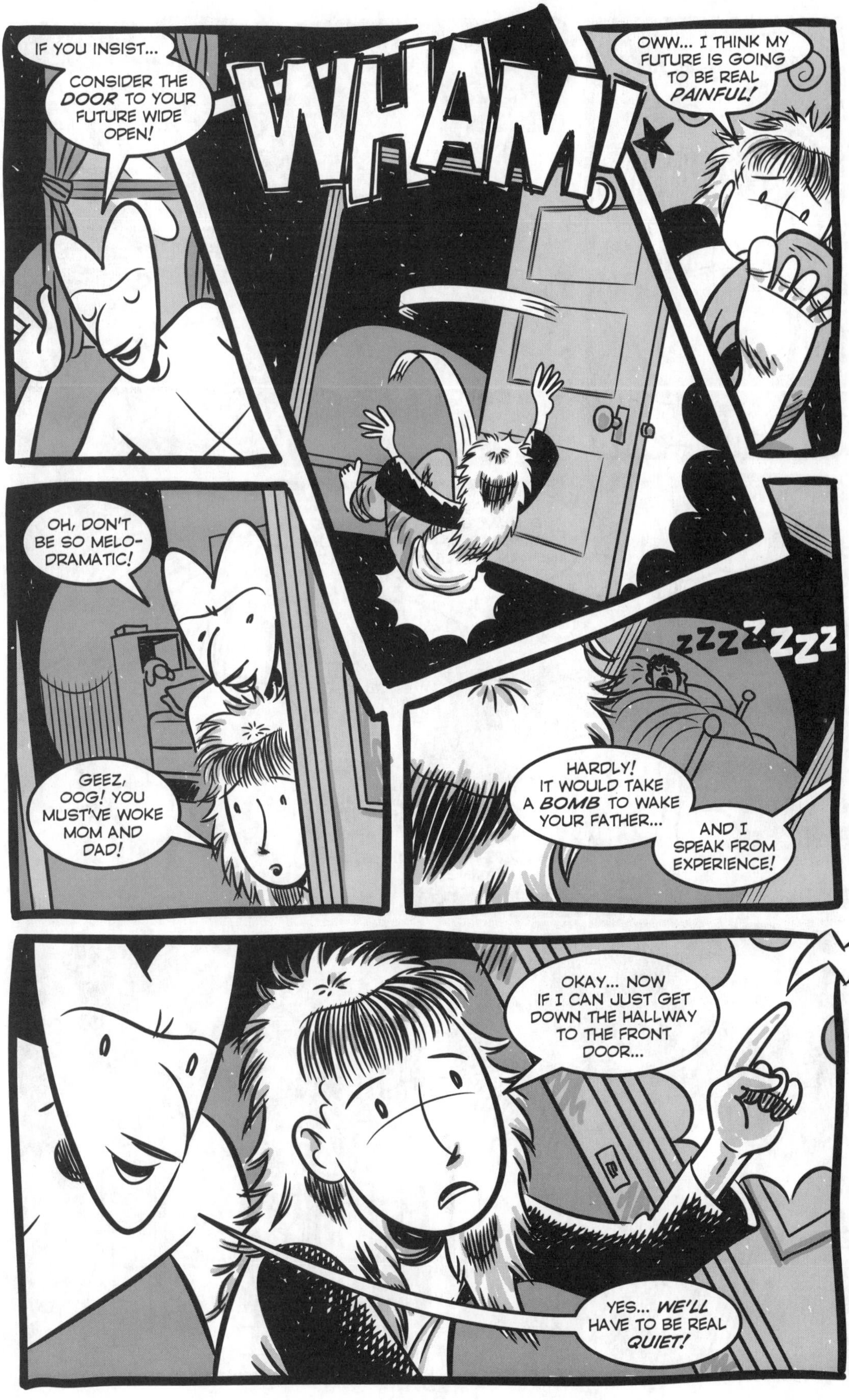
IF YOU INSIST...
CONSIDER THE DOOR TO YOUR FUTURE WIDE OPEN!
WHAM!
OWW... I THINK MY FUTURE IS GOING TO BE REAL PAINFUL!
OH, DON'T BE SO MELO-DRAMATIC!
GEEZ, OOG! YOU MUST'VE WOKE MOM AND DAD!
ZZZZZZZ
HARDLY! IT WOULD TAKE A BOMB TO WAKE YOUR FATHER...
AND I SPEAK FROM EXPERIENCE!
OKAY... NOW IF I CAN JUST GET DOWN THE HALLWAY TO THE FRONT DOOR...
YES... WE'LL HAVE TO BE REAL QUIET!

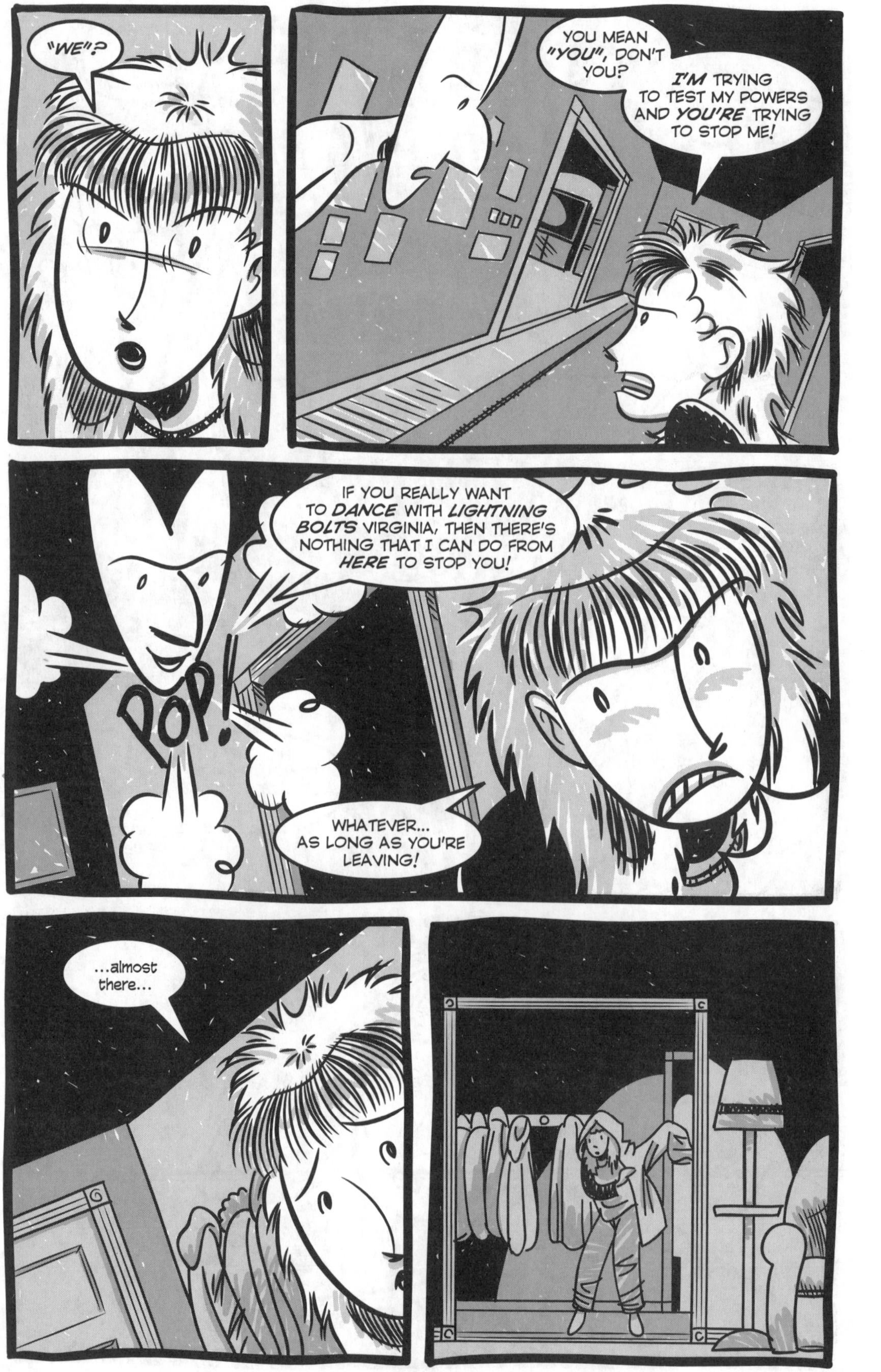
"WE"?
YOU MEAN "YOU", DON'T YOU?
I'M TRYING TO TEST MY POWERS AND YOU'RE TRYING TO STOP ME!
IF YOU REALLY WANT TO DANCE WITH LIGHTNING BOLTS VIRGINIA, THEN THERE'S NOTHING THAT I CAN DO FROM HERE TO STOP YOU!
POP!
WHATEVER... AS LONG AS YOU'RE LEAVING!
...almost there...

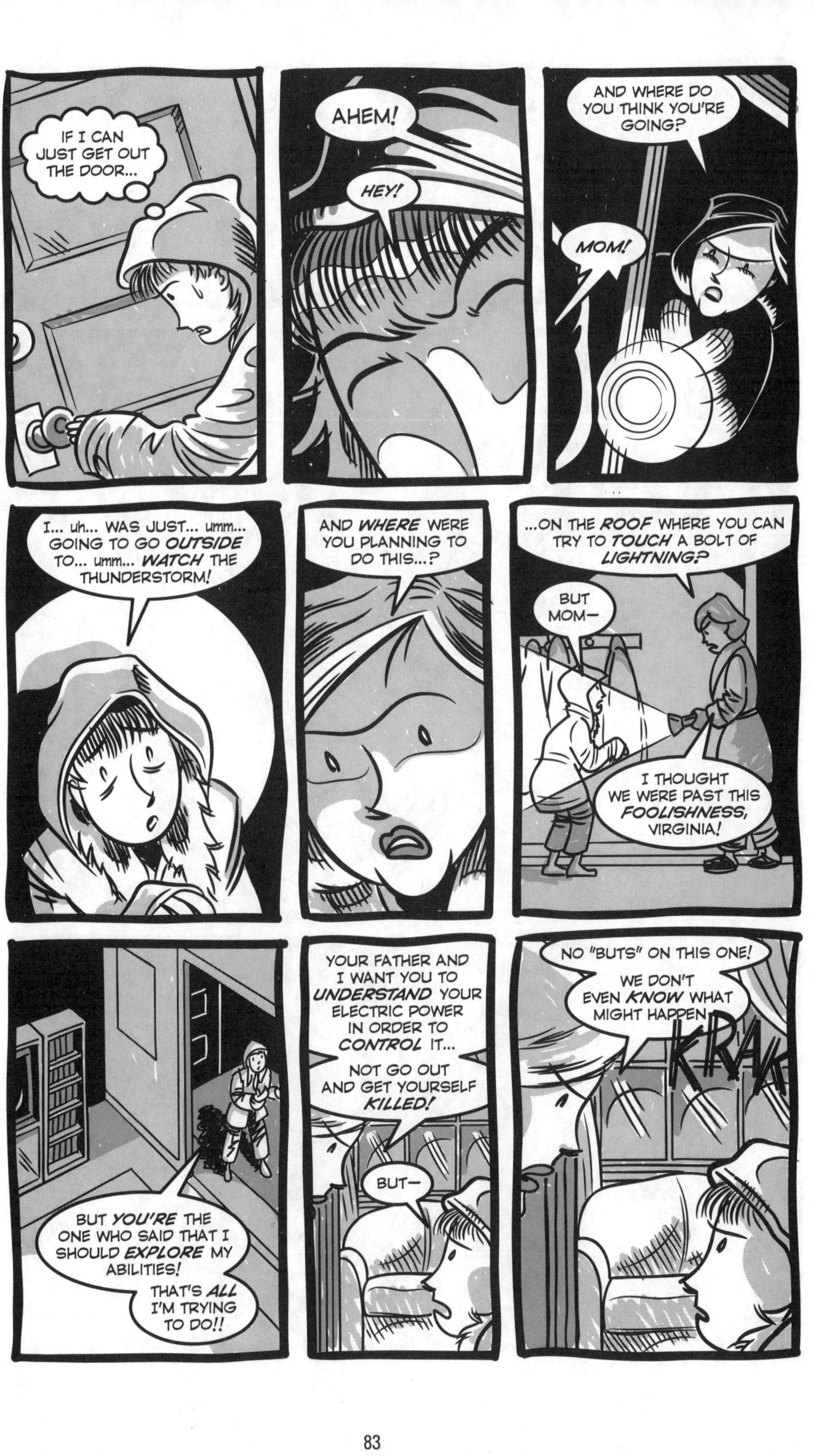
IF I CAN JUST GET OUT THE DOOR...
AHEM!
HEY!
AND WHERE DO YOU THINK YOU'RE GOING?
MOM!
I... uh... WAS JUST... umm... GOING TO GO OUTSIDE TO... umm... WATCH THE THUNDERSTORM!
AND WHERE WERE YOU PLANNING TO DO THIS...?
...ON THE ROOF WHERE YOU CAN TRY TO TOUCH A BOLT OF LIGHTNING?
BUT MOM—
I THOUGHT WE WERE PAST THIS FOOLISHNESS, VIRGINIA!
BUT YOU'RE THE ONE WHO SAID THAT I SHOULD EXPLORE MY ABILITIES!
THAT'S ALL I'M TRYING TO DO!!
YOUR FATHER AND I WANT YOU TO UNDERSTAND YOUR ELECTRIC POWER IN ORDER TO CONTROL IT...
NOT GO OUT AND GET YOURSELF KILLED!
BUT—
NO "BUTS" ON THIS ONE!
WE DON'T EVEN KNOW WHAT MIGHT HAPPEN
KRAK

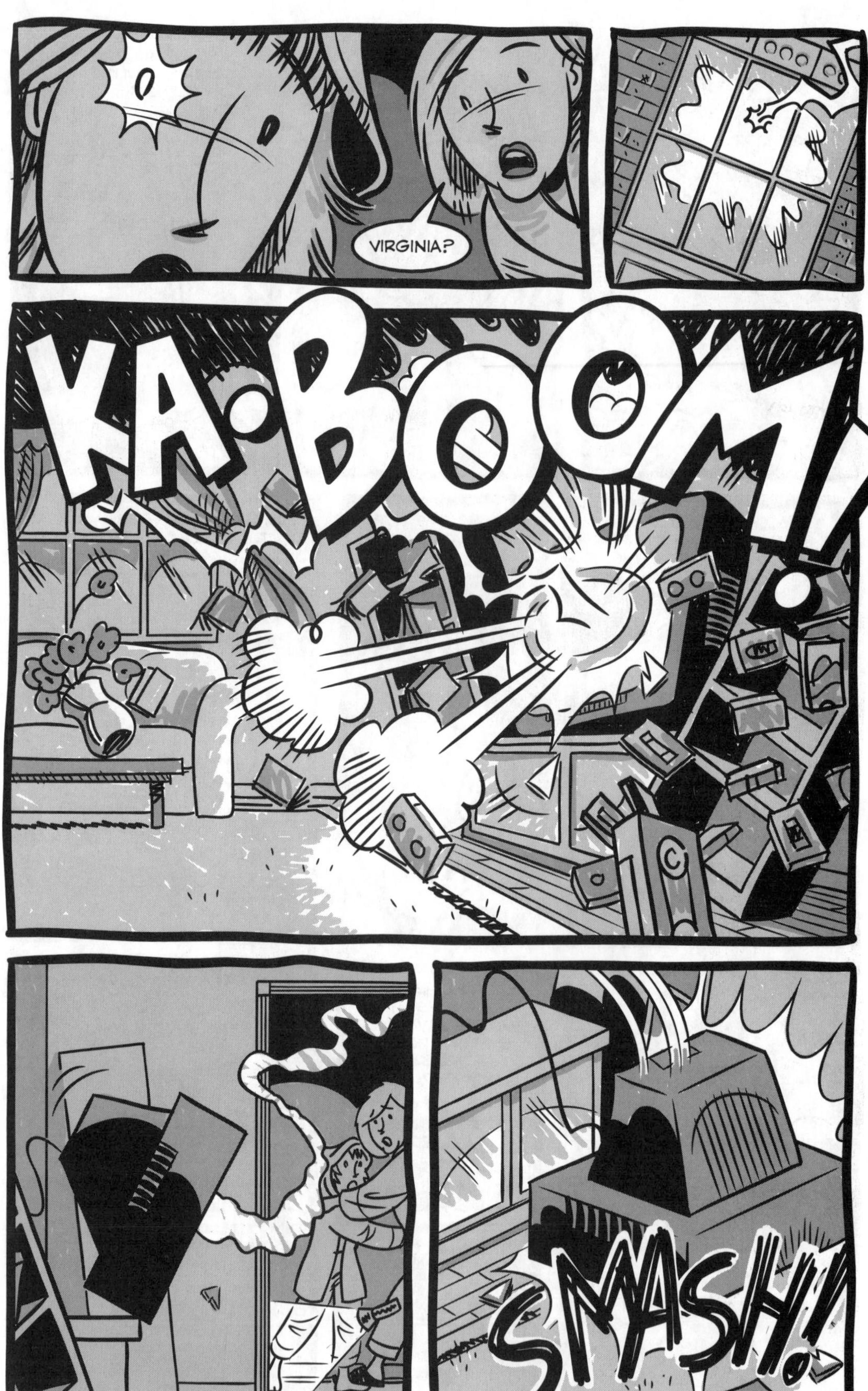
VIRGINIA?
KA-BOOM!
SMASH!

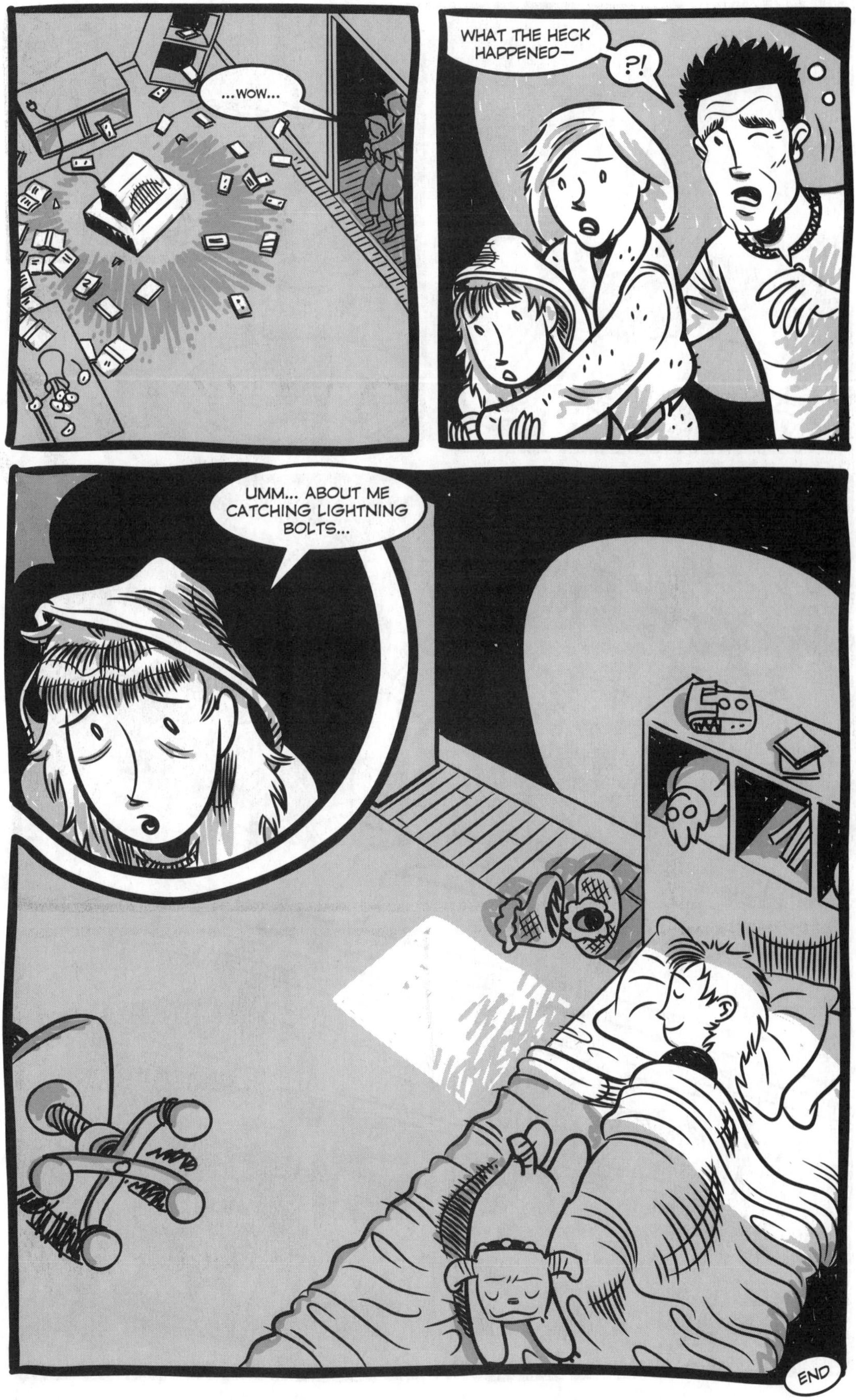
...WOW...
WHAT THE HECK HAPPENED—
?!
UMM... ABOUT ME CATCHING LIGHTNING BOLTS...
END

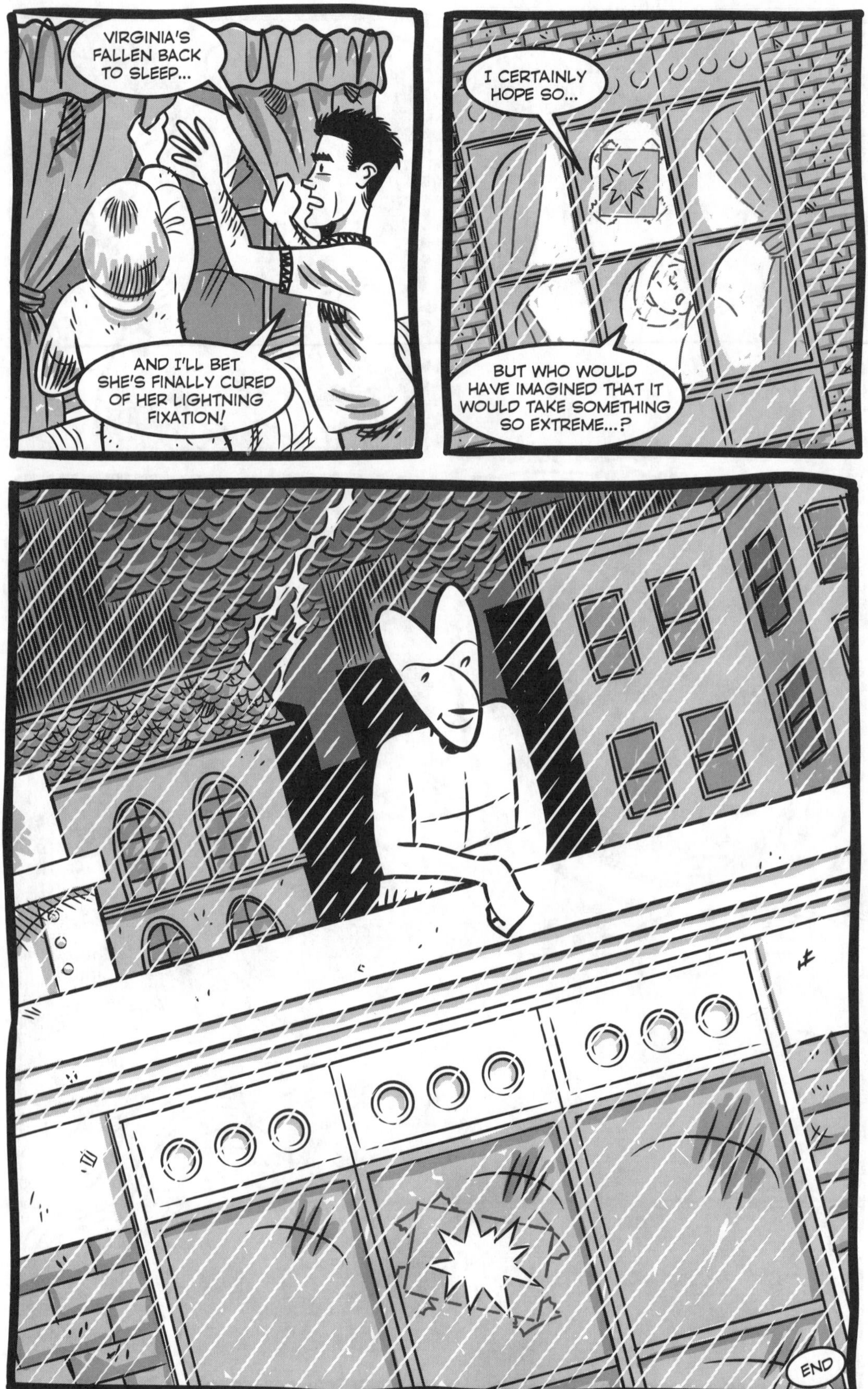
VIRGINIA'S FALLEN BACK TO SLEEP...
AND I'LL BET SHE'S FINALLY CURED OF HER LIGHTNING FIXATION!
I CERTAINLY HOPE SO...
BUT WHO WOULD HAVE IMAGINED THAT IT WOULD TAKE SOMETHING SO EXTREME...?
END

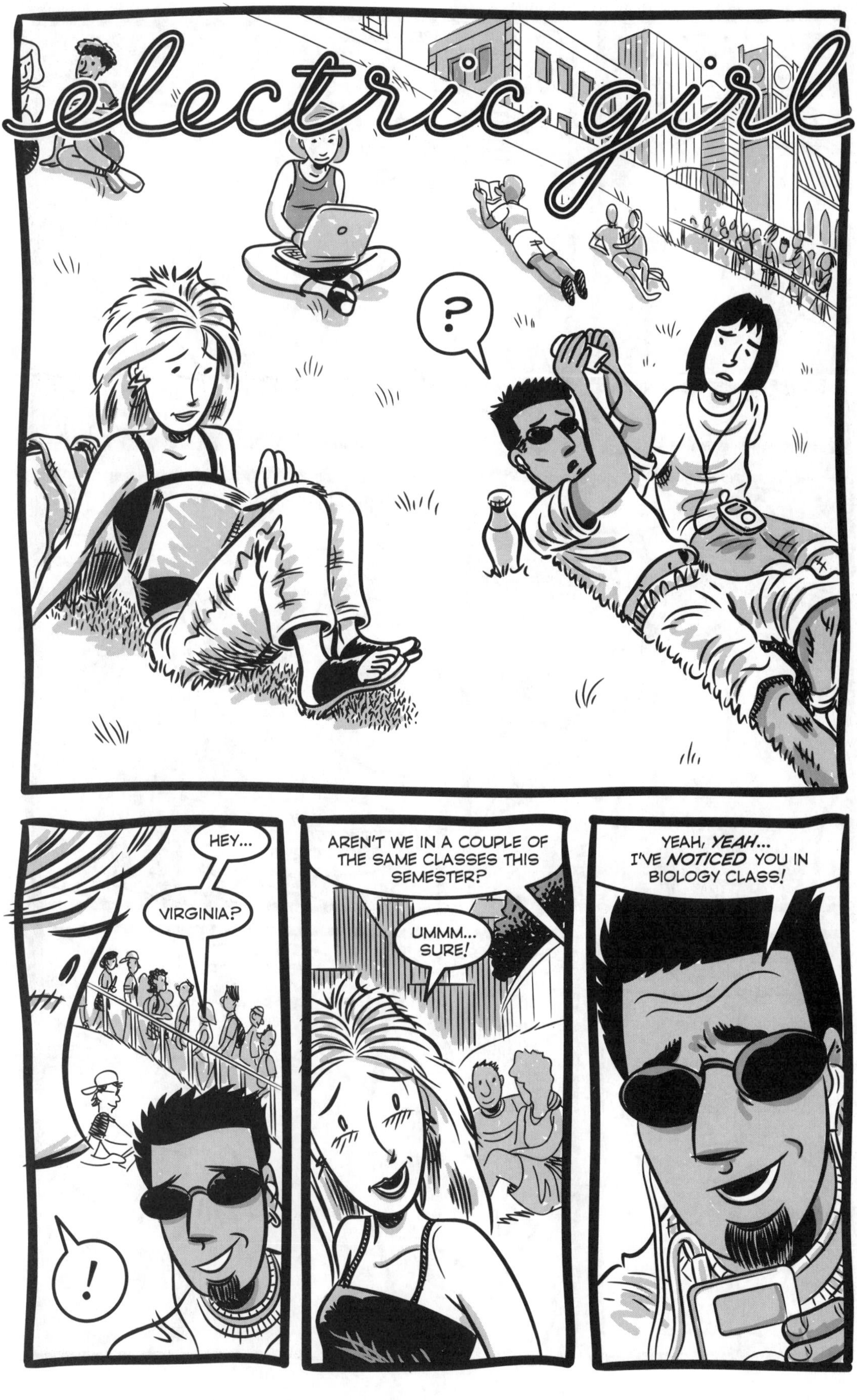
electric girl
?
HEY...
VIRGINIA?
!
AREN'T WE IN A COUPLE OF THE SAME CLASSES THIS SEMESTER?
UMMM... SURE!
YEAH, *YEAH*... I'VE ***NOTICED*** YOU IN BIOLOGY CLASS!

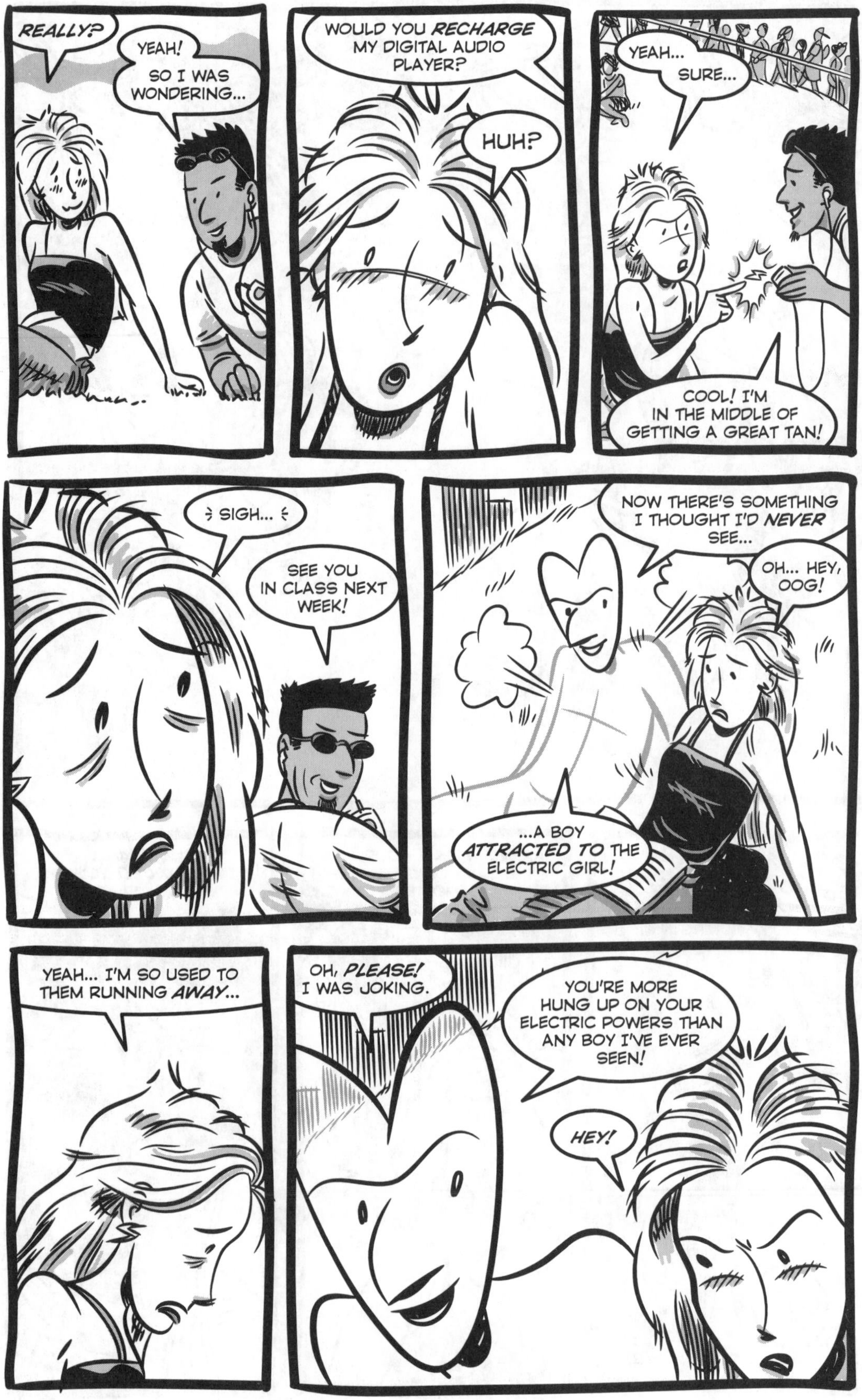
REALLY?
YEAH!
SO I WAS WONDERING...
WOULD YOU RECHARGE MY DIGITAL AUDIO PLAYER?
HUH?
YEAH... SURE...
COOL! I'M IN THE MIDDLE OF GETTING A GREAT TAN!
SIGH...
SEE YOU IN CLASS NEXT WEEK!
NOW THERE'S SOMETHING I THOUGHT I'D NEVER SEE...
OH... HEY, OOG!
...A BOY ATTRACTED TO THE ELECTRIC GIRL!
YEAH... I'M SO USED TO THEM RUNNING AWAY...
OH, PLEASE! I WAS JOKING.
YOU'RE MORE HUNG UP ON YOUR ELECTRIC POWERS THAN ANY BOY I'VE EVER SEEN!
HEY!

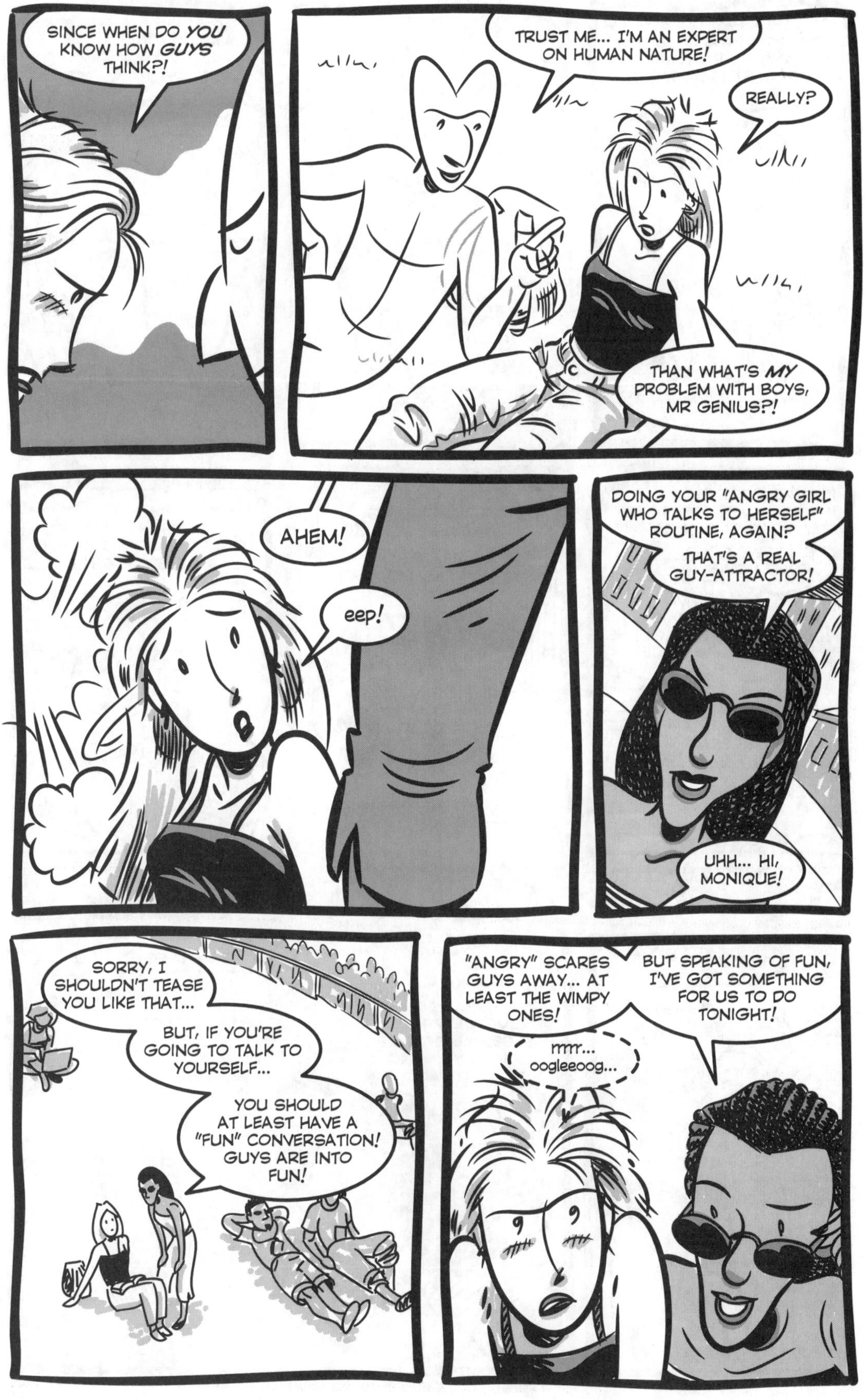
SINCE WHEN DO YOU KNOW HOW GUYS THINK?!
TRUST ME... I'M AN EXPERT ON HUMAN NATURE!
REALLY?
THAN WHAT'S MY PROBLEM WITH BOYS, MR GENIUS?!
AHEM!
eep!
DOING YOUR "ANGRY GIRL WHO TALKS TO HERSELF" ROUTINE, AGAIN?
THAT'S A REAL GUY-ATTRACTOR!
UHH... HI, MONIQUE!
SORRY, I SHOULDN'T TEASE YOU LIKE THAT...
BUT, IF YOU'RE GOING TO TALK TO YOURSELF...
YOU SHOULD AT LEAST HAVE A "FUN" CONVERSATION! GUYS ARE INTO FUN!
"ANGRY" SCARES GUYS AWAY... AT LEAST THE WIMPY ONES!
BUT SPEAKING OF FUN, I'VE GOT SOMETHING FOR US TO DO TONIGHT!
rrrr... oogleeoog...

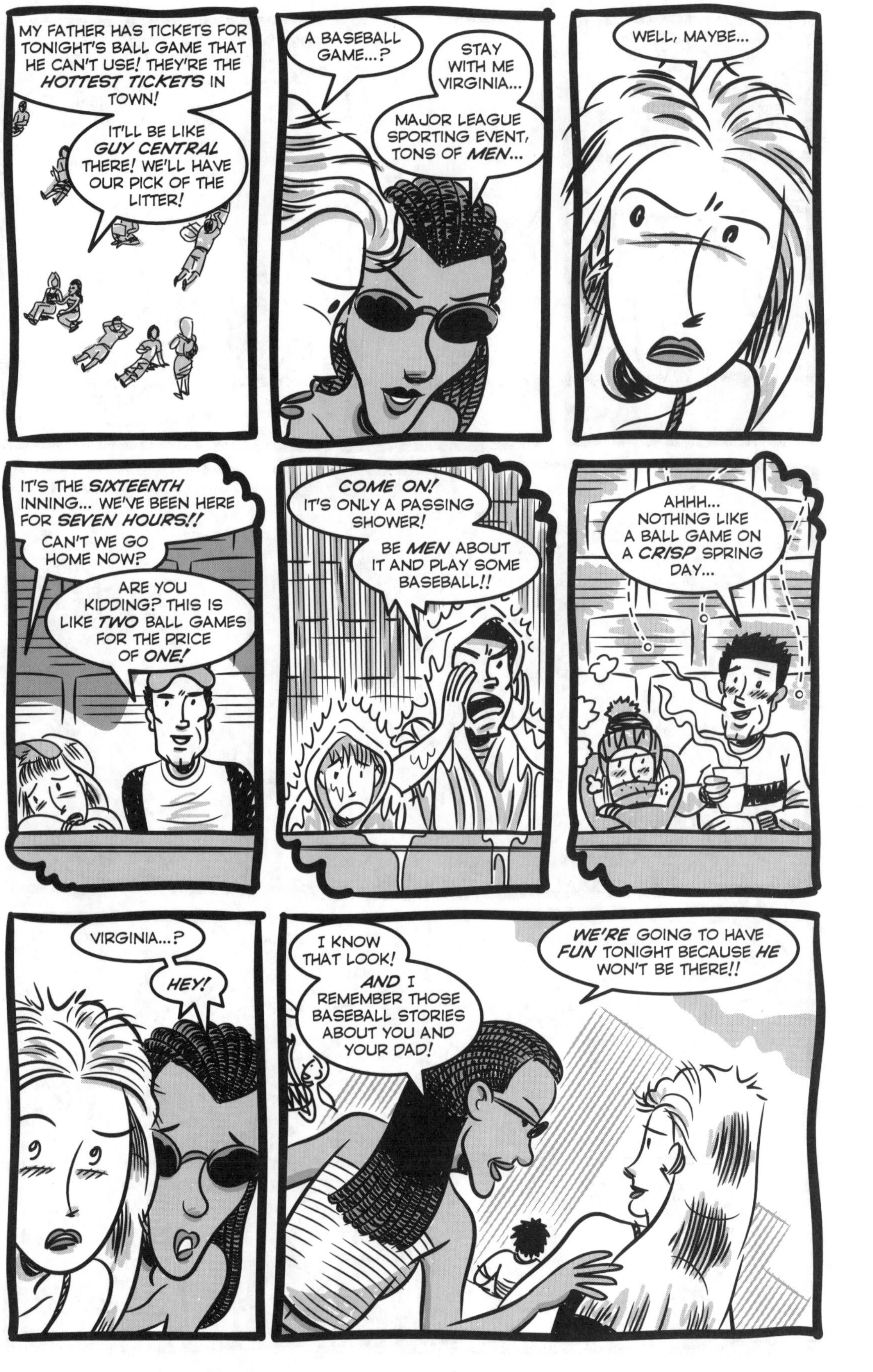
MY FATHER HAS TICKETS FOR TONIGHT'S BALL GAME THAT HE CAN'T USE! THEY'RE THE HOTTEST TICKETS IN TOWN!
IT'LL BE LIKE GUY CENTRAL THERE! WE'LL HAVE OUR PICK OF THE LITTER!
A BASEBALL GAME...?
STAY WITH ME VIRGINIA...
MAJOR LEAGUE SPORTING EVENT, TONS OF MEN...
WELL, MAYBE...
IT'S THE SIXTEENTH INNING... WE'VE BEEN HERE FOR SEVEN HOURS!!
CAN'T WE GO HOME NOW?
ARE YOU KIDDING? THIS IS LIKE TWO BALL GAMES FOR THE PRICE OF ONE!
COME ON! IT'S ONLY A PASSING SHOWER!
BE MEN ABOUT IT AND PLAY SOME BASEBALL!!
AHHH... NOTHING LIKE A BALL GAME ON A CRISP SPRING DAY...
VIRGINIA...?
HEY!
I KNOW THAT LOOK!
AND I REMEMBER THOSE BASEBALL STORIES ABOUT YOU AND YOUR DAD!
WE'RE GOING TO HAVE FUN TONIGHT BECAUSE HE WON'T BE THERE!!

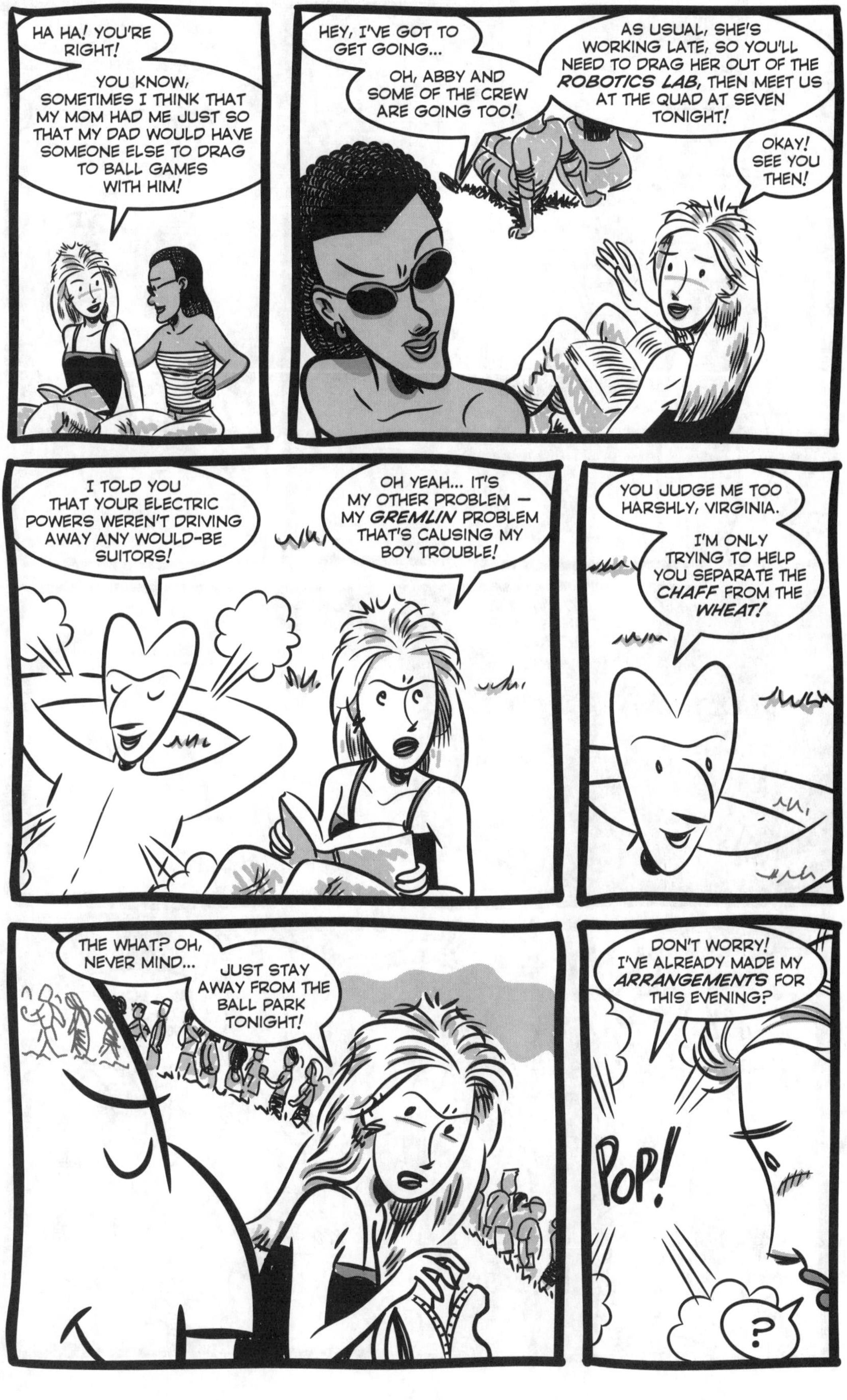
HA HA! YOU'RE RIGHT!
YOU KNOW, SOMETIMES I THINK THAT MY MOM HAD ME JUST SO THAT MY DAD WOULD HAVE SOMEONE ELSE TO DRAG TO BALL GAMES WITH HIM!
HEY, I'VE GOT TO GET GOING...
OH, ABBY AND SOME OF THE CREW ARE GOING TOO!
AS USUAL, SHE'S WORKING LATE, SO YOU'LL NEED TO DRAG HER OUT OF THE ROBOTICS LAB, THEN MEET US AT THE QUAD AT SEVEN TONIGHT!
OKAY! SEE YOU THEN!
I TOLD YOU THAT YOUR ELECTRIC POWERS WEREN'T DRIVING AWAY ANY WOULD-BE SUITORS!
OH YEAH... IT'S MY OTHER PROBLEM — MY GREMLIN PROBLEM THAT'S CAUSING MY BOY TROUBLE!
YOU JUDGE ME TOO HARSHLY, VIRGINIA.
I'M ONLY TRYING TO HELP YOU SEPARATE THE CHAFF FROM THE WHEAT!
THE WHAT? OH, NEVER MIND...
JUST STAY AWAY FROM THE BALL PARK TONIGHT!
DON'T WORRY! I'VE ALREADY MADE MY ARRANGEMENTS FOR THIS EVENING?
POP!
?

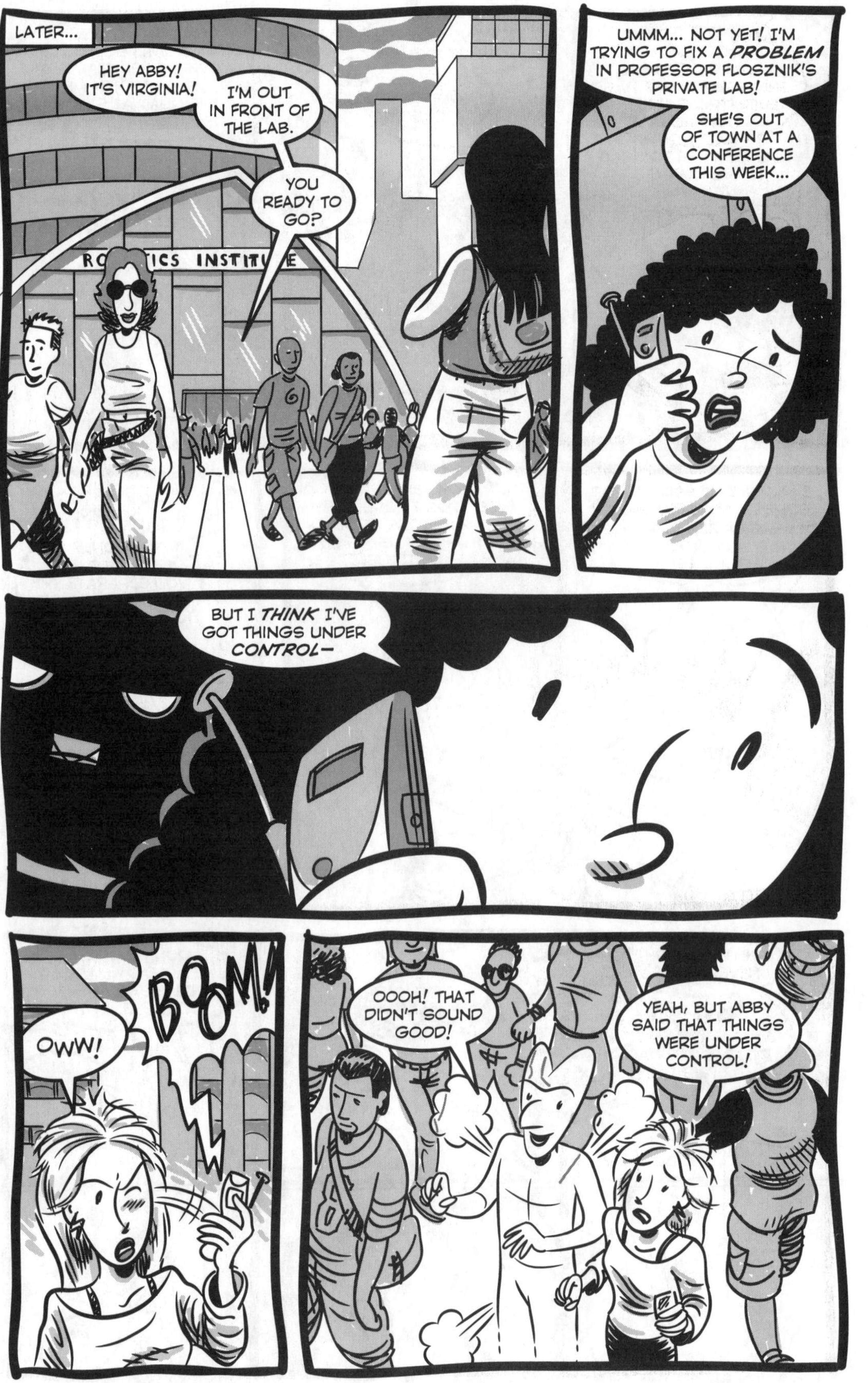
LATER...
HEY ABBY! IT'S VIRGINIA!
I'M OUT IN FRONT OF THE LAB.
YOU READY TO GO?
ROBOTICS INSTITUTE
UMMM... NOT YET! I'M TRYING TO FIX A PROBLEM IN PROFESSOR FLOSZNIK'S PRIVATE LAB!
SHE'S OUT OF TOWN AT A CONFERENCE THIS WEEK...
BUT I THINK I'VE GOT THINGS UNDER CONTROL—
BOOM!
OWW!
OOOH! THAT DIDN'T SOUND GOOD!
YEAH, BUT ABBY SAID THAT THINGS WERE UNDER CONTROL!

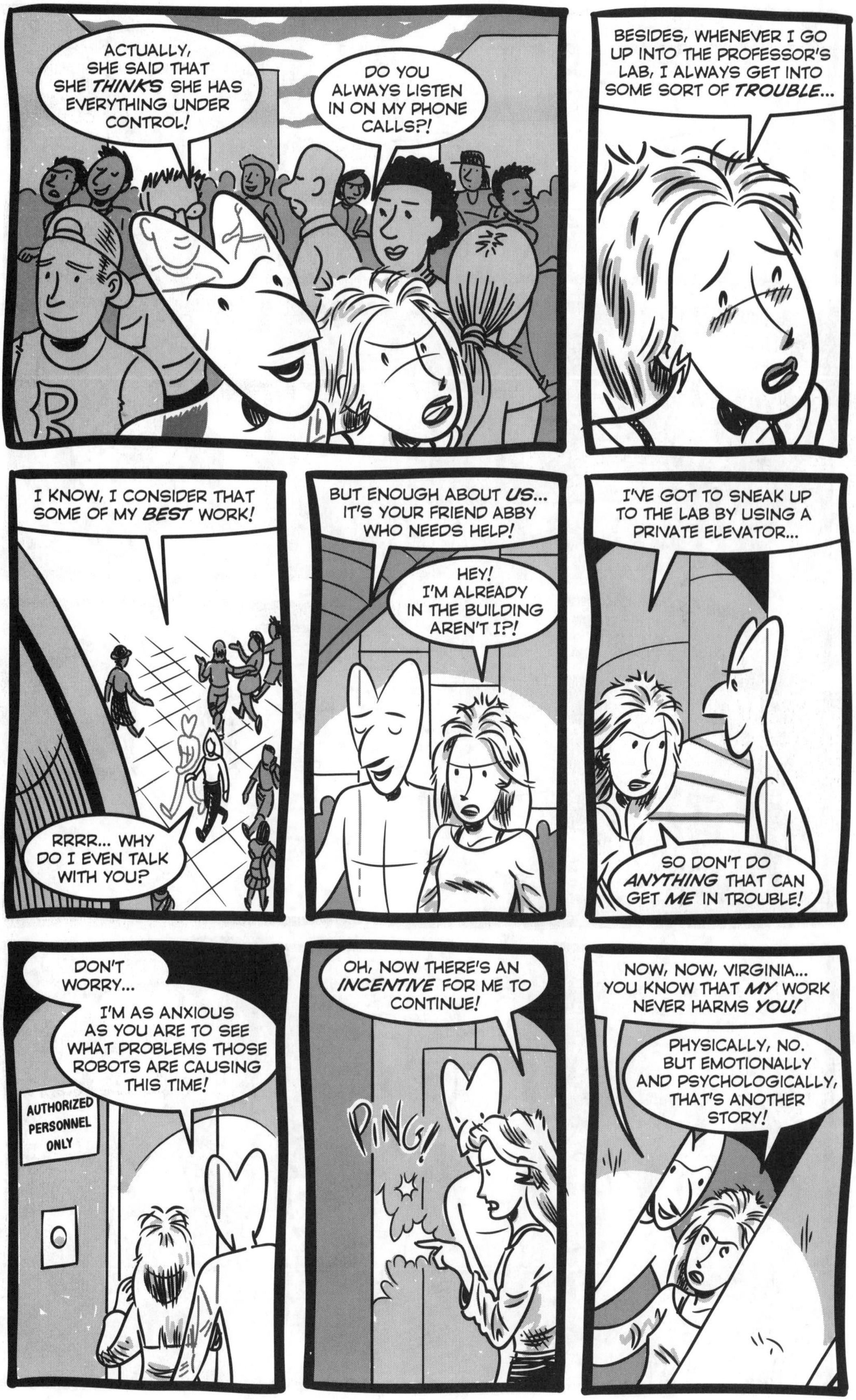
ACTUALLY, SHE SAID THAT SHE THINKS SHE HAS EVERYTHING UNDER CONTROL!
DO YOU ALWAYS LISTEN IN ON MY PHONE CALLS?!
BESIDES, WHENEVER I GO UP INTO THE PROFESSOR'S LAB, I ALWAYS GET INTO SOME SORT OF TROUBLE...
I KNOW, I CONSIDER THAT SOME OF MY BEST WORK!
RRRR... WHY DO I EVEN TALK WITH YOU?
BUT ENOUGH ABOUT US... IT'S YOUR FRIEND ABBY WHO NEEDS HELP!
HEY! I'M ALREADY IN THE BUILDING AREN'T I?!
I'VE GOT TO SNEAK UP TO THE LAB BY USING A PRIVATE ELEVATOR...
SO DON'T DO ANYTHING THAT CAN GET ME IN TROUBLE!
DON'T WORRY...
I'M AS ANXIOUS AS YOU ARE TO SEE WHAT PROBLEMS THOSE ROBOTS ARE CAUSING THIS TIME!
AUTHORIZED PERSONNEL ONLY
OH, NOW THERE'S AN INCENTIVE FOR ME TO CONTINUE!
PING!
NOW, NOW, VIRGINIA... YOU KNOW THAT MY WORK NEVER HARMS YOU!
PHYSICALLY, NO. BUT EMOTIONALLY AND PSYCHOLOGICALLY, THAT'S ANOTHER STORY!

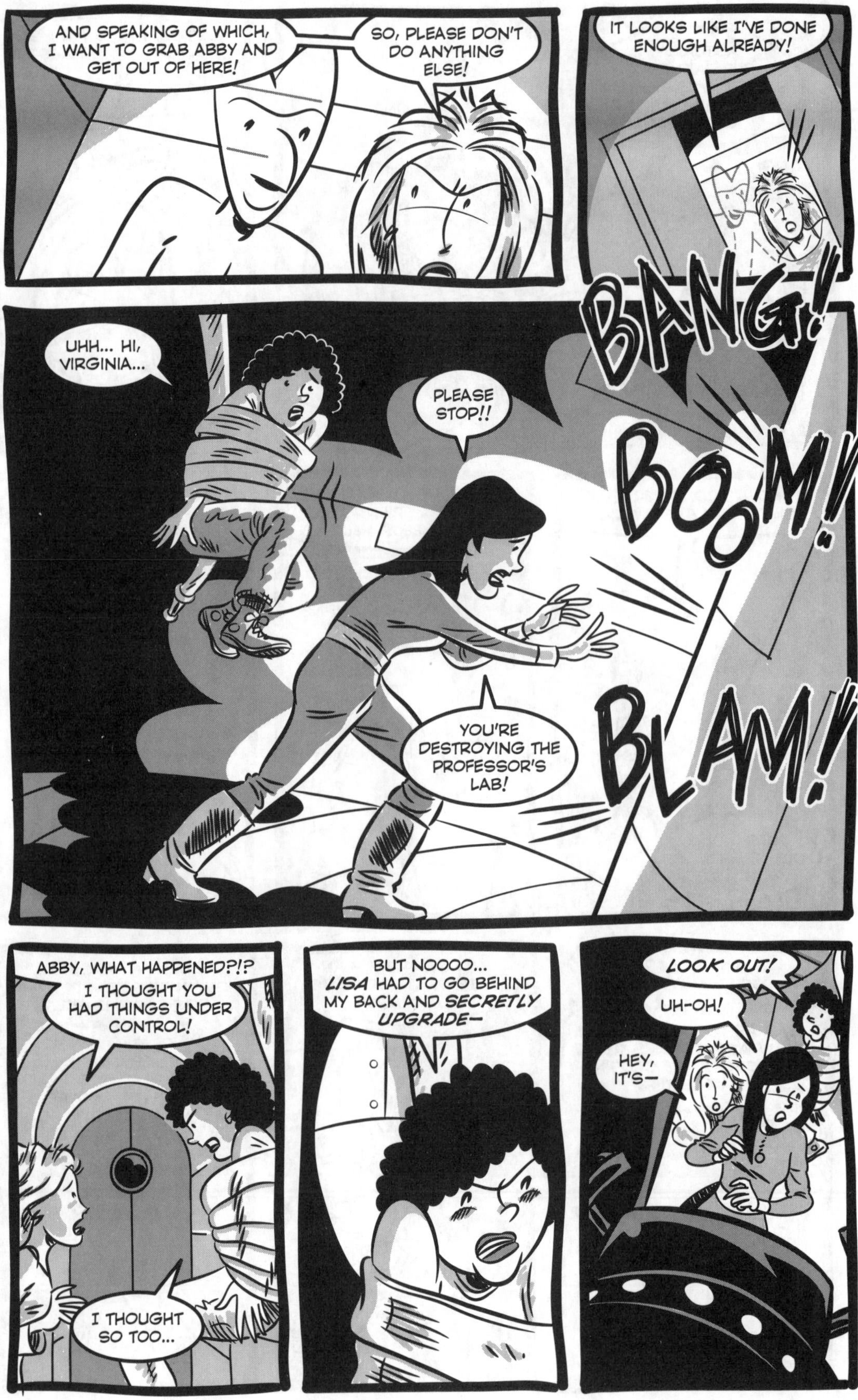
AND SPEAKING OF WHICH, I WANT TO GRAB ABBY AND GET OUT OF HERE!
SO, PLEASE DON'T DO ANYTHING ELSE!
IT LOOKS LIKE I'VE DONE ENOUGH ALREADY!
BANG!
UHH... HI, VIRGINIA...
PLEASE STOP!!
BOOM!!
YOU'RE DESTROYING THE PROFESSOR'S LAB!
BLAM!
ABBY, WHAT HAPPENED?!?
I THOUGHT YOU HAD THINGS UNDER CONTROL!
I THOUGHT SO TOO...
BUT NOOOO... LISA HAD TO GO BEHIND MY BACK AND SECRETLY UPGRADE—
LOOK OUT!
UH-OH!
HEY, IT'S—

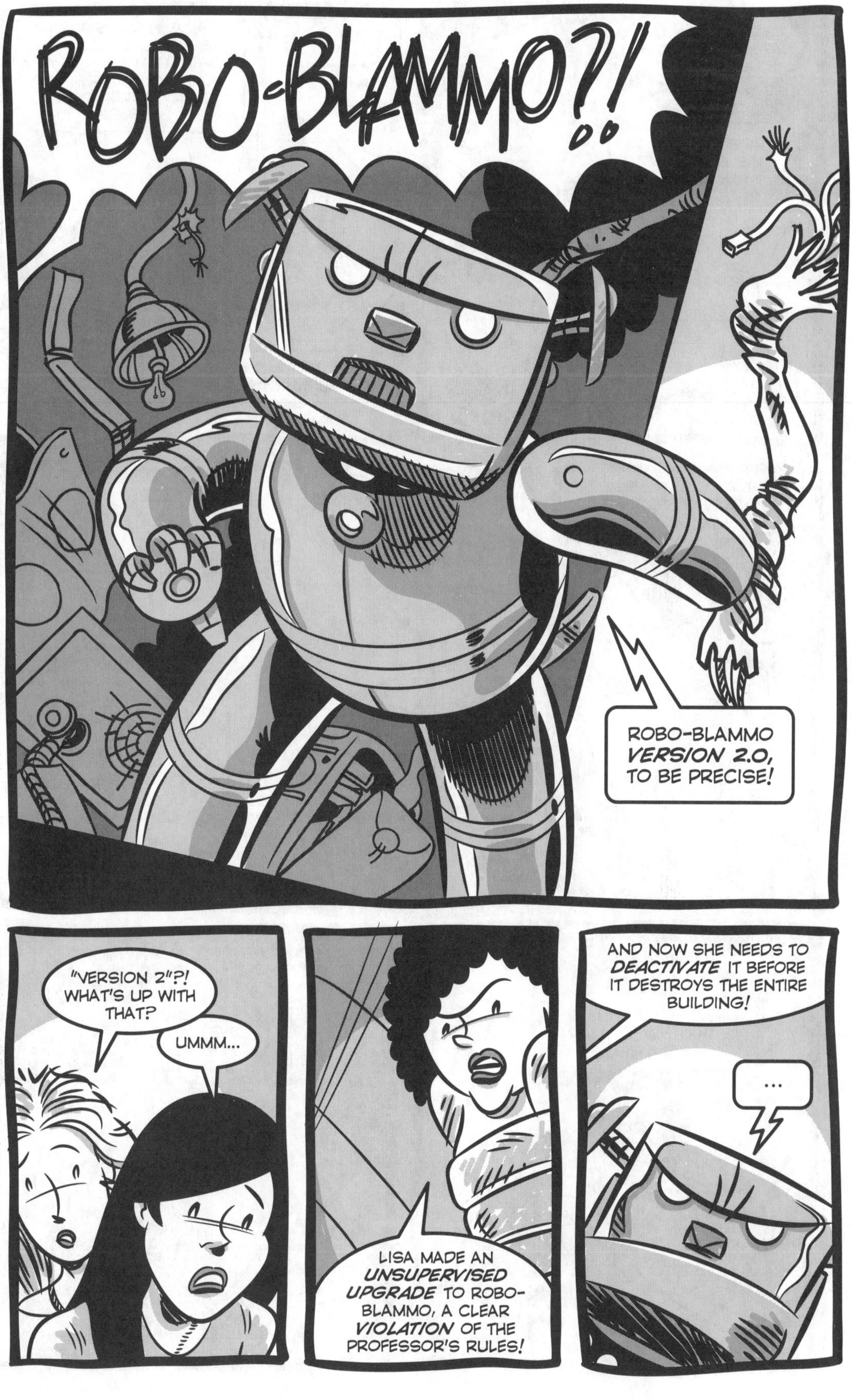
ROBO-BLAMMO?!
ROBO-BLAMMO VERSION 2.0, TO BE PRECISE!
"VERSION 2"?! WHAT'S UP WITH THAT?
UMMM...
LISA MADE AN UNSUPERVISED UPGRADE TO ROBO-BLAMMO, A CLEAR VIOLATION OF THE PROFESSOR'S RULES!
AND NOW SHE NEEDS TO DEACTIVATE IT BEFORE IT DESTROYS THE ENTIRE BUILDING!
...

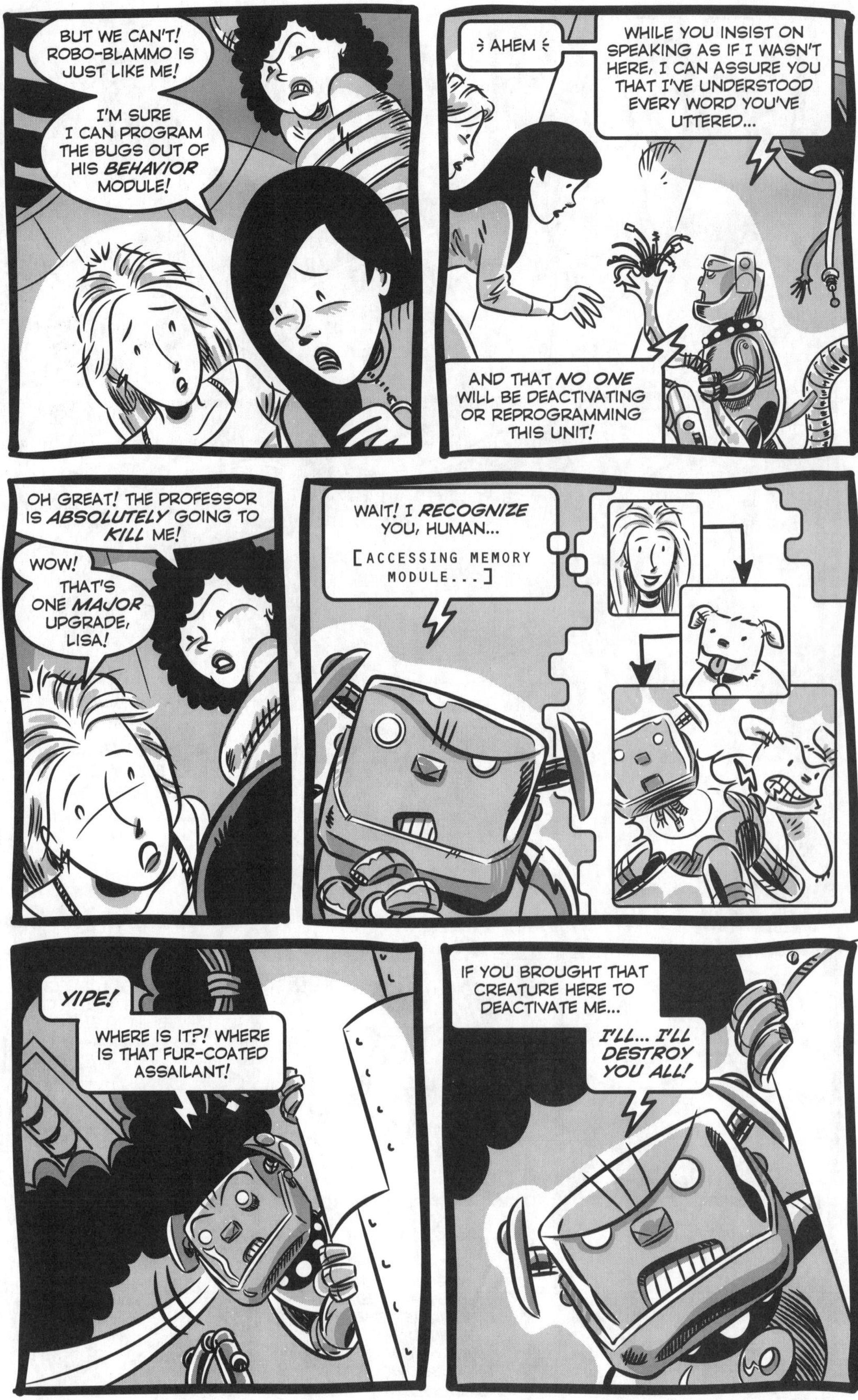
BUT WE CAN'T! ROBO-BLAMMO IS JUST LIKE ME!
I'M SURE I CAN PROGRAM THE BUGS OUT OF HIS *BEHAVIOR* MODULE!
AHEM
WHILE YOU INSIST ON SPEAKING AS IF I WASN'T HERE, I CAN ASSURE YOU THAT I'VE UNDERSTOOD EVERY WORD YOU'VE UTTERED...
AND THAT *NO ONE* WILL BE DEACTIVATING OR REPROGRAMMING THIS UNIT!
OH GREAT! THE PROFESSOR IS *ABSOLUTELY* GOING TO *KILL* ME!
WOW! THAT'S ONE *MAJOR* UPGRADE, LISA!
WAIT! I *RECOGNIZE* YOU, HUMAN...
[ACCESSING MEMORY MODULE...]
YIPE!
WHERE IS IT?! WHERE IS THAT FUR-COATED ASSAILANT!
IF YOU BROUGHT THAT CREATURE HERE TO DEACTIVATE ME...
I'LL... I'LL DESTROY YOU ALL!

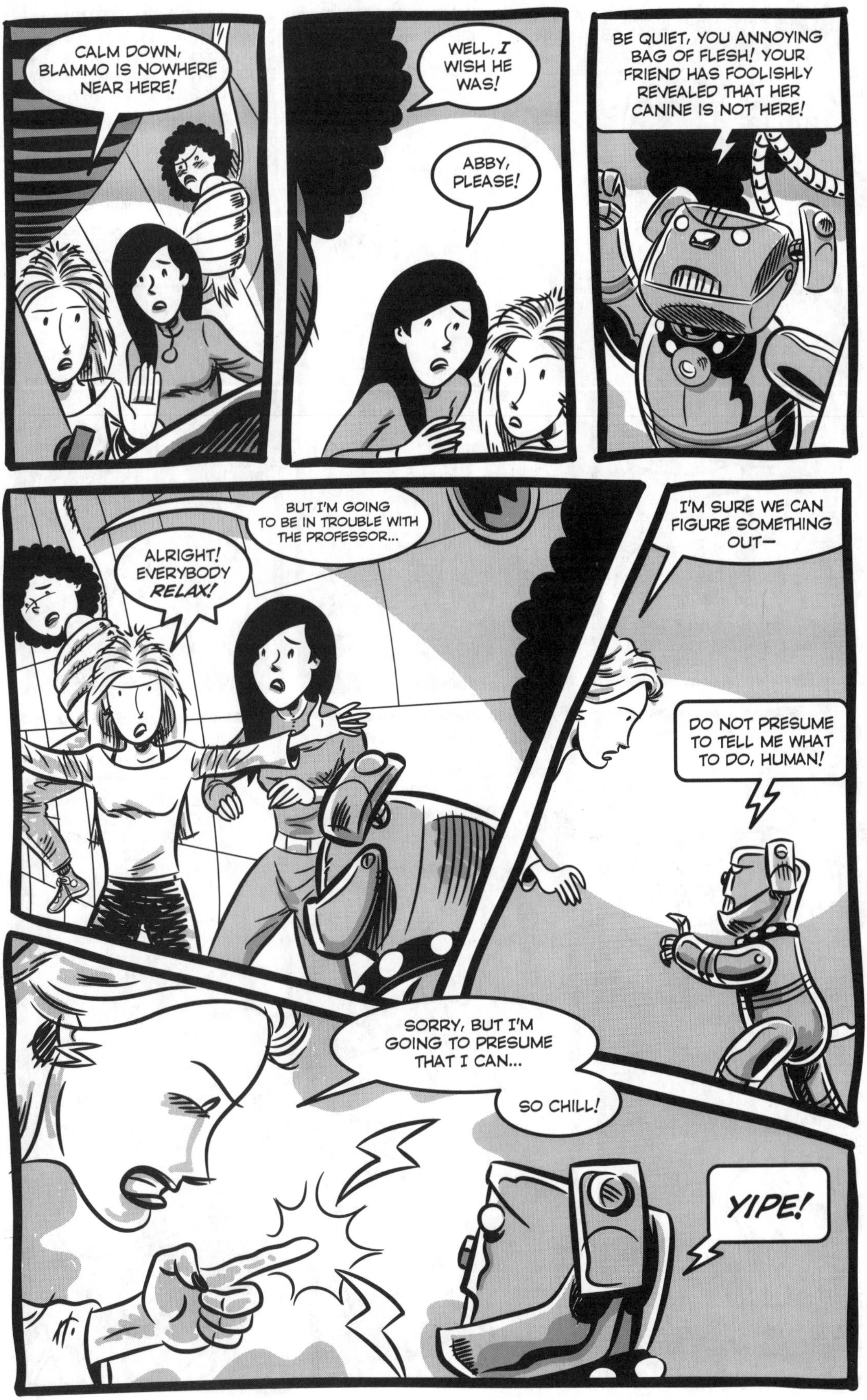
CALM DOWN, BLAMMO IS NOWHERE NEAR HERE!
WELL, I WISH HE WAS!
ABBY, PLEASE!
BE QUIET, YOU ANNOYING BAG OF FLESH! YOUR FRIEND HAS FOOLISHLY REVEALED THAT HER CANINE IS NOT HERE!
ALRIGHT! EVERYBODY RELAX!
BUT I'M GOING TO BE IN TROUBLE WITH THE PROFESSOR...
I'M SURE WE CAN FIGURE SOMETHING OUT—
DO NOT PRESUME TO TELL ME WHAT TO DO, HUMAN!
SORRY, BUT I'M GOING TO PRESUME THAT I CAN...
SO CHILL!
YIPE!

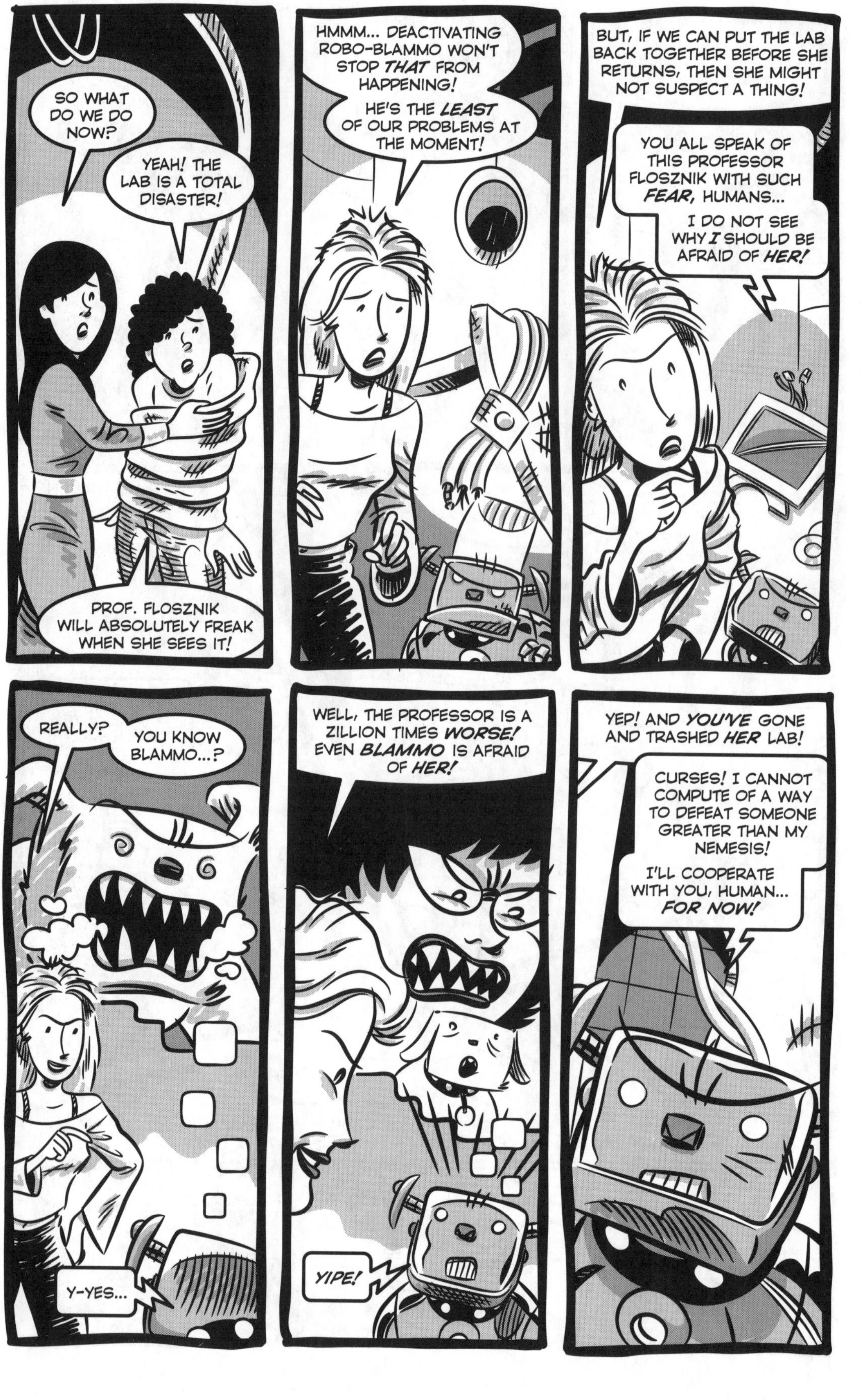
SO WHAT DO WE DO NOW?
YEAH! THE LAB IS A TOTAL DISASTER!
PROF. FLOSZNIK WILL ABSOLUTELY FREAK WHEN SHE SEES IT!
HMMM... DEACTIVATING ROBO-BLAMMO WON'T STOP THAT FROM HAPPENING!
HE'S THE LEAST OF OUR PROBLEMS AT THE MOMENT!
BUT, IF WE CAN PUT THE LAB BACK TOGETHER BEFORE SHE RETURNS, THEN SHE MIGHT NOT SUSPECT A THING!
YOU ALL SPEAK OF THIS PROFESSOR FLOSZNIK WITH SUCH FEAR, HUMANS...
I DO NOT SEE WHY I SHOULD BE AFRAID OF HER!
REALLY?
YOU KNOW BLAMMO...?
Y-YES...
WELL, THE PROFESSOR IS A ZILLION TIMES WORSE! EVEN BLAMMO IS AFRAID OF HER!
YIPE!
YEP! AND YOU'VE GONE AND TRASHED HER LAB!
CURSES! I CANNOT COMPUTE OF A WAY TO DEFEAT SOMEONE GREATER THAN MY NEMESIS!
I'LL COOPERATE WITH YOU, HUMAN... FOR NOW!

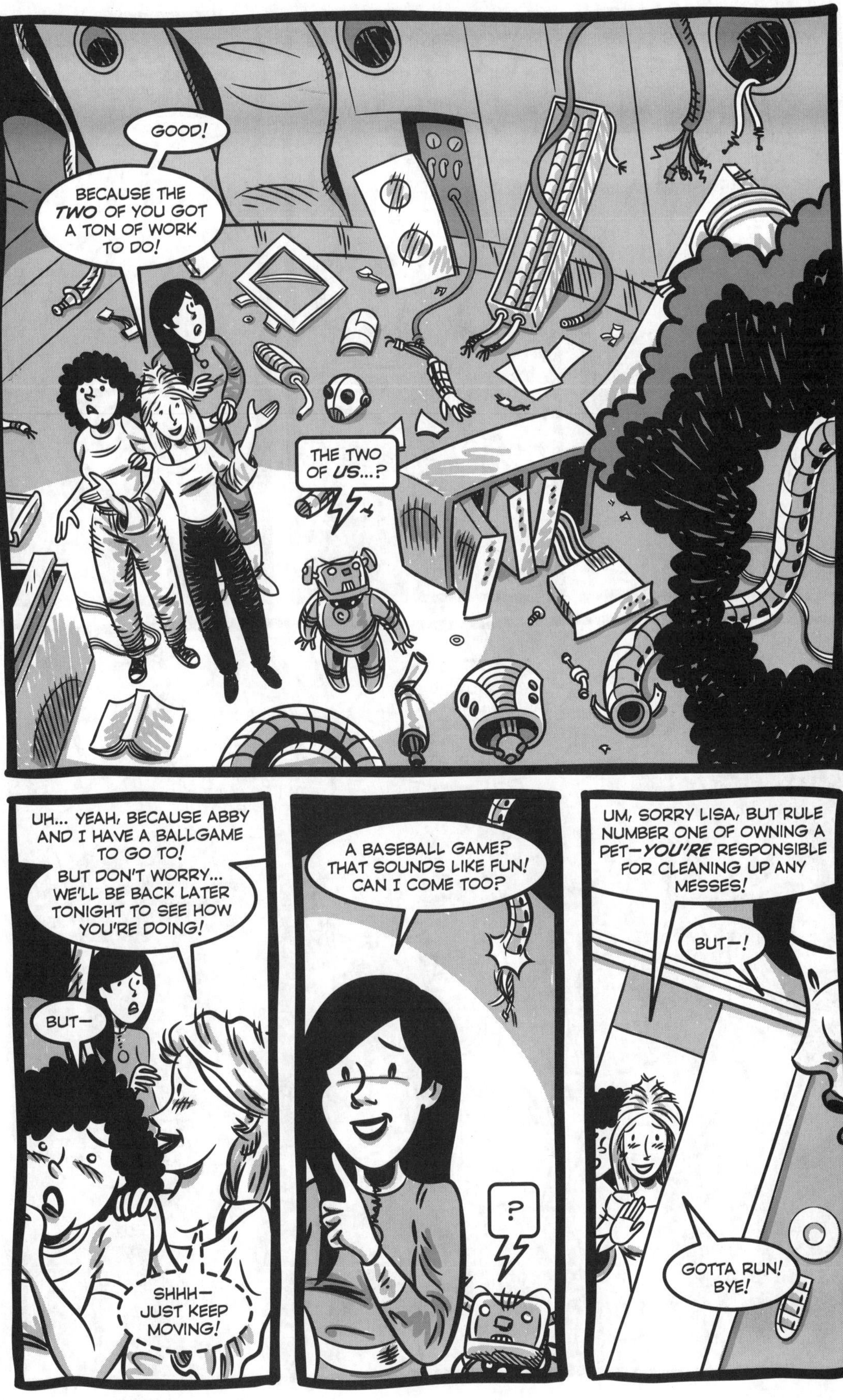
GOOD!
BECAUSE THE TWO OF YOU GOT A TON OF WORK TO DO!
THE TWO OF US...?
UH... YEAH, BECAUSE ABBY AND I HAVE A BALLGAME TO GO TO!
BUT DON'T WORRY... WE'LL BE BACK LATER TONIGHT TO SEE HOW YOU'RE DOING!
BUT—
SHHH— JUST KEEP MOVING!
A BASEBALL GAME? THAT SOUNDS LIKE FUN! CAN I COME TOO?
?
UM, SORRY LISA, BUT RULE NUMBER ONE OF OWNING A PET—YOU'RE RESPONSIBLE FOR CLEANING UP ANY MESSES!
BUT—!
GOTTA RUN! BYE!

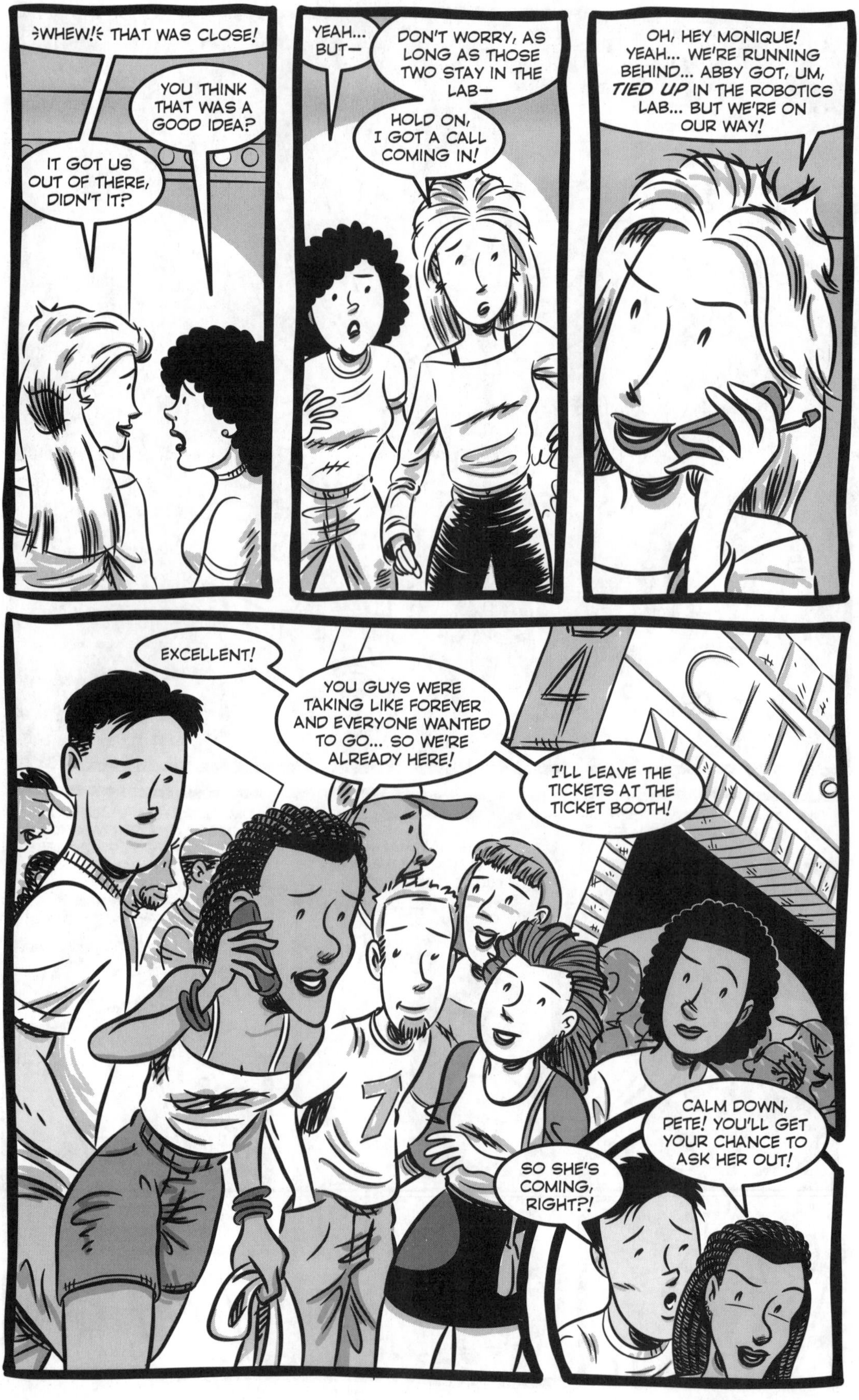
WHEW! THAT WAS CLOSE!
YOU THINK THAT WAS A GOOD IDEA?
IT GOT US OUT OF THERE, DIDN'T IT?
YEAH... BUT—
DON'T WORRY, AS LONG AS THOSE TWO STAY IN THE LAB—
HOLD ON, I GOT A CALL COMING IN!
OH, HEY MONIQUE! YEAH... WE'RE RUNNING BEHIND... ABBY GOT, UM, *TIED UP* IN THE ROBOTICS LAB... BUT WE'RE ON OUR WAY!
EXCELLENT!
YOU GUYS WERE TAKING LIKE FOREVER AND EVERYONE WANTED TO GO... SO WE'RE ALREADY HERE!
I'LL LEAVE THE TICKETS AT THE TICKET BOOTH!
SO SHE'S COMING, RIGHT?!
CALM DOWN, PETE! YOU'LL GET YOUR CHANCE TO ASK HER OUT!

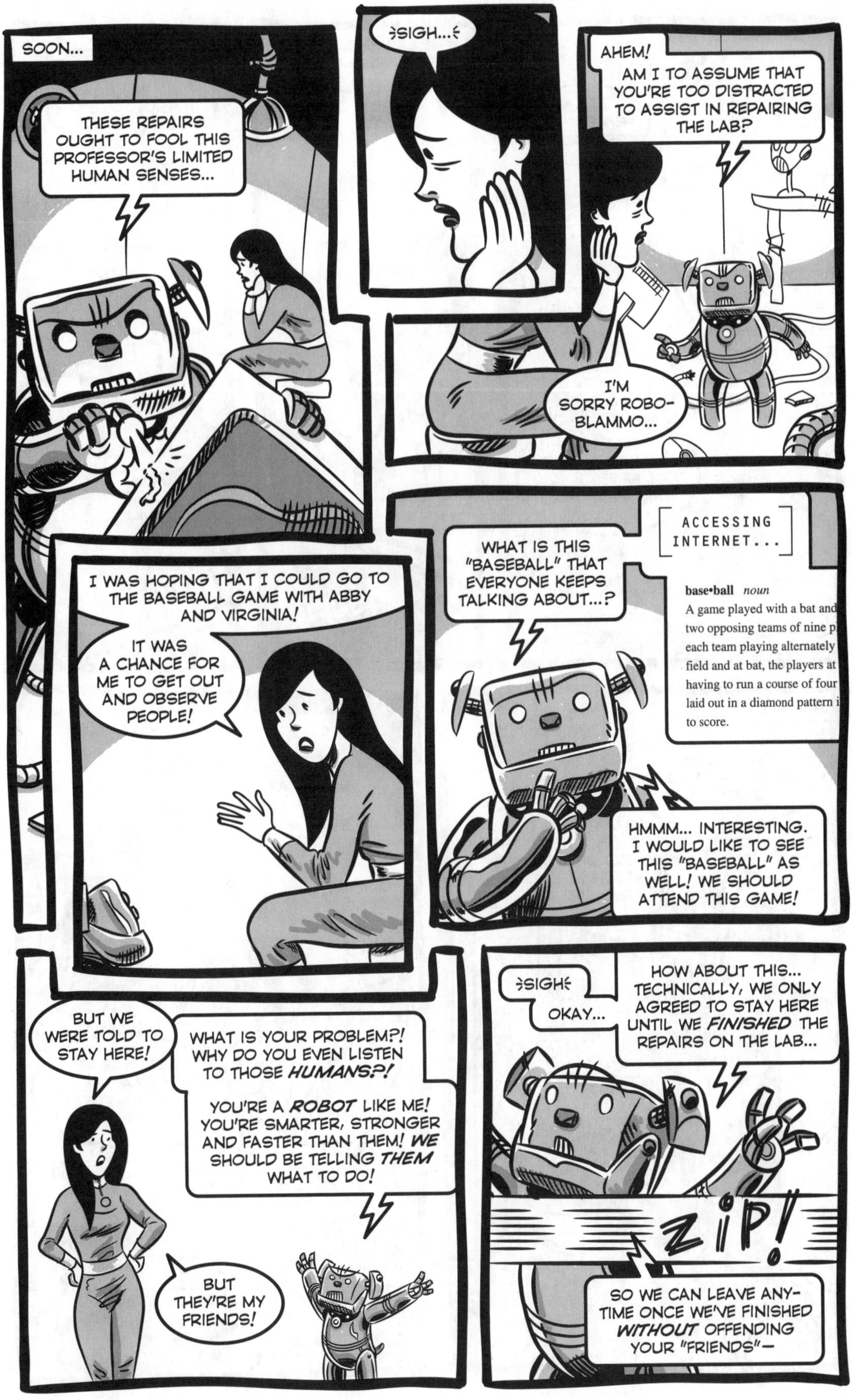
SOON...
THESE REPAIRS OUGHT TO FOOL THIS PROFESSOR'S LIMITED HUMAN SENSES...
SIGH...
AHEM!
AM I TO ASSUME THAT YOU'RE TOO DISTRACTED TO ASSIST IN REPAIRING THE LAB?
I'M SORRY ROBO-BLAMMO...
I WAS HOPING THAT I COULD GO TO THE BASEBALL GAME WITH ABBY AND VIRGINIA!
IT WAS A CHANCE FOR ME TO GET OUT AND OBSERVE PEOPLE!
WHAT IS THIS "BASEBALL" THAT EVERYONE KEEPS TALKING ABOUT...?
ACCESSING INTERNET...
base•ball noun
A game played with a bat and
two opposing teams of nine p
each team playing alternately
field and at bat, the players at
having to run a course of four
laid out in a diamond pattern i
to score.
HMMM... INTERESTING. I WOULD LIKE TO SEE THIS "BASEBALL" AS WELL! WE SHOULD ATTEND THIS GAME!
BUT WE WERE TOLD TO STAY HERE!
WHAT IS YOUR PROBLEM?! WHY DO YOU EVEN LISTEN TO THOSE HUMANS?!
YOU'RE A ROBOT LIKE ME! YOU'RE SMARTER, STRONGER AND FASTER THAN THEM! WE SHOULD BE TELLING THEM WHAT TO DO!
BUT THEY'RE MY FRIENDS!
SIGH
OKAY...
HOW ABOUT THIS... TECHNICALLY, WE ONLY AGREED TO STAY HERE UNTIL WE FINISHED THE REPAIRS ON THE LAB...
ZIP!
SO WE CAN LEAVE ANY-TIME ONCE WE'VE FINISHED WITHOUT OFFENDING YOUR "FRIENDS"—

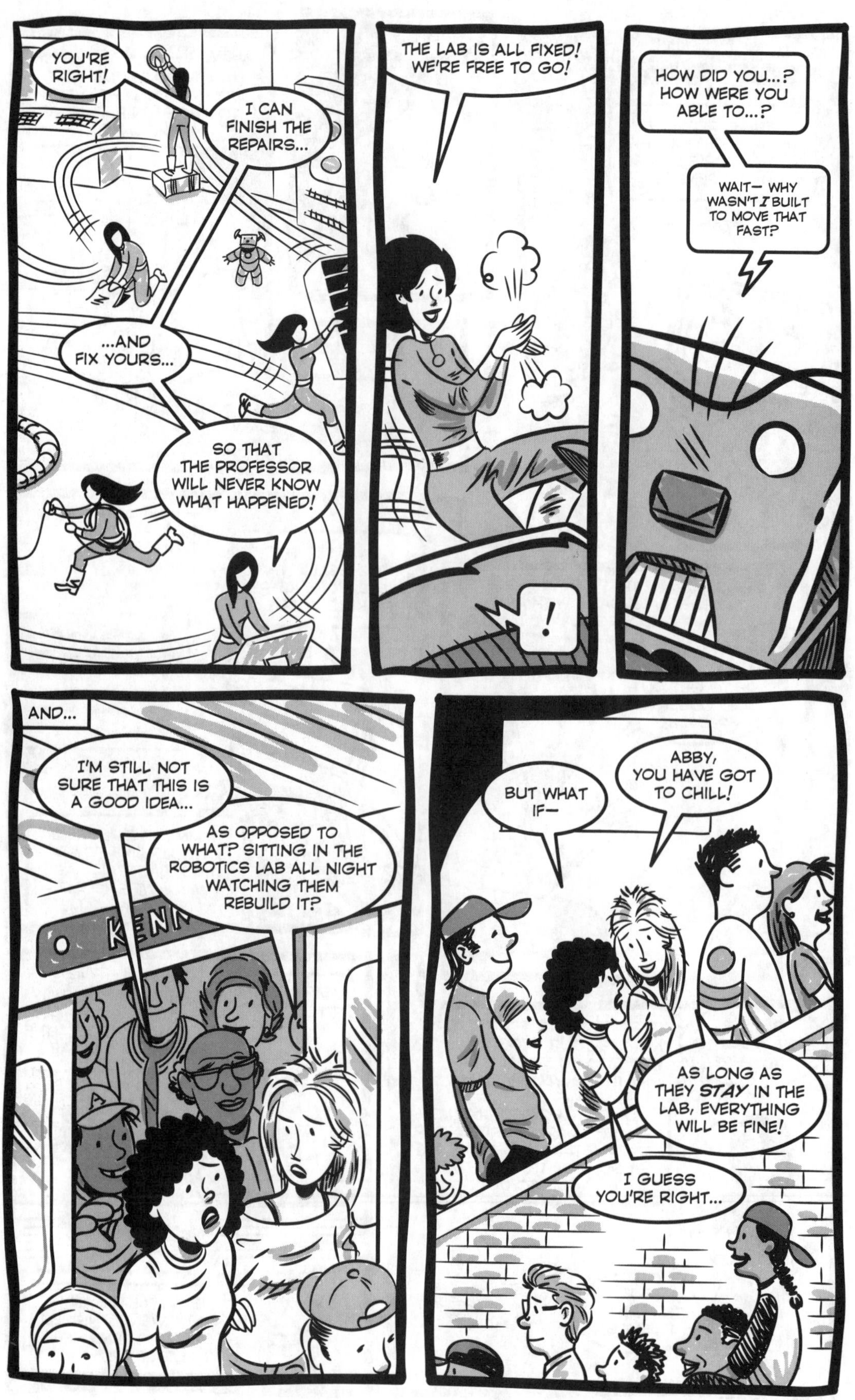
YOU'RE RIGHT!
I CAN FINISH THE REPAIRS...
...AND FIX YOURS...
SO THAT THE PROFESSOR WILL NEVER KNOW WHAT HAPPENED!
THE LAB IS ALL FIXED! WE'RE FREE TO GO!
!
HOW DID YOU...? HOW WERE YOU ABLE TO...?
WAIT— WHY WASN'T I BUILT TO MOVE THAT FAST?
AND...
I'M STILL NOT SURE THAT THIS IS A GOOD IDEA...
AS OPPOSED TO WHAT? SITTING IN THE ROBOTICS LAB ALL NIGHT WATCHING THEM REBUILD IT?
KENN
BUT WHAT IF—
ABBY, YOU HAVE GOT TO CHILL!
AS LONG AS THEY STAY IN THE LAB, EVERYTHING WILL BE FINE!
I GUESS YOU'RE RIGHT...

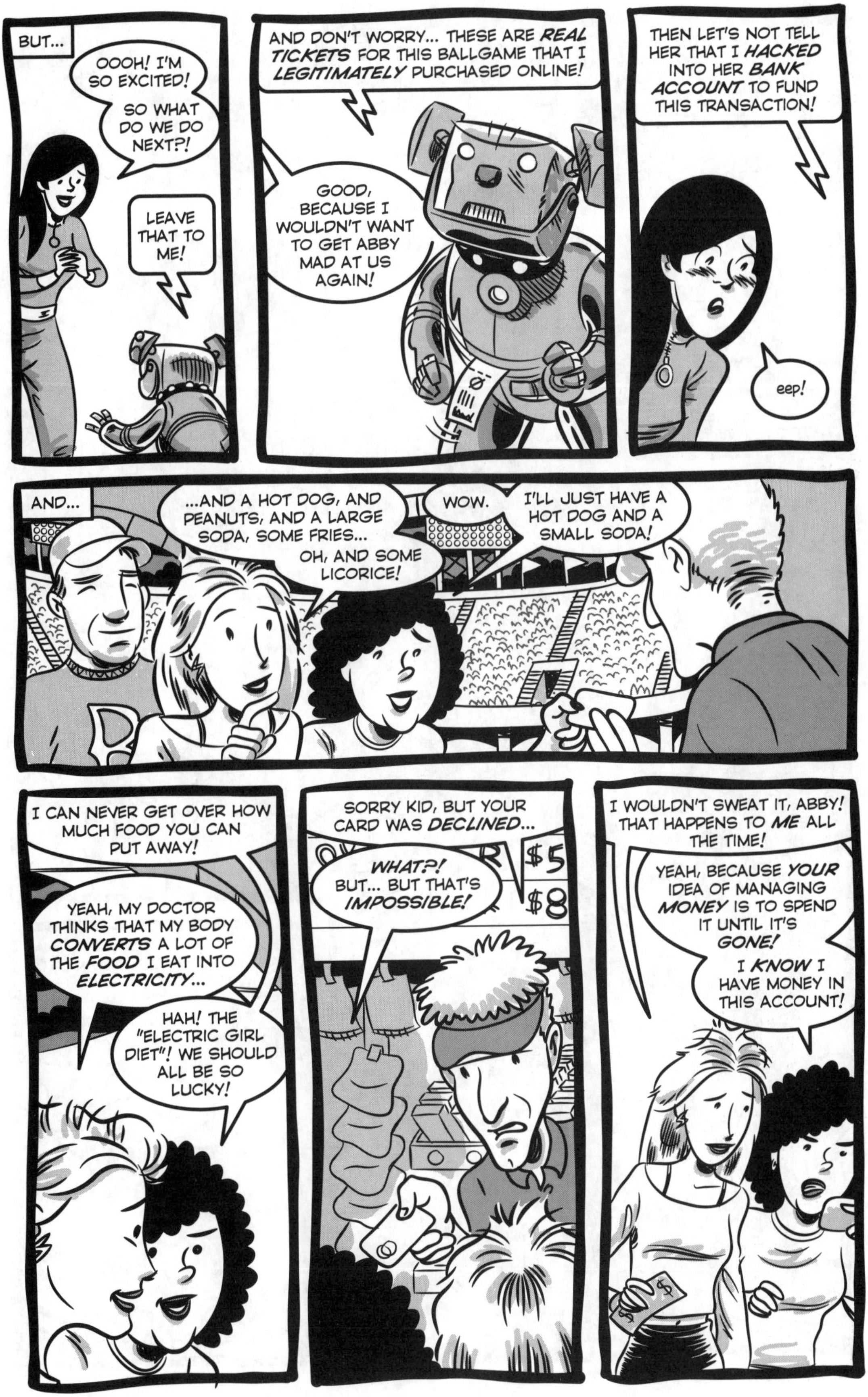

BUT...
OOOH! I'M SO EXCITED!
SO WHAT DO WE DO NEXT?!
LEAVE THAT TO ME!
AND DON'T WORRY... THESE ARE *REAL TICKETS* FOR THIS BALLGAME THAT I *LEGITIMATELY* PURCHASED ONLINE!
GOOD, BECAUSE I WOULDN'T WANT TO GET ABBY MAD AT US AGAIN!
THEN LET'S NOT TELL HER THAT I *HACKED* INTO HER *BANK ACCOUNT* TO FUND THIS TRANSACTION!
eep!
AND...
...AND A HOT DOG, AND PEANUTS, AND A LARGE SODA, SOME FRIES...
OH, AND SOME LICORICE!
WOW.
I'LL JUST HAVE A HOT DOG AND A SMALL SODA!
I CAN NEVER GET OVER HOW MUCH FOOD YOU CAN PUT AWAY!
YEAH, MY DOCTOR THINKS THAT MY BODY *CONVERTS* A LOT OF THE *FOOD* I EAT INTO *ELECTRICITY*...
HAH! THE "ELECTRIC GIRL DIET"! WE SHOULD ALL BE SO LUCKY!
SORRY KID, BUT YOUR CARD WAS *DECLINED*...
WHAT?! BUT... BUT THAT'S *IMPOSSIBLE!*
$5
$8
I WOULDN'T SWEAT IT, ABBY! THAT HAPPENS TO *ME* ALL THE TIME!
YEAH, BECAUSE *YOUR* IDEA OF MANAGING *MONEY* IS TO SPEND IT UNTIL IT'S *GONE!*
I *KNOW* I HAVE MONEY IN THIS ACCOUNT!

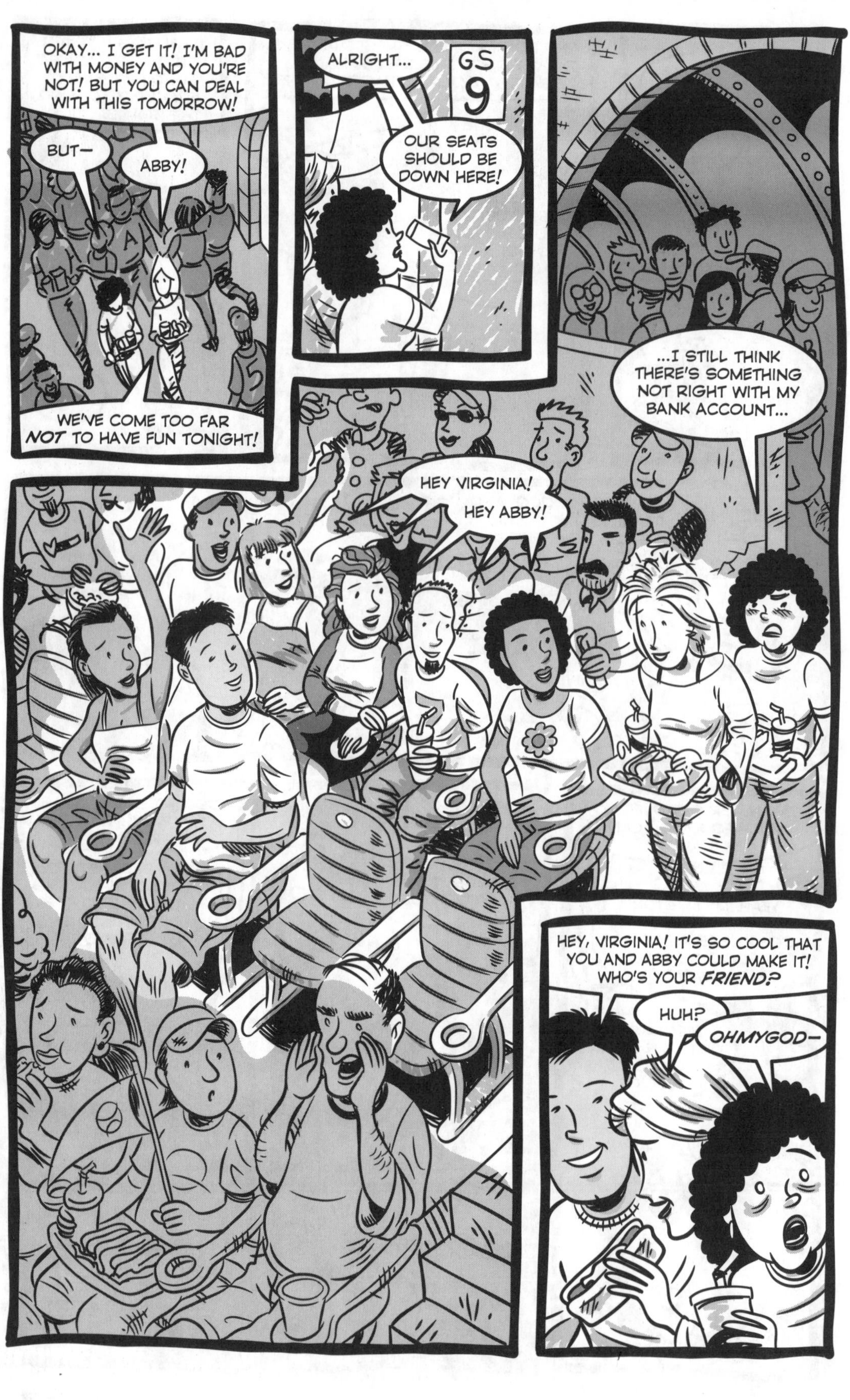
OKAY... I GET IT! I'M BAD WITH MONEY AND YOU'RE NOT! BUT YOU CAN DEAL WITH THIS TOMORROW!
BUT—
ABBY!
WE'VE COME TOO FAR NOT TO HAVE FUN TONIGHT!
ALRIGHT...
GS 9
OUR SEATS SHOULD BE DOWN HERE!
...I STILL THINK THERE'S SOMETHING NOT RIGHT WITH MY BANK ACCOUNT...
HEY VIRGINIA!
HEY ABBY!
HEY, VIRGINIA! IT'S SO COOL THAT YOU AND ABBY COULD MAKE IT! WHO'S YOUR FRIEND?
HUH?
OHMYGOD—

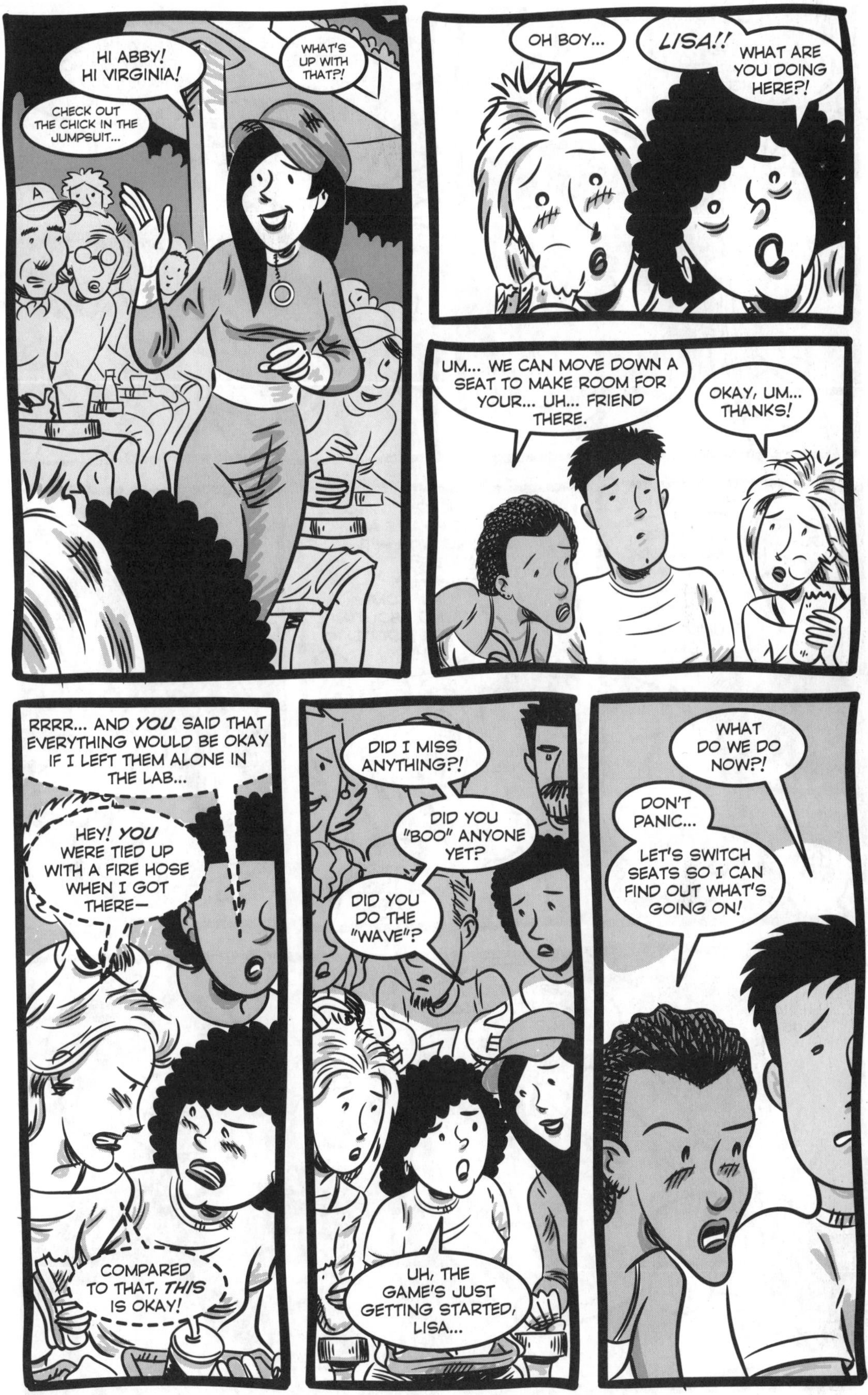
HI ABBY! HI VIRGINIA!
CHECK OUT THE CHICK IN THE JUMPSUIT...
WHAT'S UP WITH THAT?!
OH BOY...
LISA!! WHAT ARE YOU DOING HERE?!
UM... WE CAN MOVE DOWN A SEAT TO MAKE ROOM FOR YOUR... UH... FRIEND THERE.
OKAY, UM... THANKS!
RRRR... AND YOU SAID THAT EVERYTHING WOULD BE OKAY IF I LEFT THEM ALONE IN THE LAB...
HEY! YOU WERE TIED UP WITH A FIRE HOSE WHEN I GOT THERE—
COMPARED TO THAT, THIS IS OKAY!
DID I MISS ANYTHING?!
DID YOU "BOO" ANYONE YET?
DID YOU DO THE "WAVE"?
UH, THE GAME'S JUST GETTING STARTED, LISA...
WHAT DO WE DO NOW?!
DON'T PANIC...
LET'S SWITCH SEATS SO I CAN FIND OUT WHAT'S GOING ON!

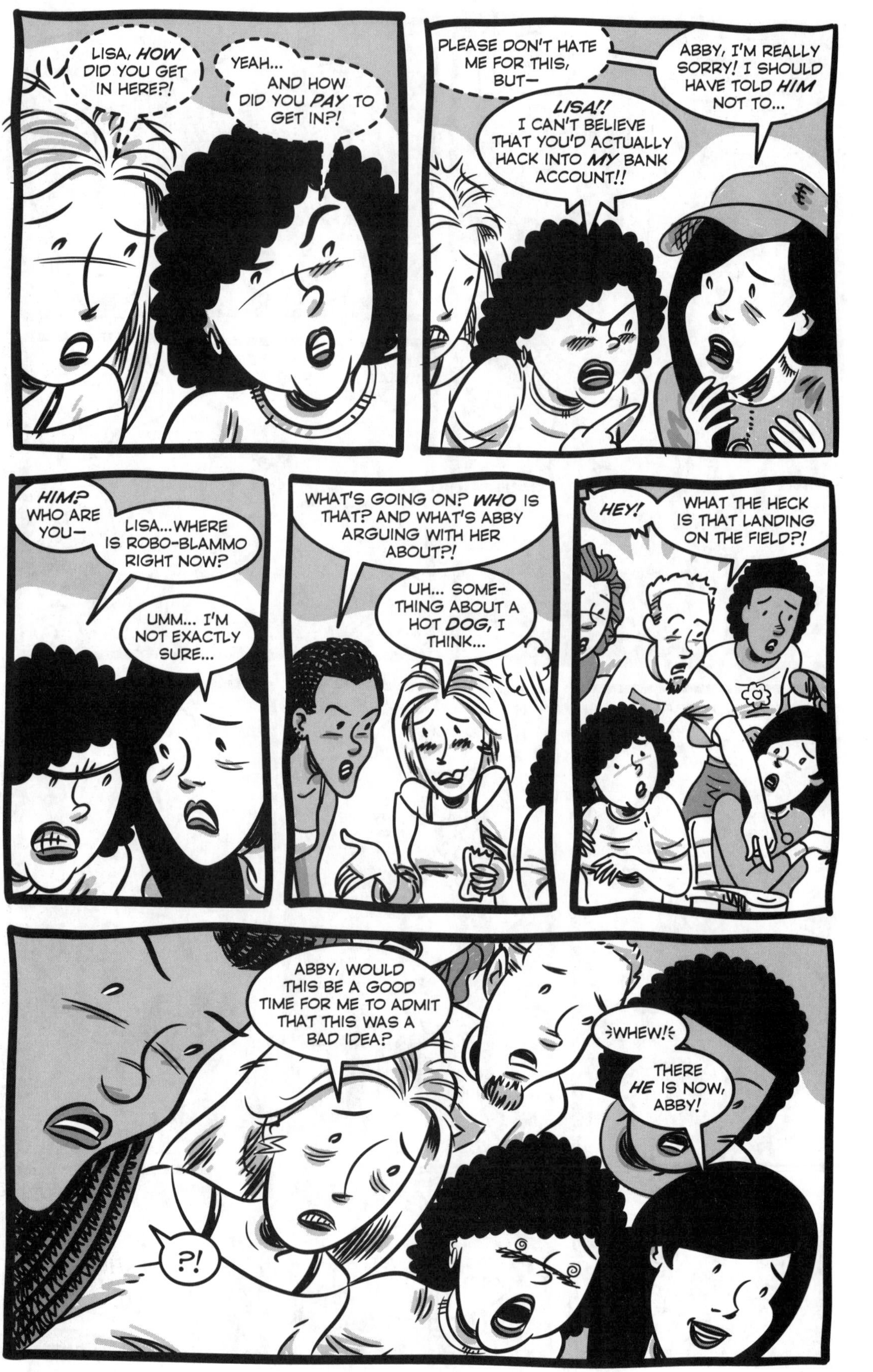
LISA, HOW DID YOU GET IN HERE?!
YEAH... AND HOW DID YOU PAY TO GET IN?!
PLEASE DON'T HATE ME FOR THIS, BUT—
LISA!! I CAN'T BELIEVE THAT YOU'D ACTUALLY HACK INTO MY BANK ACCOUNT!!
ABBY, I'M REALLY SORRY! I SHOULD HAVE TOLD HIM NOT TO...
HIM? WHO ARE YOU—
LISA...WHERE IS ROBO-BLAMMO RIGHT NOW?
UMM... I'M NOT EXACTLY SURE...
WHAT'S GOING ON? WHO IS THAT? AND WHAT'S ABBY ARGUING WITH HER ABOUT?!
UH... SOMETHING ABOUT A HOT DOG, I THINK...
HEY!
WHAT THE HECK IS THAT LANDING ON THE FIELD?!
ABBY, WOULD THIS BE A GOOD TIME FOR ME TO ADMIT THAT THIS WAS A BAD IDEA?
?!
WHEW!
THERE HE IS NOW, ABBY!

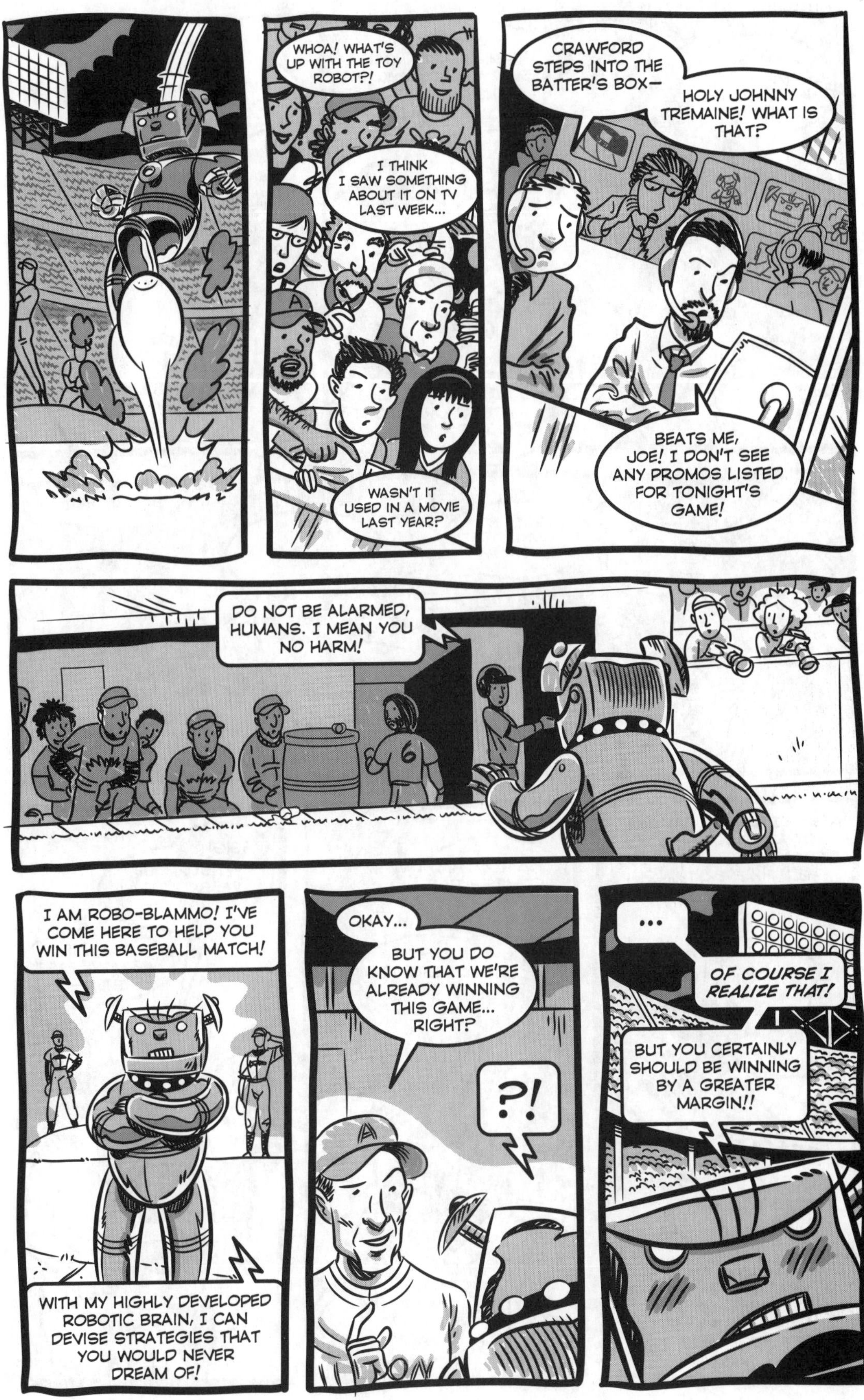
WHOA! WHAT'S UP WITH THE TOY ROBOT?!
I THINK I SAW SOMETHING ABOUT IT ON TV LAST WEEK...
WASN'T IT USED IN A MOVIE LAST YEAR?
CRAWFORD STEPS INTO THE BATTER'S BOX—
HOLY JOHNNY TREMAINE! WHAT IS THAT?
BEATS ME, JOE! I DON'T SEE ANY PROMOS LISTED FOR TONIGHT'S GAME!
DO NOT BE ALARMED, HUMANS. I MEAN YOU NO HARM!
I AM ROBO-BLAMMO! I'VE COME HERE TO HELP YOU WIN THIS BASEBALL MATCH!
WITH MY HIGHLY DEVELOPED ROBOTIC BRAIN, I CAN DEVISE STRATEGIES THAT YOU WOULD NEVER DREAM OF!
OKAY...
BUT YOU DO KNOW THAT WE'RE ALREADY WINNING THIS GAME... RIGHT?
?!
...
OF COURSE I REALIZE THAT!
BUT YOU CERTAINLY SHOULD BE WINNING BY A GREATER MARGIN!!

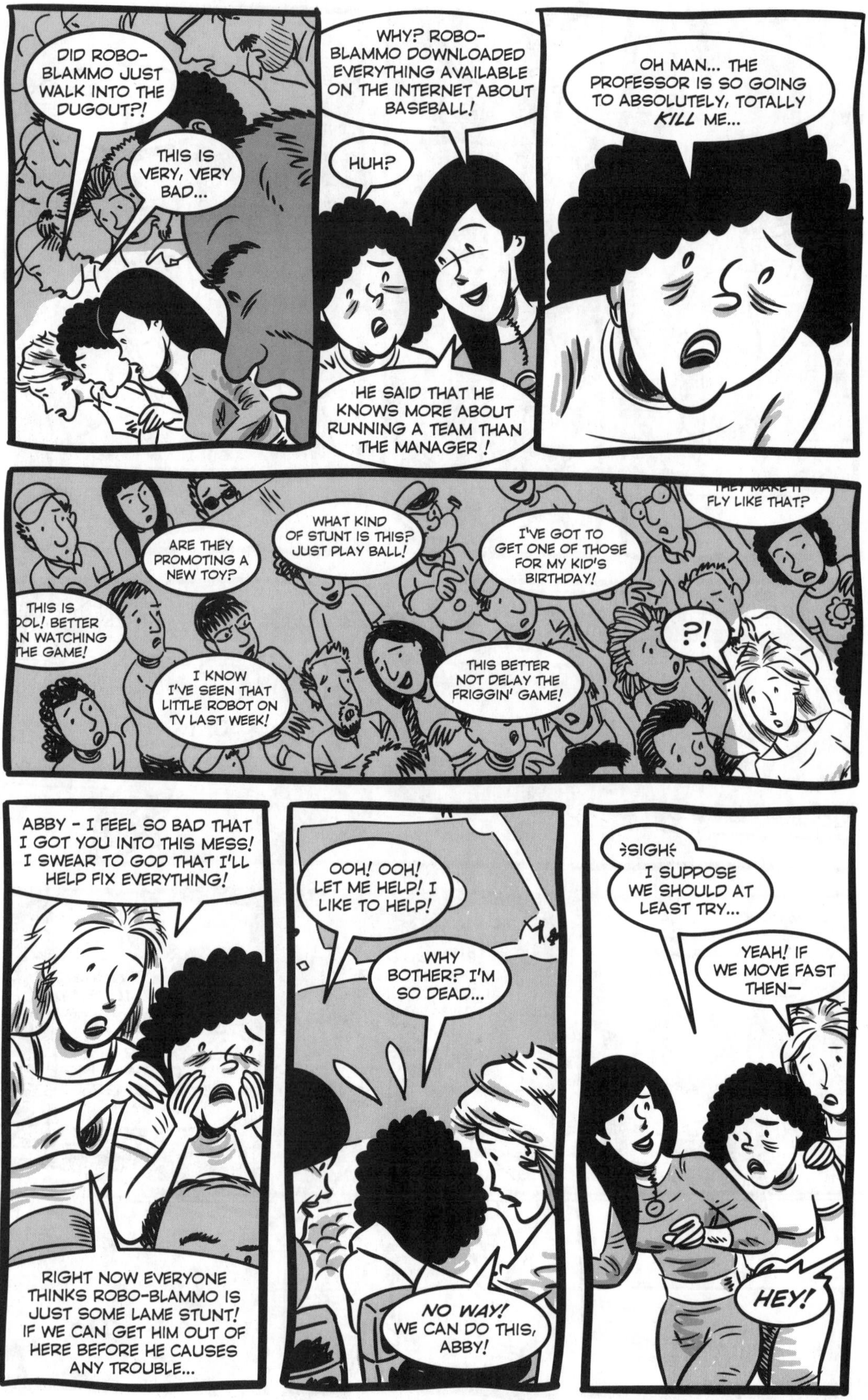
DID ROBO-BLAMMO JUST WALK INTO THE DUGOUT?!
THIS IS VERY, VERY BAD...
WHY? ROBO-BLAMMO DOWNLOADED EVERYTHING AVAILABLE ON THE INTERNET ABOUT BASEBALL!
HUH?
HE SAID THAT HE KNOWS MORE ABOUT RUNNING A TEAM THAN THE MANAGER!
OH MAN... THE PROFESSOR IS SO GOING TO ABSOLUTELY, TOTALLY KILL ME...
ARE THEY PROMOTING A NEW TOY?
WHAT KIND OF STUNT IS THIS? JUST PLAY BALL!
I'VE GOT TO GET ONE OF THOSE FOR MY KID'S BIRTHDAY!
FLY LIKE THAT?
THIS IS
OOL! BETTER
N WATCHING
THE GAME!
?!
I KNOW I'VE SEEN THAT LITTLE ROBOT ON TV LAST WEEK!
THIS BETTER NOT DELAY THE FRIGGIN' GAME!
ABBY - I FEEL SO BAD THAT I GOT YOU INTO THIS MESS! I SWEAR TO GOD THAT I'LL HELP FIX EVERYTHING!
RIGHT NOW EVERYONE THINKS ROBO-BLAMMO IS JUST SOME LAME STUNT! IF WE CAN GET HIM OUT OF HERE BEFORE HE CAUSES ANY TROUBLE...
OOH! OOH! LET ME HELP! I LIKE TO HELP!
WHY BOTHER? I'M SO DEAD...
NO WAY! WE CAN DO THIS, ABBY!
SIGH
I SUPPOSE WE SHOULD AT LEAST TRY...
YEAH! IF WE MOVE FAST THEN—
HEY!

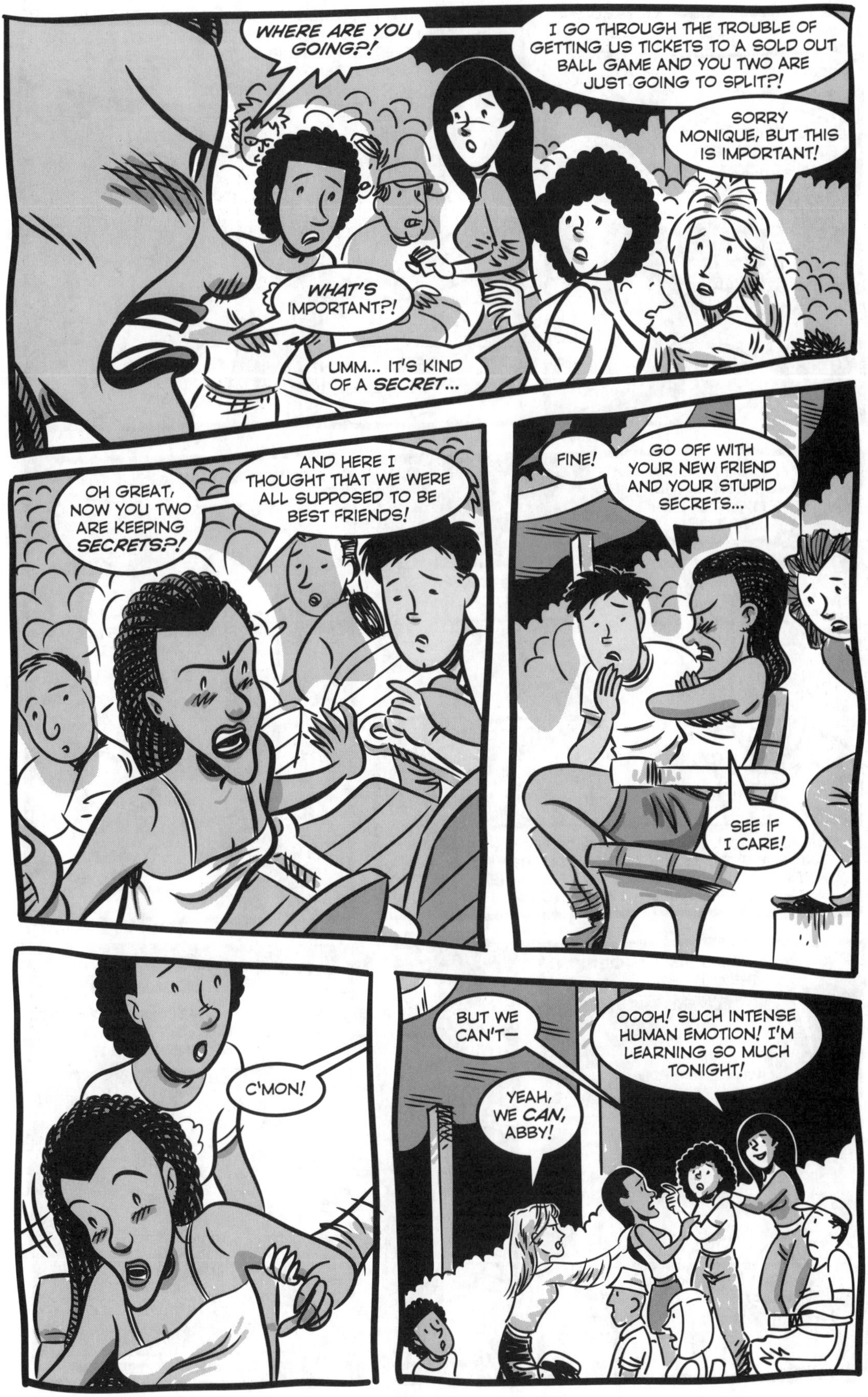
WHERE ARE YOU GOING?!
I GO THROUGH THE TROUBLE OF GETTING US TICKETS TO A SOLD OUT BALL GAME AND YOU TWO ARE JUST GOING TO SPLIT?!
SORRY MONIQUE, BUT THIS IS IMPORTANT!
WHAT'S IMPORTANT?!
UMM... IT'S KIND OF A SECRET...
OH GREAT, NOW YOU TWO ARE KEEPING SECRETS?!
AND HERE I THOUGHT THAT WE WERE ALL SUPPOSED TO BE BEST FRIENDS!
FINE!
GO OFF WITH YOUR NEW FRIEND AND YOUR STUPID SECRETS...
SEE IF I CARE!
C'MON!
BUT WE CAN'T—
OOOH! SUCH INTENSE HUMAN EMOTION! I'M LEARNING SO MUCH TONIGHT!
YEAH, WE CAN, ABBY!

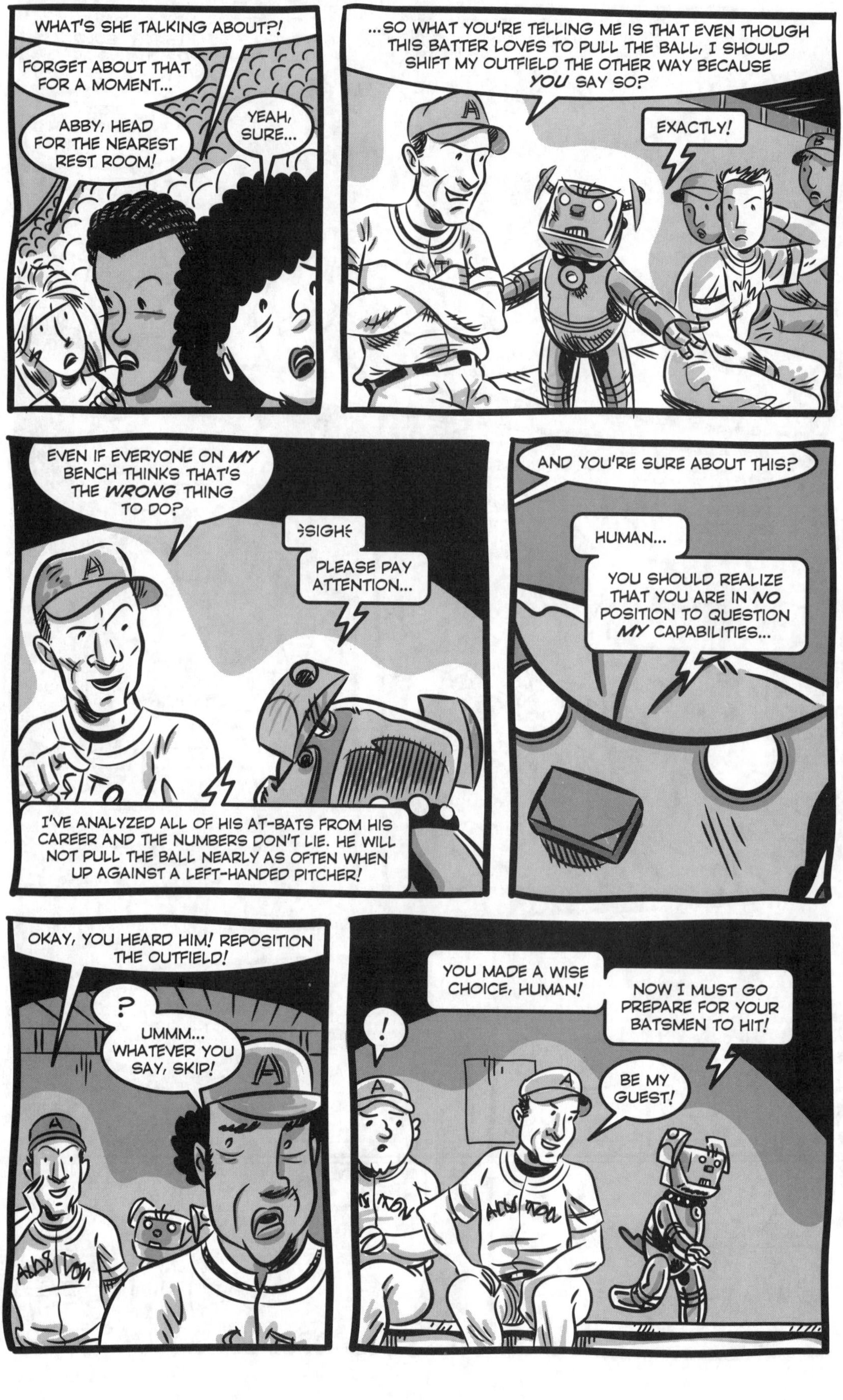
WHAT'S SHE TALKING ABOUT?!
FORGET ABOUT THAT FOR A MOMENT...
ABBY, HEAD FOR THE NEAREST REST ROOM!
YEAH, SURE...
...SO WHAT YOU'RE TELLING ME IS THAT EVEN THOUGH THIS BATTER LOVES TO PULL THE BALL, I SHOULD SHIFT MY OUTFIELD THE OTHER WAY BECAUSE YOU SAY SO?
EXACTLY!
EVEN IF EVERYONE ON MY BENCH THINKS THAT'S THE WRONG THING TO DO?
SIGH
PLEASE PAY ATTENTION...
I'VE ANALYZED ALL OF HIS AT-BATS FROM HIS CAREER AND THE NUMBERS DON'T LIE. HE WILL NOT PULL THE BALL NEARLY AS OFTEN WHEN UP AGAINST A LEFT-HANDED PITCHER!
AND YOU'RE SURE ABOUT THIS?
HUMAN...
YOU SHOULD REALIZE THAT YOU ARE IN NO POSITION TO QUESTION MY CAPABILITIES...
OKAY, YOU HEARD HIM! REPOSITION THE OUTFIELD!
?
UMMM... WHATEVER YOU SAY, SKIP!
!
YOU MADE A WISE CHOICE, HUMAN!
NOW I MUST GO PREPARE FOR YOUR BATSMEN TO HIT!
BE MY GUEST!

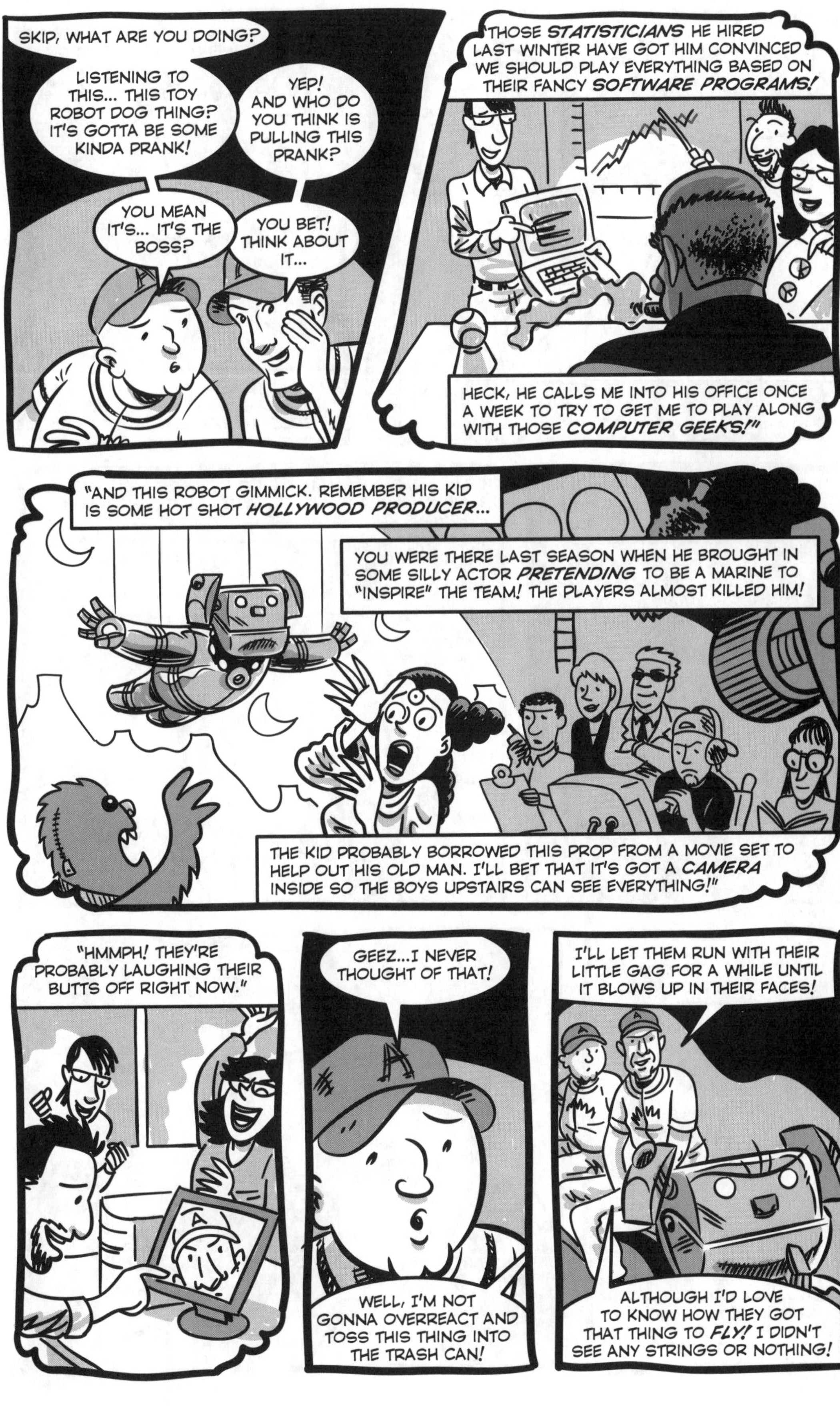
SKIP, WHAT ARE YOU DOING?
LISTENING TO THIS... THIS TOY ROBOT DOG THING? IT'S GOTTA BE SOME KINDA PRANK!
YEP! AND WHO DO YOU THINK IS PULLING THIS PRANK?
YOU MEAN IT'S... IT'S THE BOSS?
YOU BET! THINK ABOUT IT...
THOSE *STATISTICIANS* HE HIRED LAST WINTER HAVE GOT HIM CONVINCED WE SHOULD PLAY EVERYTHING BASED ON THEIR FANCY *SOFTWARE PROGRAMS!*
HECK, HE CALLS ME INTO HIS OFFICE ONCE A WEEK TO TRY TO GET ME TO PLAY ALONG WITH THOSE *COMPUTER GEEKS!"*
"AND THIS ROBOT GIMMICK. REMEMBER HIS KID IS SOME HOT SHOT *HOLLYWOOD PRODUCER...*
YOU WERE THERE LAST SEASON WHEN HE BROUGHT IN SOME SILLY ACTOR *PRETENDING* TO BE A MARINE TO "INSPIRE" THE TEAM! THE PLAYERS ALMOST KILLED HIM!
THE KID PROBABLY BORROWED THIS PROP FROM A MOVIE SET TO HELP OUT HIS OLD MAN. I'LL BET THAT IT'S GOT A *CAMERA* INSIDE SO THE BOYS UPSTAIRS CAN SEE EVERYTHING!"
"HMMPH! THEY'RE PROBABLY LAUGHING THEIR BUTTS OFF RIGHT NOW."
GEEZ...I NEVER THOUGHT OF THAT!
WELL, I'M NOT GONNA OVERREACT AND TOSS THIS THING INTO THE TRASH CAN!
I'LL LET THEM RUN WITH THEIR LITTLE GAG FOR A WHILE UNTIL IT BLOWS UP IN THEIR FACES!
ALTHOUGH I'D LOVE TO KNOW HOW THEY GOT THAT THING TO *FLY!* I DIDN'T SEE ANY STRINGS OR NOTHING!

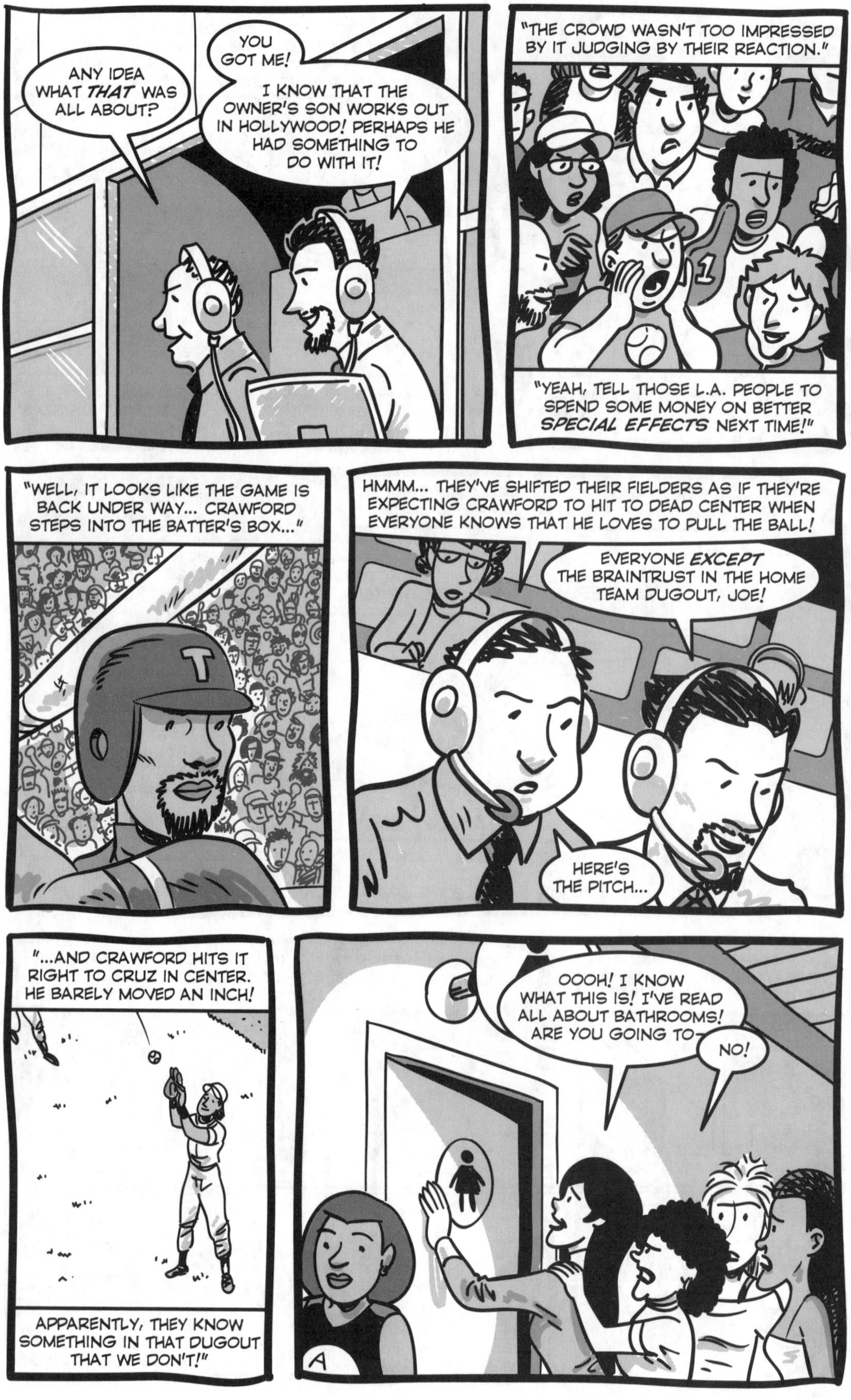
ANY IDEA WHAT *THAT* WAS ALL ABOUT?
YOU GOT ME!
I KNOW THAT THE OWNER'S SON WORKS OUT IN HOLLYWOOD! PERHAPS HE HAD SOMETHING TO DO WITH IT!
"THE CROWD WASN'T TOO IMPRESSED BY IT JUDGING BY THEIR REACTION."
"YEAH, TELL THOSE L.A. PEOPLE TO SPEND SOME MONEY ON BETTER *SPECIAL EFFECTS* NEXT TIME!"
"WELL, IT LOOKS LIKE THE GAME IS BACK UNDER WAY... CRAWFORD STEPS INTO THE BATTER'S BOX..."
HMMM... THEY'VE SHIFTED THEIR FIELDERS AS IF THEY'RE EXPECTING CRAWFORD TO HIT TO DEAD CENTER WHEN EVERYONE KNOWS THAT HE LOVES TO PULL THE BALL!
EVERYONE *EXCEPT* THE BRAINTRUST IN THE HOME TEAM DUGOUT, JOE!
HERE'S THE PITCH...
"...AND CRAWFORD HITS IT RIGHT TO CRUZ IN CENTER. HE BARELY MOVED AN INCH!
APPARENTLY, THEY KNOW SOMETHING IN THAT DUGOUT THAT WE DON'T!"
OOOH! I KNOW WHAT THIS IS! I'VE READ ALL ABOUT BATHROOMS! ARE YOU GOING TO—
NO!

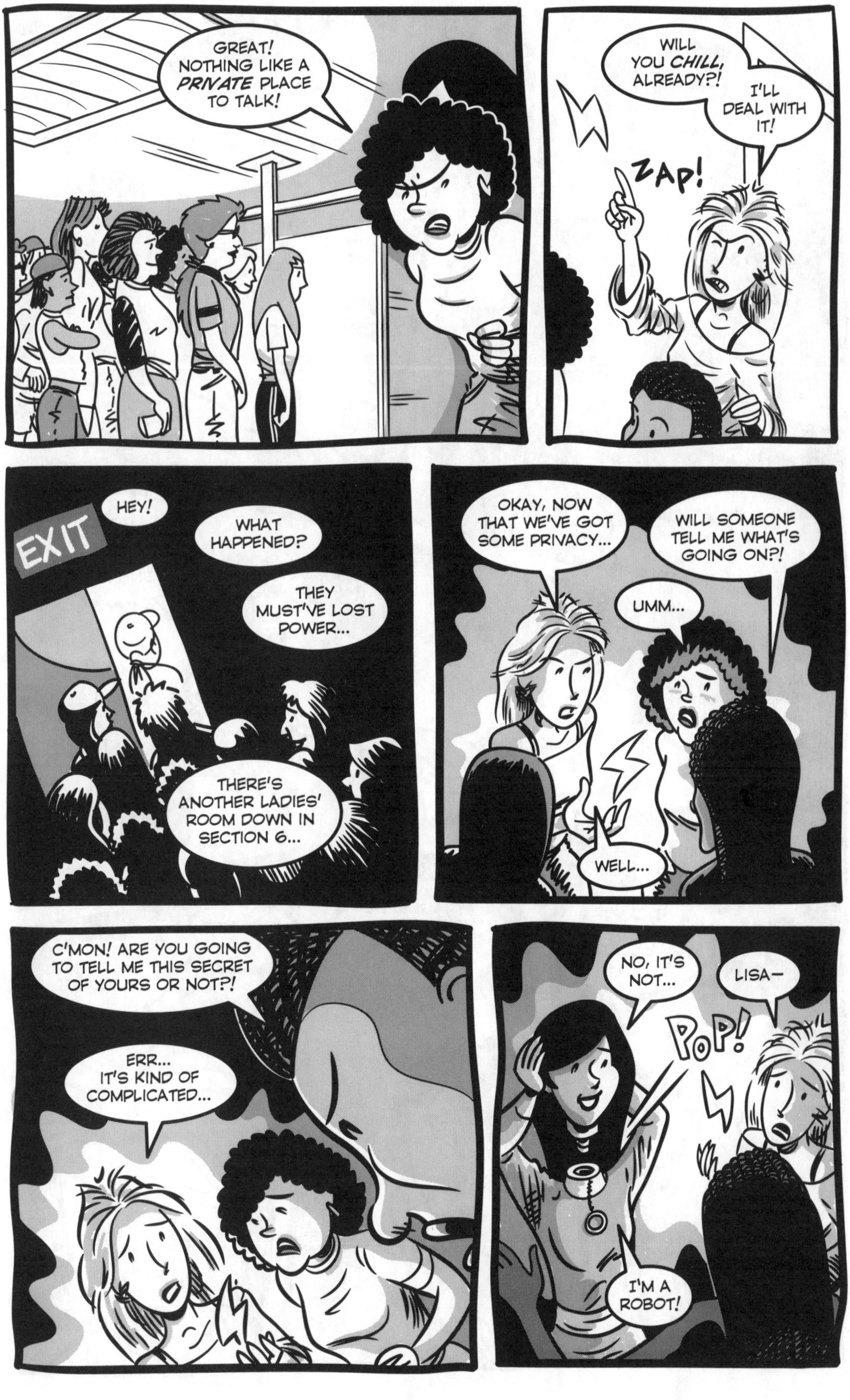
GREAT! NOTHING LIKE A PRIVATE PLACE TO TALK!
WILL YOU CHILL, ALREADY?!
I'LL DEAL WITH IT!
ZAP!
HEY!
WHAT HAPPENED?
THEY MUST'VE LOST POWER...
EXIT
THERE'S ANOTHER LADIES' ROOM DOWN IN SECTION 6...
OKAY, NOW THAT WE'VE GOT SOME PRIVACY...
WILL SOMEONE TELL ME WHAT'S GOING ON?!
UMM...
WELL...
C'MON! ARE YOU GOING TO TELL ME THIS SECRET OF YOURS OR NOT?!
ERR... IT'S KIND OF COMPLICATED...
NO, IT'S NOT...
LISA—
POP!
I'M A ROBOT!

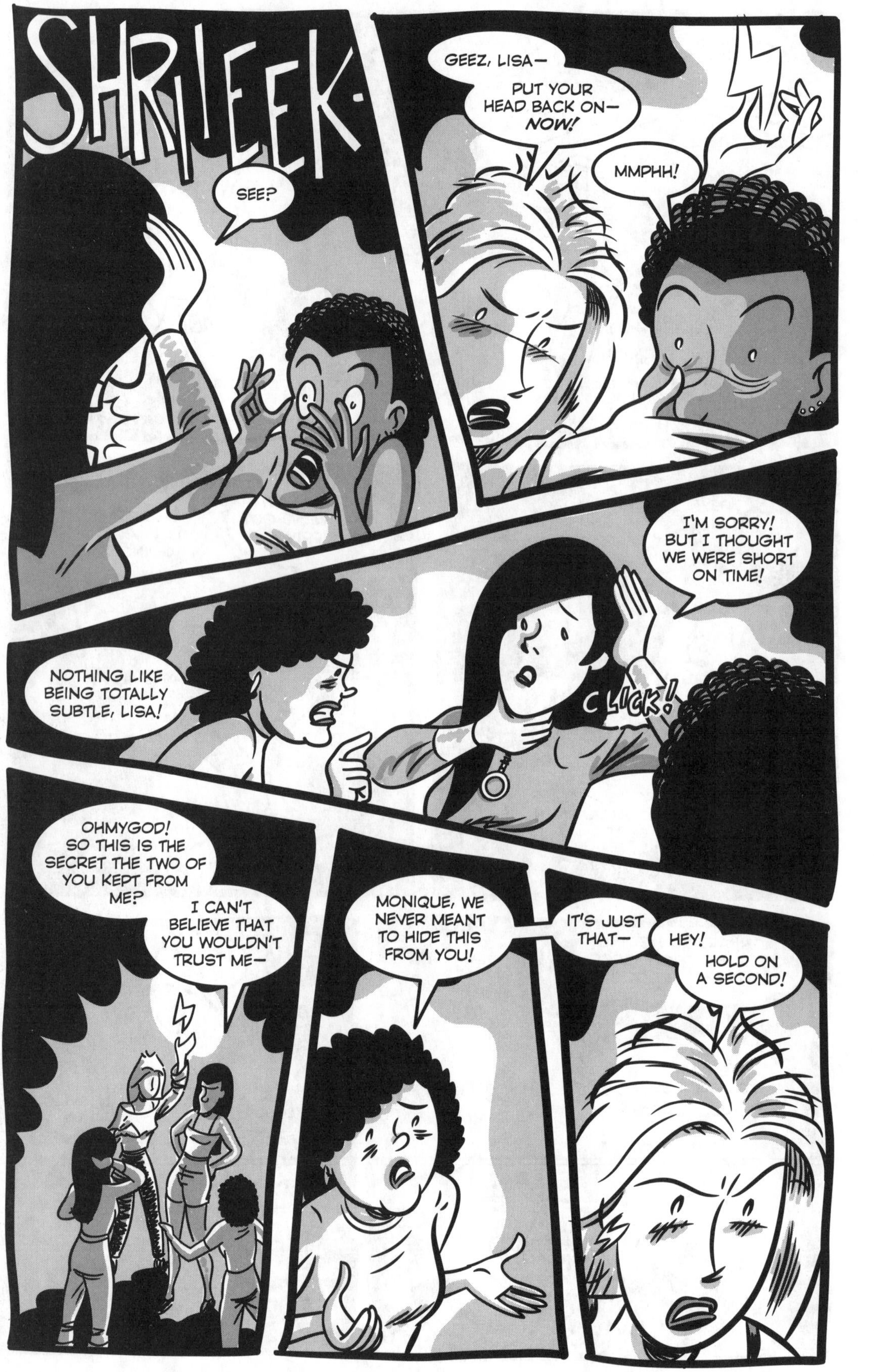
SHRIIEEK
SEE?
GEEZ, LISA—
PUT YOUR HEAD BACK ON— *NOW!*
MMPHH!
I'M SORRY! BUT I THOUGHT WE WERE SHORT ON TIME!
NOTHING LIKE BEING TOTALLY SUBTLE, LISA!
CLICK!
OHMYGOD! SO THIS IS THE SECRET THE TWO OF YOU KEPT FROM ME?
I CAN'T BELIEVE THAT YOU WOULDN'T TRUST ME—
MONIQUE, WE NEVER MEANT TO HIDE THIS FROM YOU!
IT'S JUST THAT—
HEY!
HOLD ON A SECOND!

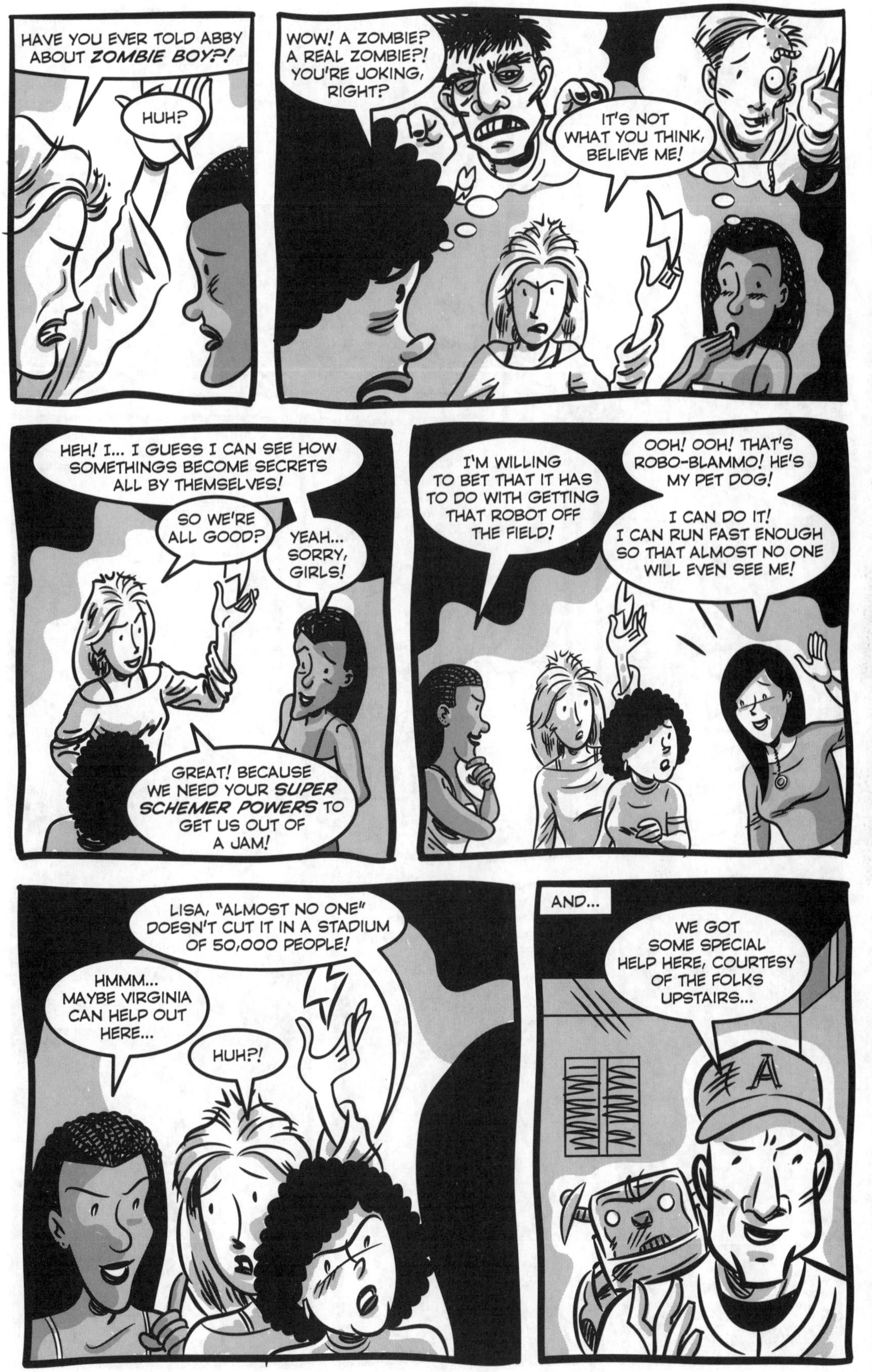
HAVE YOU EVER TOLD ABBY ABOUT ZOMBIE BOY?!
HUH?
WOW! A ZOMBIE? A REAL ZOMBIE?! YOU'RE JOKING, RIGHT?
IT'S NOT WHAT YOU THINK, BELIEVE ME!
HEH! I... I GUESS I CAN SEE HOW SOMETHINGS BECOME SECRETS ALL BY THEMSELVES!
SO WE'RE ALL GOOD?
YEAH... SORRY, GIRLS!
GREAT! BECAUSE WE NEED YOUR SUPER SCHEMER POWERS TO GET US OUT OF A JAM!
I'M WILLING TO BET THAT IT HAS TO DO WITH GETTING THAT ROBOT OFF THE FIELD!
OOH! OOH! THAT'S ROBO-BLAMMO! HE'S MY PET DOG!
I CAN DO IT! I CAN RUN FAST ENOUGH SO THAT ALMOST NO ONE WILL EVEN SEE ME!
LISA, "ALMOST NO ONE" DOESN'T CUT IT IN A STADIUM OF 50,000 PEOPLE!
HMMM... MAYBE VIRGINIA CAN HELP OUT HERE...
HUH?!
AND...
WE GOT SOME SPECIAL HELP HERE, COURTESY OF THE FOLKS UPSTAIRS...
A

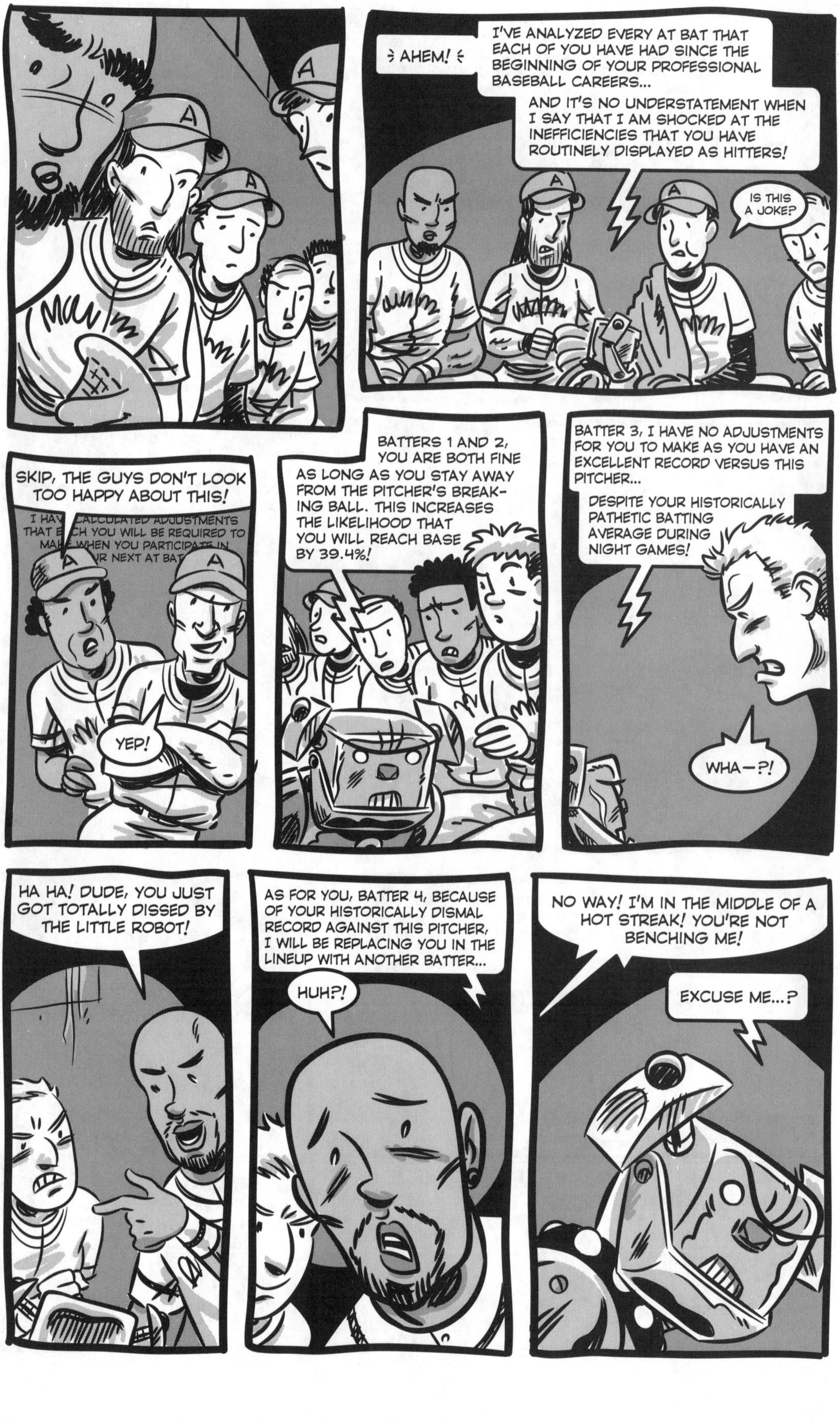

AHEM!
I'VE ANALYZED EVERY AT BAT THAT EACH OF YOU HAVE HAD SINCE THE BEGINNING OF YOUR PROFESSIONAL BASEBALL CAREERS...
AND IT'S NO UNDERSTATEMENT WHEN I SAY THAT I AM SHOCKED AT THE INEFFICIENCIES THAT YOU HAVE ROUTINELY DISPLAYED AS HITTERS!
IS THIS A JOKE?
SKIP, THE GUYS DON'T LOOK TOO HAPPY ABOUT THIS!
YEP!
BATTERS 1 AND 2, YOU ARE BOTH FINE AS LONG AS YOU STAY AWAY FROM THE PITCHER'S BREAKING BALL. THIS INCREASES THE LIKELIHOOD THAT YOU WILL REACH BASE BY 39.4%!
BATTER 3, I HAVE NO ADJUSTMENTS FOR YOU TO MAKE AS YOU HAVE AN EXCELLENT RECORD VERSUS THIS PITCHER...
DESPITE YOUR HISTORICALLY PATHETIC BATTING AVERAGE DURING NIGHT GAMES!
WHA—?!
HA HA! DUDE, YOU JUST GOT TOTALLY DISSED BY THE LITTLE ROBOT!
AS FOR YOU, BATTER 4, BECAUSE OF YOUR HISTORICALLY DISMAL RECORD AGAINST THIS PITCHER, I WILL BE REPLACING YOU IN THE LINEUP WITH ANOTHER BATTER...
HUH?!
NO WAY! I'M IN THE MIDDLE OF A HOT STREAK! YOU'RE NOT BENCHING ME!
EXCUSE ME...?

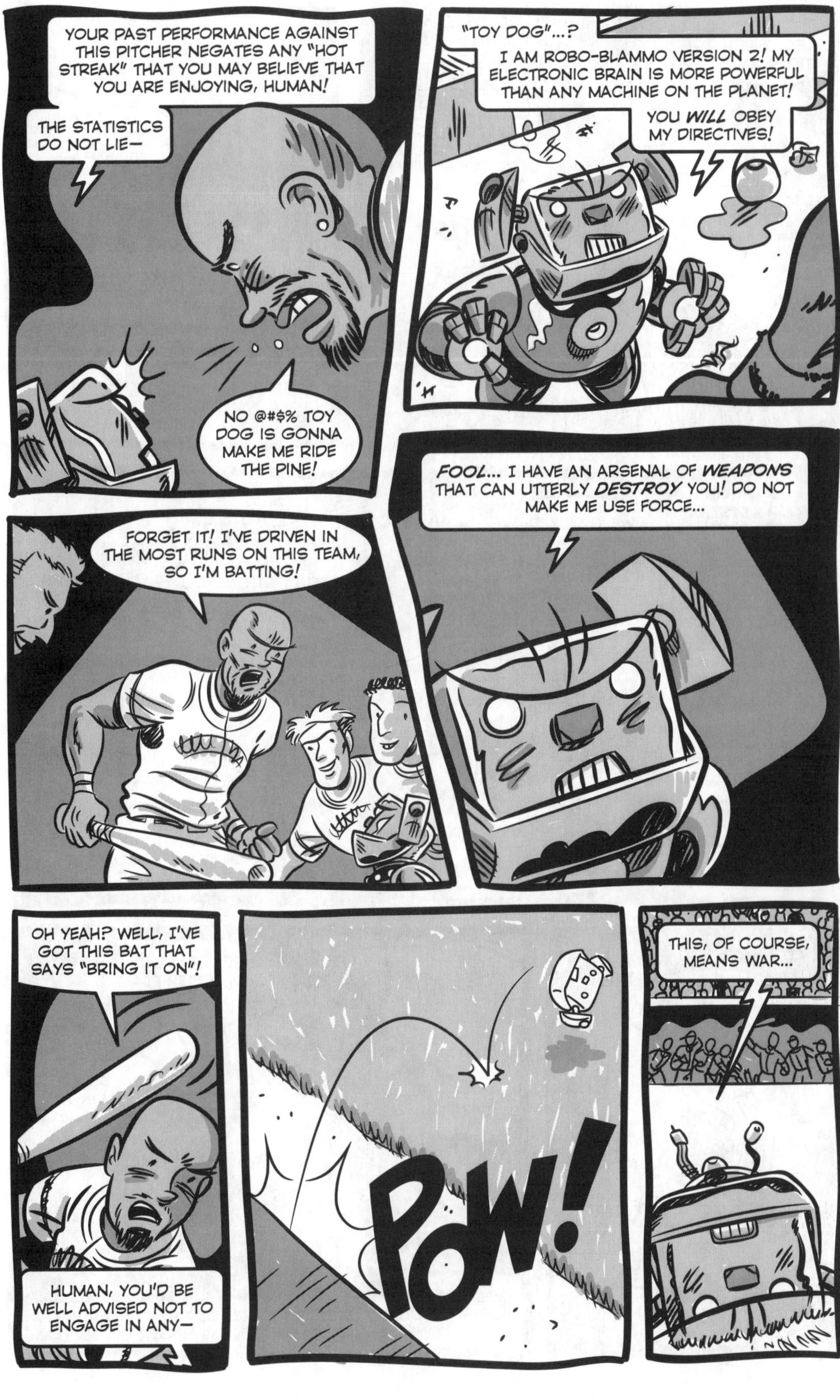
YOUR PAST PERFORMANCE AGAINST THIS PITCHER NEGATES ANY "HOT STREAK" THAT YOU MAY BELIEVE THAT YOU ARE ENJOYING, HUMAN!
THE STATISTICS DO NOT LIE—
NO @#$% TOY DOG IS GONNA MAKE ME RIDE THE PINE!
"TOY DOG"...?
I AM ROBO-BLAMMO VERSION 2! MY ELECTRONIC BRAIN IS MORE POWERFUL THAN ANY MACHINE ON THE PLANET!
YOU WILL OBEY MY DIRECTIVES!
FORGET IT! I'VE DRIVEN IN THE MOST RUNS ON THIS TEAM, SO I'M BATTING!
FOOL... I HAVE AN ARSENAL OF WEAPONS THAT CAN UTTERLY DESTROY YOU! DO NOT MAKE ME USE FORCE...
OH YEAH? WELL, I'VE GOT THIS BAT THAT SAYS "BRING IT ON"!
HUMAN, YOU'D BE WELL ADVISED NOT TO ENGAGE IN ANY—
POW!
THIS, OF COURSE, MEANS WAR...

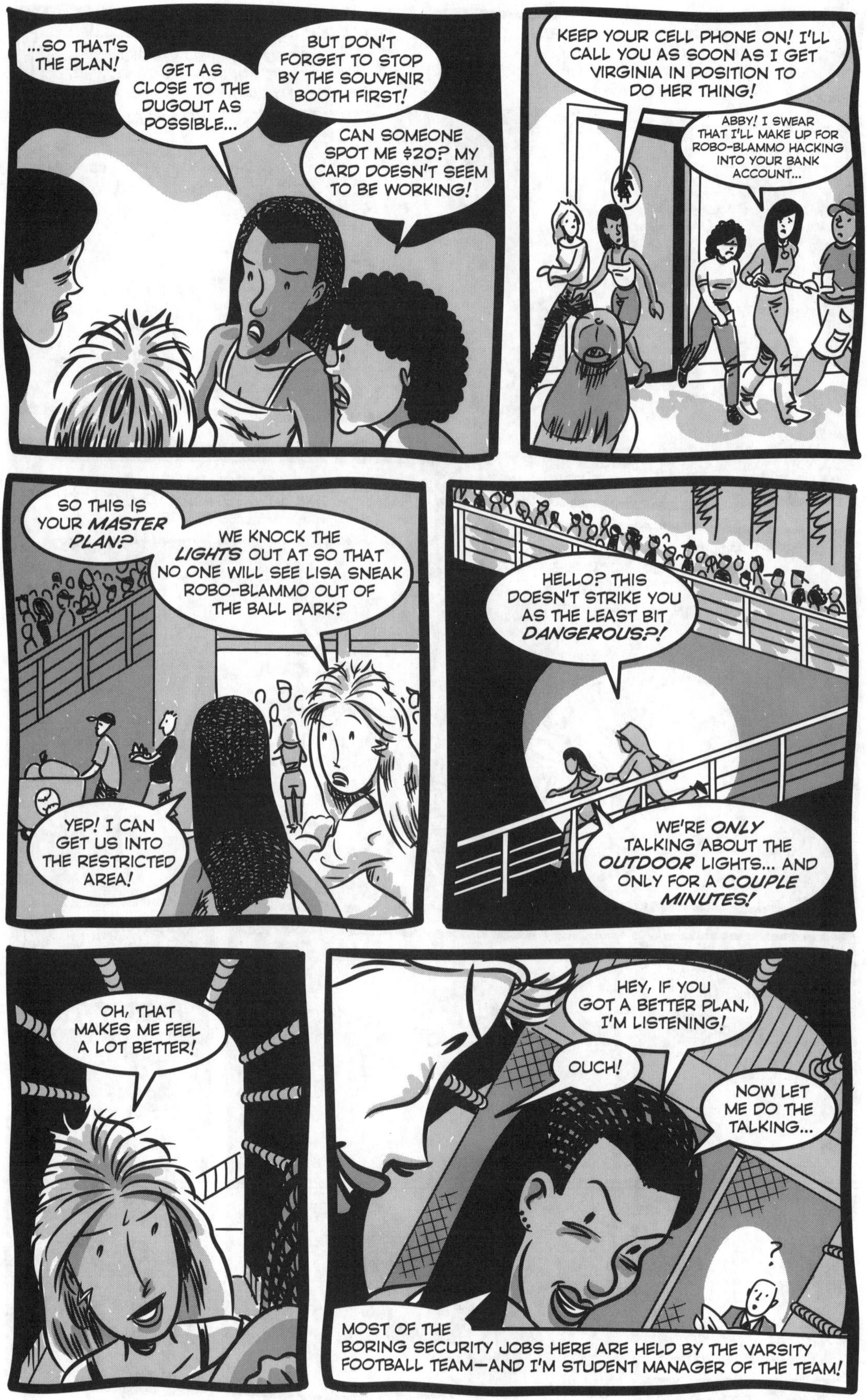
...SO THAT'S THE PLAN!
GET AS CLOSE TO THE DUGOUT AS POSSIBLE...
BUT DON'T FORGET TO STOP BY THE SOUVENIR BOOTH FIRST!
CAN SOMEONE SPOT ME $20? MY CARD DOESN'T SEEM TO BE WORKING!
KEEP YOUR CELL PHONE ON! I'LL CALL YOU AS SOON AS I GET VIRGINIA IN POSITION TO DO HER THING!
ABBY! I SWEAR THAT I'LL MAKE UP FOR ROBO-BLAMMO HACKING INTO YOUR BANK ACCOUNT...
SO THIS IS YOUR MASTER PLAN?
WE KNOCK THE LIGHTS OUT AT SO THAT NO ONE WILL SEE LISA SNEAK ROBO-BLAMMO OUT OF THE BALL PARK?
YEP! I CAN GET US INTO THE RESTRICTED AREA!
HELLO? THIS DOESN'T STRIKE YOU AS THE LEAST BIT DANGEROUS?!
WE'RE ONLY TALKING ABOUT THE OUTDOOR LIGHTS... AND ONLY FOR A COUPLE MINUTES!
OH, THAT MAKES ME FEEL A LOT BETTER!
HEY, IF YOU GOT A BETTER PLAN, I'M LISTENING!
OUCH!
NOW LET ME DO THE TALKING...
?
MOST OF THE BORING SECURITY JOBS HERE ARE HELD BY THE VARSITY FOOTBALL TEAM—AND I'M STUDENT MANAGER OF THE TEAM!

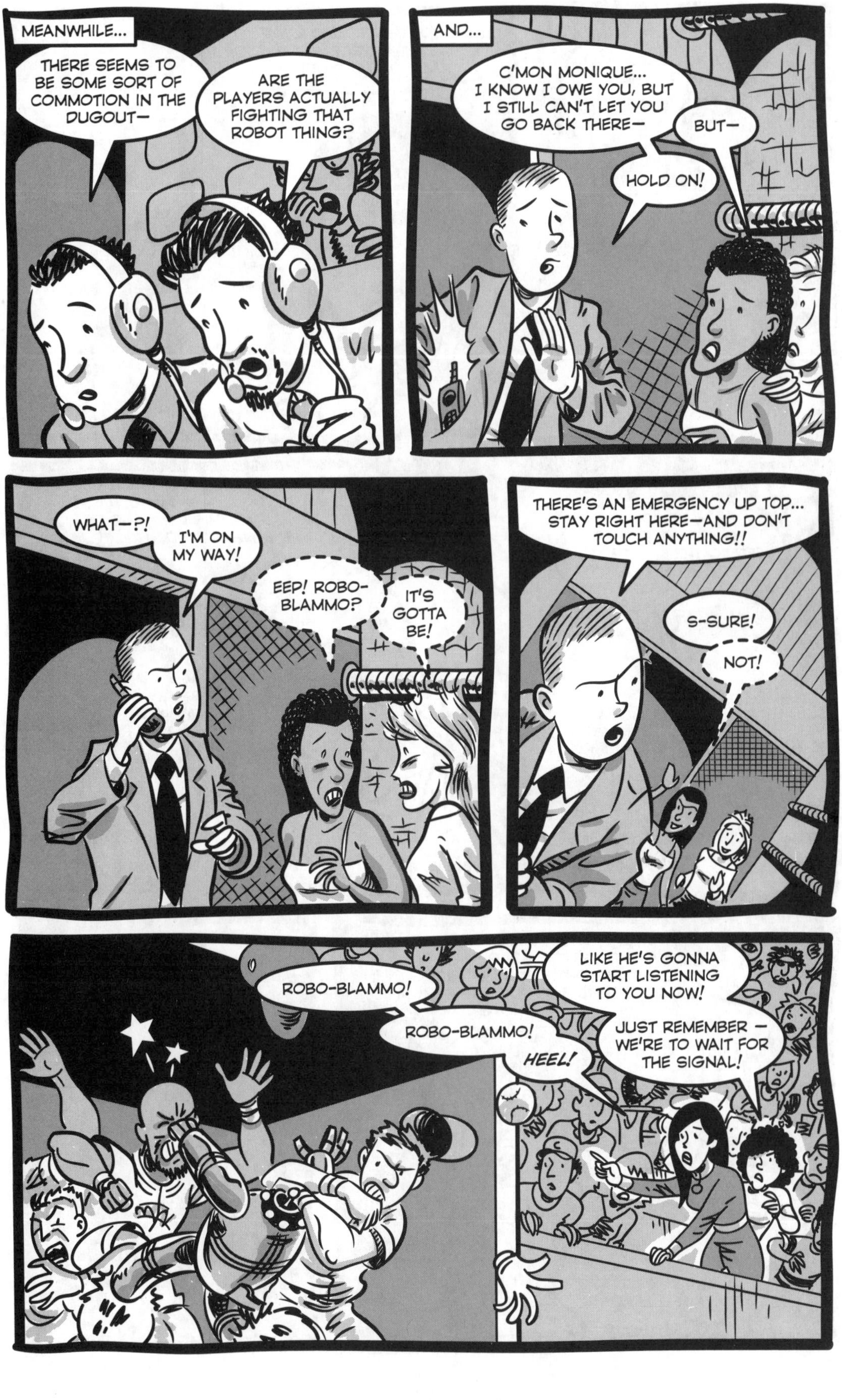
MEANWHILE...
THERE SEEMS TO BE SOME SORT OF COMMOTION IN THE DUGOUT—
ARE THE PLAYERS ACTUALLY FIGHTING THAT ROBOT THING?
AND...
C'MON MONIQUE... I KNOW I OWE YOU, BUT I STILL CAN'T LET YOU GO BACK THERE—
BUT—
HOLD ON!
WHAT—?!
I'M ON MY WAY!
EEP! ROBO-BLAMMO?
IT'S GOTTA BE!
THERE'S AN EMERGENCY UP TOP... STAY RIGHT HERE—AND DON'T TOUCH ANYTHING!!
S-SURE!
NOT!
ROBO-BLAMMO!
ROBO-BLAMMO!
HEEL!
LIKE HE'S GONNA START LISTENING TO YOU NOW!
JUST REMEMBER — WE'RE TO WAIT FOR THE SIGNAL!

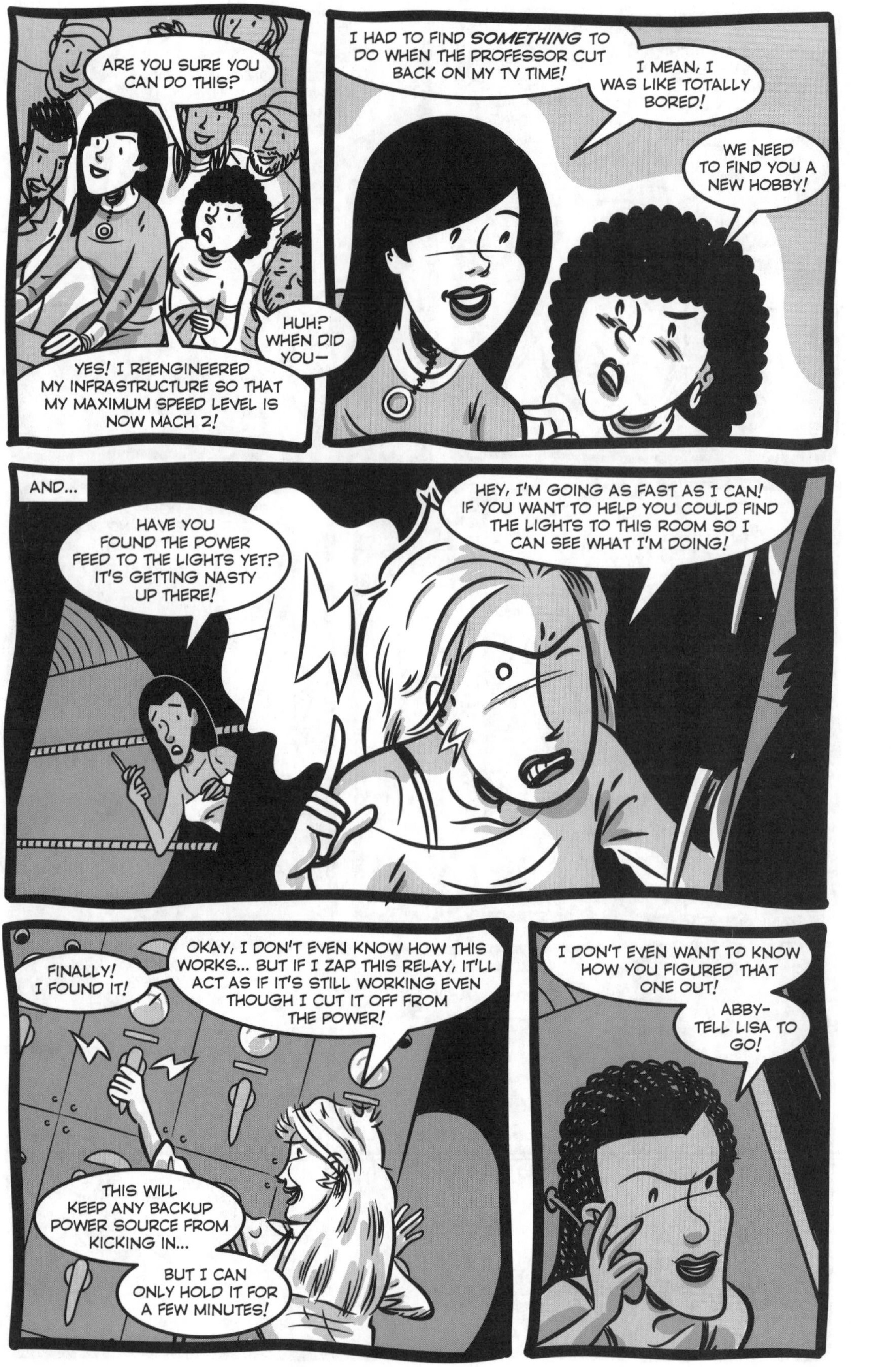
ARE YOU SURE YOU CAN DO THIS?
YES! I REENGINEERED MY INFRASTRUCTURE SO THAT MY MAXIMUM SPEED LEVEL IS NOW MACH 2!
HUH? WHEN DID YOU—
I HAD TO FIND SOMETHING TO DO WHEN THE PROFESSOR CUT BACK ON MY TV TIME!
I MEAN, I WAS LIKE TOTALLY BORED!
WE NEED TO FIND YOU A NEW HOBBY!
AND...
HAVE YOU FOUND THE POWER FEED TO THE LIGHTS YET? IT'S GETTING NASTY UP THERE!
HEY, I'M GOING AS FAST AS I CAN! IF YOU WANT TO HELP YOU COULD FIND THE LIGHTS TO THIS ROOM SO I CAN SEE WHAT I'M DOING!
FINALLY! I FOUND IT!
OKAY, I DON'T EVEN KNOW HOW THIS WORKS... BUT IF I ZAP THIS RELAY, IT'LL ACT AS IF IT'S STILL WORKING EVEN THOUGH I CUT IT OFF FROM THE POWER!
THIS WILL KEEP ANY BACKUP POWER SOURCE FROM KICKING IN...
BUT I CAN ONLY HOLD IT FOR A FEW MINUTES!
I DON'T EVEN WANT TO KNOW HOW YOU FIGURED THAT ONE OUT!
ABBY- TELL LISA TO GO!

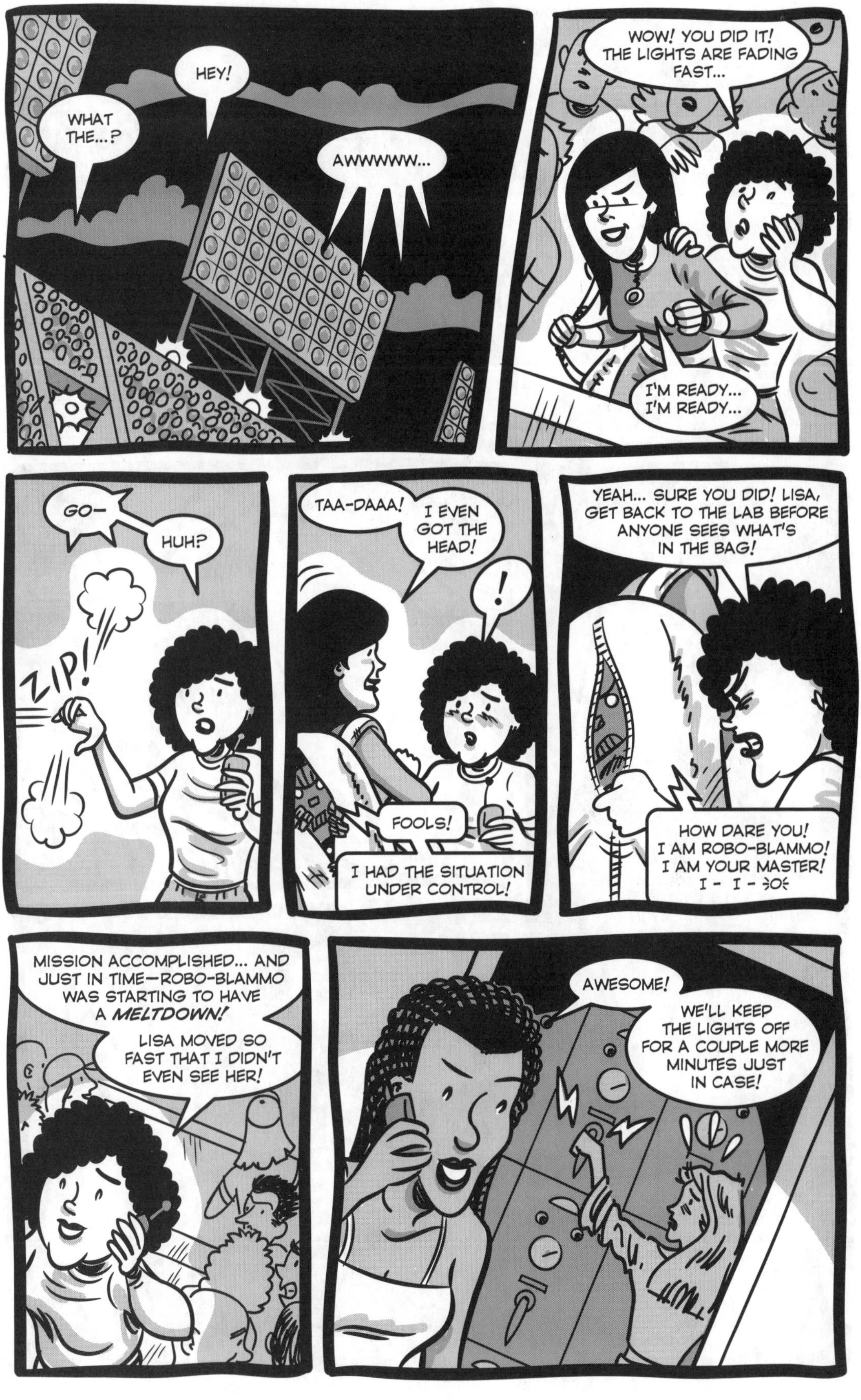
WHAT THE...?
HEY!
AWWWWW...
WOW! YOU DID IT! THE LIGHTS ARE FADING FAST...
I'M READY... I'M READY...
GO—
HUH?
ZIP!!
TAA-DAAA!
I EVEN GOT THE HEAD!
!
FOOLS!
I HAD THE SITUATION UNDER CONTROL!
YEAH... SURE YOU DID! LISA, GET BACK TO THE LAB BEFORE ANYONE SEES WHAT'S IN THE BAG!
HOW DARE YOU! I AM ROBO-BLAMMO! I AM YOUR MASTER! I - I -
MISSION ACCOMPLISHED... AND JUST IN TIME—ROBO-BLAMMO WAS STARTING TO HAVE A *MELTDOWN!*
LISA MOVED SO FAST THAT I DIDN'T EVEN SEE HER!
AWESOME!
WE'LL KEEP THE LIGHTS OFF FOR A COUPLE MORE MINUTES JUST IN CASE!

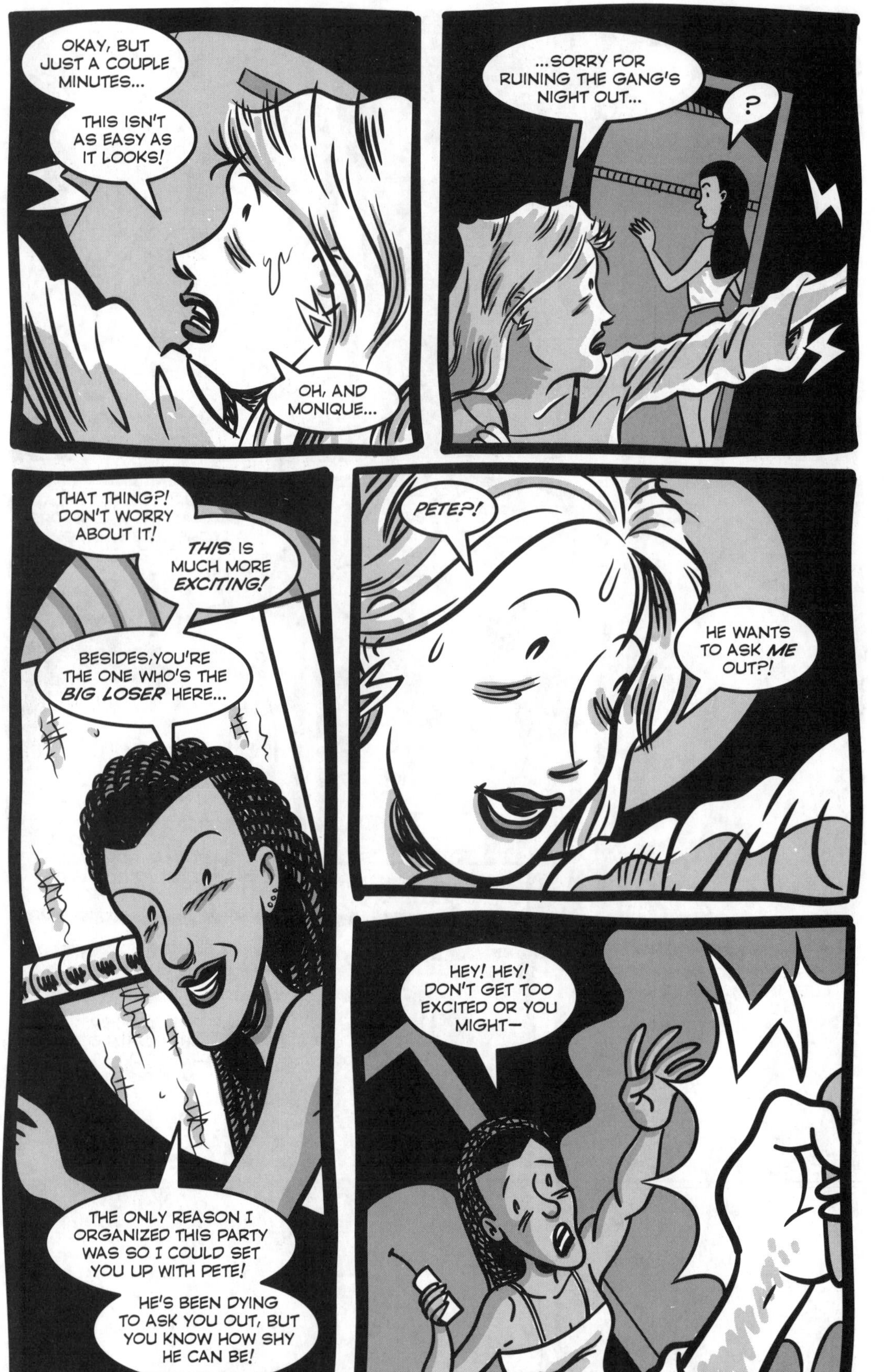
OKAY, BUT JUST A COUPLE MINUTES...
THIS ISN'T AS EASY AS IT LOOKS!
OH, AND MONIQUE...
...SORRY FOR RUINING THE GANG'S NIGHT OUT...
?
THAT THING?! DON'T WORRY ABOUT IT!
THIS IS MUCH MORE *EXCITING!*
BESIDES,YOU'RE THE ONE WHO'S THE *BIG LOSER* HERE...
THE ONLY REASON I ORGANIZED THIS PARTY WAS SO I COULD SET YOU UP WITH PETE!
HE'S BEEN DYING TO ASK YOU OUT, BUT YOU KNOW HOW SHY HE CAN BE!
PETE?!
HE WANTS TO ASK *ME* OUT?!
HEY! HEY! DON'T GET TOO EXCITED OR YOU MIGHT—

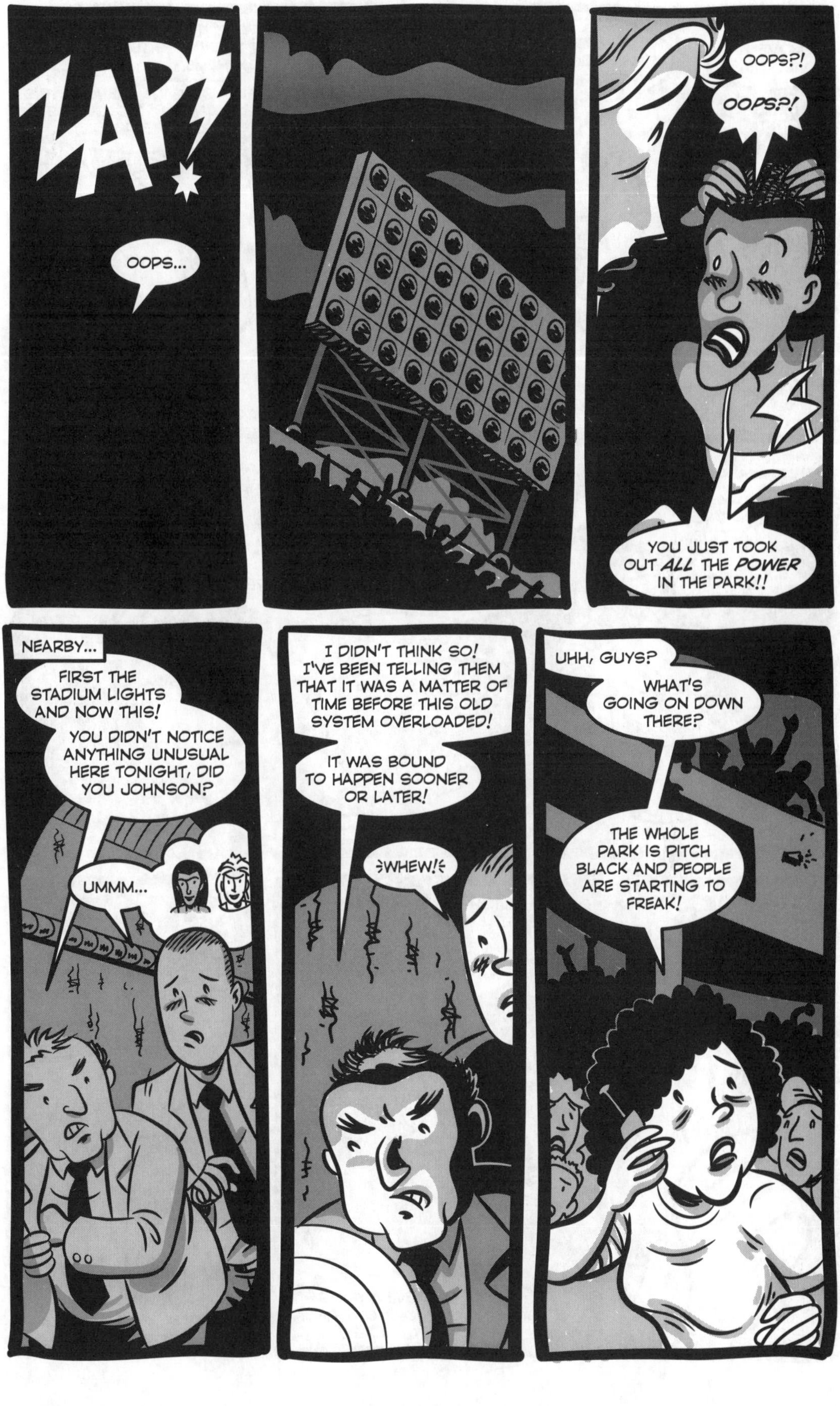
ZAP!
OOPS...
OOPS?!
OOPS?!
YOU JUST TOOK OUT ALL THE POWER IN THE PARK!!
NEARBY...
FIRST THE STADIUM LIGHTS AND NOW THIS!
YOU DIDN'T NOTICE ANYTHING UNUSUAL HERE TONIGHT, DID YOU JOHNSON?
UMMM...
I DIDN'T THINK SO! I'VE BEEN TELLING THEM THAT IT WAS A MATTER OF TIME BEFORE THIS OLD SYSTEM OVERLOADED!
IT WAS BOUND TO HAPPEN SOONER OR LATER!
WHEW!
UHH, GUYS?
WHAT'S GOING ON DOWN THERE?
THE WHOLE PARK IS PITCH BLACK AND PEOPLE ARE STARTING TO FREAK!

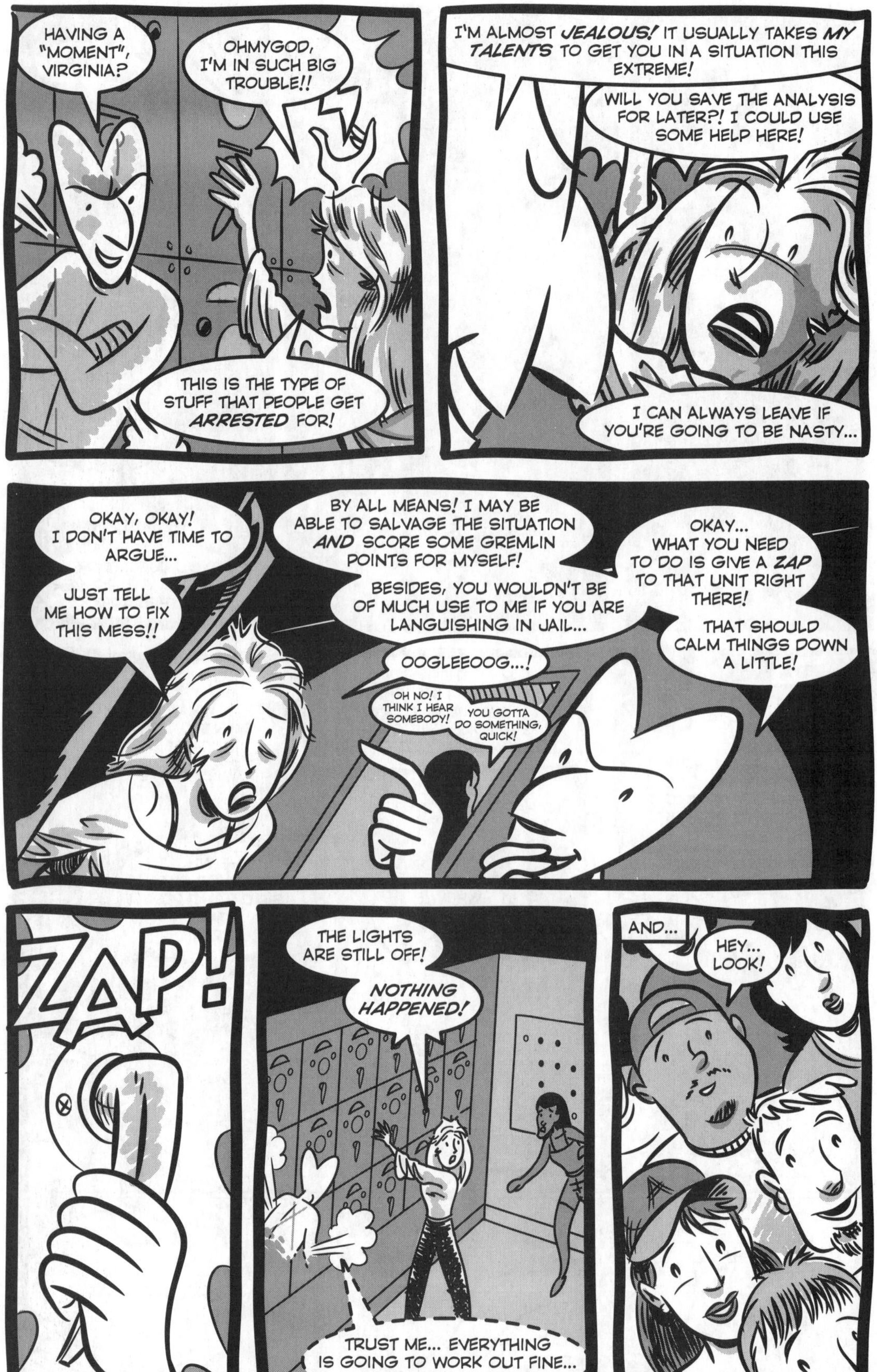
HAVING A "MOMENT", VIRGINIA?
OHMYGOD, I'M IN SUCH BIG TROUBLE!!
THIS IS THE TYPE OF STUFF THAT PEOPLE GET ARRESTED FOR!
I'M ALMOST JEALOUS! IT USUALLY TAKES MY TALENTS TO GET YOU IN A SITUATION THIS EXTREME!
WILL YOU SAVE THE ANALYSIS FOR LATER?! I COULD USE SOME HELP HERE!
I CAN ALWAYS LEAVE IF YOU'RE GOING TO BE NASTY...
OKAY, OKAY! I DON'T HAVE TIME TO ARGUE...
JUST TELL ME HOW TO FIX THIS MESS!!
BY ALL MEANS! I MAY BE ABLE TO SALVAGE THE SITUATION AND SCORE SOME GREMLIN POINTS FOR MYSELF!
BESIDES, YOU WOULDN'T BE OF MUCH USE TO ME IF YOU ARE LANGUISHING IN JAIL...
OOGLEEOOG...!
OH NO! I THINK I HEAR SOMEBODY!
YOU GOTTA DO SOMETHING, QUICK!
OKAY... WHAT YOU NEED TO DO IS GIVE A ZAP TO THAT UNIT RIGHT THERE!
THAT SHOULD CALM THINGS DOWN A LITTLE!
ZAP!
THE LIGHTS ARE STILL OFF!
NOTHING HAPPENED!
TRUST ME... EVERYTHING IS GOING TO WORK OUT FINE... FOR ME, AT LEAST!
AND...
HEY... LOOK!

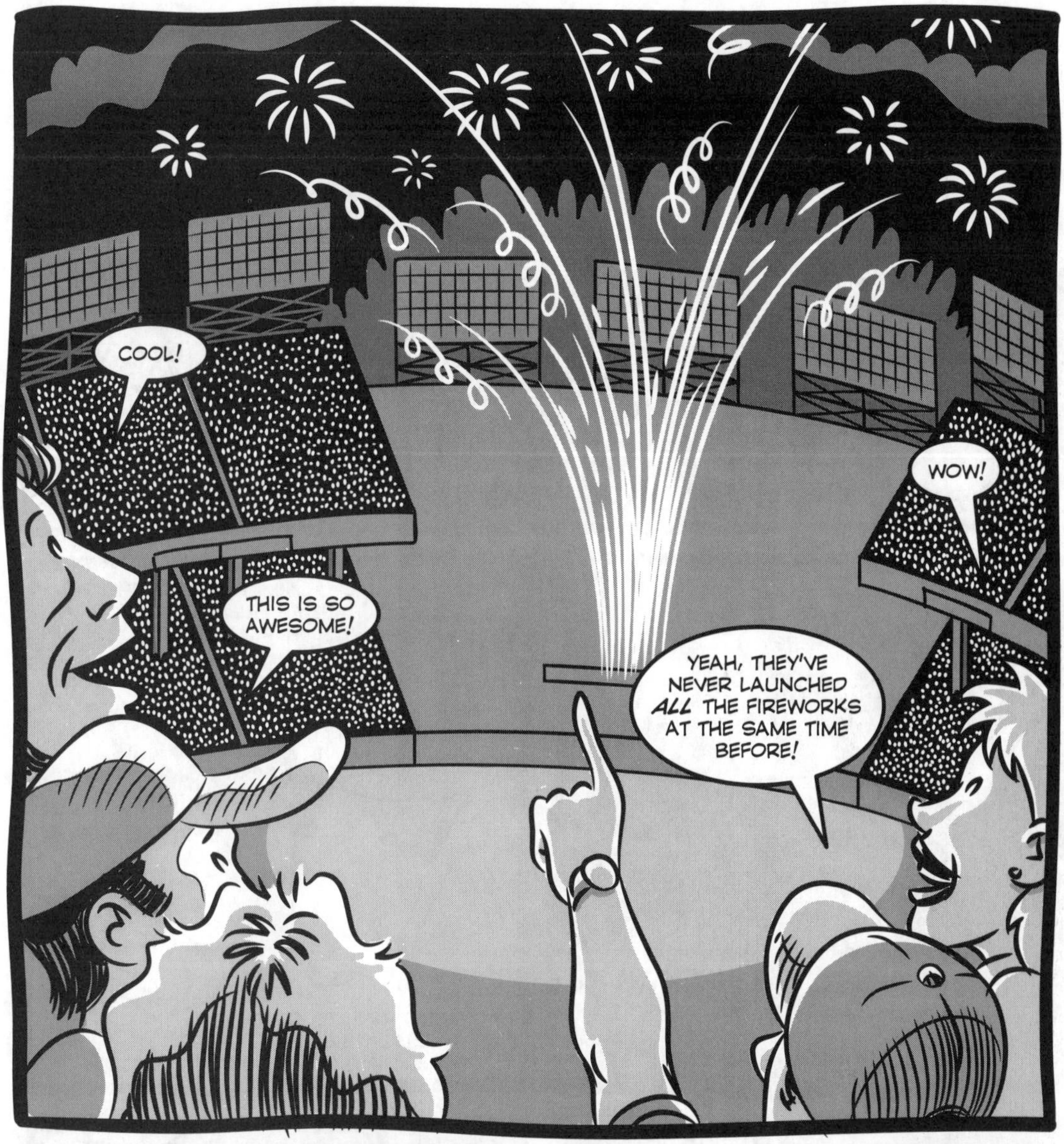
COOL!
THIS IS SO AWESOME!
WOW!
YEAH, THEY'VE NEVER LAUNCHED ALL THE FIREWORKS AT THE SAME TIME BEFORE!

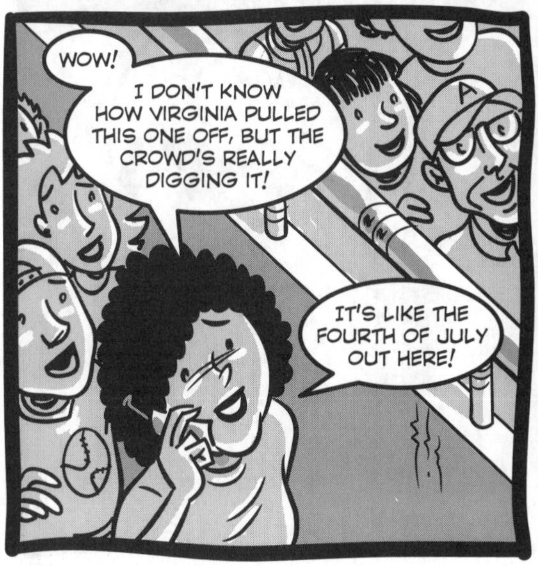
WOW!
I DON'T KNOW HOW VIRGINIA PULLED THIS ONE OFF, BUT THE CROWD'S REALLY DIGGING IT!
IT'S LIKE THE FOURTH OF JULY OUT HERE!

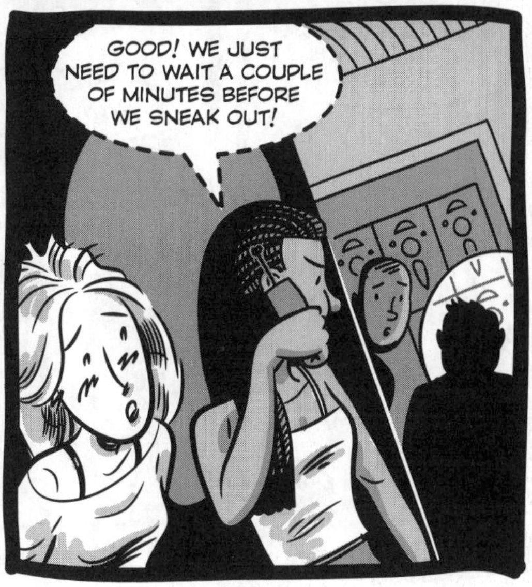
GOOD! WE JUST NEED TO WAIT A COUPLE OF MINUTES BEFORE WE SNEAK OUT!

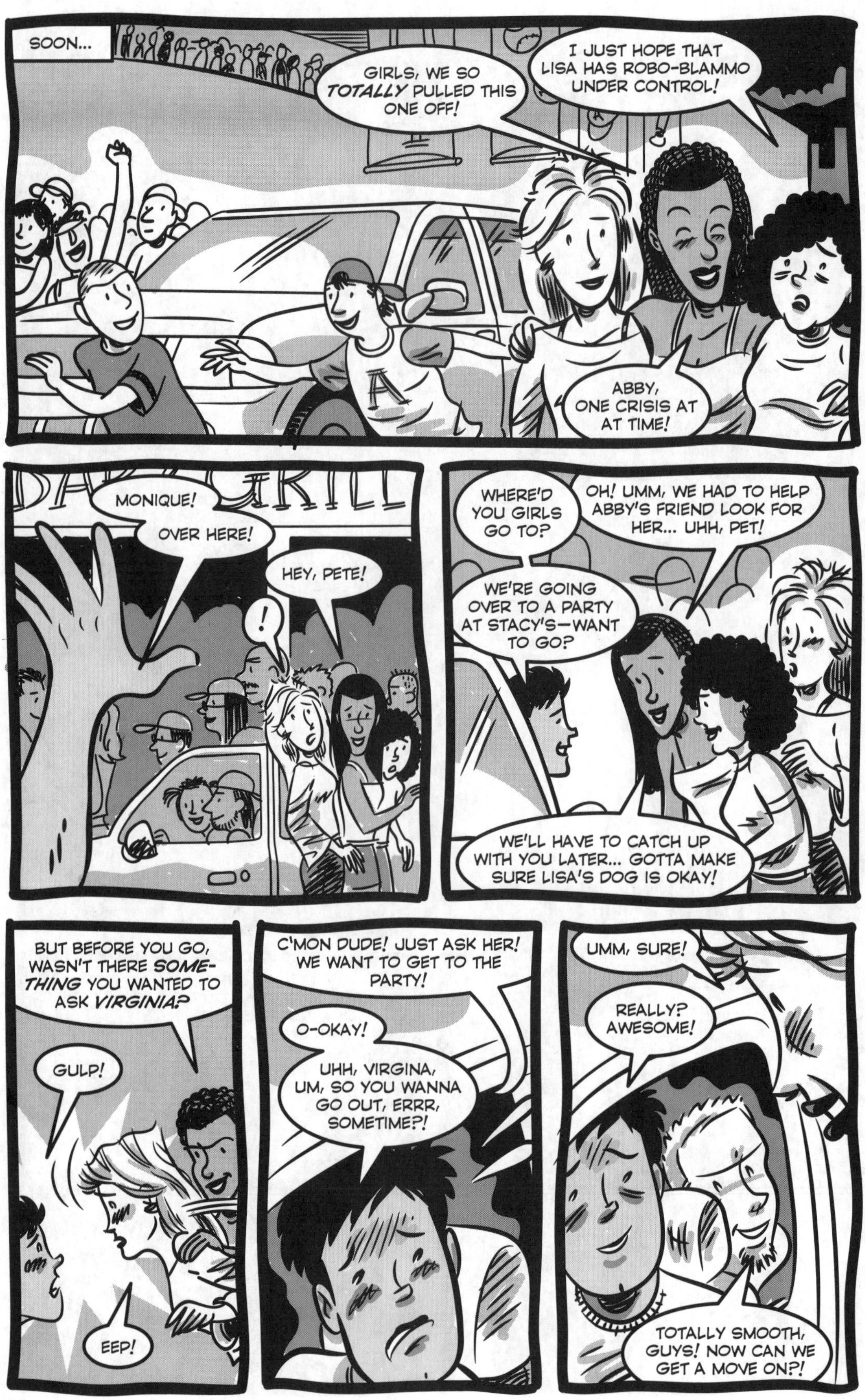
SOON...
GIRLS, WE SO *TOTALLY* PULLED THIS ONE OFF!
I JUST HOPE THAT LISA HAS ROBO-BLAMMO UNDER CONTROL!
ABBY, ONE CRISIS AT AT TIME!
MONIQUE!
OVER HERE!
HEY, PETE!
!
WHERE'D YOU GIRLS GO TO?
OH! UMM, WE HAD TO HELP ABBY'S FRIEND LOOK FOR HER... UHH, PET!
WE'RE GOING OVER TO A PARTY AT STACY'S—WANT TO GO?
WE'LL HAVE TO CATCH UP WITH YOU LATER... GOTTA MAKE SURE LISA'S DOG IS OKAY!
BUT BEFORE YOU GO, WASN'T THERE *SOMETHING* YOU WANTED TO ASK *VIRGINIA*?
GULP!
EEP!
C'MON DUDE! JUST ASK HER! WE WANT TO GET TO THE PARTY!
O-OKAY!
UHH, VIRGINA, UM, SO YOU WANNA GO OUT, ERRR, SOMETIME?!
UMM, SURE!
REALLY? AWESOME!
TOTALLY SMOOTH, GUYS! NOW CAN WE GET A MOVE ON?!

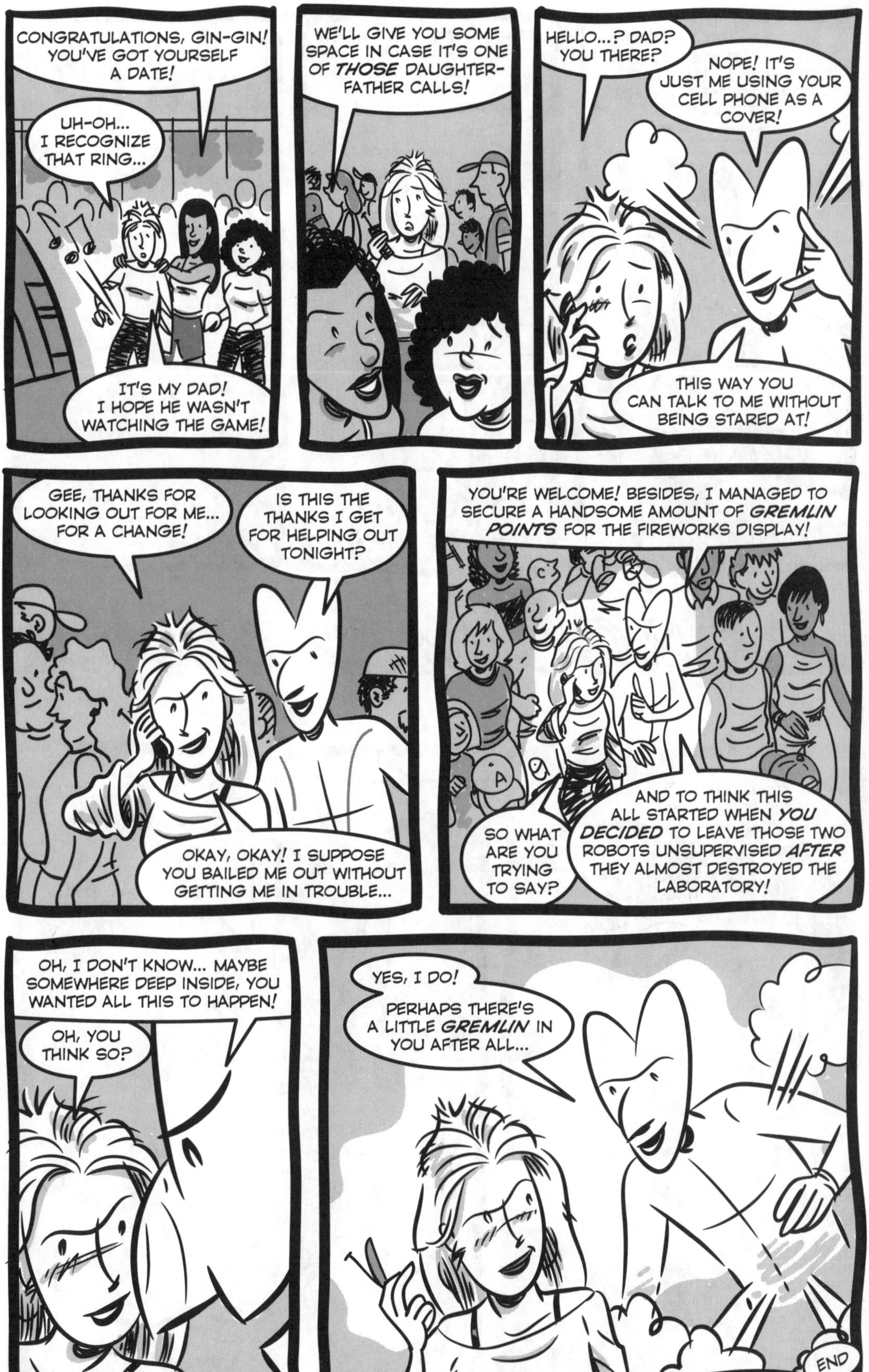
CONGRATULATIONS, GIN-GIN! YOU'VE GOT YOURSELF A DATE!
UH-OH... I RECOGNIZE THAT RING...
IT'S MY DAD! I HOPE HE WASN'T WATCHING THE GAME!
WE'LL GIVE YOU SOME SPACE IN CASE IT'S ONE OF *THOSE* DAUGHTER-FATHER CALLS!
HELLO...? DAD? YOU THERE?
NOPE! IT'S JUST ME USING YOUR CELL PHONE AS A COVER!
THIS WAY YOU CAN TALK TO ME WITHOUT BEING STARED AT!
GEE, THANKS FOR LOOKING OUT FOR ME... FOR A CHANGE!
IS THIS THE THANKS I GET FOR HELPING OUT TONIGHT?
OKAY, OKAY! I SUPPOSE YOU BAILED ME OUT WITHOUT GETTING ME IN TROUBLE...
YOU'RE WELCOME! BESIDES, I MANAGED TO SECURE A HANDSOME AMOUNT OF *GREMLIN POINTS* FOR THE FIREWORKS DISPLAY!
AND TO THINK THIS ALL STARTED WHEN *YOU DECIDED* TO LEAVE THOSE TWO ROBOTS UNSUPERVISED *AFTER* THEY ALMOST DESTROYED THE LABORATORY!
SO WHAT ARE YOU TRYING TO SAY?
OH, I DON'T KNOW... MAYBE SOMEWHERE DEEP INSIDE, YOU WANTED ALL THIS TO HAPPEN!
OH, YOU THINK SO?
YES, I DO!
PERHAPS THERE'S A LITTLE *GREMLIN* IN YOU AFTER ALL...
END

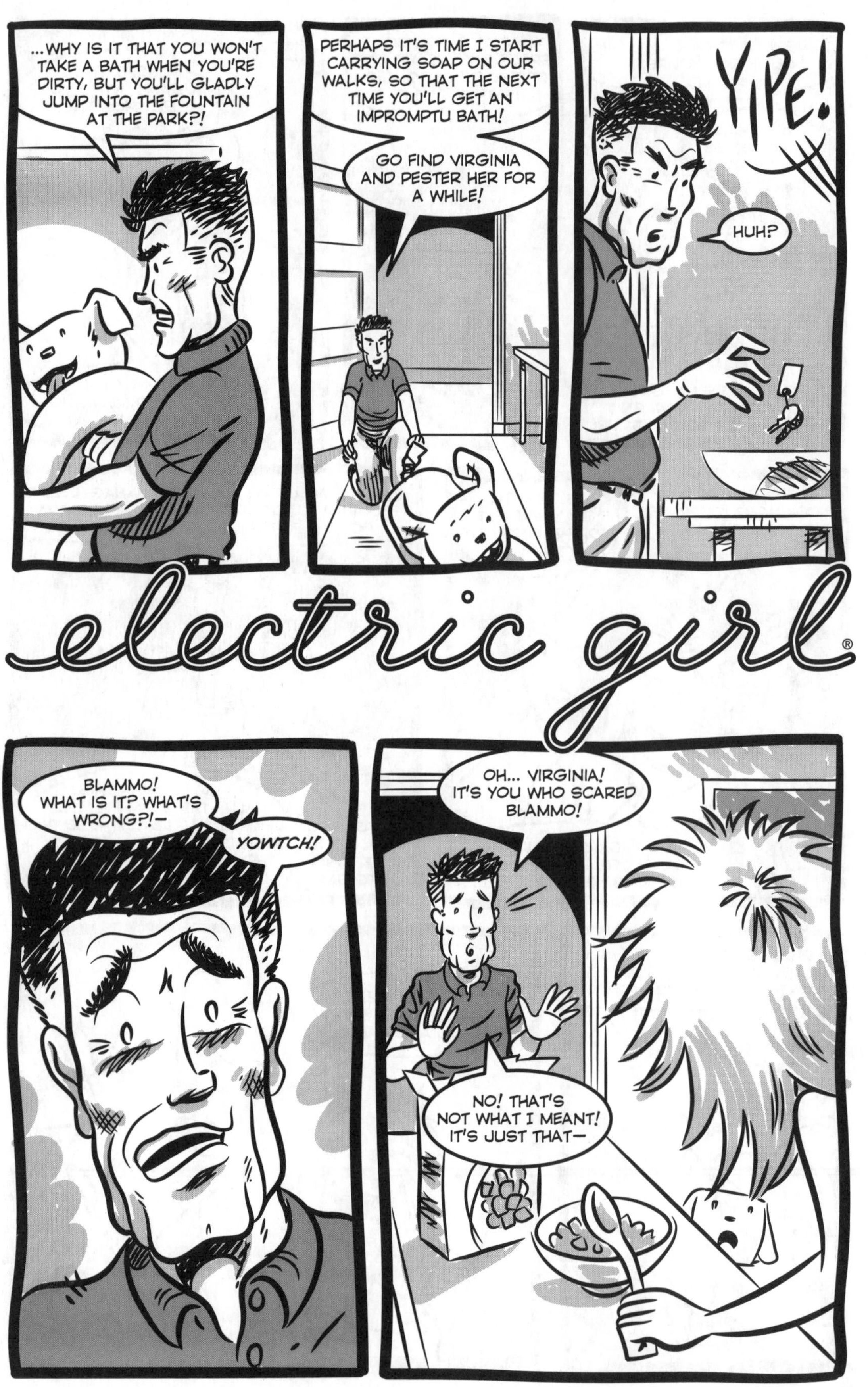
...WHY IS IT THAT YOU WON'T TAKE A BATH WHEN YOU'RE DIRTY, BUT YOU'LL GLADLY JUMP INTO THE FOUNTAIN AT THE PARK?!
PERHAPS IT'S TIME I START CARRYING SOAP ON OUR WALKS, SO THAT THE NEXT TIME YOU'LL GET AN IMPROMPTU BATH!
GO FIND VIRGINIA AND PESTER HER FOR A WHILE!
YIPE!
HUH?
electric girl®
BLAMMO! WHAT IS IT? WHAT'S WRONG?!–
YOWTCH!
OH... VIRGINIA! IT'S YOU WHO SCARED BLAMMO!
NO! THAT'S NOT WHAT I MEANT! IT'S JUST THAT–

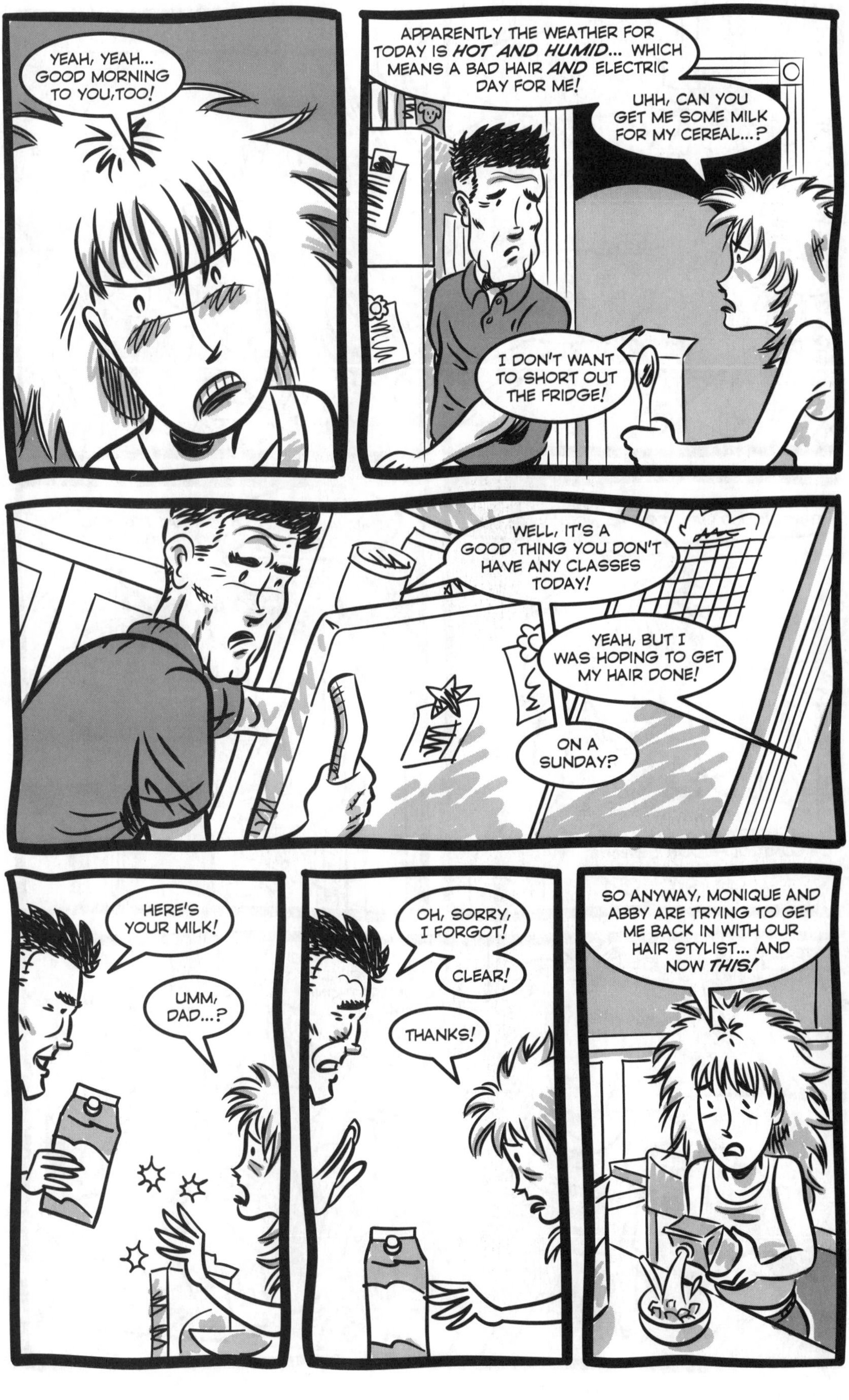
YEAH, YEAH... GOOD MORNING TO YOU,TOO!
APPARENTLY THE WEATHER FOR TODAY IS *HOT AND HUMID*... WHICH MEANS A BAD HAIR *AND* ELECTRIC DAY FOR ME!
UHH, CAN YOU GET ME SOME MILK FOR MY CEREAL...?
I DON'T WANT TO SHORT OUT THE FRIDGE!
WELL, IT'S A GOOD THING YOU DON'T HAVE ANY CLASSES TODAY!
YEAH, BUT I WAS HOPING TO GET MY HAIR DONE!
ON A SUNDAY?
HERE'S YOUR MILK!
UMM, DAD...?
OH, SORRY, I FORGOT!
CLEAR!
THANKS!
SO ANYWAY, MONIQUE AND ABBY ARE TRYING TO GET ME BACK IN WITH OUR HAIR STYLIST... AND NOW *THIS!*

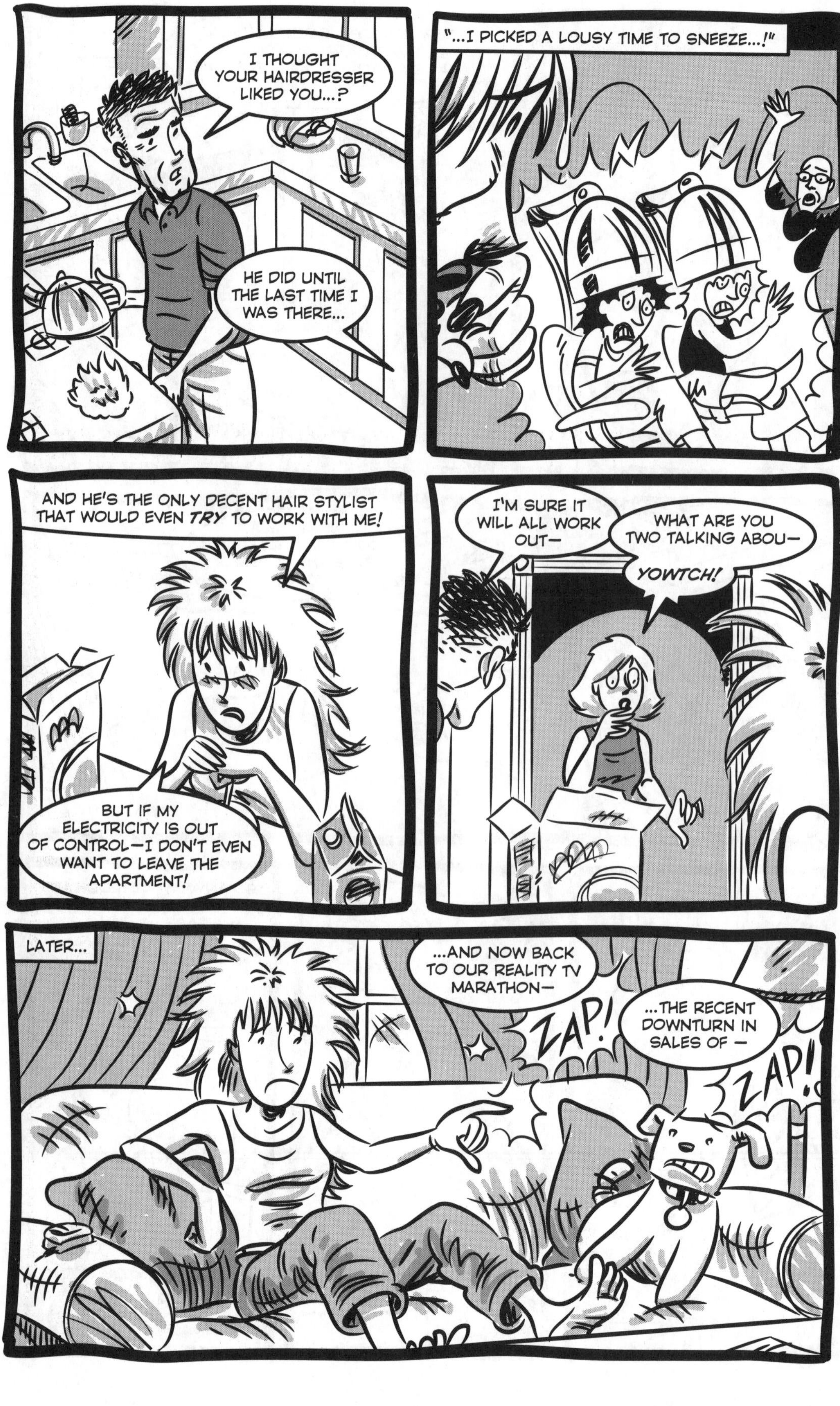
I THOUGHT YOUR HAIRDRESSER LIKED YOU...?
HE DID UNTIL THE LAST TIME I WAS THERE...
"...I PICKED A LOUSY TIME TO SNEEZE...!"
AND HE'S THE ONLY DECENT HAIR STYLIST THAT WOULD EVEN *TRY* TO WORK WITH ME!
BUT IF MY ELECTRICITY IS OUT OF CONTROL—I DON'T EVEN WANT TO LEAVE THE APARTMENT!
I'M SURE IT WILL ALL WORK OUT—
WHAT ARE YOU TWO TALKING ABOU—
YOWTCH!
LATER...
...AND NOW BACK TO OUR REALITY TV MARATHON—
ZAP!
...THE RECENT DOWNTURN IN SALES OF —
ZAP!

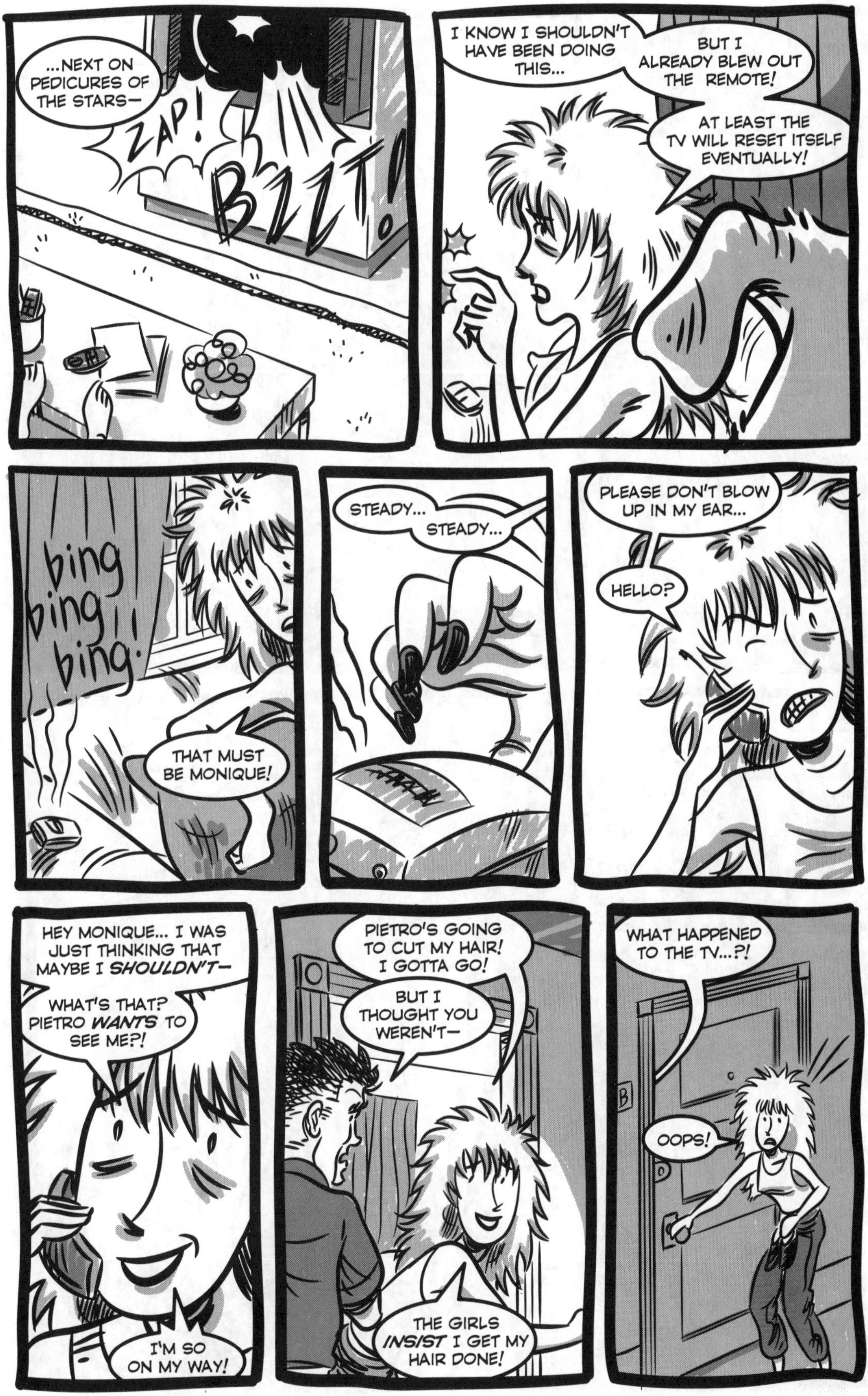
...NEXT ON PEDICURES OF THE STARS—
ZAP!
BZZT!
I KNOW I SHOULDN'T HAVE BEEN DOING THIS...
BUT I ALREADY BLEW OUT THE REMOTE!
AT LEAST THE TV WILL RESET ITSELF EVENTUALLY!
bing bing bing!
THAT MUST BE MONIQUE!
STEADY...
STEADY...
PLEASE DON'T BLOW UP IN MY EAR...
HELLO?
HEY MONIQUE... I WAS JUST THINKING THAT MAYBE I *SHOULDN'T*—
WHAT'S THAT? PIETRO *WANTS* TO SEE ME?!
I'M SO ON MY WAY!
PIETRO'S GOING TO CUT MY HAIR! I GOTTA GO!
BUT I THOUGHT YOU WEREN'T—
THE GIRLS *INSIST* I GET MY HAIR DONE!
WHAT HAPPENED TO THE TV...?!
B
OOPS!

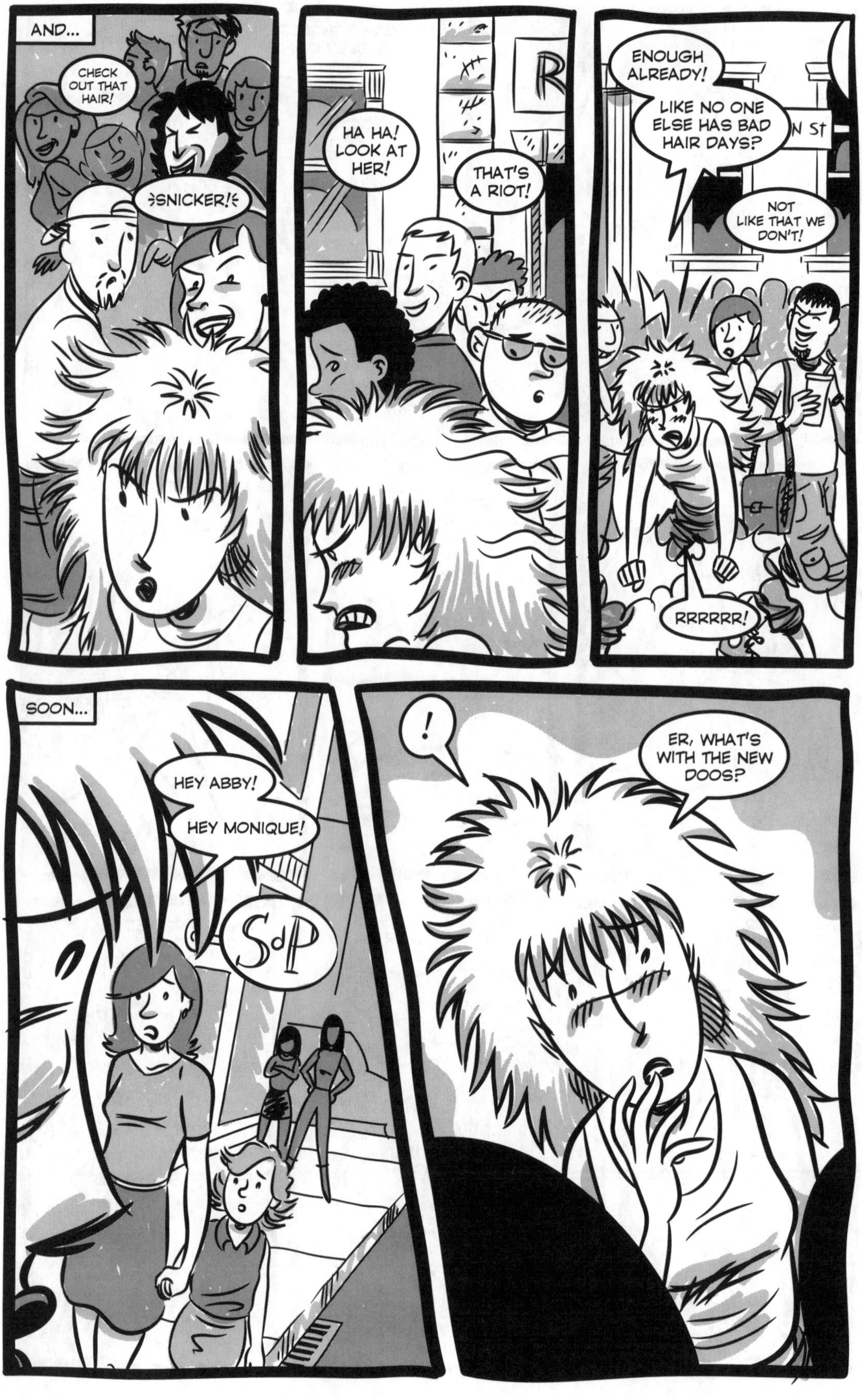
AND...
CHECK OUT THAT HAIR!
SNICKER!
HA HA! LOOK AT HER!
THAT'S A RIOT!
ENOUGH ALREADY!
LIKE NO ONE ELSE HAS BAD HAIR DAYS?
NOT LIKE THAT WE DON'T!
RRRRRR!
SOON...
HEY ABBY!
HEY MONIQUE!
!
ER, WHAT'S WITH THE NEW DOOS?

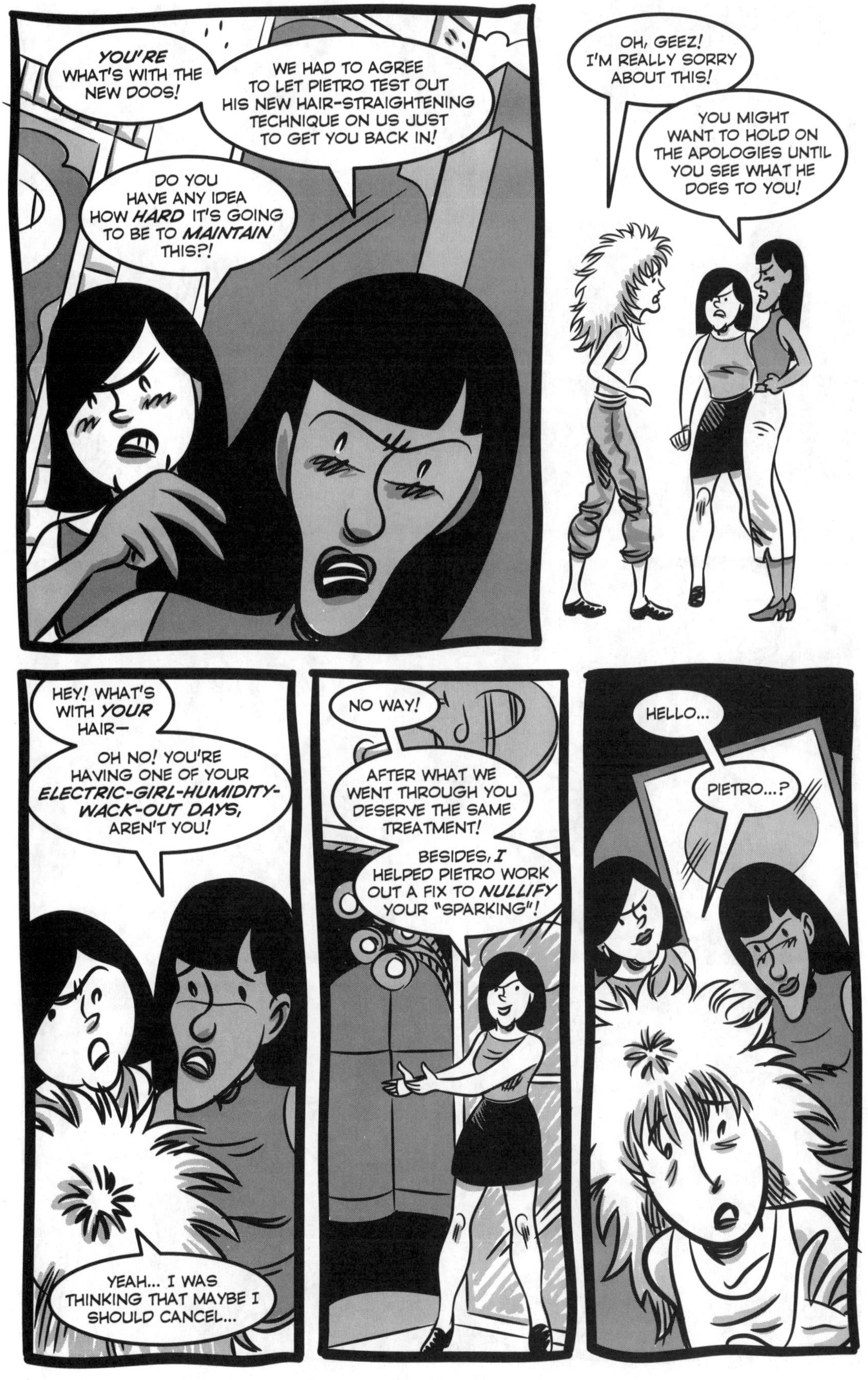
YOU'RE WHAT'S WITH THE NEW DOOS!
WE HAD TO AGREE TO LET PIETRO TEST OUT HIS NEW HAIR-STRAIGHTENING TECHNIQUE ON US JUST TO GET YOU BACK IN!
DO YOU HAVE ANY IDEA HOW HARD IT'S GOING TO BE TO MAINTAIN THIS?!
OH, GEEZ! I'M REALLY SORRY ABOUT THIS!
YOU MIGHT WANT TO HOLD ON THE APOLOGIES UNTIL YOU SEE WHAT HE DOES TO YOU!
HEY! WHAT'S WITH YOUR HAIR—
OH NO! YOU'RE HAVING ONE OF YOUR ELECTRIC-GIRL-HUMIDITY-WACK-OUT DAYS, AREN'T YOU!
YEAH... I WAS THINKING THAT MAYBE I SHOULD CANCEL...
NO WAY!
AFTER WHAT WE WENT THROUGH YOU DESERVE THE SAME TREATMENT!
BESIDES, I HELPED PIETRO WORK OUT A FIX TO NULLIFY YOUR "SPARKING"!
HELLO...
PIETRO...?

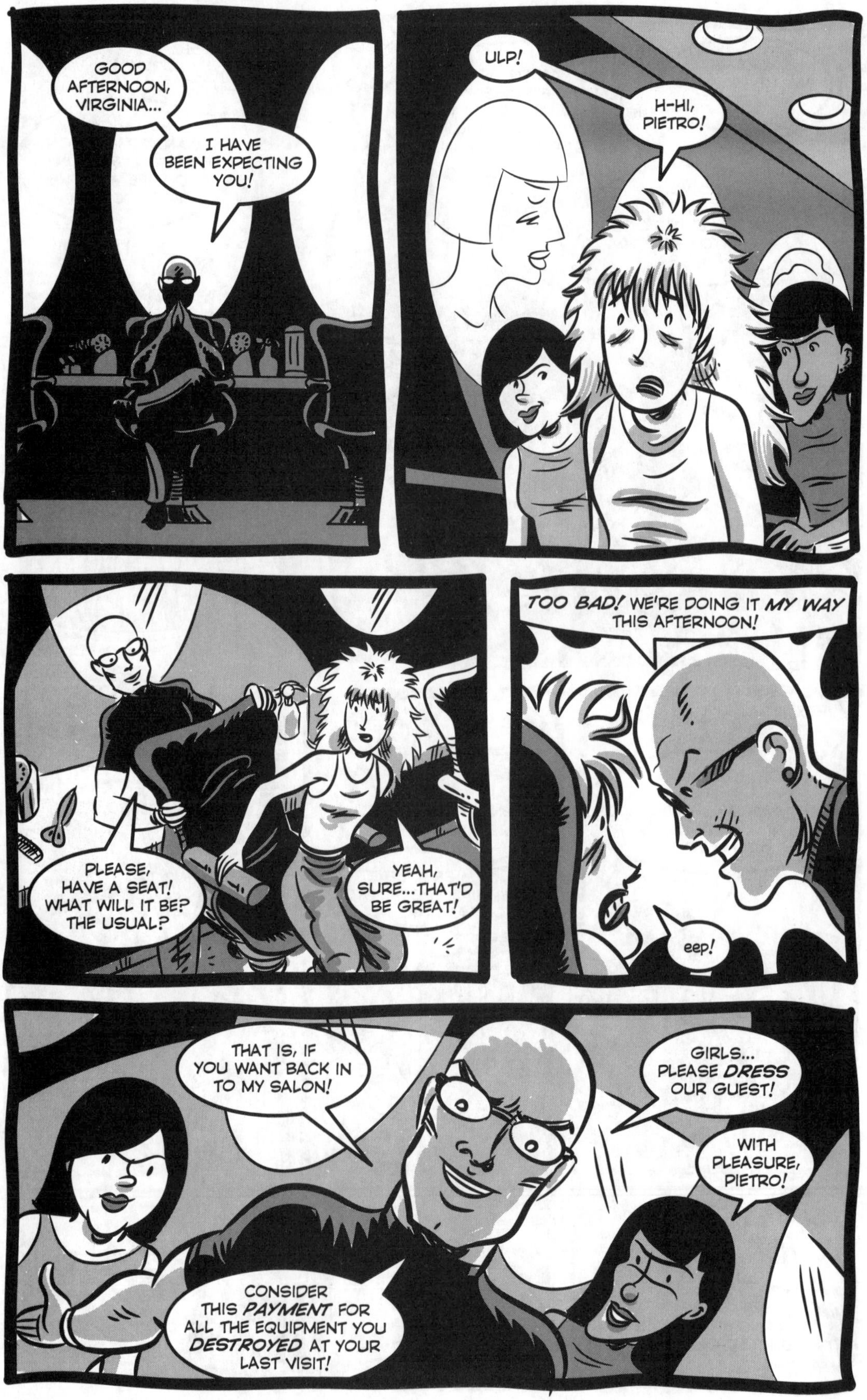
GOOD AFTERNOON, VIRGINIA...
I HAVE BEEN EXPECTING YOU!
ULP!
H-HI, PIETRO!
PLEASE, HAVE A SEAT! WHAT WILL IT BE? THE USUAL?
YEAH, SURE...THAT'D BE GREAT!
TOO BAD! WE'RE DOING IT MY WAY THIS AFTERNOON!
eep!
THAT IS, IF YOU WANT BACK IN TO MY SALON!
GIRLS... PLEASE DRESS OUR GUEST!
WITH PLEASURE, PIETRO!
CONSIDER THIS PAYMENT FOR ALL THE EQUIPMENT YOU DESTROYED AT YOUR LAST VISIT!

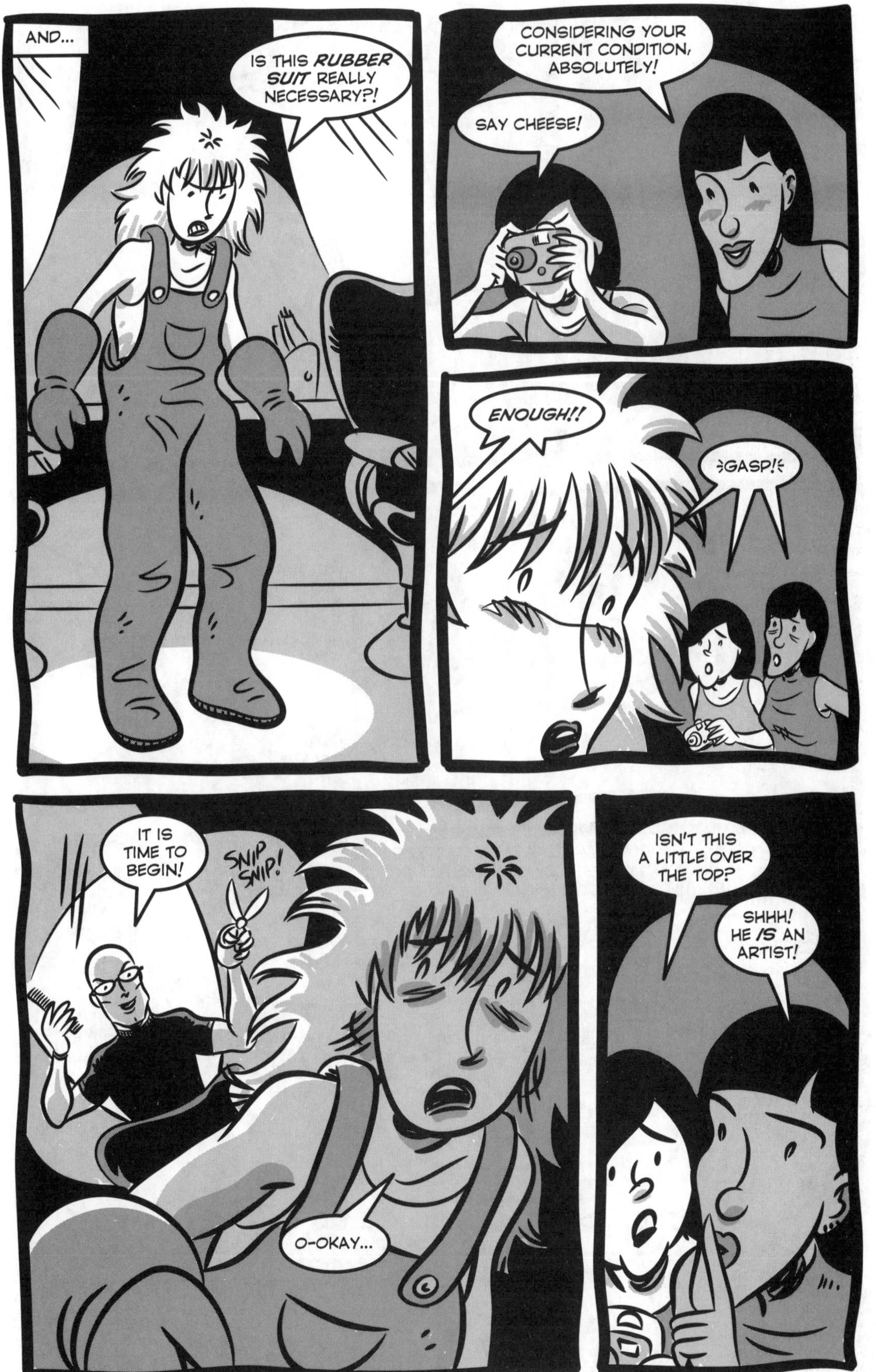
AND...
IS THIS RUBBER SUIT REALLY NECESSARY?!
CONSIDERING YOUR CURRENT CONDITION, ABSOLUTELY!
SAY CHEESE!
ENOUGH!!
GASP!
IT IS TIME TO BEGIN!
SNIP SNIP!
O-OKAY...
ISN'T THIS A LITTLE OVER THE TOP?
SHHH! HE IS AN ARTIST!

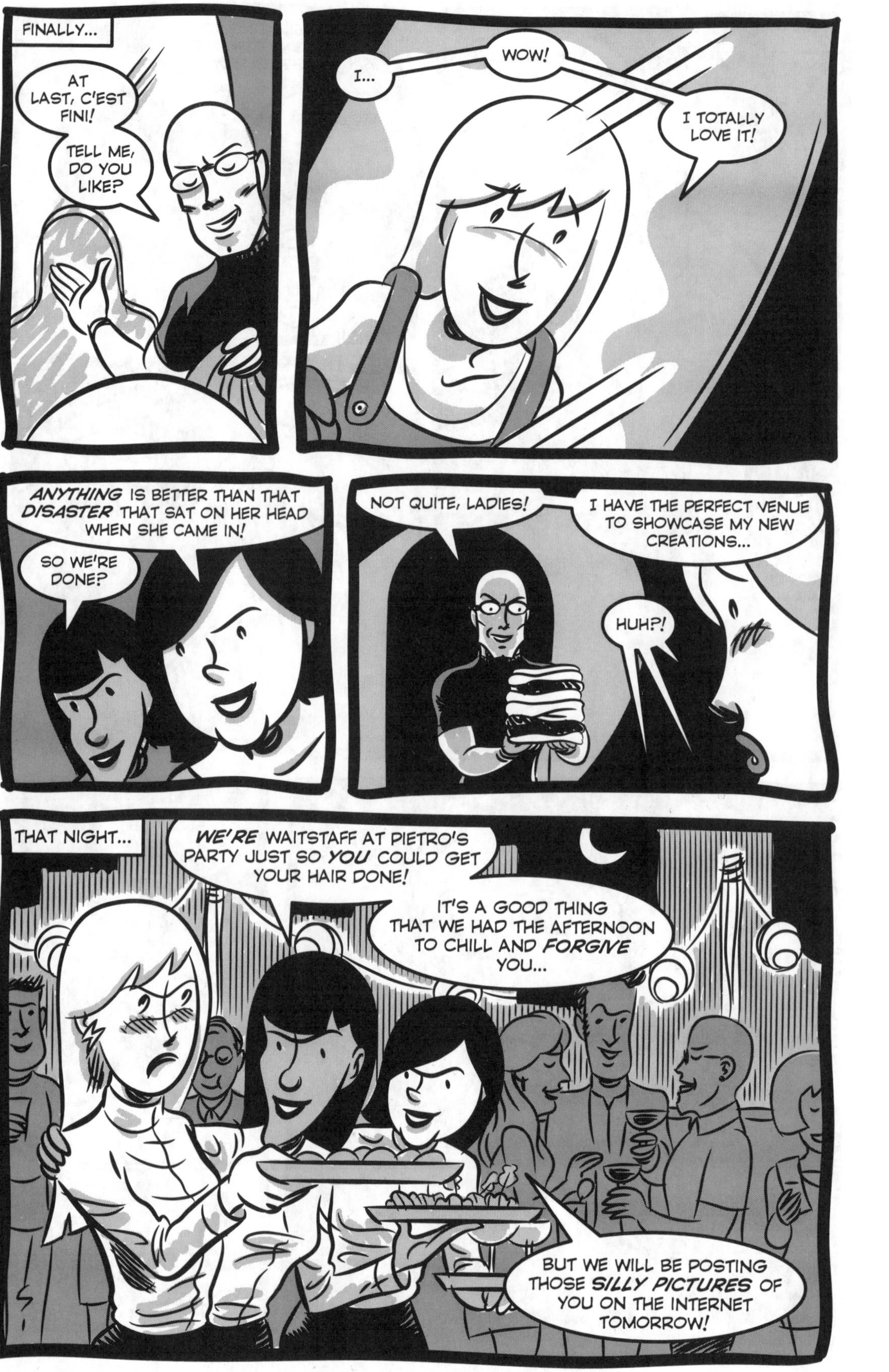
FINALLY...
AT LAST, C'EST FINI!
TELL ME, DO YOU LIKE?
I...
WOW!
I TOTALLY LOVE IT!
ANYTHING IS BETTER THAN THAT DISASTER THAT SAT ON HER HEAD WHEN SHE CAME IN!
SO WE'RE DONE?
NOT QUITE, LADIES!
I HAVE THE PERFECT VENUE TO SHOWCASE MY NEW CREATIONS...
HUH?!
THAT NIGHT...
WE'RE WAITSTAFF AT PIETRO'S PARTY JUST SO YOU COULD GET YOUR HAIR DONE!
IT'S A GOOD THING THAT WE HAD THE AFTERNOON TO CHILL AND FORGIVE YOU...
BUT WE WILL BE POSTING THOSE SILLY PICTURES OF YOU ON THE INTERNET TOMORROW!

electric girl etcetera

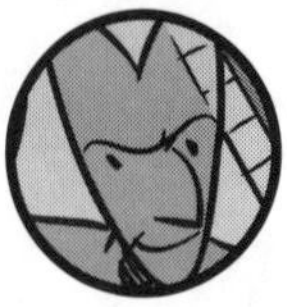

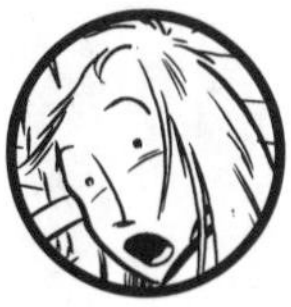

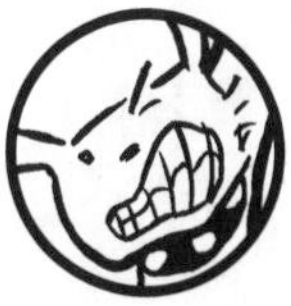

Covers and mini-posters from Electric Girl #9 and Electric Girl #10, and a pre-Electric Girl #1 story showing a slightly different approach to the Electric Girl characters...

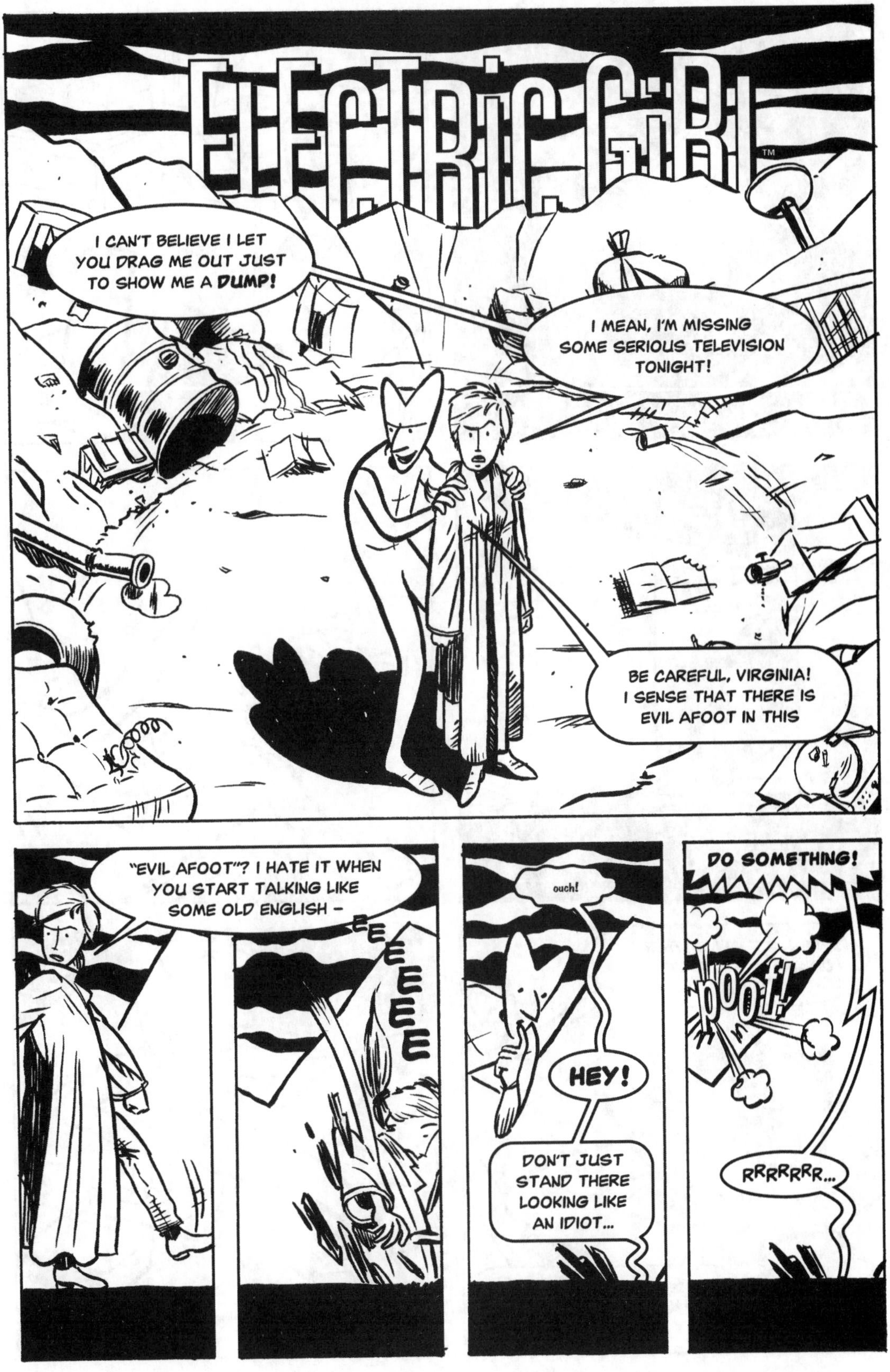
ELECTRIC GIRL™
I CAN'T BELIEVE I LET YOU DRAG ME OUT JUST TO SHOW ME A DUMP!
I MEAN, I'M MISSING SOME SERIOUS TELEVISION TONIGHT!
BE CAREFUL, VIRGINIA! I SENSE THAT THERE IS EVIL AFOOT IN THIS
"EVIL AFOOT"? I HATE IT WHEN YOU START TALKING LIKE SOME OLD ENGLISH –
EEEEEE
ouch!
HEY!
DON'T JUST STAND THERE LOOKING LIKE AN IDIOT...
DO SOMETHING!
pOOf!
RRRRRR...

This was the first take on the main story featured in the first Electric Girl comic book. While I eventually created a different version of the story to expand upon the characters' interactions, I always liked this different visual style that I experimented with. (created in 1996)

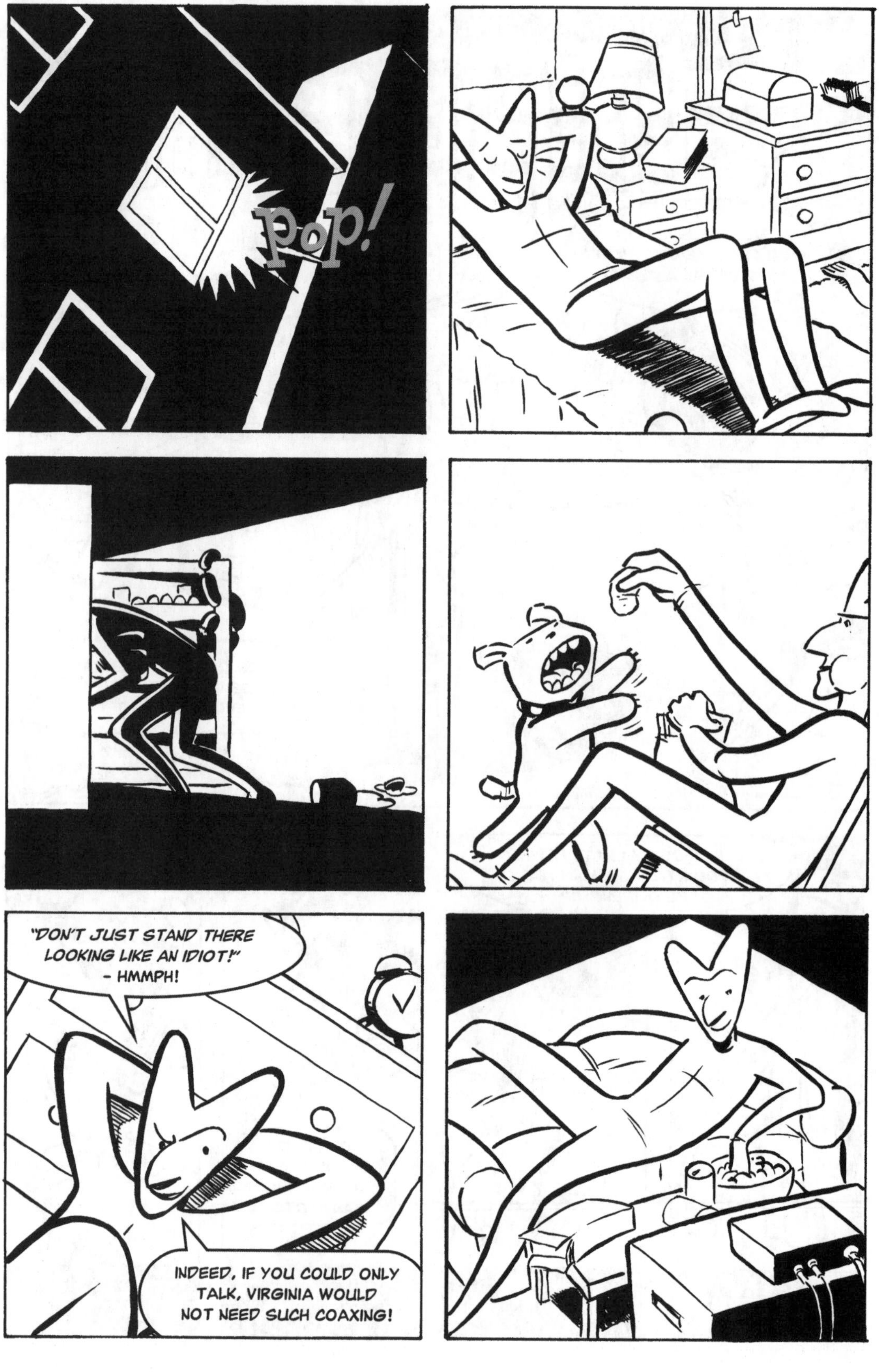
Pop!
"DON'T JUST STAND THERE LOOKING LIKE AN IDIOT!" - HMMPH!
INDEED, IF YOU COULD ONLY TALK, VIRGINIA WOULD NOT NEED SUCH COAXING!

I CERTAINLY HOPE THAT VIRGINIA HURRIES BACK SOON... I AM RUNNING OUT OF THINGS TO DO TO ENTERTAIN MYSELF!

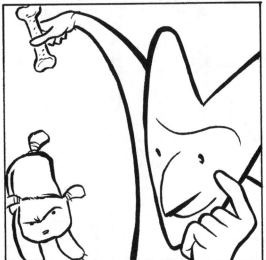

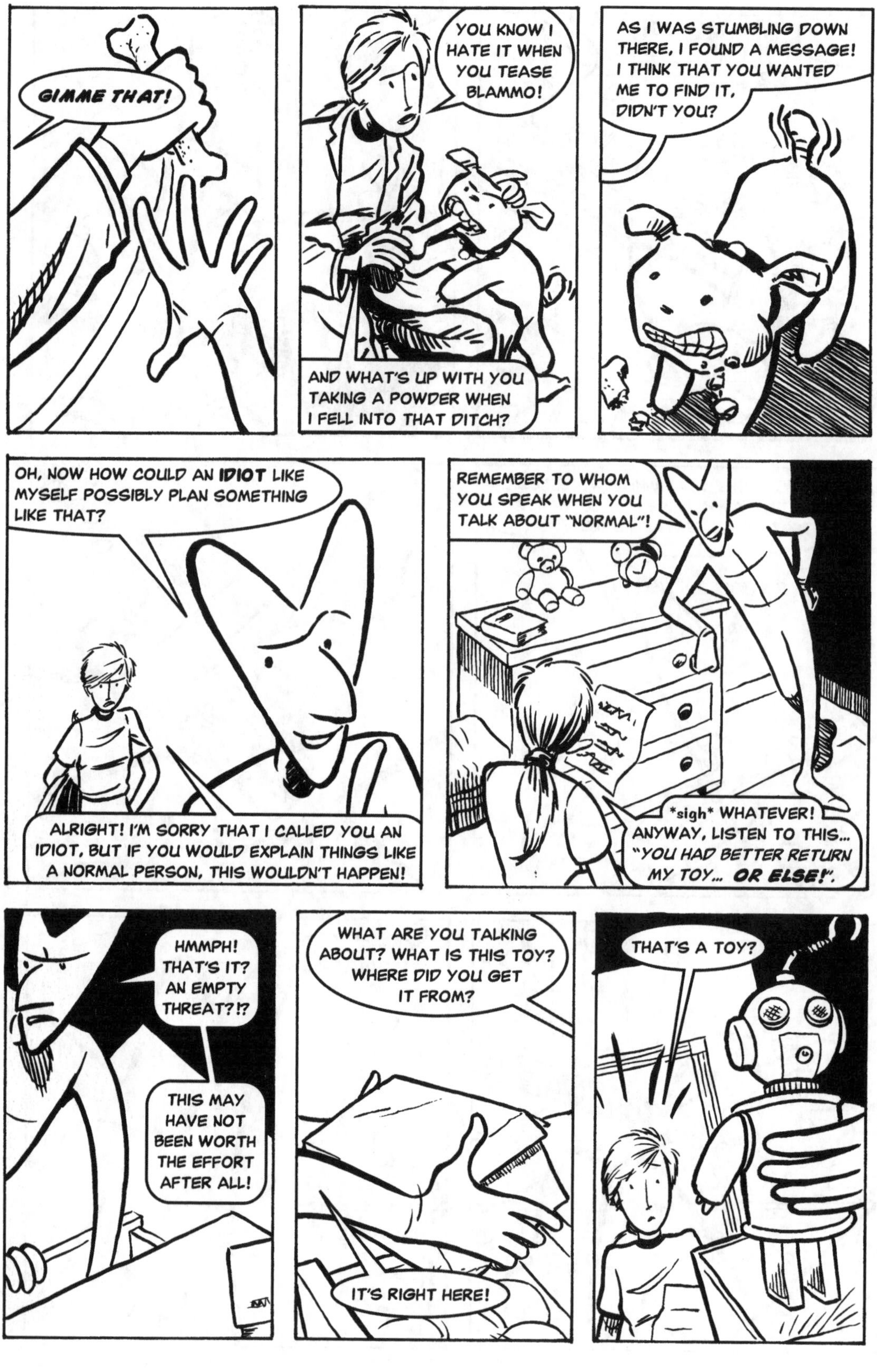
GIMME THAT!
YOU KNOW I HATE IT WHEN YOU TEASE BLAMMO!
AND WHAT'S UP WITH YOU TAKING A POWDER WHEN I FELL INTO THAT DITCH?
AS I WAS STUMBLING DOWN THERE, I FOUND A MESSAGE! I THINK THAT YOU WANTED ME TO FIND IT, DIDN'T YOU?
OH, NOW HOW COULD AN IDIOT LIKE MYSELF POSSIBLY PLAN SOMETHING LIKE THAT?
ALRIGHT! I'M SORRY THAT I CALLED YOU AN IDIOT, BUT IF YOU WOULD EXPLAIN THINGS LIKE A NORMAL PERSON, THIS WOULDN'T HAPPEN!
REMEMBER TO WHOM YOU SPEAK WHEN YOU TALK ABOUT "NORMAL"!
sigh WHATEVER! ANYWAY, LISTEN TO THIS... "YOU HAD BETTER RETURN MY TOY... OR ELSE!".
HMMPH! THAT'S IT? AN EMPTY THREAT?!?
THIS MAY HAVE NOT BEEN WORTH THE EFFORT AFTER ALL!
WHAT ARE YOU TALKING ABOUT? WHAT IS THIS TOY? WHERE DID YOU GET IT FROM?
IT'S RIGHT HERE!
THAT'S A TOY?

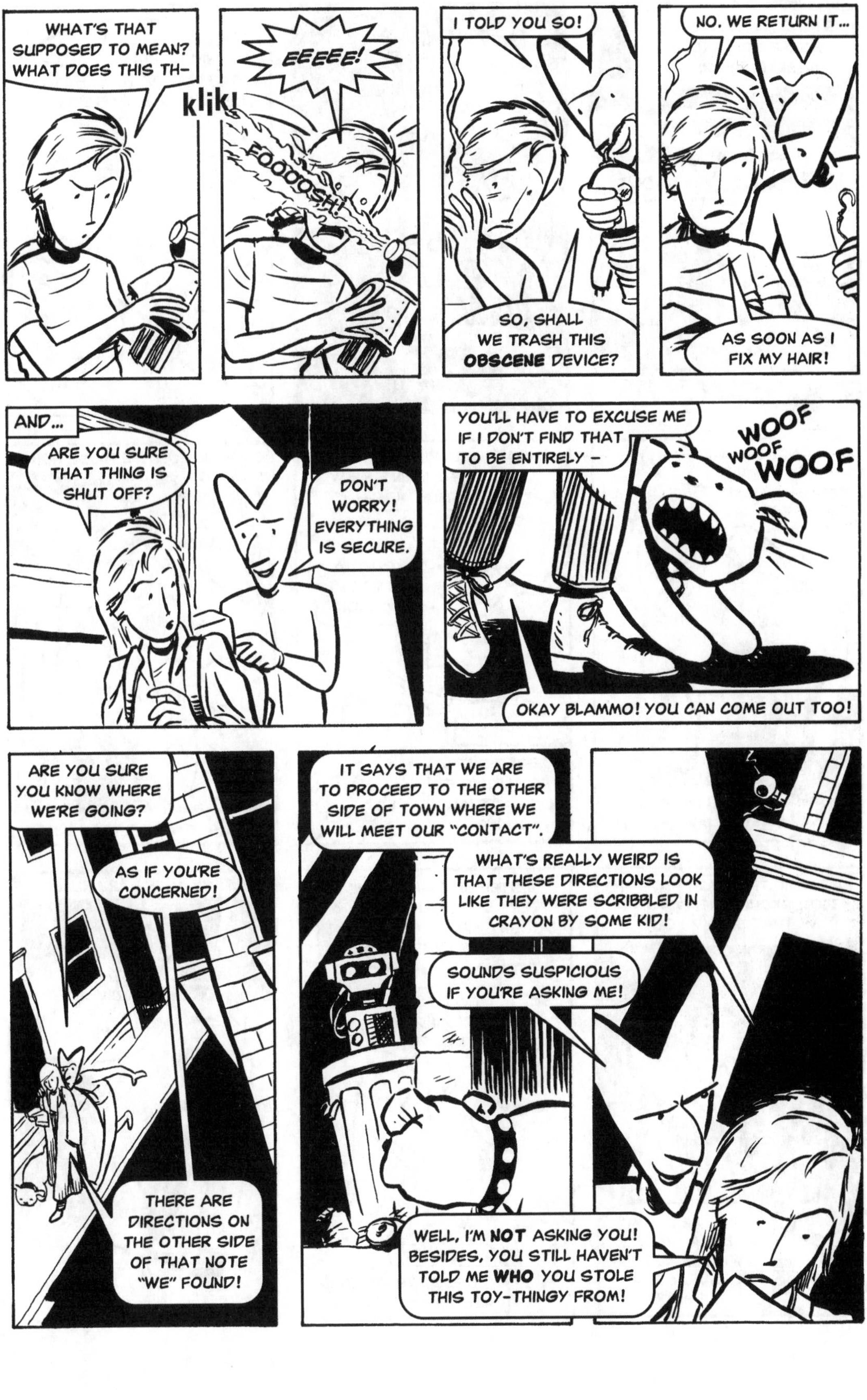
WHAT'S THAT SUPPOSED TO MEAN? WHAT DOES THIS TH-
klik!
EEEEE!
FOOOOOSH!
I TOLD YOU SO!
SO, SHALL WE TRASH THIS **OBSCENE** DEVICE?
NO. WE RETURN IT...
AS SOON AS I FIX MY HAIR!
AND...
ARE YOU SURE THAT THING IS SHUT OFF?
DON'T WORRY! EVERYTHING IS SECURE.
YOU'LL HAVE TO EXCUSE ME IF I DON'T FIND THAT TO BE ENTIRELY –
WOOF WOOF WOOF
OKAY BLAMMO! YOU CAN COME OUT TOO!
ARE YOU SURE YOU KNOW WHERE WE'RE GOING?
AS IF YOU'RE CONCERNED!
THERE ARE DIRECTIONS ON THE OTHER SIDE OF THAT NOTE "WE" FOUND!
IT SAYS THAT WE ARE TO PROCEED TO THE OTHER SIDE OF TOWN WHERE WE WILL MEET OUR "CONTACT".
WHAT'S REALLY WEIRD IS THAT THESE DIRECTIONS LOOK LIKE THEY WERE SCRIBBLED IN CRAYON BY SOME KID!
SOUNDS SUSPICIOUS IF YOU'RE ASKING ME!
WELL, I'M **NOT** ASKING YOU! BESIDES, YOU STILL HAVEN'T TOLD ME **WHO** YOU STOLE THIS TOY-THINGY FROM!

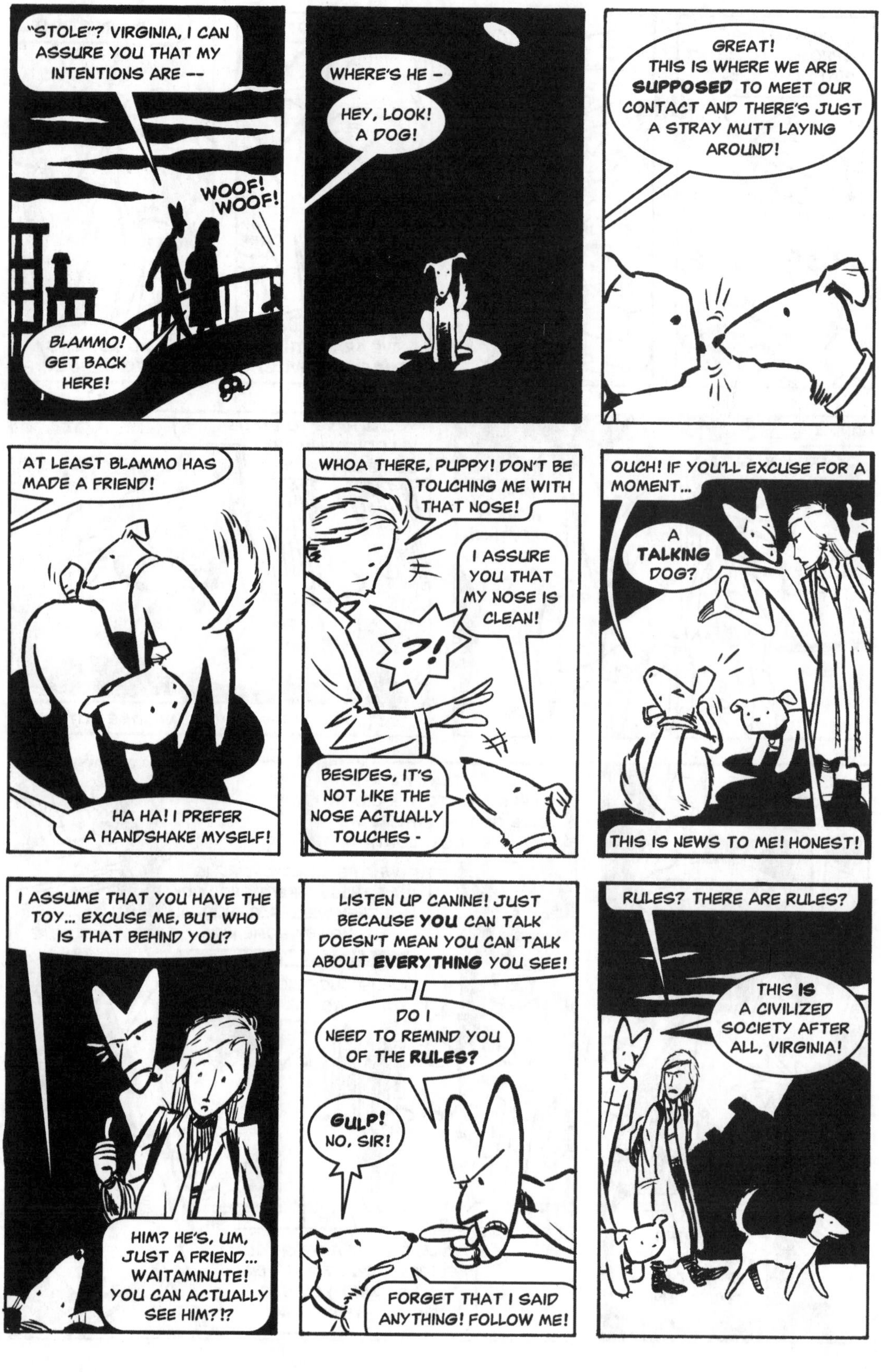
"STOLE"? VIRGINIA, I CAN ASSURE YOU THAT MY INTENTIONS ARE --
WOOF! WOOF!
BLAMMO! GET BACK HERE!
WHERE'S HE -
HEY, LOOK! A DOG!
GREAT! THIS IS WHERE WE ARE SUPPOSED TO MEET OUR CONTACT AND THERE'S JUST A STRAY MUTT LAYING AROUND!
AT LEAST BLAMMO HAS MADE A FRIEND!
HA HA! I PREFER A HANDSHAKE MYSELF!
WHOA THERE, PUPPY! DON'T BE TOUCHING ME WITH THAT NOSE!
?!
I ASSURE YOU THAT MY NOSE IS CLEAN!
BESIDES, IT'S NOT LIKE THE NOSE ACTUALLY TOUCHES -
OUCH! IF YOU'LL EXCUSE FOR A MOMENT...
A TALKING DOG?
THIS IS NEWS TO ME! HONEST!
I ASSUME THAT YOU HAVE THE TOY... EXCUSE ME, BUT WHO IS THAT BEHIND YOU?
HIM? HE'S, UM, JUST A FRIEND... WAITAMINUTE! YOU CAN ACTUALLY SEE HIM?!?
LISTEN UP CANINE! JUST BECAUSE YOU CAN TALK DOESN'T MEAN YOU CAN TALK ABOUT EVERYTHING YOU SEE!
DO I NEED TO REMIND YOU OF THE RULES?
GULP! NO, SIR!
FORGET THAT I SAID ANYTHING! FOLLOW ME!
RULES? THERE ARE RULES?
THIS IS A CIVILIZED SOCIETY AFTER ALL, VIRGINIA!

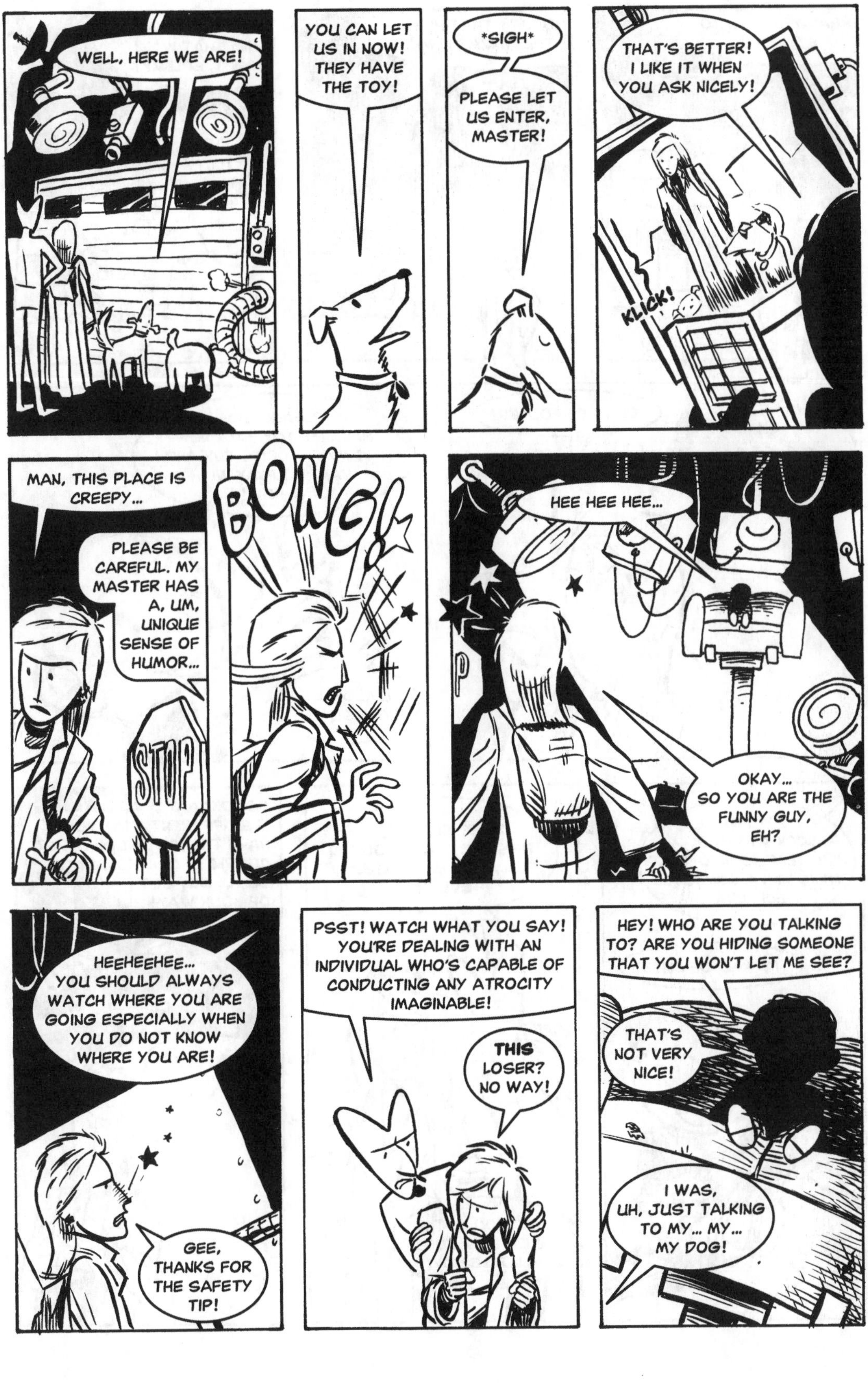

WELL, HERE WE ARE!
YOU CAN LET US IN NOW! THEY HAVE THE TOY!
SIGH
PLEASE LET US ENTER, MASTER!
THAT'S BETTER! I LIKE IT WHEN YOU ASK NICELY!
KLICK!
MAN, THIS PLACE IS CREEPY...
PLEASE BE CAREFUL. MY MASTER HAS A, UM, UNIQUE SENSE OF HUMOR...
STOP
BONG!
HEE HEE HEE...
OKAY... SO YOU ARE THE FUNNY GUY, EH?
HEEHEEHEE... YOU SHOULD ALWAYS WATCH WHERE YOU ARE GOING ESPECIALLY WHEN YOU DO NOT KNOW WHERE YOU ARE!
GEE, THANKS FOR THE SAFETY TIP!
PSST! WATCH WHAT YOU SAY! YOU'RE DEALING WITH AN INDIVIDUAL WHO'S CAPABLE OF CONDUCTING ANY ATROCITY IMAGINABLE!
THIS LOSER? NO WAY!
HEY! WHO ARE YOU TALKING TO? ARE YOU HIDING SOMEONE THAT YOU WON'T LET ME SEE?
THAT'S NOT VERY NICE!
I WAS, UH, JUST TALKING TO MY... MY... MY DOG!

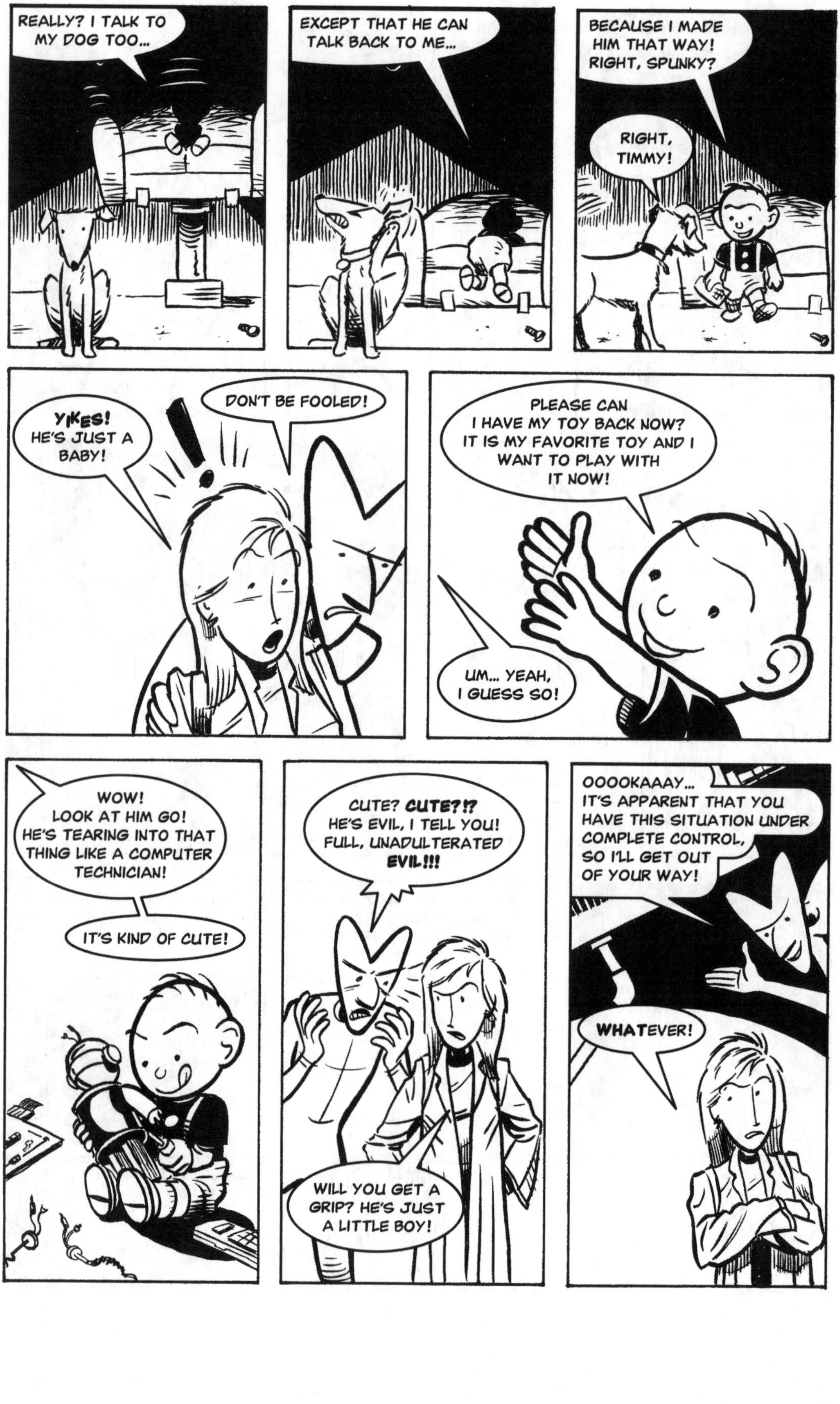
REALLY? I TALK TO MY DOG TOO...
EXCEPT THAT HE CAN TALK BACK TO ME...
BECAUSE I MADE HIM THAT WAY! RIGHT, SPUNKY?
RIGHT, TIMMY!
YIKES! HE'S JUST A BABY!
DON'T BE FOOLED!
PLEASE CAN I HAVE MY TOY BACK NOW? IT IS MY FAVORITE TOY AND I WANT TO PLAY WITH IT NOW!
UM... YEAH, I GUESS SO!
WOW! LOOK AT HIM GO! HE'S TEARING INTO THAT THING LIKE A COMPUTER TECHNICIAN!
IT'S KIND OF CUTE!
CUTE? CUTE?!? HE'S EVIL, I TELL YOU! FULL, UNADULTERATED EVIL!!!
WILL YOU GET A GRIP? HE'S JUST A LITTLE BOY!
OOOOKAAAY... IT'S APPARENT THAT YOU HAVE THIS SITUATION UNDER COMPLETE CONTROL, SO I'LL GET OUT OF YOUR WAY!
WHATEVER!

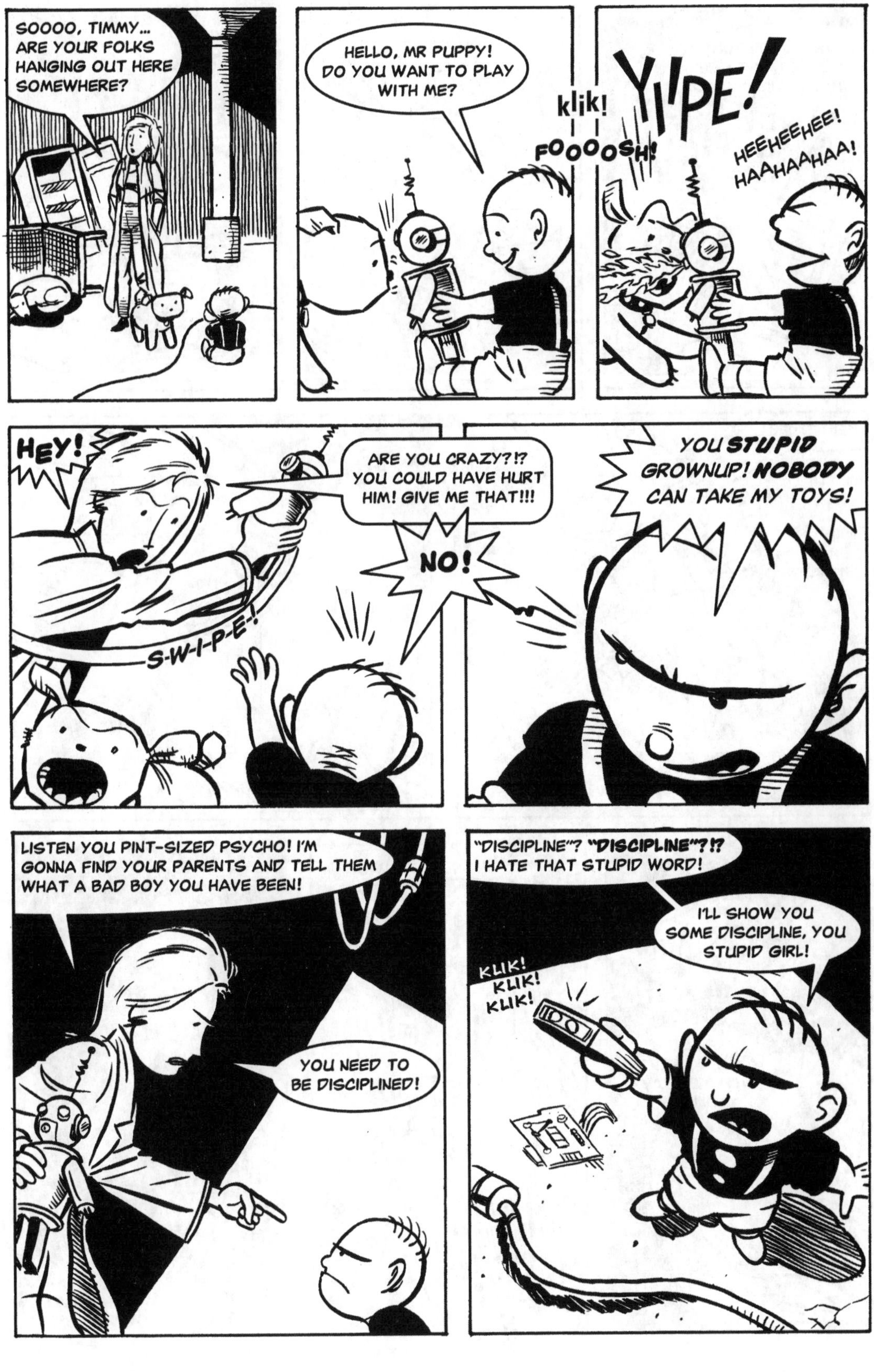
SOOOO, TIMMY... ARE YOUR FOLKS HANGING OUT HERE SOMEWHERE?
HELLO, MR PUPPY! DO YOU WANT TO PLAY WITH ME?
klik!
YIIPE!
FOOOOOSH!
HEEHEEHEE! HAAHAAHAA!
HEY!
ARE YOU CRAZY?!? YOU COULD HAVE HURT HIM! GIVE ME THAT!!!
S-W-I-P-E-!
NO!
YOU STUPID GROWNUP! NOBODY CAN TAKE MY TOYS!
LISTEN YOU PINT-SIZED PSYCHO! I'M GONNA FIND YOUR PARENTS AND TELL THEM WHAT A BAD BOY YOU HAVE BEEN!
YOU NEED TO BE DISCIPLINED!
"DISCIPLINE"? "DISCIPLINE"?!? I HATE THAT STUPID WORD!
I'LL SHOW YOU SOME DISCIPLINE, YOU STUPID GIRL!
KLIK! KLIK! KLIK!

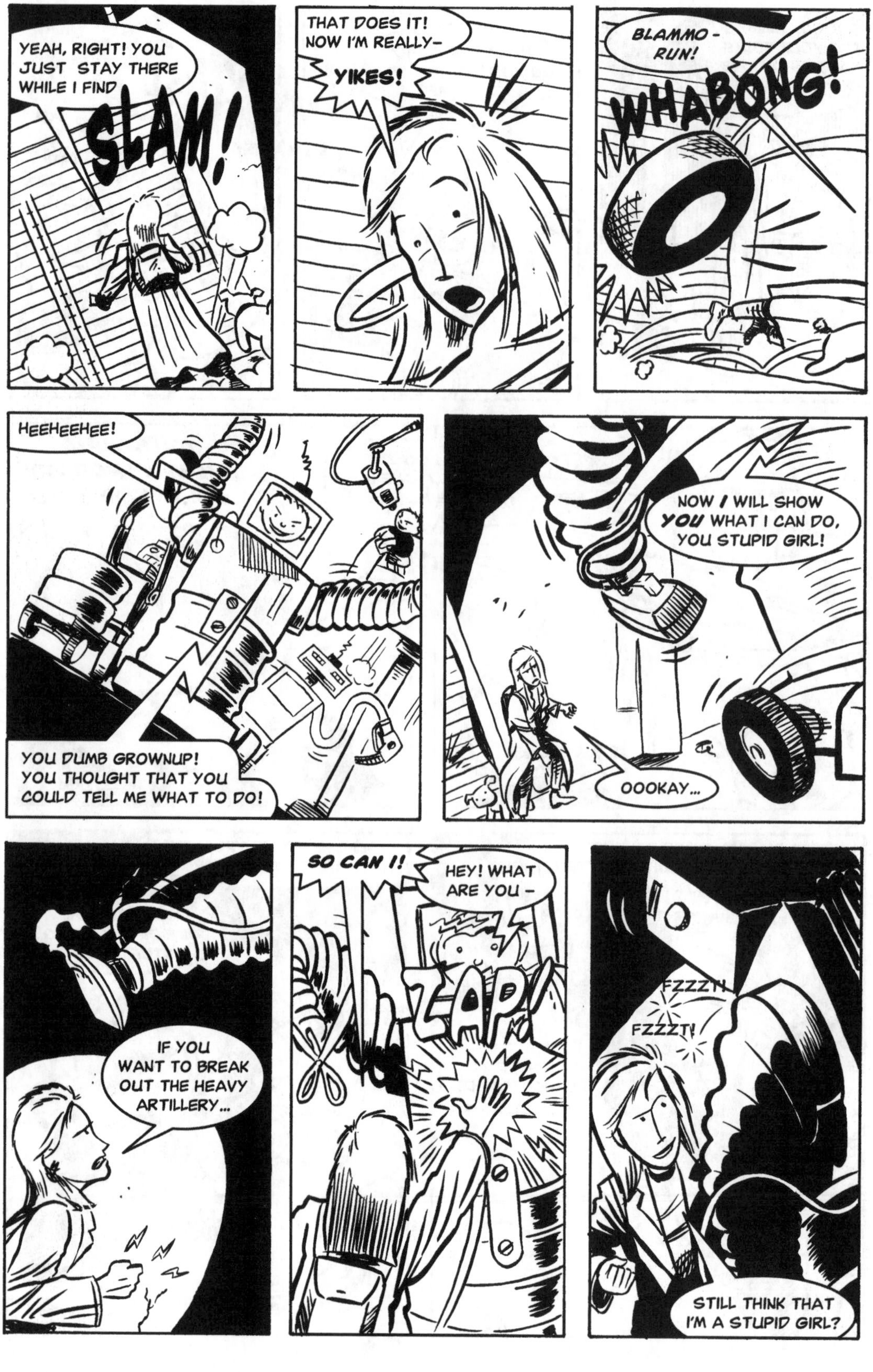
YEAH, RIGHT! YOU JUST STAY THERE WHILE I FIND
SLAM!
THAT DOES IT! NOW I'M REALLY–
YIKES!
BLAMMO-RUN!
WHABONG!
HEEHEEHEE!
YOU DUMB GROWNUP! YOU THOUGHT THAT YOU COULD TELL ME WHAT TO DO!
NOW I WILL SHOW YOU WHAT I CAN DO, YOU STUPID GIRL!
OOOKAY...
IF YOU WANT TO BREAK OUT THE HEAVY ARTILLERY...
SO CAN I!
HEY! WHAT ARE YOU –
ZAP!
FZZZT!
FZZZT!
STILL THINK THAT I'M A STUPID GIRL?

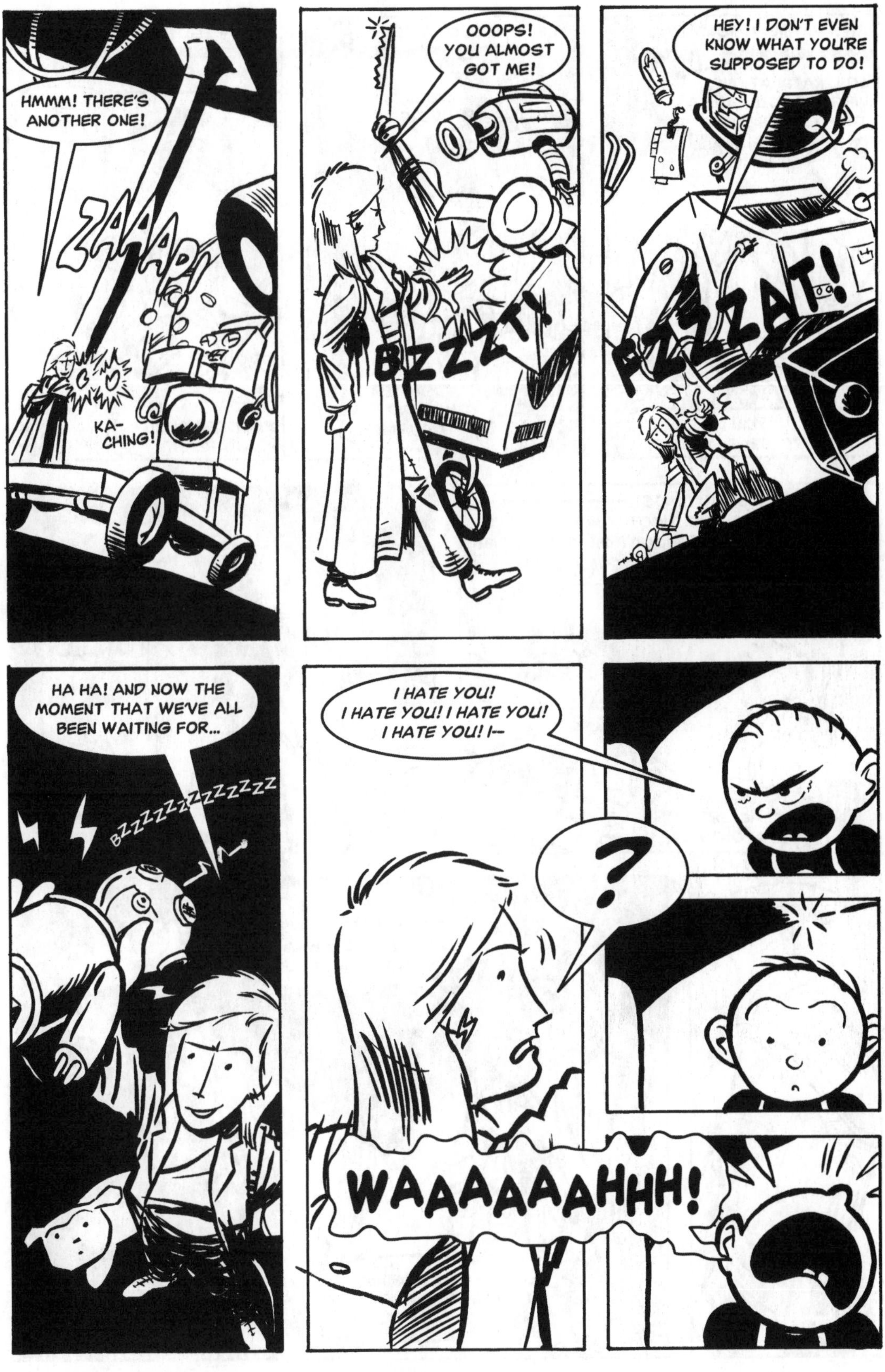
HMMM! THERE'S ANOTHER ONE!
ZAAAP!
KA-CHING!
OOOPS! YOU ALMOST GOT ME!
BZZZT!
HEY! I DON'T EVEN KNOW WHAT YOU'RE SUPPOSED TO DO!
FZZZAT!
HA HA! AND NOW THE MOMENT THAT WE'VE ALL BEEN WAITING FOR...
BZZZZZZZZZZZZZ
I HATE YOU! I HATE YOU! I HATE YOU! I HATE YOU! I--
?
WAAAAAAAHHH!

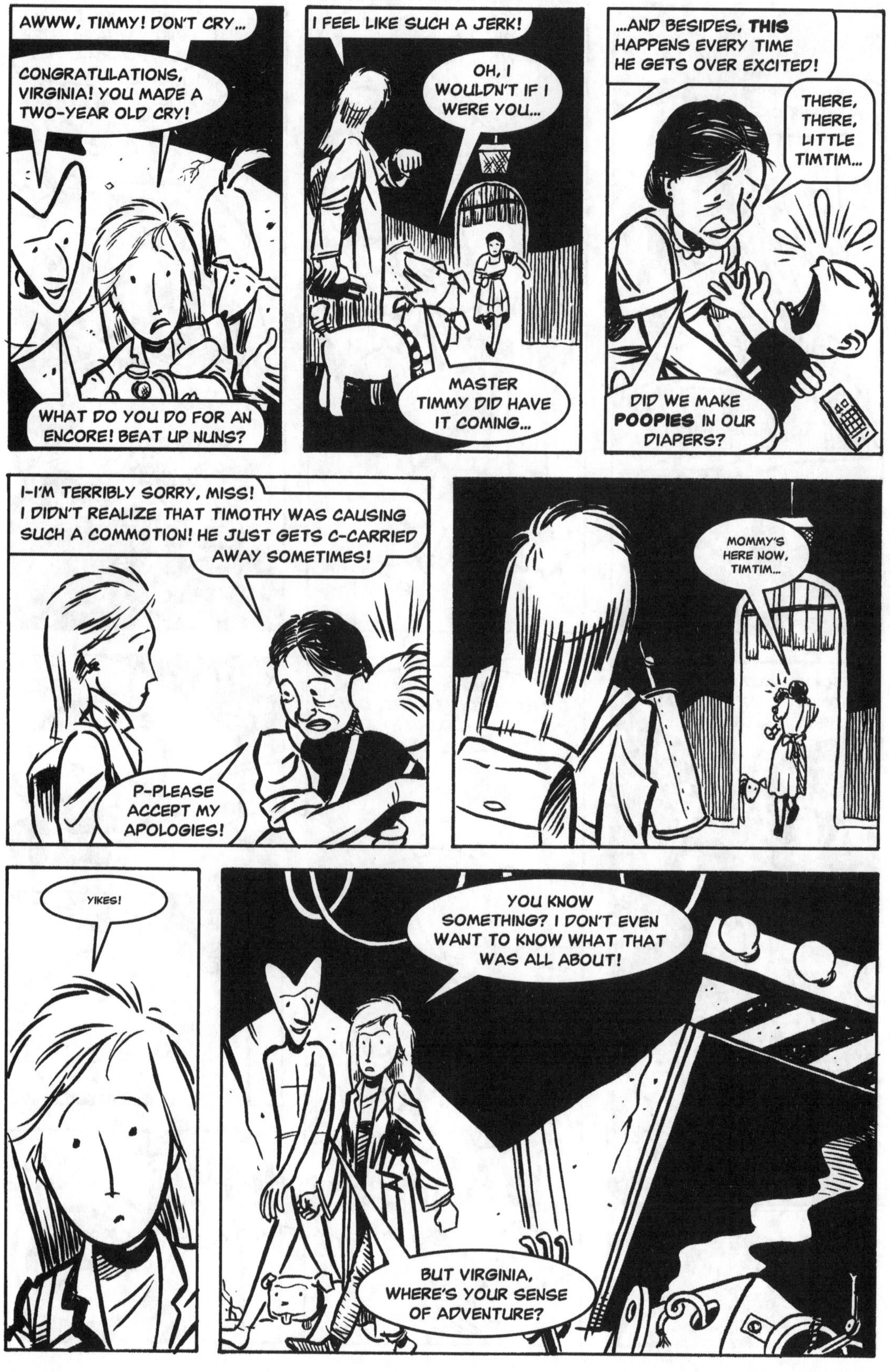
AWWW, TIMMY! DON'T CRY...
CONGRATULATIONS, VIRGINIA! YOU MADE A TWO-YEAR OLD CRY!
WHAT DO YOU DO FOR AN ENCORE! BEAT UP NUNS?
I FEEL LIKE SUCH A JERK!
OH, I WOULDN'T IF I WERE YOU...
MASTER TIMMY DID HAVE IT COMING...
...AND BESIDES, THIS HAPPENS EVERY TIME HE GETS OVER EXCITED!
THERE, THERE, LITTLE TIMTIM...
DID WE MAKE POOPIES IN OUR DIAPERS?
I-I'M TERRIBLY SORRY, MISS! I DIDN'T REALIZE THAT TIMOTHY WAS CAUSING SUCH A COMMOTION! HE JUST GETS C-CARRIED AWAY SOMETIMES!
P-PLEASE ACCEPT MY APOLOGIES!
MOMMY'S HERE NOW, TIMTIM...
YIKES!
YOU KNOW SOMETHING? I DON'T EVEN WANT TO KNOW WHAT THAT WAS ALL ABOUT!
BUT VIRGINIA, WHERE'S YOUR SENSE OF ADVENTURE?

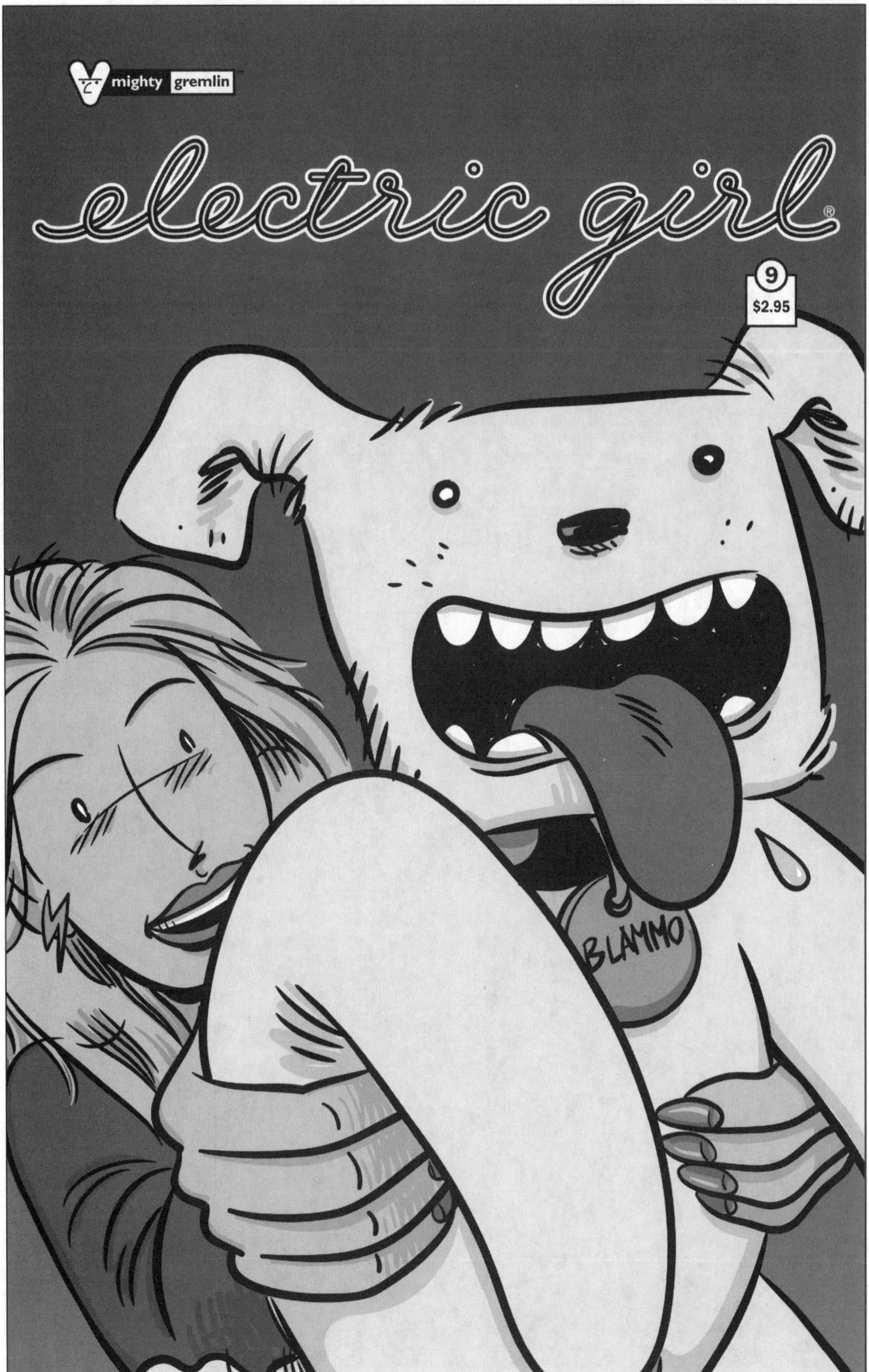
mighty gremlin
electric girl
9
$2.95
BLAMMO

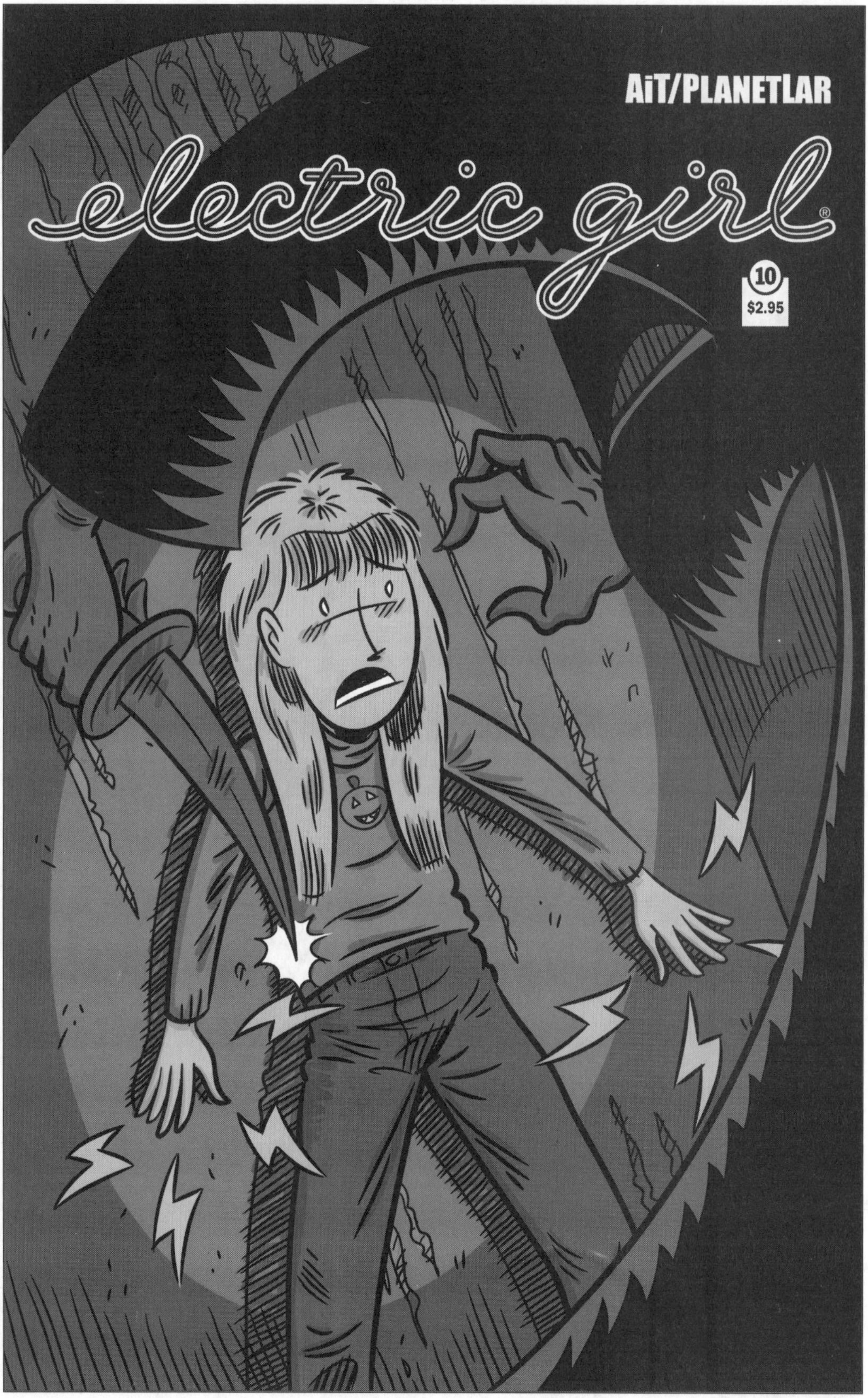
AiT/PLANETLAR
electric girl®
10
$2.95

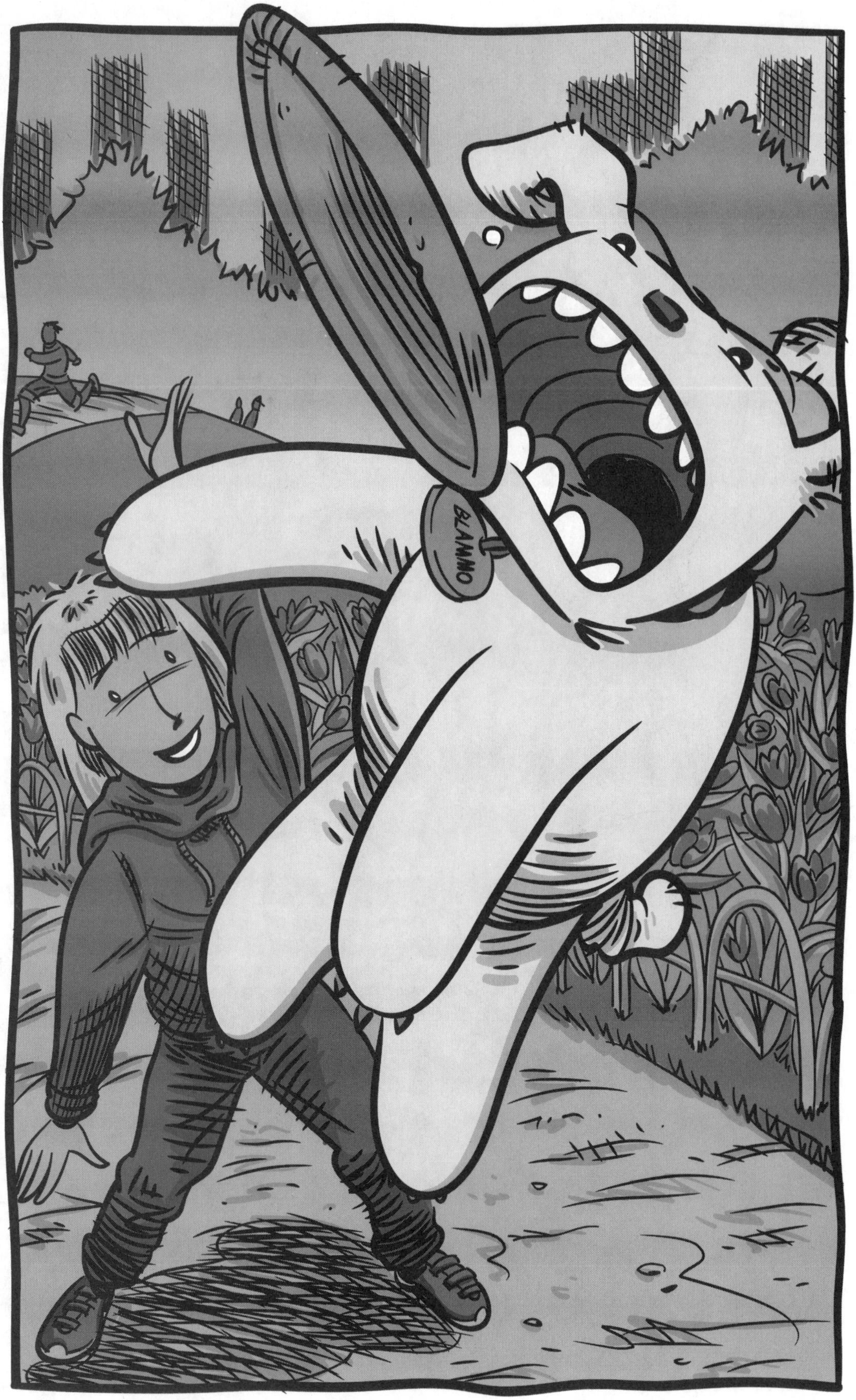
BLAMMO

(the next four pages were originally published in Electric Girl #9)

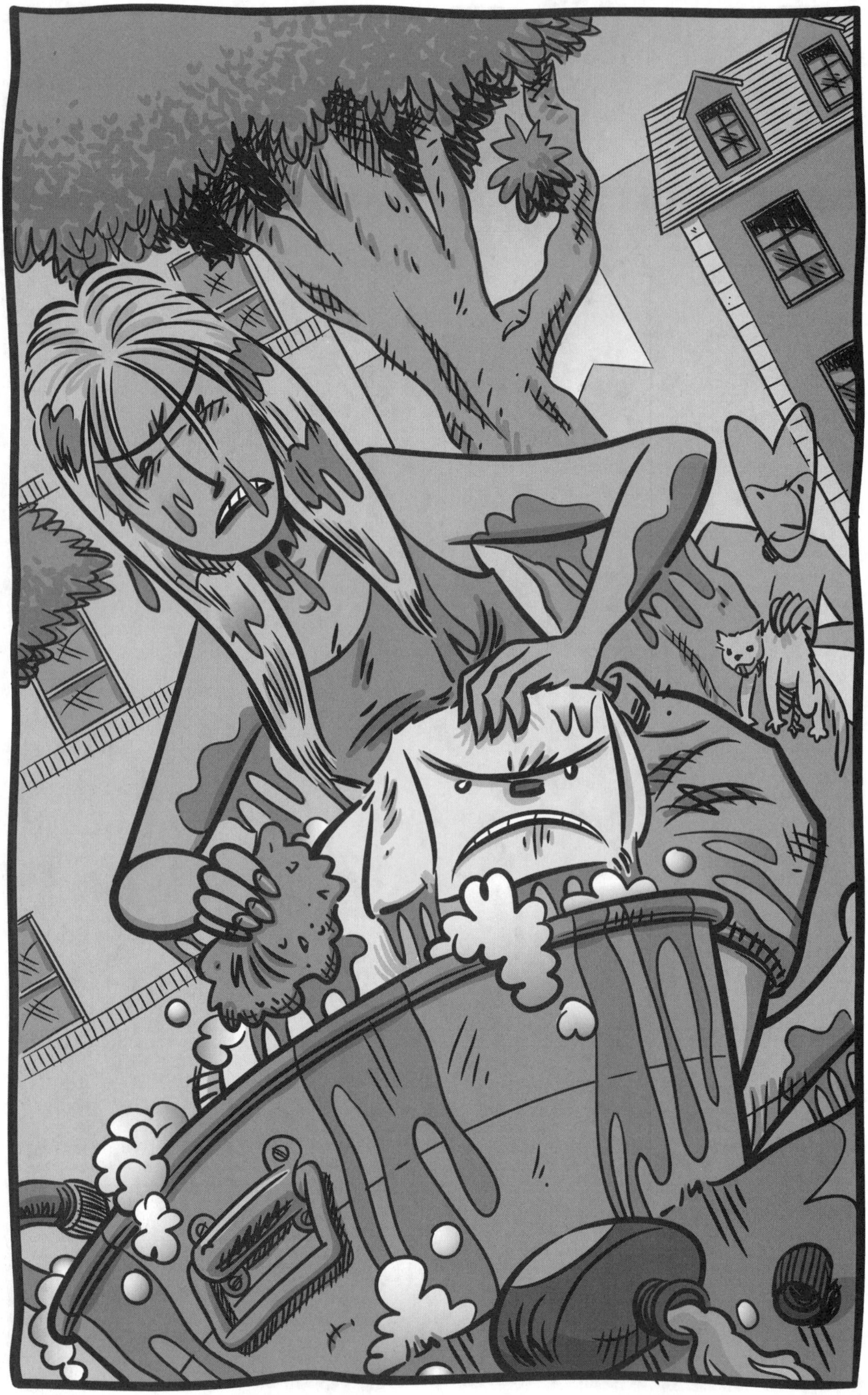

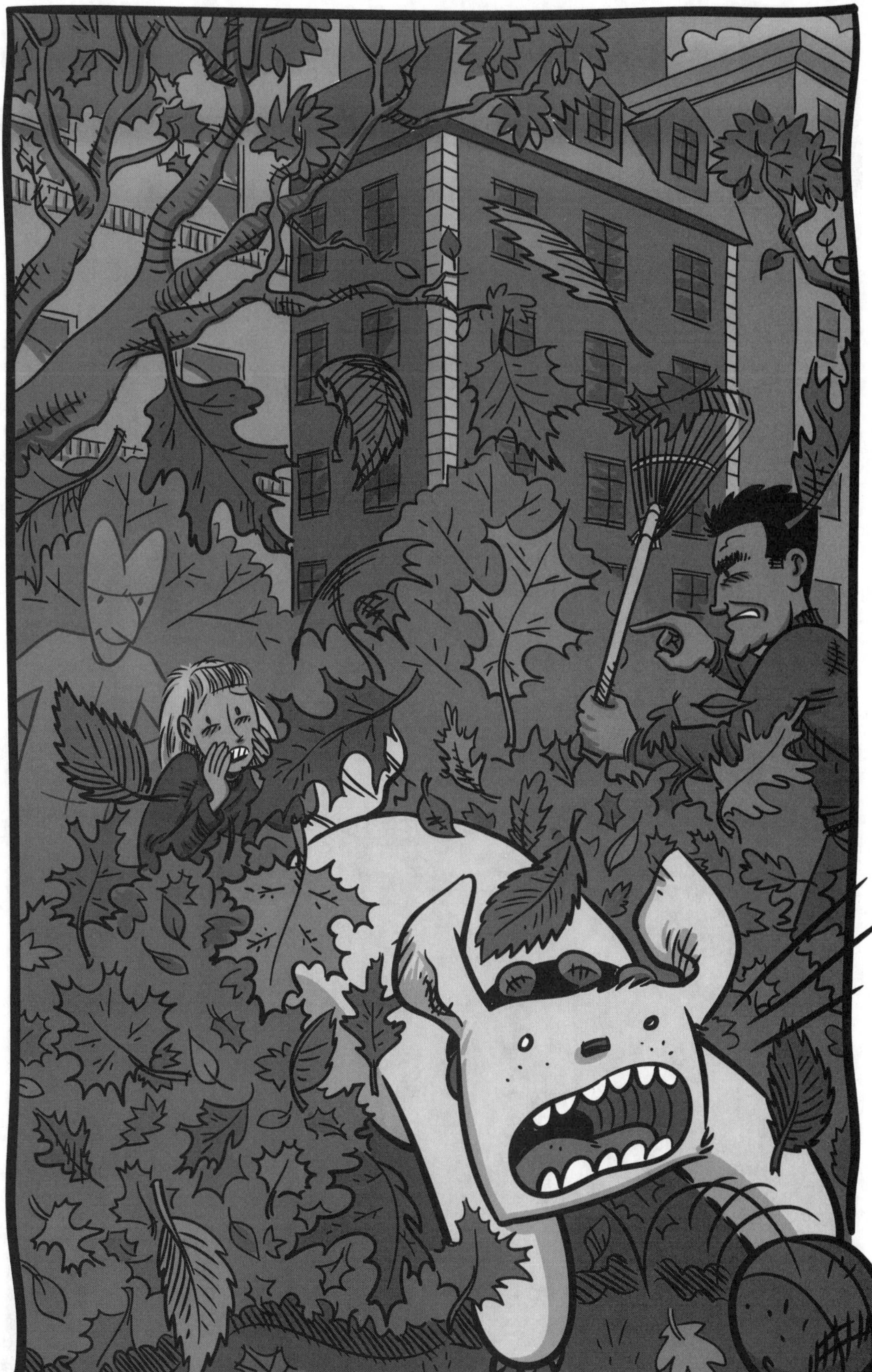

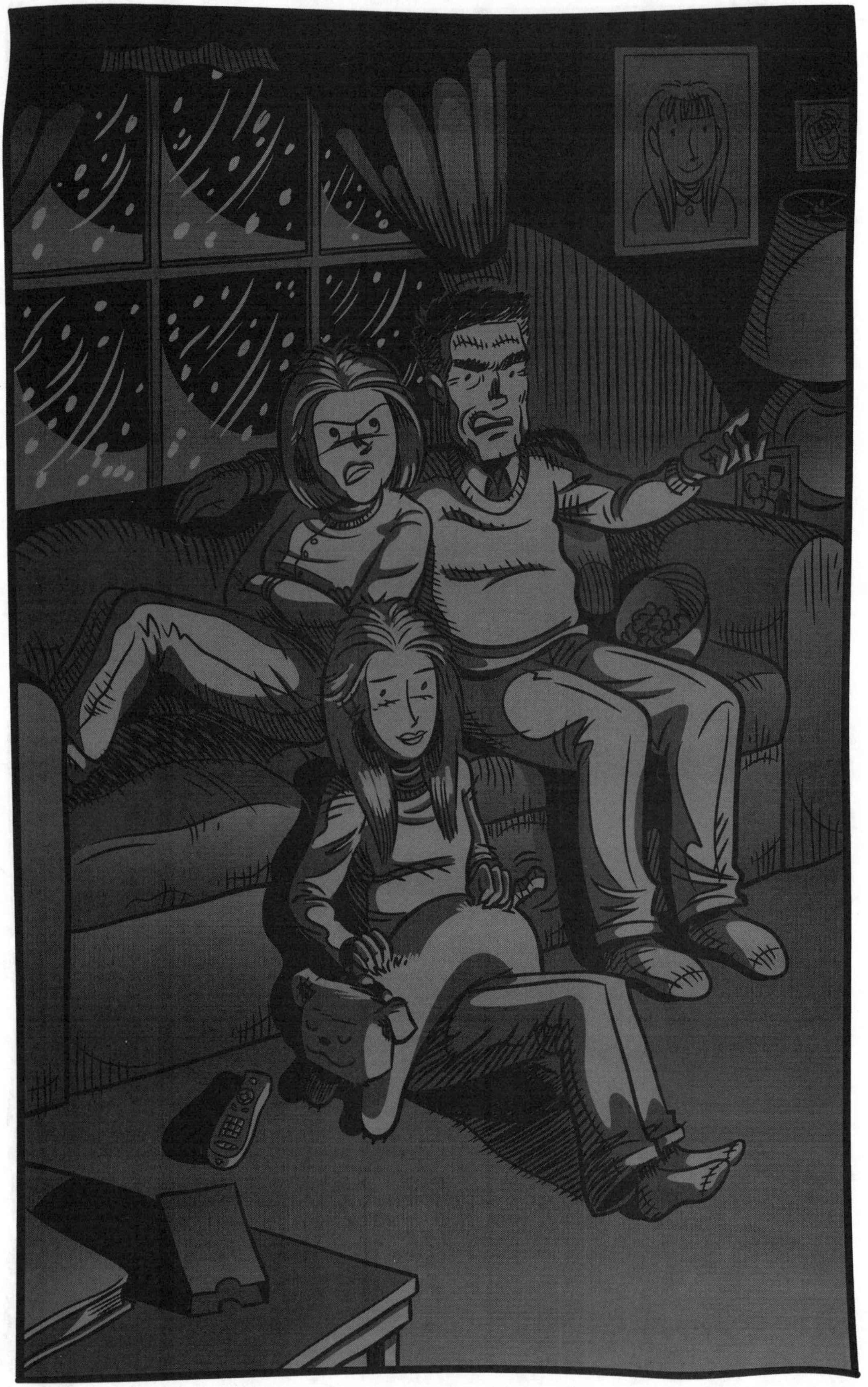

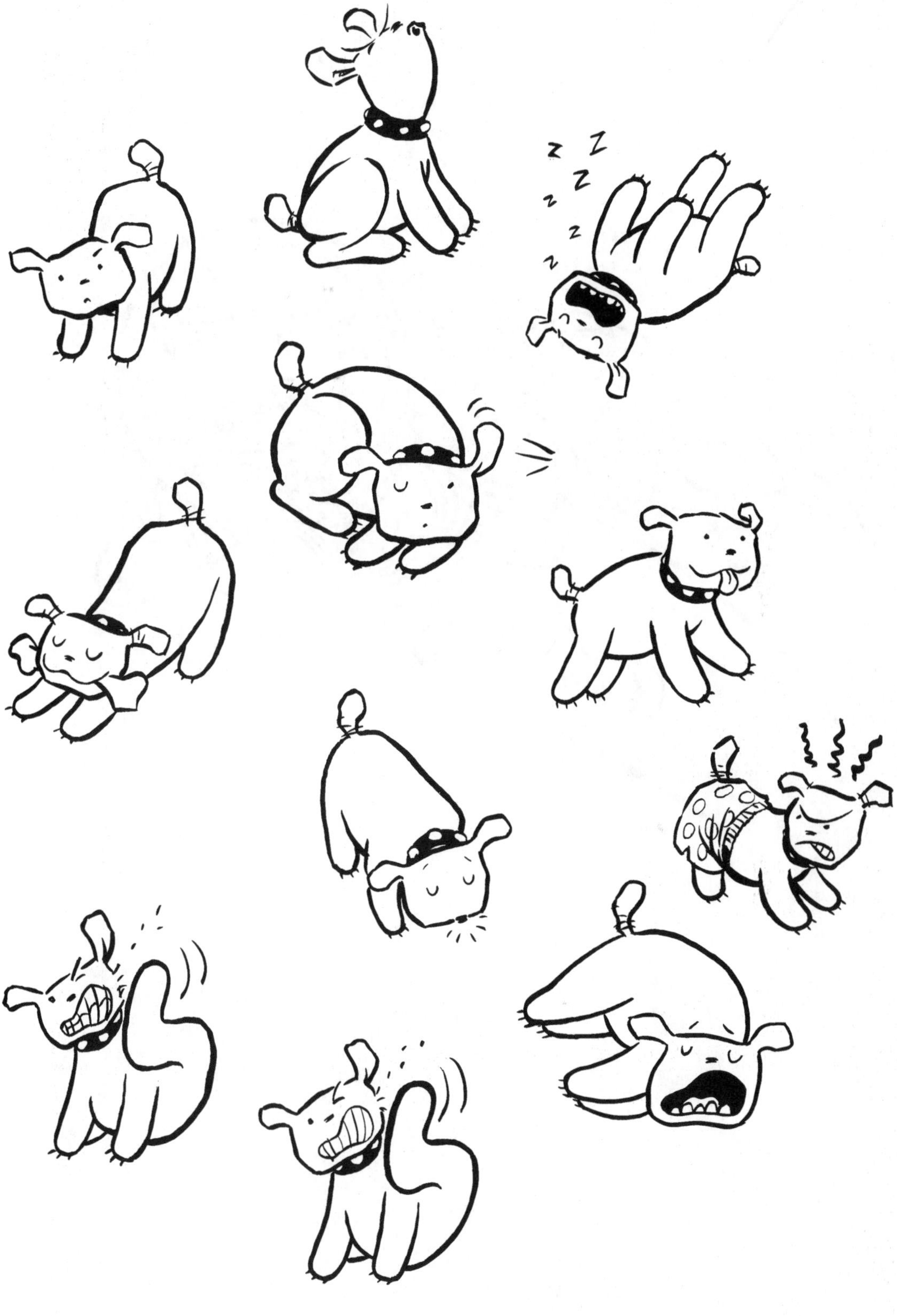

A series of Blammo character drawings that I did some time before starting the Electric Girl comic books. I developed an affection for him and started using him as my mascot for my illustration work before bringing him into the EG stories.

"Blammo in Space"!

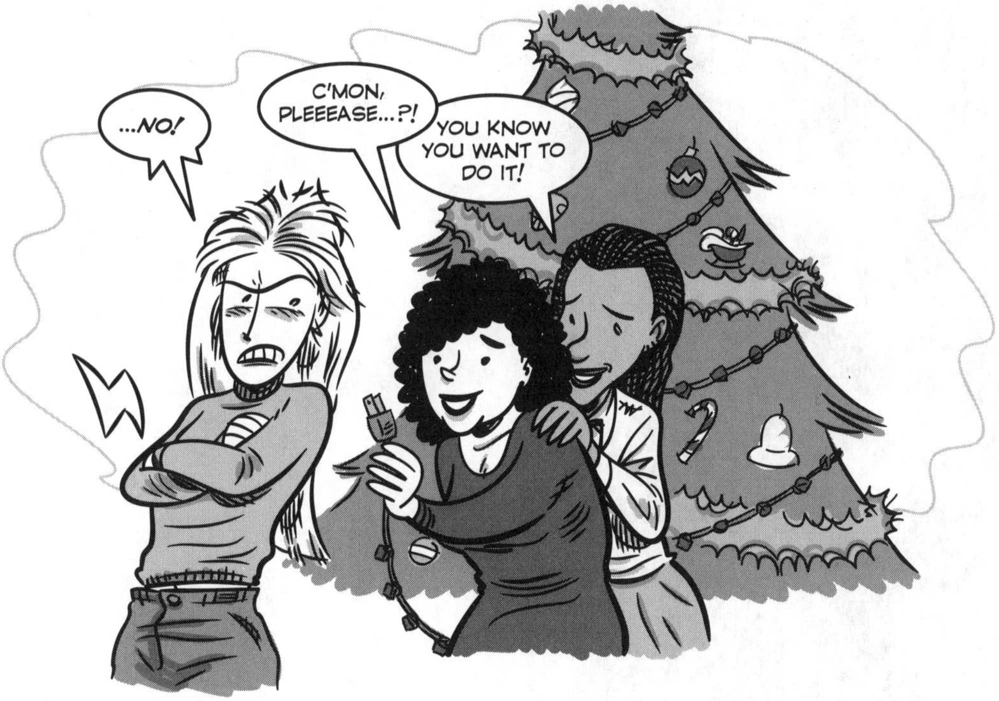
...NO!
C'MON, PLEEEASE...?!
YOU KNOW YOU WANT TO DO IT!

An idea for a Electric Girl-themed Christmas card...

Michael Brennan was born in the coastal town of Gloucester, MA, where he developed an aversion to both the ocean and seafood. He attended Massachusetts College of Art where he received his BFA with a concentration in Illustration.

In 1990, Michael started on the precursor to **Electric Girl** in the form of a comic strip. After rejections from all the major syndicates, he retooled the concept in his spare time and the first issue of the **Electric Girl** comic book was published in 1998.

Mike's work has received critical recognition since the first printing of **Electric Girl Volume 1,** when he was nominated for an Eisner Award – one of the comic book industry's highest honors – in 2001. **EGv1** has also been named to the "Popular Paperbacks for Young Adults 2002" list by the Young Adult Library Services Association. (a division of the American Library Association)